David Zopfi-Jordan
53 Suzanne Ave.
Vadnais Heights MN 55127-4118

shment and social
ontrol

PUNISHMENT AND SOCIAL CONTROL

SOCIAL INSTITUTIONS AND SOCIAL CHANGE
An Aldine de Gruyter Series of Texts and Monographs
EDITED BY
James D. Wright

Larry Barnett, **Legal Construct, Social Concept: A Macrosociological Perspective on Law**

Vern L. Bengtson and W. Andrew Achenbaum, **The Changing Contract Across Generations**

Thomas G. Blomberg and Stanley Cohen (eds.), **Punishment and Social Control: Essays in Honor of Sheldon L. Messinger**

Remi Clignet, **Death, Deeds, and Descendants: Inheritance in Modern America**

Mary Ellen Colten and Susan Gore (eds.), **Adolescent Stress: Causes and Consequences**

Rand D. Conger and Glen H. Elder, Jr., **Families in Troubled Times: Adapting to Change in Rural America**

Joel A. Devine and James D. Wright, **The Greatest of Evils: Urban Poverty and the American Underclass**

G. William Domhoff, **The Power Elite and the State: How Policy is Made in America**

Paula S. England, **Comparable Worth: Theories and Evidence**

Paula S. England, **Theory on Gender/Feminism on Theory**

R. G. Evans, M. L. Barer, and T. R. Marmor, **Why Are Some People Healthy and Others Not? The Determinants of Health of Populations**

J. Rogers Hollingsworth and Ellen Jane Hollingsworth (eds.), **Care of the Chronically and Severely Ill: Comparative Social Policies**

Gary Kleck, **Point Blank: Guns and Violence in America**

James R. Kluegel, David S. Mason, and Bernd Wegener (eds.), **Social Justice and Political Change: Public Opinion in Capitalist and Post-Communist States**

Dean Knudsen and JoAnn L. Miller (eds.), **Abused and Battered: Social and Legal Responses to Family Violence**

Theodore R. Marmor, **The Politics of Medicare** *(Second Edition)*

Clark McPhail, **The Myth of the Madding Crowd**

Steven L. Nock, **The Costs of Privacy: Surveillance and Reputation in America**

Talcott Parsons on National Socialism *(Edited and with an Introduction by Uta Gerhardt)*

Carolyn C. and Robert Perrucci, Dena B. and Harry R. Targ, **Plant Closings: International Context and Social Costs**

Robert Perrucci and Harry R. Potter (eds.), **Networks of Power: Organizational Actors at the National, Corporate, and Community Levels**

Robert Perrucci, **Japanese Auto Transplants in the Heartland: Corporatism and Community**

James T. Richardson, Joel Best, and David G. Bromley (eds.), **The Satanism Scare**

Alice S. Rossi and Peter H. Rossi, **Of Human Bonding: Parent-Child Relations Across the Life Course**

Joseph F. Sheley and James D. Wright: **In the Line of Fire: Youth, Guns, and Violence in Urban America**

David G. Smith, **Paying for Medicare: The Politics of Reform**

James D. Wright, **Address Unknown: The Homeless in America**

James D. Wright and Peter H. Rossi, **Armed and Considered Dangerous: A Survey of Felons and Their Firearms**

James D. Wright, Peter H. Rossi, and Kathleen Daly, **Under the Gun: Weapons, Crime, and Violence in America**

Mary Zey, **Banking on Fraud: Drexel, Junk Bonds, and Buyouts**

PUNISHMENT AND SOCIAL CONTROL
Essays in Honor of Sheldon L. Messinger

Thomas G. Blomberg and Stanley Cohen
EDITORS

ALDINE DE GRUYTER
New York

About the Editors

Thomas G. Blomberg is Professor of Criminology at Florida State University. His major research has been concerned with the meaning and consequences of penal reform. Dr. Blomberg has published numerous journal articles and is the author of *Courts and Diversion* (1979), *Juvenile Court and Community Corrections* (1984), and *American Corrections: Past, Present and Future* (forthcoming).

Stanley Cohen is Professor of Criminology at the Hebrew University, Jerusalem, and has also taught in Britain and the United States. He is presently working on the subject of human rights violations. Dr. Cohen is the author of many books, among them *Social Control and the State* (1983); *Visions of Social Control* (1985) and *Against Criminology* (1988).

Copyright © 1995 Walter de Gruyter, Inc., New York
All rights reserved. No part of this publication may be reproduced or transmitted in any form, or by any means, electronic or mechanical, including photocopy, recording, or any information storage or retrieval system, without permission in writing from the publisher.

ALDINE DE GRUYTER
A division of Walter de Gruyter, Inc.
200 Saw Mill River Road
Hawthrone, New York 10532

This publication is printed on acid-free paper ∞

Library of Congress Cataloging-in-Publication Data
Punishment and social control : essays in honor of Sheldon L. Messinger / Thomas G. Blomberg and Stanley Cohen, editors.
   p.   cm. — (Social institutions and social change)
   Includes bibliographical references and index.
   ISBN 0-202-30497-3 (cloth : alk. paper)
   1. Prisons—Government policy—United States. 2. Punishment—Government policy—United States. 3. Social control—United States. 4. Criminal justice, Administration of—United States. 5. Alternatives to imprisonment—United States. 6. United States—Social policy. 7. Messinger, Sheldon L. I. Messinger, Sheldon L. II. Blomberg, Thomas G. III. Cohen, Stanley. IV. Series.
HV9469.P88 1995
364.6'0973—dc20   95-19596
                                                                  CIP

Manufactured in the United States of America
10 9 8 7 6 5 4 3 2

Contents

Foreword xi

PART I INTRODUCTION

1 Editorial Introduction:
  Punishment and Social Control
  Thomas G. Blomberg and Stanley Cohen — 3

2 Sheldon L. Messinger:
  The Man, His Work, and The Carceral Society
  Jerome H. Skolnick — 15

PART II THE PRISON:
Reforms and Alternatives

3 More of the Same:
  American Criminal Justice Policies in the 1990s
  David J. Rothman — 29

4 Beyond Metaphors:
  Penal Reform As Net-Widening
  Thomas G. Blomberg — 45

5 Judicial Impact on Prison Reform
  James B. Jacobs — 63

6 The Structural-Functional Perspective
  on Imprisonment
  Gresham M. Sykes — 77

PART III CRIMINAL JUSTICE:
Policing and Sentencing

7 Staffing and Training Problem-Oriented Police
   Egon Bittner — 87

8 Recent Developments in Undercover Policing
   Gary T. Marx — 95

9 The Future of the Proportionate Sentence
   Andrew von Hirsch — 123

PART IV SOCIAL CONTROL:
Changing Strategies and Meanings

10 True Crime:
   The New Penology and Public Discourse on Crime
   Jonathan Simon and Malcolm M. Feeley — 147

11 Penal Modernism and Postmodernism
   David Garland — 181

12 Virginia, Criminology, and the Antisocial Control of Women
   Pat Carlen — 211

13 Controlling Drug Use:
   The Great Prohibition
   David Matza and Patricia Morgan — 229

PART V MEASURING CRIME AND CONTROL

14 Statistical Assumptions as Empirical Commitments
   Richard A. Berk and David A. Freedman — 245

15 Stability of Punishment:
   What Happened and What Next?
   Alfred Blumstein — 259

PART VI EPILOGUE

16 The Limits of Academic Tolerance:
    The Discontinuance of the School of Criminology
    at Berkeley
        Gilbert Geis   277

Biographical Sketches of the Contributors   305

Index   309

Foreword

This impressive volume is a fitting tribute to my old friend and colleague, Sheldon L. Messinger. It is heartwarming to see how much he is appreciated by the many scholars who have benefited from his insights, suggestions, and criticisms. Indeed, he has been a special kind of teacher, one for whom every student is a colleague and every colleague is a student. He has always been ready to make someone else's problems his own; and in doing so he has brought to bear a sharp mind and a creative imagination. In this way, Messinger has quietly exerted a wide and beneficial influence.

A major base for that influence has been Berkeley's Center for the Study of Law and Society. Shelly's willingness to join me in founding the Center, in 1961, made all the difference for my own decision to go forward. From its earliest beginnings he played a major part in its work and direction. He had a wholehearted commitment to the enterprise, and he gave liberally of time and faith to a wide variety of people and projects. Messinger was the glue that held the place together. I hope my displays of confidence were as evident in those years as were my anxieties and demands.

I believe I learned from Messinger, more than from anyone else, how important is the "postulate of humanity" in social science, and especially in sociology. This is the idea that the people we study are fully human and must be respected as such. They respond in characteristically human ways to situations of stress, deprivation, and oppression; and they take advantage of opportunities that make sense to them within the situations they encounter. The presumption is that people on welfare or in prison are "one of us." We understand their motives and choices because we know our own frailties, and because we can see ourselves responding in similar ways under similar conditions. This awareness encourages both empathy and realism—a combination that, in Shelly's case, produced a strong sense of irony. That irony, as his friends can testify, never became a disabling cynicism. Shelly has known how to make criticism constructive, how to take responsibility despite qualms and doubts, how to be both in and out of the game.

I thank the editors of this book for the opportunity to join them in this very appropriate expression of our gratitude, respect, and admiration.

Philip Selznick

I
INTRODUCTION

1

Editorial Introduction:
Punishment and Social Control

THOMAS G. BLOMBERG and STANLEY COHEN

This collection of essays is being published to mark the retirement of Sheldon L. Messinger in 1992 from the Center for the Study of Law and Society, University of California, Berkeley.

Volumes of this type—*festschrifts*—fall into two main categories. At the one extreme, there is the self-indulgently personal: reminiscences and tributes that place the person being honored at the center of the stage, obsessively tracking down his or her every lifetime contribution. At the other extreme, there is the ascetically intellectual: detached scholarship that virtually ignores any personal references and seems only obliquely related to the biographical record of the person honored.

With the exception of two contributions—Jerome Skolnick's personal introduction and Gilbert Geis's epilogue on a historic phase in Messinger's academic milieu in Berkeley—our collection appears to be closer to the second extreme. This apparent detachment, however, certainly does not derive from any lack of personal warmth toward Shelly Messinger. On the contrary, all of us, editors and contributors, have been—sometimes over a period of more than thirty years—collaborators, colleagues, students, and friends of Messinger's and deeply indebted to him. In each of these roles, we instantly came to appreciate his sociological mind, personal charm, help, and support.

Anyone who has ever received his comments on a draft will testify to a degree of concern, care, and precision well beyond the usual academic norms. Much of this has been low-visibility work—not receiving (or requesting) any public acclaim. In our collective area of interest—the study of crime, punishment, law, and social control—Messinger has been the sociologist's sociologist, the criminologist's criminologist: supporting, encouraging, and advising behind the scenes.

It is precisely because Messinger himself has been so self effacing—and would only be embarrassed by a set of kitsch personal tributes—that we chose to invite substantive contributions that stand on their own right. As it happens, a quite impersonal classification of the main preoccupations in these areas of study over the last thirty years would correspond rather closely to Messinger's personal interests. He has, in fact, written on a far wider range of subjects than represented here: on the transformation of social movements, on the dramaturgical interpretation of social life, on the families of schizophrenics, and on the social construction of "trouble." But the dominant thread in all his work, has been the application of the sociological imagination to the study of law, punishment, and social control.

PUNISHMENT AND "SOCIAL CONTROL"

While crime, law, and punishment are subjects that have everyday meanings not very far from their academic representations, *social control* is one of those terms that appear in the sociological discourse without any corresponding everyday usage. This concept has a rather mixed lineage.

One of its branches can be traced back to the tradition of classic political and social theory associated with the emergence of the liberal democratic state. Here the political problem was how a government could achieve a degree of control over its citizens that did not infringe on their rights and liberties. The conceptual problem was how to understand this social space that was created between the individual and the state. In both political and conceptual terms, the problem of social control was part of a broader discourse about regulation, citizenship, and the social order.

This connotation of the term *social control* all but disappeared within the political discourse of Western democratic societies. The concept appears mostly in standard futuristic and dystopian images (such as *1984* and *Brave New World*) about overcontrolled societies, or it is reserved to describe more totalitarian regimes, as in "Saddam Hussein controls the Iraqi population through fear." More recently, however, debates about civil society and "governance," both in the West and in postcommunist societies, have revived earlier classic interests (Cohen 1994).

The concept's other and quite different branch emerged from the twentieth-century academic institutionalization of sociology in the United States. Here, the political dimension gave way to a concern with the universal social processes by which societies were integrated and social conformity induced. Integration, in functionalist theory, was explained in terms of the interdependency between different social institutions. (As Gresham Sykes describes in Chapter 6, this theory was later applied to institutions like the prison.) Conformity was explained at the family level or cultural levels ("informal social control") and employed a Freudian metapsychology that talked about internalization, socialization, and conscience formation. The superego was the "policeman in the head." The Chicago school version, in which social control was very much a central concept, looked more at processes rather than structures and employed a symbolic-interactionist rather than Freudian theory of learning. Social control and its breakdown (social disorganization) were not macropolitical issues; they were observed in the more immediate settings of city, neighborhood, peer group, and gang.

Despite differences of emphasis between schools of sociology, the assumption—still more or less present in introductory sociology textbooks—was that the "informal" and universal processes of inducing conformity normally worked. Only when they "failed"—that is, through some breakdown, disintegration, or pathology—were the "formal" methods of social control, notably the police, criminal law, and justice system, brought into play. These formal methods themselves were the proprietary subject matter of disciplines such as criminology, which, until at least the beginning of the sixties, were regarded as intellectually marginal precisely because they were not concerned with what normally happened.

The contemporary discourse on social control—from which most of the contributions to this volume originate—did not at first have any obvious genealogical connection with either the political or the functionalist streams. It emerged from the new sociology of deviance movement of the early to mid-1960s—usually called *labeling theory*—and derived from symbolic interactionism (onto which phenomenology and ethnomethodology were sometimes grafted). Through ties of collaborative work and friendship, Messinger was very much associated with this early movement. He was part of the same generation and intellectual subculture as sociologists such as Erving Goffman, Howard Becker, John Kitsuse, David Matza, and Aaron Cicourel. Their contribution was to place the microsociology of social control—the construction of deviance and deviant identities—onto the wider sociological agenda.

The debate continues on how this tradition has contributed to our understanding of deviance. Students still wrestle with the same paradoxical and ironical relationships between deviance and social control that were suggested by labeling theory—and are illustrated explicitly in Gary Marx's chapter on undercover policing (Chapter 8 in this volume). And even those uninterested in theoretical subtleties about social control "creating" deviance, came to adopt the rather distinctive notion of social control that emerged from this tradition and that informs this volume. Social control, that is, is understood as the repertoire of organized social responses to deviance.

Given the earlier broader connotations of the term, whether political or sociological, it was rather odd that this very restrictive notion came to monopolize the discourse for so long. The explanation probably lies in the imaginative ways in which this apparently narrow base was extended beyond the restricted domains of criminology and the criminal justice system to the resonant subjects of the wider sixties culture: drugs, sexuality, madness, political protest, and a celebration of cultural diversity. This gave rise to facile dichotomies: control and repression on the one hand; diversity, freedom and tolerance on the other. It also left behind a distinctive vision of ideal social control (Cohen 1985): informal, decentralized, inclusive and non-stigmatic, lying somewhere outside the tentacles of the organized state systems of law, criminal justice, imprisonment, and punishment.

Sociologists of deviance and crime began to apply this notion of social control at three levels. First, there was the micro-, interpersonal, or face-to-face level: how stigmatic meanings, identities, and roles were constructed and negotiated. Second, there was the organizational level: how formal bureaucracies and professions (the police, courts, corrections, welfare, and treatment agencies) went about their business of deviance-processing. Third, there was the macro or historical level: how particular deviant categories (such as drug abuse), or laws (such as prohibition), or institutions (such as the juvenile court) were established in the first place.

Whatever conceptual or substantive unity held all this together—in truth, not very much—was already breaking up by the end of the sixties. The more political direction taken by key figures such as Tony Platt laid ground for the conflicts that Geis describes in Chapter 16. The British version of the deviance-control paradigm almost immediately took on a committed political character missing in the United States. By focusing on the political origins and enforcement of the criminal law, it also returned to a more state-centered view of social control and restored some connections with classical European social theory. Other key figures from the original subculture, such as Howard Becker began drifting away from the deviance area altogether. Only a few of the cohort, such as John Kitsuse, remained faithful to its original preoccupations; their line of enquiry culminated in the current highly influential "social constructionist" model of social problems.

Others from the original (Californian if not specifically Berkeley-based) group directed their concerns to the criminal justice system: Messinger himself on prison, parole, and corrections; Skolnick on the police and law; their students like Krisberg on juvenile justice and Blomberg on diversion and alternatives to custody. No one, of course, used the concepts of law, punishment, and social control as if they were interchangeable. But these three areas were contemplated within the same discourse—a discourse that soon included the "law and society" tradition (sociolegal studies, sociology of law, the Berkeley type of "jurisprudence and social policy"), and, later in a somewhat different way, critical legal studies. A distinctive policy-driven agenda also emerged around issues such as the critique of imprisonment, skepticism about rehabilitation, the search for "alternatives," the emergence of the "back to justice" model, and the implementation of determinate sentencing reforms.

Messinger played a distinctive and eclectic role in these developments. He always took the middle ground: first, by tuning in to mainstream policy concerns as well as more critical or marginal thinking; and second by using abstract theory as well as hard-nosed empirical methodology (for example, his collaboration with Johnson, Berk, and others in unraveling the operations of the Californian correctional system).

He looked for the middle ground in yet another sense: the level between historical explanations of correctional change and the actual strategies deployed by correctional agencies. He would stress, for example, how the imperative to control and dispose of deviant populations finds its expression not just in the wider political economy or vaguely defined "social forces," but in certain identifiable organizational practices, imperatives, and contingencies. His interest became focused on organizational decision-making. In an influential underground manuscript that circulated at the end of the sixties (Messinger 1969), he analyzed the "strategies of control" through which the Californian correctional system had developed its elaborate system of internal concentration and segregation to deal with recalcitrant prisoners. When one of us came to study long-term imprisonment in England in this period, it was Messinger's "Chinese-box" model that provided the best way to understand the organizational strategies of the system (Cohen and Taylor 1972).

By the middle of the 1970s, this literature had become enriched by contributions from directions well outside its original theoretical sources. Most notably there was the first wave of "revisionist" literature about the origins of the asylum or total institution: prisons, mental hospitals, and juvenile correctional institutions. The historical accounts by Rothman (on the early nineteenth-century American penitentiary), Ignatieff (on the equivalent developments in England), and—more complicatedly—Foucault all opened the theoretical landscape well beyond their apparently specialized subject matter. The return to the historical roots of the prison in the early nineteenth century also signaled a return to the original wider meaning of the concept of social control. Indeed there was an almost exaggerated use of the prison as an emblem for the emergence of the modern state. (As Blomberg suggests in Chapter 4, our understanding of social control continues to be shaped by metaphors.)

By this time, Foucault had become the dominating presence. His work became (as he wanted it to be) a series of open texts that allowed all sorts of quite different readings and directions. Various versions of radical, feminist, and critical theory began to find resonant messages in his gnomic writings about power, discipline, and control. Even interactionists and social constructionists appropriated Foucault for a model of deviance construction similar to the more liberal, culture-centered theories of the mid-sixties. Areas such as mental illness, the self, the body, and sexuality appeared at the center of the theoretical stage.

The emerging phase of academic work took two directions, both close to Messinger's concerns. The first, more theoretical and historical, was the continued attempt to explain changes in state-organized systems of social control: ideologies, master patterns, strategies, tactics, and alliances. Various systems of punishment, treatment, welfare, and rehabilitation became the subjects of a new style of sociological enquiry best exemplified by David Garland's (1985) study of the emerging juvenile justice system in late nineteenth-century Britain.

The second direction was more driven by policy (and sometimes, visionary political) directions: the continued escalation of crime rates and the continued looming presence of the prison. Here came yet another round in the historical quest for "alternatives." More than ever before, this quest revealed the paradox that as the critique of imprisonment became more obvious and the implementation of alternatives more frenzied, so the prison came even more to dominate the punitive landscape. Strategies such as diversion, community corrections, and intermediate punishment were implemented—without lowering the rates of either crime or imprisonment. Soon, the standard net-widening critique emerged: that alternatives were really becoming supplements, the system was increasing its reach. At this point, Messinger was less interested in the innovative and headline-catching alternatives, such as electronic monitoring or house arrest, than the traditional noncustodial alternatives within the old system, particularly probation and parole.

Current explorations of these issues—whether Christie's disturbing critique of the apparently infinite expansion of the American crime control industry (Christie 1993), Feeley and Simon's account of the "new penology" (Feeley and Simon 1992), or Garland's more theoretical exploration on the sociology of punishment (Garland 1990)—all vindicate the message shared by Messinger and the contributors to this volume. This is simply that forms of punishment and social control, far from being residual or marginal, are closely related to social trends, such as managerialism, the end of ideology, population and actuarial control, free-market ideology, and rationality. In this volume, the chapters by Simon and Feeley (Chapter 10) and Garland (Chapter 11) show the complexity of these relationships. The correctional system is not driven by its surface utilitarian justification ("what works") but both reflects and creates these wider social trends. It needs no great theoretical sophistication to understand the current political significance of crime in American society: in public talk about fear and insecurity, in new laws, in the political symbiosis between resentment and punitiveness, in massive budgetary reallocations, in shaping election results. If only for this reason, the social control literature has begun to restore its connection with its original political lineage.

At the same time—more subtly—this literature makes it possible to return to the wider and more generic sociological meaning of social control. This is happening in two directions.

First—as the European abolitionists have always been saying in their visionary style—it should be quite obvious that the punitive/criminal law model must be seen as only one form of social control. It is entirely misleading to talk of "alternatives" to punishment as if punishment through the criminal law were the normal method of social control. In fact, it is this mode of social control that is really the "alternative." This point is also reflected in the recent (rather arid) style typologies of the entire social control repertoire (Black 1991; Horwitz 1990). These place punitive controls alongside other forms of control such as therapy, mediation, restitution, compensation, tolerance, and avoidance.

A second direction comes from feminism—both in the wider sense of understanding gender as a form of social control and in the narrower sense of uncovering the gender base of decision-making within the formal social control system. Both senses are covered in Pat Carlen's contribution (Chapter 12)—which shows how concerns that seem specific to feminism raise broader issues about inclusive and exclusive forms of control. This literature describes how institutions, for example, for the treatment of such problems as anorexia and eating disorders, are sensitive to wider social processes—in this case, not just the control over the (female) body, but the commodification of "social control" as a property to be bought and sold (Ewick 1993).

THIS VOLUME

There are three ways in which we might organize and classify the contributions to this volume.

The first would be to follow the intellectual chronology of the field that we have just summarized. Many key figures in this story have been associated with Messinger and appear as contributors to this volume. From the original stage, beginning in the late 1950s/early 1960s, there are names such as Gresham Sykes on prison subculture, Egon Bittner on the police, David Matza on the social control of drugs, and Jerome Skolnick on the Center for Law and Society. From the middle phase, starting from the 1970s, there are Thomas G. Blomberg on alternatives to imprisonment and Andrew von Hirsch on proportionality in punishment. Then, from the current wave of scholarship, there are David Garland on penality and Pat Carlen on the social control of women.

A second, more straightforward, classification would be according to subject matter. Thus the papers in Part II deal with the prison: its history and sociology, the attempts to reform it from within, and the search for alternatives. Part III deals with selected issues and institutions in the legal and criminal justice process, such as trends in policing and the debate about proportionality in sentencing. Part IV contains various contributions from the theoretical interface between, on the one hand, the narrow fields of corrections and punishment and, on the other, the broader sociological study of social control. Part V raises issues about the measurement of crime and control.

These subjects obviously overlap at several points. It would be difficult to understand the specifics of prison reform without looking at broader changes in the theory and methods of punishment. And, as Rothman's and von Hirsch's chapters show (with quite different conclusions), the study of determinate sentencing leads "backward" into one of its origins as a way to limit incarceration and "forward" into its alleged role in *increasing* incarceration.

A third, and perhaps more interesting form of classification would be to list the common theoretical issues raised by all these contributions (and which have also been central to Messinger's work). Together, these three issues make up an open agenda for future work:

1. Master Shifts

The original features of deviancy control systems associated with the birth of the modern democratic state were (1) the consolidation of state power through the criminal law, (2) the segregation of deviants in closed institutions such as prisons, and (3) the foundation of professional and academic classificatory systems (like criminology itself). A number of contributors to this volume keep returning to these original traces before trying to detect later shifts in thinking about and implementing social control policy.

Observers of current developments are preoccupied with what is new, different, or continuous with what went before. Thus, Marx reflects on his studies of undercover policing that reveal "new" forms of surveillance and control that are "more" intrusive, technical, and penetrating than before; von Hirsch traces changes in recent thinking about the principle of proportionality in sentencing; Feeley and Simon return to asking what is "new" about the "new penology;" Blomberg considers how some common metaphors might help or hinder our ability to detect such changes. Even more ambitiously, Garland asks whether the seismic shifts of modernism and postmodernism have any bearing on the changing ideas and practice of punishment.

In each case, a common set of questions appears: Is what is alleged to be "new" really new? Are continuities more striking than discontinuities? How do we explain any changes—and are these indeed, in Foucault's sense, instances of "strategies without a strategist"? What effect do these changes have? And does any of this matter?

2. Ideas and Policy

Any study of these overall changes, real or putative, raises the vexed question of the relationship between ideas and policy. Putative reforms or policy shifts—for example, in parole or the determinate sentencing model, the areas Messinger has studied intensively—may be viewed in two ways. First, there are the ideas, concepts, theory, ideologies, and knowledge (or knowledge claims) that are supposed to have informed this policy. Second, there are the observable ways in which the policy has been practiced or implemented. These two aspects—theory and practice, ideas and implementation, knowledge and power—are related, but they are not the "same." As Foucault sardonically remarked, if knowledge and power were the same—as some of his readers claim him to be saying—then he would have wasted all his intellectual life trying to understand just what this relationship was.

This relationship might also be seen—as many of our contributions do—as a relationship between intentions and consequences. For many observers, the entire history of social control over crime and deviance is a story of good intentions leading to bad consequences. But what goes wrong? What accounts for this apparently permanent gap? This question is central, because without this gap, neither criticism nor Messinger's style of empirical research on correctional policy would ever be needed. For some observers, things go wrong at the implementation stage: the original intentions are not understood, there are not enough resources or appropriate staff, the mistakes are technical. For others, the original intentions are undermined by bureaucratic convenience or professional self-interest. In yet other versions, the original intentions are themselves suspect—riddled by ideological contradictions or mere masks for political economic interest and other historical imperatives.

Virtually all of our contributors are working at this interface between ideas and policy. The various discussions about prison reform, alternatives to imprisonment, and determinate sentencing are obvious examples. Our contributors do not always agree with each other: to Rothman, for example, the "good intentions–bad consequences" model applies to the link between the ideal of proportional sentencing and the escalation of imprisonment rates; for von Hirsch, current policy does not result from the logic of proportionality.

This work leads not only in a theoretical direction (how to conceptualize the link between knowledge and power) but also directly bears on the question of evaluation: How do we judge whether a policy has succeeded or failed? The logic of standard criminological research about "what works" tends to lead to a ritual confirmation of the null hypothesis: policy X works sometimes with some offenders in some places but it cannot be proven to have worked better than policy Y. Instead of technical solutions to this nihilism—more sophisticated statistics, larger samples—evaluation needs to be studied in a more historical and contextualized way. The question raised by David Matza and Patricia Morgan's chapter on the prohibition of drug use—How can such a massive project of social engineering continue despite a widely shared sense of total failure?—can be projected onto many other policies. So too could James Jacobs's question about the impact of judicial reform on prison: What would count as a significant social reform? For Richard Berk and David Freedman, though, *count* still raises the statistical problem of measuring the impact of policies.

3. Deviance and Control, Crime and Punishment

A final and even more theoretically subtle theme runs through some other contributions. The problem began with Durkheim's original formulations about the relativity of deviance and the positive functions of control. It reappears more than half a century later in the interactionist speculations about deviance and control. What is the relationship between the raw phenomena of deviance and crime—street crime, victimization, corporate crime, family violence, drug abuse—and the systems of control supposed to deal with all this?

The commonsense answer to this disingenuous question looks for rationality and correspondence: the response to crime is, first, appropriate to its character; second, proportionate to its extent; and third, sequentially related (that is, the crime comes first, then the control system reacts). It is just the simplicity of the rationality/correspondence model—its assumptions both of isomorphism and of sequence—that has for so long been at issue.

There are numerous theoretical alternatives. These include the assertion that systems of control, and punishment are transformed almost entirely by "external" social, political and economic forces. Another possibility is that any real or putative rationality is a property of crime control organizations; these organizations are "self-regulated" rather than responsive to changes in patterns of crime. Yet another alternative—one that has intrigued Messinger and his colleagues—is the Durkheimian-derived "stability of punishment" hypothesis (Berk, Rauma, Messinger, and Cooley 1981). How this hypothesis makes sense of continually rising prison rates is reviewed in Chapter 15 by Alfred Blumstein, one of the leading contributors to this debate.

Another different objection to the correspondence model questions the very possibility of distinguishing between crime and deviance as "raw phenomena" to which any response, least of all a sequential response, can be identified. In this version, forms of crime, deviance, and social problems are to be wholly understood as socially constructed categories. This construction is an artefact of such processes as criminalization or the invention of new diagnostic categories.

At the theoretical level, these issues are more subtle than they appear. But one hardly requires much subtlety to see the complete lack of any correspondence and rationality at the policy level. Just living in contemporary United States should be enough for one to know that current systems of punishment and control do not work—and are themselves out of control. How does one explain the current U.S. correctional budget of thirty billion dollars: a rational compromise between the contradictory demands of getting tough on criminals and reducing government spending? What lies behind policies such as "three strikes and you're out" in the thirty billion dollar 1994 Clinton anticrime bill?

It is tempting to dismiss these policies as thoughtless, yet another ritualistic round in the endless "war against crime." But, as Foucault reminds us about the prison system, even the most stupid institutions do have ideas. Messinger has spent his academic life studying these ideas and their consequences. His own ideas have had consequences for all of us in this volume as well as his many other friends, colleagues, students, and anyone else interested in our subject.

Messinger's first postretirement project was to start a research project about the methods of compensation and insurance used to help victims of the devastating 1992 fires in Berkeley and Oakland. We wish him well in this work and we are pleased that he has not really retired.

REFERENCES

Berk, Richard A., David Rauma, Sheldon L. Messinger, and Thomas Cooley. 1981. "A Test of the Stability of Punishment Hypothesis: The Case of California, 1851–1970." *American Sociological Review* 46:805–29.

Black, Donald. 1991."The Elementary Forms of Conflict Management." Pp. 43–69, *New Directions in the Study of Justice, Law and Social Control*, edited by School of Justice Studies. New York: Plenum.

Christie, Nils. 1993. *Crime Control as Industry*. London: Routledge.

Cohen, Stanley. 1985. *Visions of Social Control*. Cambridge: Polity.

———. 1994. "Social Control and the Politics of Reconstruction." Pp. 63–88 in *The Futures of Criminology*, edited by D. Nelken. London: Sage.

Cohen, Stanley and Laurie Taylor. 1972. *Psychological Survival: The Experience of Long Term Imprisonment*. Harmondsworth: Penguin.
Ewick, Patricia. 1993. "Corporate Cures: The Commodification of Social Control." *Studies in Law, Politics and Society* 13:137–57.
Feeley, Malcolm and Jonathan Simon. 1992. "Reflections on the New Penology." *Criminology* 30:449–74.
Garland, David. 1985. *Punishment and Welfare*. Aldershot: Gower.
———. 1990. *Punishment and Modern Society*. Oxford: Oxford University Press.
Horwitz, Alan. 1990. *The Logic of Social Control*. New York: Plenum.
Messinger, Sheldon. 1969. "Strategies of Control." Unpublished M.S. thesis, Center for the Study of Law and Society, University of California, Berkeley.

2
Sheldon L. Messinger:
The Man, His Work, and The Carceral Society

JEROME H. SKOLNICK

I first met Sheldon L. Messinger in January 1962 at the Center for the Study of Law and Society, then housed in a small set of rented offices on Telegraph Avenue. The Center had been launched on July 1, 1961, with Philip Selznick as chairman and Sheldon L. Messinger as vice-chairman. Along with Phil Selznick, Shelly Messinger set a tone that combined intellectual challenge with easy informality. More than anyone, however, it was Messinger to whom students and colleagues turned to discuss inchoate theories, half-baked ideas, and plans for research.

Time and again, like a magnificent editor who sees in a manuscript what the author *really* wants to say, Messinger would cut to the essence of the author's thesis or project, clarify the underlying argument, and show how to conceive of the idea as representing a higher theoretical concept or issue. It was also Shelly's manner that drew students and colleagues to him. He made them, us, feel that he really cared about our work, and that its success, the success of the other, was important to him. After some years of this combination of intellectual precision and generosity of spirit, Shelly Messinger became something of a legend around the Center. He became fabled as a supportive wizard of reconceptualization to whom several generations of students and colleagues were intellectually indebted, as acknowledgments in their dissertations, books, and articles were to show.

Such qualities led to Messinger's appointment as professor and dean of the School of Criminology from 1970 to 1977. By the time this appointment occurred, he had also written significant articles on the transformation of social movements (Messinger 1955), the dramaturgical interpretation of social life (Messinger 1962), the social life of inmates (Sykes and Messinger 1960), and had coauthored several noteworthy articles and studies, including a major study of schizophrenic women (Sampson, Messinger, and Towne 1964) and an unusually influential article (later to be a book) on civil justice and the poor (Carlin, Howard, and Messinger 1964).

I was his colleague at the School of Criminology and admired his calm and fortitude in an especially difficult time. Being a dean has rarely been a trouble-free business, especially on the Berkeley campus in the 1960s and 1970s, but a combination of circumstances made the deanship particularly vexing in the School of Criminology. As a "professional school" supporting an ambiguous profession—policing and corrections—the school's mandate had never been entirely clear. Neither had the goal of training such professionals ever achieved a wholly comfortable fit with the scholarly aspirations of the larger Berkeley campus. Although by no means of a piece, by 1970, the School of Criminology's faculty and students had mostly rejected the assignment of training professional police and corrections officials. Instead they, we, concentrated on studying the etiology of crime; police, courts, and corrections; and criminal justice policy.

Crime and criminal justice policies such as criminal responsibility, the death penalty, drug legalization, victim's rights, determinate and indeterminate sentencing, and the rights of the accused draw powerful resonances from across the political spectrum. This was especially true in a time, like the 1960s and early 1970s, of political conflict, protest, and sometimes violent confrontation. By the early 1970s, a substantial and visible group of criminology students and faculty had become active participants in local radical activities, while outside law enforcement agencies were being called to Berkeley and the campus to quell civil disturbances. Understandably, local and even statewide law enforcement officials, who once had supported the school, felt they had been betrayed.

Consequently, as dean, Messinger often found himself perched precariously between a rock and a hard place. The radical faculty and students were, after all, *his* faculty and students, and, like an understanding father, he tried to protect them. At the same time, he was, after all, an administrator appointed by the university administration, which did not look fondly on this patch of radicalism. It says something about his human qualities and moral character that throughout this difficult period Sheldon Messinger lost no friends and even picked up a few. He was fair to all points of view within and outside the school, and maintained an equanimity that eluded most of his faculty. He tried to save the school, but sooner or later the school seemed destined to fall. It did, and was phased out in the mid-1970s.

What was to be done with the dozen faculty positions held by the former School of Criminology? Committees were formed, meetings were held, votes were taken. Instead of distributing the faculty positions to schools and departments across the campus, Vice-Chancellor Ira M. Heyman, aided and abetted by Dean Sanford Kadish and Philip Selznick, guided the discussion toward the development of the Jurisprudence and Social Policy program. The program began in 1976, with Selznick as chair. Messinger assumed the chairmanship from 1980 to 1982, and then again from 1984 to 1987. After the retirement of Caleb Foote, with whom he had worked closely, Messinger was designated the Elizabeth J. Boalt Chair in the School of Law, which had formerly been held by Caleb Foote.

During the 1980s and until the present, Messinger's scholarly interests have resolved more centrally toward the sociology and history of punishment and punitive institutions. And, as has been his style, much of his writing is collaborative, including an article on determinate sentencing with Philip Johnson (Messinger and Johnson 1978) and a major and continuing study of the history and consequences of parole in California, with a variety of collaborators, especially Richard A. Berk, John E. Berecochea, and David Rauma (Berk, Messinger, Rauma, and Berecochea 1981; Berk, Messinger, Rauma, and Berecochea 1982; Berk, Messinger, Rauma, and Berecochea 1983).

He has himself largely been a macrotheorist of social control, by which I mean to say that he seems always to be endeavoring to reconcile and explain the particular into longer-term trends. For example, his article with Berecochea, Rauma, and Berk (1985) on the history and development of parole in California concludes with two important lessons for those who would explain penal innovations: First, that "inquiries into the origins of penal reforms should be specific about the times and places studied" (p. 103); and second, that such inquiries "must be alert to changes over time in the problems of the organizations they serve" (ibid.). Thus, parole was adopted to address complaints about justice, but was transformed fifteen years later to relieve prison overcrowding. As a parole supervision organization developed, still further problems arose, including the need for a revised justification. As a result, parole eventually was justified as a rehabilitative program. More recently, parole has come to be justified as a public safety measure, offering protection for the community through the "supervision and surveillance" of parolees.

CONTEMPORARY CRIME POLICY

In early January 1994, Shelly Messinger and I were sipping coffee at the International House terrace in midafternoon, overlooking San Francisco Bay. Over the years, many of our discussions have taken place like this, informally, as friends and colleagues. We were discussing California's crime policy and the impending "three strikes and you're out" legislation, which passed shortly afterward on February 28, 1994. The "three strikes" law is complicated, but unquestionably casts the widest habitual-offender net in the nation. The first two strikes are defined as "serious" felonies, but the third strike is *any* felony. Six months after the law was passed, more than half of the "three strikes" cases filed in some California counties (the more rural and suburban) have involved such nonviolent felonies as shoplifting, auto burglary, theft of cigarettes and—in one Los Angeles case—theft of a pizza. A juvenile can be convicted of two residential burglaries. Years later, convicted of passing a bad check, he or she can be sent to prison for life.

On September 13, 1994, six months after the law passed, Los Angeles officials told the Board of Supervisors that the law was slowing down the criminal justice system almost to a halt. Sheriff Sherman Block testified that during the first six months since the law's enactment, the Los Angeles County jail, already under court order to limit overcrowding, has added 1,700 inmates. Block, District Attorney Gil Garcetti, and a panel of judges warned that the gridlock in the courts could force the release of thousands of petty criminals. The law enforcement officials were gloomy. The only solutions they could envision, they warned, were cutbacks in public services or a rise in taxes.

I had recently written an op-ed piece in the *Los Angeles Times* (16 December 1993) explaining how it could happen that such a vicious, dangerous criminal as Richard Allen Davis, whose kidnapping and strangulation of twelve-year-old Polly Klaas outraged the public and laid the popular justification for "three strikes and you're out," could slip through the cracks of California's criminal justice system—and what that suggested for penal reform.

I traced the freedom of Richard Allen Davis to California's 1977 prison sentencing reforms, which were supported by an unlikely coalition of hard-line conservatives and prisoner advocates. Before 1977, California was a pioneer in indeterminate prison sentencing for felony offenders. A Richard Allen Davis might receive a sentence of one year to life for such felonies as second-degree murder, robbery, and rape. In fact, that sentence was apportioned to Davis in the spring of 1977 for the crimes he had committed in 1976—kidnapping, assault, robbery, and burglary.

Nevertheless, many legislators thought that the indeterminate system was too soft on criminals, and perhaps it was. For example, in 1965, the median time served by prisoners released on parole ranged from a high of 5.4 years for second-degree murder to a low of 3 years for burglary. But on the other side, many prisoners believed that the board's vast discretion produced unfair disparities, since people convicted of the same crime could serve significantly different sentences. They charged that indeterminate sentencing offered prison administrators an arbitrary and potent instrument for inmate control. Their complaint was summed up for writer Jessica Mitford by a convict whom she had interviewed: "From the vindictive guard who sets out to build a record against some individual to the parole board, the indeterminate sentence grants Corrections the power to play God with the lives of prisoners" (Mitford 1973:83).

In 1977, the legislature, spurred by critics from both political sides, changed to a determinate sentencing system. The new law required that Davis's term be recalculated to six years, a reduction mandated despite the prescient presentencing report of San Mateo County probation officer Adele Shiells, who warned of what she called Davis's propensity for crime and apparent accelerating potential for violence.

Shiells's predictions were unfortunately proven true when, after his automatic release, Davis and an accomplice robbed, kidnapped, and assaulted a Redwood City woman in 1984. Sentenced to sixteen years, he earned time off for work and good behavior and had to be released in eight. If the indeterminate sentence had been in effect, someone with Davis's personality and criminal history might have been imprisoned, if not for life, then for decades.

I concluded by acknowledging that the indeterminate sentencing system unquestionably had its flaws, but could be improved by making qualified professional appointments to the parole board and providing guidelines for release. In any case, I argued, a modified indeterminate sentencing system would be preferable to the rigidities of determinate sentencing and to the add-ons, such as "three strikes and you're out" that are being proposed to shore up a fundamentally flawed structure.

I wanted to know what Sheldon Messinger thought of all this, especially as some California legislators were taking an interest in penal reform. He wasn't especially impressed one way or another. He told me, "There's nothing new in any of this. Everything you need to know about penal reform is in the concluding chapter of Michel Foucault's *Discipline and Punish.*"

And so I turned to Foucault's (1977) last chapter. There I learned that in 1840, at Mettray, the inmates were divided into five groups: the family, to offer brotherhood and role models; the army, which stressed hierarchy, discipline, and cleanliness; the workshop, which taught skills, especially to younger inmates; the school, which taught "lessons;" and the court, where justice was meted out to punish even the most minor offenses very severely. That does, indeed, sound familiar.

I also learned, according to Foucault, that although we have moved far from the tortures, gibbets, gallows, and pillories of the eighteenth century, we have adopted "not a network of forces, but a multiple network of diverse elements—walls, space, institution, rules, discourse" (p. 307) that make up the "carceral city."

Although Foucault's vision is dismal and pessimistic, it may not be grim enough when measures like "three strikes and you're out" threaten to render the twenty-first a carceral century—and it needs to be put into the recent historical context of the United States.

THE 1960s: FROM PROTEST TO CRIME

Twenty-six years ago, in 1969, the 1960s had gone into history as the decade of protest and civil disorder. Bitter and divisive race riots shook dozens of cities from Los Angeles to Detroit to Newark. Protest against American involvement in Vietnam had become so familiar that it had almost acquired the status of an institution. We researchers were asked to explain why protest, confrontation, and violence had become, in the words of black activist H. Rap Brown, "as American as apple pie."

By comparison, there wasn't much fear of crime in the early 1960s. In fact, the nation's prisons had empty beds in the middle of the decade. This is not to suggest that crime wasn't an issue. But as a recent Gallup Poll showed, the public was not so nearly frustrated then with what it now sees as an impotent and ineffective criminal-justice system.

The war protests ended with our withdrawal from Vietnam. And civil disorder in the ghettos of the nation also came to an end. It was forcibly suppressed.

As protest and civil disorder declined, the crime rate rose precipitously. Prison populations were to double in the 1970s, triple in the 1980s, and quadruple in the 1990s even as increasingly punitive sentencing laws were supposed to raise the price of crime.

But could there be a connection, an explanation for the inverse correlation between the decline in civil disorder and the rise in crime? I suggest there is. High-protest areas were transformed into high-crime, and especially high-homicide areas. Arguably, crime became a "functional alternative" to protest. From that perspective, crime began to replace protest and civil disorder to express the alienation and frustration felt by those relegated to the economic sidestreams of American society. And when the opportunities to sell drugs heightened with the development of crack cocaine in the mid 1980s, many of these unemployed kids turned to drug selling as an alternative.

From the perspective of the larger society, the connection between the suppression of civil disorder and the rise in crime lay in the failure of the polity to heed clear warnings. The commissions that studied the civil disorders and protests of the 1960s—the National Advisory Commission on Civil Disorders and the National Commission on the Causes and Prevention of Violence—were largely composed of moderate and Establishment figures who could scarcely be described as political radicals. Otto Kerner was governor of Illinois and a product of its politics. Milton Eisenhower, the former president's brother, was a distinguished educator. The executive directors, David Ginsberg of the Kerner Commission and Lloyd Cutler of the Violence Commission, were prominent Washington lawyers whose firms represented major U.S. corporations. The findings of the commissioners and their staffs were not all of a piece, but they all recognized that the ghettos of America were in crisis. Perhaps the most famous and disturbing conclusion was from the Kerner Report: "What white Americans have never fully understood—but what the Negro can never forget—is that white society is deeply implicated in the ghetto. White institutions created it, white institutions maintain it and white society condones it" (p. vii).

The ghetto has never offered much opportunity to its residents. The Kerner Report observed that a large proportion of riot participants were young, between fifteen and twenty-four years old. Since the end of World War II, this is the age group in the black community that has experienced extraordinarily high unemployment rates. This age group is also responsible for a disproportionately high crime rate. For many of these kids, crime and drug dealing have become a way of life.

Although the causal relationship between street crime and employment opportunity is complex, there is no question that there is one. People who have reasonably well-paying jobs are unlikely to rob convenience stores, burglarize homes, and mug the elderly. Aside from its economic rewards, employment is a form of social control. Its responsibilities discipline one's daily rounds. It also supports family life. But jobless youth—who tend to be impetuous, who engage in male bonding activities that we call gangs—are even more likely than other jobless people to be free from ordinary social constraints. Nor are they likely to be deterred by the threat of imprisonment, partly because the threat is not entirely credible, but mostly because they have few alternatives.

The threat of imprisonment can be assimilated by even a rational risk assessor who has little to lose and much to gain by a life of crime, especially the entrepreneurial activity of drug marketing. The risks of drug dealing, as the RAND study *Money from Crime* (Reuter, MacCoun, and Murphy 1990) finds, are quite high, but drug dealers pass on the costs through high prices. About half of the average drug dealer's earnings can be considered as compensation for "incurring the risk of imprisonment or of . . . a market-related killing." Whether through stealing or, more likely, selling drugs, young, male, outlaw capitalists have found an alternative economic path.

As we move from an industrial economy that promised jobs to a broad range of workers to a postindustrial world that increasingly offers rich rewards to skilled professionals but low-paying service jobs to the least educated, we see an increase in economic inequality as well as in poverty. The

Reagan and Bush years also have reduced such opportunities as "jobs for youth" and other social programs as alternatives for potential gang kids.

Capitalism offers few, if any, moral cautions against moderate risk-taking—a point underscored by the peccadilloes of such presumably exemplary capitalists as Wall Street investment bankers and Sunbelt savings and loan executives. Although the wrongs of the rich do not justify the wrongs of the poor, they send a message of widespread rule breaking. Capitalism needs moral and regulatory institutions, whether religious or secular, to restrain risk-takers at every rung of the social ladder.

The criminal law is one of these institutions, but it works very effectively only when most of us accept it as a moral force. Most of us do not refrain from killing, robbing, and raping because we expect punishment for crime, but because we believe those acts are morally wrong. In the Hobbesian world of gang enterprise, the criminal law must rely primarily on its capacity to deter through threat of punishment. The threat simply does not work very well. Gang members are young and tough, and risks of arrest and imprisonment are already quite high. Moreover, as the RAND study found, "Death and serious injury resulting from the actions of other participants [in the drug trade] may be more important in determining both who participates and what they earn than are risks imposed by the criminal justice system."

The commissions of the 1960s did caution the nation about its underlying social needs, even as counterinsurgency strategies prevailed, but today we can see an increasing emphasis on the symbolism of repression—curfews, sweeps, boot camps, death penalty, "three strikes and you're out," and more prisons. Just as economists observe that there is no free lunch, sociologists warn that there is no costless social neglect. "The Politics of Protest," my 1969 report to the National Commission on the Causes and Prevention of Violence, concluded by saying:

> A democratic society cannot depend upon force as its recurrent answer to longstanding and legitimate grievances. This nation cannot have it both ways: Either it will carry through a firm commitment to massive and widespread social reform, or it will develop into a society of garrison cities where order is enforced without due process of law and without the consent of the governed. (Skolnick 1969:346)

A CIVIL OR CARCERAL SOCIETY?

Surely all of us—liberals as well as conservatives—aspire to live in a society marked by self-discipline, civil behavior, family stability, and public safety. The real issue is why some of us believe that we can rely upon penal institutions to achieve those admirable goals. Foucault (and Messinger) remind us that human deviance is a function of marginality, rather than the reverse. Yet politicians, spurred by public alarm, are reluctant to offer that message, even when they believe it.

At a time when crime has been identified in polls in the United States as our number one social problem, the political world, instead of showing leadership, has reverted to the simplistic banality of being "tough on crime," a reversion reminiscent of the preenlightenment intuitions that governed social control in the seventeenth century. In this respect, our current penological state is even worse than Foucault imagined, and Messinger's pessimism is unfortunately justified. We are approaching a critical time in penal history, and the future appears gloomily punitive.

The prospect in California is particularly ominous. This is not merely a parochial observation. Even without "three strikes" legislation, California is already the nation's largest jailer, with one out of every eight U.S. prisoners occupying its cells. During the past sixteen years its prison population has grown 600 percent, while violent crime in the state has increased by 40 percent. As Franklin E. Zimring and Gordon Hawkins (1994) demonstrate in a recent issue of the *British Journal of Criminology,* correctional growth in California was in a class by itself in the 1980s. The three next largest state prison systems (New York, Texas, and Florida) experienced half the growth of California, and Western European nations about a quarter.

To pay for a fivefold increase in the corrections budget since 1980, Californians have had to sacrifice other services. In 1984, California devoted 14 percent of its state budget to higher education and 4 percent to prisons. In 1994, it gave 9 percent to both. Under "three strikes," the balance is expected to shift sharply in favor of prisons. The California Department of Corrections has estimated that "three strikes" will require an additional twenty prisons to be added to the present twenty-eight and the twelve already on the drawing board. By 2001, California anticipates 109,000 more prisoners behind bars serving life sentences.

If the crime problem were properly defined, and the lessons of past efforts were fully absorbed, this could be an opportunity to set national crime policy on a positive course. Instead it is a moment of dangerous anxiety and thoughtless intuition that is driving the nation toward desperate and ineffectual measures. These will drive up the costs of imprisonment, divert tax dollars from other vital purposes, and leave the public as insecure and dissatisfied as ever.

In any case, when I consider imprisonment and its wider networks of social control, probation, parole, diversion, I am aware that I, like so many others, have benefited from Sheldon L. Messinger's insights and contributions to criminal justice research and theory. These were recognized in 1992 by the American Justice Institute, which awarded him the Richard A. McGee prize for his "outstanding contributions to criminal justice research."

Dr. Messinger has had a number of collaborators over the years for the very good reason that people enjoy his company, conversation, wit, humor, and selflessness. To collaborate and talk with Sheldon L. Messinger is an experience that many of those who have contributed to this volume, as students, colleagues and friends, have enjoyed and benefited from. And we are all the better for it.

REFERENCES

Berk, Richard, Sheldon L. Messinger, David Rauma, and John E. Berecochea. 1981. "A Test of the Stability of Punishment Hypothesis: The Case of California, 1851–1970." *American Sociological Review* 40:805–28.

———. 1982. "A Further Test of the Stability of Punishment Hypothesis." Pp. 39–64 in *Quantitative Criminology: Innovations and Applications*, edited by John Hagan. Beverly Hills, CA: Sage.

———. 1983. "Prisons as Self-Regulating Systems: A Comparison of Historical Patterns in California for Male and Female Offenders." *Law and Society Review* 17:547–86.

Carlin, Jerome E., Jan Howard, and Sheldon L. Messinger. 1964. *Civil Justice and the Poor: Issues for Sociological Change*. Berkeley, CA: Center for the Study of Law and Society.

Foucault, Michel. 1977. *Discipline and Punish: The Birth of the Prison*. New York: Pantheon.

Messinger, Sheldon. 1955. "Organizational Transformation: A Study of a Declining Social Movement." *American Sociological Review* 20:3–10.

———. 1962. "Life as Theatre: Some Notes on the Dramaturgical Approach to Social Reality." *Sociometry* 25:98–110.

Messinger, Sheldon, and Phillip E. Johnson. 1978. "California's Determinate Sentence Statute: History and Issues." Pp. 13–58 in *Determinate Sentencing: Reform or Regression?* Proceedings of the Special Conference on Determinate Sentencing, National Institute of Law Enforcement and Criminal Justice, Law Enforcement Assistance Administration, U.S. Department of Justice. Washington, DC: USGPO.

Messinger, Sheldon, John E. Berecochea, David Rauma, and Richard A. Berk. 1985. "The Foundation of Parole in California." *Law and Society Review* 19:69–106.

Mitford, Jessica. 1973. *Kind and Usual Punishment: The Prison Business*. New York: Knopf.

Reuter, Peter, Robert MacCoun, and Patrick Murphy. 1990. *Money From Crime: A Study of the Economics of Drug Dealing in Washington, D.C.* Santa Monica, CA: Rand Corporation.

Sampson, Harold, Sheldon L. Messinger, and Robert D. Towne. 1964. *Schizophrenic Women: Studies in Marital Crisis.* New York: Atherton.

Skolnick, Jerome H. 1969. *The Politics of Protest.* New York: Simon & Schuster.

Sykes, Gresham and Sheldon Messinger. 1960. "The Inmate Social System." Pp. 5–19 in *Theoretical Studies In Social Organization of the Prison,* edited by Richard A. Cloward, Donald R. Cressey, George H. Grosser, Richard McCleery, Sheldon L. Messinger, Lloyd E. Ohlin, and Gresham M. Sykes. New York: Social Sciences Research Council.

Zimring, Franklin E. and Gordon Hawkins. 1994. "The Growth of Imprisonment in California." *British Journal of Criminology* 34:83–95.

II

THE PRISON:
Reforms and Alternatives

We referred in our Editorial Introduction to the continued presence of the prison. It would be hard to imagine another institution with such apparently specialized functions that has been so intensively scrutinized. Historians have debated about its origins; sociologists have studied its internal structure and culture; policy analysts have tried to evaluate its effectiveness; social critics, reformers, and prisoners themselves have exposed its inhumanity. The prison invariably emerges from this scrutiny as little more than a crude instrument for punishment and disposal: of dubious utility and near-certain harm. Yet prison systems throughout the world not only remain intact but keep expanding. They are seemingly impervious to criticism and resistant to attempts to replace them by alternatives that are more humane, efficient, and cheaper.

The chapters in this section offer merely some examples from this vast literature. In Chapter 3, the historian David Rothman, whose 1971 book *The Discovery of the Asylum* was a breakthrough in understanding the origins of the penitentiary and mental asylum in early nineteenth-century America, reflects on the current dramatic rise in rates of imprisonment. His emphasis on the determinate sentencing model raises important issues about the causal relationship between ideas and penal policy. In Chapter 4, Thomas G. Blomberg looks outside the prison walls to track one stream of the post-1960s movement to find alternatives to imprisonment. He emphasizes the problems in using metaphors like net-widening to capture the disappointment of many reformers at the failure of this movement to stop the expansion of the correctional system.

In Chapter 5, James Jacobs examines one particular strand of prison reform: the use of the formal legal system to improve prison conditions and protect prisoners' rights. Whether or not alternative forms of social control can be found, democratic societies cannot allow internal prison regimes to be insulated from conventional mechanisms of legal accountability. How far have the courts succeeded in penetrating the closed walls of the prison?

In 1958, Gresham Sykes published *The Society of Captives*, the pioneering sociological study of imprisonment. The themes he raised in this study—what imprisonment does to prisoners, the social relationship between inmates and staff, the prison as a miniature society—remain just as relevant and interesting today. In Chapter 6, Sykes reflects on how this line of enquiry was established.

3
More of the Same: American Criminal Justice Policies in the 1990s

DAVID J. ROTHMAN

The least controversial observation about American criminal justice today is that it is remarkably ineffective, absurdly expensive, grossly inhumane, and riddled with discrimination. The beating of Rodney King was a reminder of the ruthlessness and racism that characterizes many big city police departments. But the other aspects of the justice system, especially sentencing practices and prison conditions, are every bit as harsh and unfair. Nevertheless, a powerful political coalition remains determined to promote the very policies that perpetuate these outcomes. Despite repeated failures and inequities, the rallying cry is more of the same.

I

American prisons and sentencing practices were not always so disreputable. Immediately after the revolution, in an effort to rid the country of the relics of British imperial rule, state legislatures drastically reduced the number of capital punishments. Then in the 1820s and 1830s, American state governments were pioneers in prison design; they built huge and expensive institutions that provided each inmate with his own private cell, and, as in the Pennsylvania Penitentiary, his own private exercise yard. The prison, by excluding all corrupting influences and subjecting the inmate to steady labor and a quasi-military routine (exemplified by the lockstep), would reform the deviant and eradicate crime from the society. That a simplistic and utopian mission failed to achieve its aims is not nearly as remarkable as the influence it exerted around the world. Alexis de Tocqueville, it should be remembered, came to the United States not to write *Democracy in America* but to advise the French Assembly on American prisons.

A second phase of prison reform took place in the opening decades of the twentieth century. American states were the first to introduce indeterminate sentences, under which the inmate was to serve, say, one to five years (or in ideal form, from one day to life); the actual time of release depended on the parole board's estimate of whether the offender had been rehabilitated. The prisons introduced educational programs and psychological counseling and dropped the insistence on isolation; ostensibly, life behind walls would prepare inmates for life outside. Once more, European criminologists and legislators came to study American methods and generally admired the new measures.

But again, the realities of prison life soon contradicted the reformers' hopes. Indeterminate sentences did not result in "rehabilitation," and people who actually visited the prisons could not ignore the overcrowding and brutality, or the periodic riots, that took place. The failures, however, were attributed by such leading reformers as Thomas Osborne and Sheldon Glueck, and by the most important national commission on law enforcement, the 1931 Wickersham Commission, not to an inherent flaw in design but to the incompetence of administrators, the ignorance of the guards, or the stinginess of the legislators. To read their conclusions, the rehabilitative goals of prison administration were altogether feasible.

Beginning in the 1970s, and continuing to this day, an abundant and impressive literature demonstrates how each component of this inherited system has been discredited. Foreign analysts are appalled by current prison conditions and sentencing practices; they cannot believe that we could be so retrogressive. Nils Christie, an eminent Norwegian criminologist and author of *Crime Control as Industry*, found U.S. prisons so repellent that he opens his analysis with the apologetic phrase, "Whom one loveth, one chasteneth" (1993:79). He then goes on to draw an analogy with Nazi Germany: "The extermination camp was a product of industrialization. . .a combination of thought-patterns, social organization and technical tools. My contention is that the prison system in the USA is rapidly moving in the same direction" (p. 163). American critics display less hyperbole but no less indignation. Human Rights Watch (1991), having investigated prison conditions throughout the world, looked at home and found "numerous human rights abuses and frequent violations of the U.N. Standard Minimum Rules for the Treatment of Prisoners" (p. 4).

The most conspicuous sign of failure, cited by Christie, Human Rights Watch, and practically every other observer, is our extraordinary reliance on incarceration. The United States leads the world with a rate of 455 incarcerated per 100,000 of the population. South Africa is a distant second with 311 per 100,000. To be sure, a low rate of incarceration may reflect pervasive police brutality; in India, for example, police prefer to beat up petty felons rather than imprison them (Rothman and Neier 1981). But such conduct is irrelevant to a comparison with the Netherlands (40 per 100,000), Japan (45), France (81), or England (97) (Mauer 1992:5).

Moreover, the pace of incarceration has spiraled out of control. Between 1980 and 1992, the number of inmates in state and federal prisons rose by 168 percent, from 330,000 to 883,000, and the number is likely to reach one million in 1994. The increase of offenders on probation and parole is no less dramatic. In 1980, 1.1 million adults were serving sentences of probation, and 220,000 were on parole. By 1990, the number on probation stood at 2.5 million, with 457,000 on parole (Edna McConnell Foundation 1993:2–3).

Keeping people in prison places a heavy burden on state budgets. The Edna McConnell Clark Foundation, the leading private funder of criminal justice reform programs, estimates that in 1992 the United States spent $25 billion dollars on its prison system, making it the second fastest growing item, after Medicaid, among state government expenditures. New York, for example, between 1983 and 1990 built twenty-seven new prisons at the short-term cost of $1.6 billion, and eventual cost of $5.4 billion over thirty years if one includes the interest payable on state bonds floated for the construction. It was once commonplace to observe that a year in jail was as expensive as a year at Harvard, but by now jail costs in many cities are much higher. Maintaining one inmate for one year in New York City costs $58,000, more than twice the annual cost for students at private universities. Unforeseen contingencies push costs still higher. New York state spends $50 million a year on AZT for inmates with AIDS, and New York City, to abide by a court order, just built eighty-four isolation cells at $450,000 each, to house inmates with tuberculosis.

Despite these expenditures, prison capacity has not kept up with need. On average, federal prisons are 46 percent and state prisons are 31 percent over capacity. Cells built for one inmate often hold two or even three. At the start of 1993, forty states and the District of Columbia were under court orders to correct overcrowding and improve substandard conditions. So were one-third of all the jails in the country. The chances of these orders being carried out are not very great.

The most troubling feature of the justice system is its impact on minorities, particularly African-Americans. As Jerome Miller, the head of the National Center on Institutions and Alternatives, recently reported, 42 percent of black men in Washington, D.C. between the ages of eighteen and thirty-five are either in prison or on probation or parole, out on bail, or being sought on an arrest warrant. For black men in Baltimore, the comparable figure is 57 percent (Miller 1992; National Center on Institutions and Alternatives 1992). Nationwide, blacks make up 48 percent of prison inmates, as against 12 percent of the population. The disparity is even more flagrant if one looks, as did Michael Tonry (1993), professor of law at the University of Minnesota, at rates of confinement per one hundred thousand. For whites, it is 289; for blacks, 1860.[1] The likelihood of being in prison or in jail is seven times higher for black Americans than whites.

II

Among the many reasons why so many blacks are in prison—including high rates of unemployment and inadequate urban schools—none is more decisive than the changes in the administration of criminal justice, particularly the new sentencing practices. During the 1970s, liberal reformers became disillusioned with the indeterminate sentence and its commitment to the principle of rehabilitation. As exemplified by the reports of the American Friends Service Committee (1971), the Twentieth Century Fund (1976), and the Field Foundation Committee for the Study of Incarceration, the dominant view was that open-ended sentences adapted to the personal characteristics of the offender—his education, job, marital state, and so on—gave judges and parole boards the discretion to penalize blacks and lower-class offenders more heavily than white, middle-class ones. The reports also shared the belief that rehabilitation programs were a sham. Not only were the interventions ineffectual, but they made imprisonment seem legitimate and desirable. The rehabilitative model, as Gaylin and I assert in the introduction of *Doing Justice,* "has been more cruel and punitive than a frankly punitive model would probably be" (Von Hirsch 1976). Fostering the illusion that inmates were locked up for their own good, rehabilitation made sentences of five, ten, and fifteen years appear benevolent.

From the diagnosis came the cure: enact fixed sentences, reduce the discretion of the judge to set the penalty, restrict or even eliminate the power of the parole board to determine the moment of release. The aim was to let the crime and the prior criminal record of the offender dictate the punishment, without any reference to the social characteristics of the criminal, including race, gender, occupation, or work history. Sentencing guidelines, drawn up in advance, would determine the time to be served within narrow ranges. In this way, all first-time burglars would get a sentence of between twelve and eighteen months, regardless of whether the burglar was white or black, male or female, from the urban or rural part of the state, or standing before a judge with a reputation for leniency or for harshness.

Reformers were aware of the possibility that fixed sentences might turn out to be even longer than indeterminate ones. They recognized that this was the goal of more conservative, right-wing thinkers who also embraced the idea of fixed sentences. Such conservatives, none more vigorously than James Q. Wilson, argued that indeterminate sentences put offenders back on the streets too quickly. Since actual time served almost always turned out to be less than the maximum provided in the original sentence, the criminal was being prematurely released and allowed to return to a life in crime. When "twenty-five years to life" turned out to be eight years, because parole boards often released inmates at one-third of the minimum, the safety of the society was compromised. Thus, fixed sentences represented a long overdue return to "truth in sentencing," which would make offenders serve out their time.

The oddness of the alliance did not weaken liberals' enthusiasm. They fully expected that sentences set forth in guidelines would reduce the scale of penalties, moving step by step from the less serious to the more serious crimes, with one eye always on the number of prison cells available for confinement. Why were they so optimistic? In retrospect, they exaggerated the appeal that a claim to fairness would have. But they were also so appalled by the existing system that they were overeager to implement an alternative to it. In 1972, Marvin Frankel, then a federal judge in New York, published a highly influential book, *Criminal Sentences: Law without Order*, arguing that judges exercised "almost wholly unchecked and sweeping authority" (p. 5). He found it "terrifying and intolerable for a society that professes devotion to the rule of law" (ibid.) to perpetuate these sentencing practices. His passionate language conveys just how anxious he and others were that changes be made.

Moreover, during the early 1970s a fierce attack took place on the legitimacy of "total institutions," to use Erving Goffman's term. Partly as a result, the number of prison inmates, along with mental hospital residents, was actually declining. Indeed, the sense that prisons were losing their hold on public policy was reinforced by the reactions to the Attica riot. The official New York State report on Attica expressed shame at the wretchedness of prison conditions, not hostility to the rebellious inmates. Reformers also expected legislators to vote in accord with their constituents' pocketbooks. Since prisons were expensive and were becoming all the more so because of court-ordered improvements, they believed politicians would welcome a reduction in the number of prisoners.

Finally, reformers were attracted by the prospect of commissions or collective bodies, not individual judges or parole boards, setting the scale of penalties. In truth, advocates did not spend much time discussing who would actually serve on the commissions or how their decisions would be translated into law or practice. Rather, they were convinced that sentencing decisions should be removed from politics and the criminal-justice system insulated from popular pressures. Sentencing commissions, like other administrative bodies (most notably, the Securities and Exchange Commission and the Food and Drug Administration) would bring expertise and rational decision-making into a bitterly contested area; and once determinations of punishment were removed from arbitrary judges, overly conservative parole boards, and constituent-driven legislators, prison time would be doled out more sparingly and alternatives to prison would be used more frequently.

The reformers proved wrong on all counts. Determinate sentences were introduced in the 1980s, both in the federal system and in roughly one-third of the states. But apart from a few jurisdictions (most notably Minnesota), sentencing guidelines have increased the time served, had relatively little impact on disparity in sentences, promoted prison overcrowding, and reduced the importance of judges in sentencing by enhancing the discretion of prosecutors. The distaste for rehabilitation has contributed as well to making prisons into warehouses. If educational and training programs are mischievous and futile, why should the state spend money on them?

Hostility to indeterminate sentences has also made it easier for the federal government and the states to enact mandatory-minimum statutes, which inevitably increase the time to be served. Once the levying of punishment became more mechanical (consult the chart) than individualized (tell me your life story), mandatory minimums assumed a surface logic. There are now over one hundred such provisions in the federal code, according to University of Chicago Law School professor Stephen Schulhofer (1993), with crimes involving guns and drugs accounting for most of them. Thus, between 1984 and 1990, sentences for drug offenders who did not carry firearms increased from thirty-six months with the possibility of earlier release on parole, to sixty-six months with no parole. Moreover, mandatory minimum sentences have expanded the authority of prosecutors—in return for a guilty plea, they will indict on a lesser offense that does not carry a minimum. And prosecutors perpetuate discriminatory practices: it is whites far more often than blacks who get the chance to plead guilty to lesser crimes and thereby receive sentences below the mandatory minimums.

What had reformers missed? Why did their good intentions lead to such punitive results? Part of the answer is the changed political environment of the 1980s. Reagan and Bush were able to make crime and sentencing procedures a rallying point around which middle-class Americans could express their frustration not only with unsafe streets but with affirmative action and welfare costs. Reformers also forgot what Nils Christie (1993) emphasizes, that many bondholders and job seekers see prison maintenance and construction not as a drain upon public resources but as a sound investment and source of employment.

More important, reformers overestimated the degree of insularity from politics that sentencing commissions would provide. The history of sentencing practices in Washington state, as explained by David Boerner (1993), professor of law at the University of Puget Sound, is an apt case in point. The driving force for change was not a burgeoning crime rate but a widely shared belief that sentencing should be less discretionary and that something had to be done to reduce overcrowding in the state's prisons (which a federal court ruled violated constitutional standards). The legislation approving a sentencing commission and determinate sentences was fashioned by two representatives, Democrat Mary Kay Becker and Republican Gene Struthers, who came from such different points on the political spectrum that their collaboration, Becker quipped, was like "Jane Fonda and John Wayne coauthoring a book on Vietnam."

The Washington State sentencing commission, like most other commissions, was dominated by insiders to the criminal justice system. Its members were four judges, two prosecutors, two defense attorneys, three state criminal justice officials, the state director of finance, and three private citizens. The commission set out explicit guidelines for sentencing, which the legislature subsequently adopted and judges were obliged to follow. Prison sentences were reserved for violent offenders, with time to be served based exclusively on the crime itself and the offender's past criminal history; alternative punishments, including probation and community service, were to go to nonviolent offenders.

These guidelines initially reduced imprisonment, so that Washington State soon enjoyed a surplus of prison cells (which it leased to other states, thereby receiving added income). But beginning in 1990, the prison population swelled (up 23 percent the first year, 10 percent the second), mostly because the legislature, with the concurrence of the commission, revised the fixed sentences upward. It set tougher penalties for drug use and drug sale, responding to pressures from prosecutors that the system was too soft on dealers. In the new scheme, judges were not allowed to sentence first-time offenders to probation and treatment programs, so 92 percent of first-time drug offenders now entered prison. The legislature also increased punishments for all drug offenders so that average sentences jumped about three times. (In 1988, possession and delivery of heroin or cocaine brought on average nineteen months, in 1992, fifty-six months.) At the same time, and after an especially gruesome sex crime (the mutilation of a young boy) committed by a known sex offender who had just been released from prison after serving his maximum sentence, the commission, responding to explicit legislative directions, revised the penalties for all sex abuse crimes. Average sentences served then increased from thirty-three months to seventy-six months.

As the Washington State experience suggests, transferring authority from judges and parole boards to a commission may bring sentencing so directly into politics that potentially short-lived outrages turn into long-term changes in penal codes. A public outcry has often affected a judge's behavior. If there is a rash of robberies or a vicious child abuse case, the next person to commit such a crime may well receive a harsher sentence in the hope of deterring future crimes. But when sentencing commissioners and legislators get agitated, the repercussions go beyond an increased sentence for one highly publicized case to increased penalties for entire categories of crimes for years to come. The real problem is, as Christie shrewdly comments, that once sentencing becomes a "tool in the hands of politicians," we get "democratic crime control" (1993:173). There are no limits to punishment so long as they do not adversely affect the majority.

III

Probably the most serious flaw in the design of the 1970s reform program was the failure to anticipate the prominence that would go to drug control. This one issue has been the fulcrum around which criminal justice procedures turn.

For the most part, attempting to correlate changing crime rates with innovations in criminal policy is futile, both because measures of crime are inexact and public responses appear to be framed not by overall crime statistics as by events in people's own immediate neighborhoods or by what they read or hear about through the media. By some measures (the FBI summary of police reports), violent crime in the nation has increased over the past decade, up 23 percent between 1980 and 1990; by other counts (the U.S. Census surveys of citizens), violent crimes have gone down 11 percent. Reviewing the data, Christopher Jencks (1991) recently observed that we are a more violent country today than we were in the 1950s and 1960s (when today's middle-aged population was growing up), but less violent than we were in the late 1970s. The recent victory of a prosecutor, Rudolph Giuliani, in New York's mayoralty election was ascribed in part to a widespread belief among voters that New York was becoming increasingly dangerous; however, in December 1993, the FBI announced that over the past year, crime in the northeast had declined 8 percent, in upstate New York, 6.8 percent, and in New York City, by 5.6 percent. Opinion and data obviously need not jibe.

The one exception to these observations is drug crime and drug policy. Arrests, convictions, and imprisonment for drug offenses have skyrocketed, and everyone agrees that the increases reflect not a change in street behavior but in enforcement and punishment patterns. Marc Mauer (1993), the assistant director of the Washington-based Sentencing Project, calculates that drug arrests increased over the 1980s by 88 percent; now, one in four inmates (in 1983 it was one in eleven) is serving time or awaiting trial for a drug offense. In federal prisons, nearly 60 percent of inmates have been convicted of drug offenses, receiving on average eight-year sentences, twice the penalty meted out in 1980. In state prisons, drug offenders make up 22 percent of inmates, up from 6 percent. One-third are in for possession, two-thirds for sale or manufacture; both the distinctions have less to do with street behavior than plea bargaining. In New York, for example, offenders sentenced for possession or sale of drugs increased over 600 percent (from 1500 to 9760) between 1983 and 1989.

Drug law enforcement and punishment are aimed almost exclusively at minorities. The war on drugs is essentially a war on blacks. The black proportion of all drug possession arrests increased from 22 percent in 1981 to 37 percent in 1990. In Baltimore, among adult offenders, blacks are five times more likely than whites to be arrested for drug offenses; among juveniles, blacks are ten times more likely. In New York, of all drug possession offenders who received a prison sentence, 91 percent were black or Hispanic; in California, 71 percent of those sentenced to prison for drug possession were black or Hispanic (Boerner 1993).

With drugs, as with crime more generally, it is almost impossible to sort out whether the disparity in convictions and punishment between whites and blacks reflects actual behavior, that is, blacks committing more of the heavily penalized crimes, or frank discrimination, with police, prosecutors, and judges coming down harder on blacks than on whites. Undoubtedly both statements are true, but discrimination is especially apparent in the drug enforcement world. For example, some state penal codes punish the possession or use of heroin far more severely than cocaine, a tactic so obviously racially biased that one federal court held the provision unconstitutional. Racial discrimination also helps explain the disparity in punishment for drunk driving as against drug use. Mauer and his colleague Cathy Shine recently calculated that although drunk driving causes as many deaths as drug use, it is punished far less severely. They suggest that the difference may lie in the fact that all but a few of those convicted of drunk driving are white, while those convicted for drug offenses are black (Shine and Mauer 1993). Hence, to understand prison overcrowding, the practical disappearance of the young black urban males from the streets, and the fate of 1970s reformers' hopes for the fixed sentence, one must look to how the system responds to drugs.

IV

The short unhappy history of the new Federal sentencing code starkly demonstrates how liberal reform produced rigid and punitive policies. As the Yale Law School Professors Kate Stith and Steve Koh (1993) skillfully recount, the initiative for revising federal sentencing codes in the 1970s came from Senator Ted Kennedy. His aim was to create a commission that would bring greater equity to sentencing by not allowing such characteristics as schooling, income, and family life to alter the severity of the punishment. In Kennedy's original proposal, the commission was also to ensure that time served did not increase, that prisons did not become overcrowded, and that alternatives to incarceration were incorporated into the system. But Kennedy never could make up his mind on how tightly he wanted to tie judges' hands. Sometimes he made it seem as though the guidelines were advisory, at other times as though they were binding. His ultimate goal was to reduce discretion so as to reduce discrimination.

The Kennedy bill did not pass under the Carter administration, in part because the House was far less attracted to mandatory guidelines, and in part because sentencing became entangled with more conservative efforts to revamp the entire federal criminal code. But rather than abandon his proposal when Reagan came in, Kennedy continued to forge ahead and, along the way, too readily accepted a number of compromises. The bill that was signed into law by President Reagan in 1984 had the shell but not the nuances of the original proposal. Earlier instructions to the commission to decrease time served and not to overcrowd prisons were weakened. More important, the commissioners were appointed by the president, and when they got down to work, they adopted Reagan's commitment to "law and order," and "get tough with the criminal." Their interpretations of the statute consistently curtailed judicial discretion and maximized penalties. They ruled, for example, that sentences were to be meted out on the basis of "real offense," that is, what the offender had presumably done, not what he had pleaded guilty to in the process of plea bargaining or been convicted for in court (Stith and Koh 1993).

In day-to-day practice, as Michael Tonry (1993) explains, the judge consults the guideline schedule to reach his sentence. He starts at the "base offense level," say, burglary, which has a score of 20, and then adds points to it on the basis of how the crime was carried out. If the offender discharged a gun, he adds 7 levels. If the crime resulted in bodily injury, he adds 2, if it was serious bodily injury, another 2. If the burglary was $10,000 or less, he adds nothing. But if it was between $10,000 and $50,000, he adds 2. If more than $250,000 he adds 3, and so on.

The judge then adds up the points and consults the guideline chart, which has offense level scores running down the left, and six columns running across the top scoring the offender on the basis of his past criminal record. So if the burglar fired a gun, caused serious bodily injury, and made off with three hundred thousand dollars, he gets a score of 34; if this was his first offense, his sentence must fall between 151 and 188 months. If he has a long record, let us say IV on the scale of VI, his sentence must fall between 210 and 262 months.

The only two factors a judge may use to reduce the guideline sentence are the offender's "acceptance of responsibility," in essence, did he plead guilty (which can bring a modest reduction), and whether he provided "substantial assistance" to the government, i.e., did he turn state's evidence and implicate others (which can bring a major reduction). The judge may not reduce sentence time because of the offender's age, his employment record, his stable family life, the fact that he has children at home to support, or any other personal characteristic.

The impact of these guidelines has been to increase the numbers in prison (sentences to probation have declined), and average time served (from twenty-four months in July 1984 to forty-six months in June 1990). The guidelines have also elevated the prosecutor over the judge. Because sentences are severe, offenders might be tempted to go to trial rather than to plea bargain; to make certain this does not happen, prosecutors define the "base offense" downward to bring about a reduction in penalty, and hide their action so that the "real offense" on which the guidelines are set cannot be known. Thus, in return for a guilty plea, the prosecutor will agree to charge the defendant with robbery without the use of a weapon, although he did brandish a pistol. Defendants and their lawyers understand that judges no longer control sentencing, bound as they are to the guidelines. All the real bargaining has to be done with the prosecutors.

Have the federal guidelines managed to reduce the disparity so that convicted offenders are more likely to receive the same punishment regardless of their race or which judge they happen to appear before? Research findings are too thin to know for certain, and to the degree that prosecutors bury their tracks the answers will remain obscure. Still, the safest conclusion is that of the Government Accounting Office (1992), the research organization for Congress, which finds that at present no decline in disparity can be demonstrated. Most analysts are less cautious, convinced that disparity has not declined. What is unambiguous is that judicial authority has declined—judges are left to add numbers and read off the chart—and judicial anger and frustration have mounted. Federal Judge Jack Weinstein (1992) speaks for many of his colleagues in declaring:

> Whereas sentencing once called for hours spent reflecting on the offense and the person, we judges are becoming rubber-stamp bureaucrats. When we come to see ourselves as judicial accountants, freed from the awful responsibility of imposing a sentence, we will have abdicated our judicial role entirely. (p. 364)

Or as Michael Tonry (1993) concisely concludes, the guidelines are the "most disliked sentencing reform initiative in United States history" (p. 131).

V

At the moment, reformers are far better at diagnosis than prescription, perceptively identifying the flaws in current policies, but uncertain of what to substitute. Nils Christie (1993), who like most everyone else is critical of determinate sentences, would like to restore sentencing discretion to the judiciary, but recognizes that to do so would only revive the dilemmas faced in the 1960s, that is, that judges would exercise unchecked and sweeping authority and rediscover the rationale of rehabilitation. He believes that composing sentencing formulas is a hopeless task: "There are no guidelines except in values" (p. 184). But he refuses to suggest alternatives: "As a criminologist I feel more and more that my function is very similar to that of a book-reviewer or art critic" (ibid.). So Christie dispenses judgment, but feels no obligation to create his own product.

Norval Morris, professor of Law at the University of Chicago and one of the most astute students of criminal justice, and Michael Tonry are more ambitious. Their latest book, *Between Prison and Probation* (1990), is a sophisticated and imaginative plea for establishing a range of alternatives to incarceration. They outline a system of substantial fines, residential control, electronic monitoring, community service orders, treatment orders, and intensive probation and parole. Judges would not be forced to choose between imprisonment and sending a criminal home. Morris and Tonry recognize the problems with such a proposal. First, it is entirely possible, even likely, that judges will use the alternatives to prison mainly on behalf of white, middle-class offenders and not for blacks, thereby making the prison system even more of an apartheid institution than it is now. Second, alternatives to prison tend to become supplements to prison. What happens is that judges apply the new range of punishments not to those they consider hardened criminals but to those that they used to treat more leniently. So a sentence to twelve months of community service goes not to someone who otherwise would have entered a maximum security prison but to those who would have been released on probation with no conditions attached. The net effect, then, is to increase the severity of sanctions and the population under state control, not to reduce incarceration. Nevertheless, Morris and Tonry are right to believe that these risks are worth taking. At least some offenders guilty of nonviolent crimes (including blacks and Hispanics) will be spared the miseries of confinement. And perhaps, building on this experience, the criminal justice system will learn to deal more intelligently with all offenders. But in the short run, alternative punishments are unlikely to reduce the harms of the existing system.

Taking a more frankly political approach, the Sentencing Project (1993) recently launched a Campaign for an Effective Crime Policy, trying to bring those inside the system (correctional officials and prosecutors) together with outsiders and would-be reformers. Their proposals, however, more successfully highlight the dilemmas than the solutions. The campaign calls for a review of mandatory sentences and federal sentencing guidelines, but does not suggest what might replace them. It urges more funding for drug rehabilitation and alternatives to incarceration. But its ultimate recommendation is that the president establish a national commission on crime to improve the administration of American justice.

This open-ended proposition has merit precisely because so much uncertainty prevails about the direction that policy should take. But were such a commission created and were it responsive to the leadership of Janet Reno, what might it do? For clues it is worth looking at the half dozen speeches the Attorney General has delivered since taking office to law enforcement groups and to the U.S. Sentencing Commission. Each repeats the same themes. Reno made clear at the outset that she favors imprisoning serious offenders—"dangerous, violent recidivists are [to be] put away and kept away" (1993:13). She then observed how expensive and overcrowded prisons are, and how "the American people are fed up with people who say, let's pass tougher sentences without putting a price tag on" (p. 14). It is foolhardy, she insisted, to be bound by mandatory minimums and to incarcerate nonviolent offenders, especially drug users. They occupy cells better reserved for violent criminals and they need treatment programs, not punishment. Otherwise, they will simply return to prison again and again.

Although Reno makes these several points in the first ten to fifteen minutes of her speeches, she does not go on to elaborate on them. She says nothing about the wisdom of sentencing guidelines (even at the commission's meeting), and does not propose a complete or detailed drug policy. Instead, she typically devotes the bulk of her talk to what is obviously her favorite theme: the need to rescue America's children. "For the last thirty years in America we have forgotten and neglected our children," she tells her audiences. "Unless we reach out and join our hands together and reweave the fabric of society around too many of our children and our families, we are never going to address the problems" (p. 16).

No one would want to quarrel with these sentiments or with her idea of a National Agenda for Children. Reno is surely right that we "will never be able to build enough prisons eighteen years from now for children who are born today from drug-involved mothers unless we start now in giving that child a good chance at a strong and healthy life" (p. 16). But as important as it is to look beyond the boundaries of criminal justice, so is it vital for the attorney general to provide leadership on the many urgent and unresolved questions endemic to the system itself, and this she has failed to do.

Accordingly, no one should be surprised that the 1994 crime bill proceeded with little input from Reno, or, for that matter, pork barrel issues aside, from the White House. The legislation accelerates the trends toward fixed sentences, mandatory minimums, and a reliance upon incarceration. It does ban the manufacture, sale, and possession of nineteen types of semiautomatic weapons, including the Israeli-built Uzi. But it also provides billions of dollars for the Justice Department to build and operate ten regional high-security prisons; each will hold no less than twenty-five hundred inmates convicted in state courts of violent crimes. To enjoy this fiscal windfall (whereby the federal government assumes all costs of confinement), the participating states must adopt a "truth in sentencing" formula under which offenders must serve no less than 85 percent of sentences that are five years or longer; the states must also have in place "a binding sentencing guidelines system in which the sentencing judges' discretion is limited to ensure greater uniformity in sentencing" (Sect. 1341, p. 365).

The legislation is so enamored of incarceration that it provides several billion dollars to open boot camps for nonviolent young offenders. The camps, to be located where possible on closed military bases and to be run by one-time drill sergeants, are to compel "adherence by inmates to a highly regimented schedule that involves strict discipline, physical training, and work" (Sect. 1321, p. 345). Finally, the new bill increases the number of mandatory minimum sentences, including one that gives life in prison with no parole to all felons guilty of two or more prior convictions for drug offenses or crimes of violence.

It takes little imagination or foresight to calculate the likely impact of these measures: more minorities will be locked up, time served will increase, boot camps will become the latest feeder to prisons, prosecutors will flourish, and judges will complain. Ill-informed citizens will think that we are finally getting tough on crime and that by locking up recidivists we are making streets safer. But none of these actions are likely to reduce crime. For all the faith in prisons, rates of incarceration do not correlate with rates of crime. The number of people in prison and jail between 1980 to 1991 more than doubled, from 500,000 to 1,200,000, making a forty-five-degree angle on a graph. But the overall crime rate followed a jagged pattern—down from 1980 to 1984, then up to 1991, then down again in 1992), and so did rates for murder (U-shaped 1980 to 1991), rape (up), robbery (V-shaped) and burglary (down).[2] And there is no evidence that the staggering numbers of prisoners serving time for drug offenses are having an appreciable impact on drug use, or drug-related crimes.

Perhaps the worse feature of the 1994 legislation is that just when we desperately need to explore new solutions to crime and punishment, we are being fed programs that are mischievous, ineffectual, and costly. We need well-designed and bounded experiments to see what the impact of decriminalization would be on drug use and crime rates—instead we get a reflexive shudder when Joycelyn Elders, the surgeon general until Clinton fired her in December 1994, remarks that a different drug policy might reduce crime. We need to rethink sentencing policy on the federal and on the state level, to experiment with ways to restore judicial discretion without exacerbating judicial discrimination, and to keep sentences honest without being excessive; instead we get a bill that increases the number and length of mandatory sentences and an attorney general who will not utter a word about the issue.

We need to implement and evaluate alternatives to incarceration—not build enormous regional prisons and boot camps.

In the end, we need an honest recognition of what criminal justice sanctions can and cannot accomplish and a frank acknowledgment that increasingly severe punishments are no remedy for thwarted life circumstances. We require leadership that will help map out new directions and enable us to break out of a fixation with prisons. But by every indication, we will go on marching lockstep along the same monotonous paths.

NOTES

1. Tonry (forthcoming) notes that the United States is no worse in this respect than England (blacks), Canada (native population), and Australia (aboriginal people). His point is not to exculpate but to demonstrate how pervasive the problem is.
2. For the empirical and ethical flaws in the case for reducing crime through selective confinement, see Andrew Von Hirsch (1976).

REFERENCES

American Friends Service Committee. 1971. *Struggle for Justice.* New York: Hill and Wang.
Boerner, David. 1993. "The Role of the Legislature in Guideline Sentencing in 'The Other Washington,'" *Wake Forest Law Review* 28:381–420.
Christie, Nils. 1993. *Crime Control as Industry.* London and New York: Routledge.
Edna McConnell Clark Foundation. 1993. *Americans Behind Bars.* New York: Author.
Frankel, Marvin E. 1972. *Criminal Sentences: Law without Order.* New York: Hill and Wang.
Human Rights Watch. 1991. *Prison Conditions in the Untied States, A Human Rights Watch Report.* New York, Washington, Los Angeles: Author.
Jencks, Christopher 1991. "Is Violent Crime Increasing?" *American Prospect,* Winter:98–109.
Mauer, Marc. 1992. *Americans Behind Bars.* Washington, DC: The Sentencing Project.
Morris, Norval and Michael Tonry. 1990. *Between Prison and Probation: Intermediate Punishments in a Rational Sentencing System.* New York: Oxford University Press.
Miller, Jerome G. 1992. "Search and Destroy: The Plight of African American Males in the Criminal Justice System." Report, National Center on Institutions and Alternatives, Alexandria, Virginia.
National Center on Institutions and Alternatives. 1992. "Hobbling a Generation." Report, National Center on Institutions and Alternatives, Alexandria, Virginia.

Reno, Janet. 1993. Speech by the Honorable Janet Reno at the opening dinner of the United States Sentencing Commission Symposium, June 16.
Rothman, David and Aryeh Neier. 1991. "India's Awful Prisons," *New York Review of Books*, May 16.
Schulhofer, Stephen J. 1993. "Rethinking Mandatory Minimums." *Wake Forest Law Review* 28:199–222.
Sentencing Project. 1993. "Does the Punishment Fit the Crime? Drug Users and Drunk Drivers. Questions of Race and Class." Washington, DC: Author.
Shine, Cathy and Marc Mauer. 1993. *Does the Punishment Fit the Crime? Drug Users and Drunk Drivers, Questions of Race and Class*. Washington, DC: The Sentencing Project.
Stith, Kate and Steve Y. Koh. 1993. "The Politics of Sentencing Reform." *Wake Forest Law Review* 28:223–90.
Tonry, Michael. 1993. "The Failure of the U.S. Sentencing Commission's Guidelines." *Crime and Delinquency* 39:131–49.
Tonry, Michael. 1995. "Racial Disproportion in U.S. Prisons." *British Journal of Criminology*, forthcoming.
Twentieth Century Fund, Task Force in Criminal Sentencing. 1976. *Fair and Certain Punishment*. New York: McGraw-Hill.
United States General Accounting Office. 1992. *Sentencing Guidelines*, GAO/GGD-92-93. Washington, DC: Author.
Von Hirsch, Andrew. 1976. *Doing Justice: The Choice of Punishments*. Report of the Committee for the Study of Incarceration. New York: Hill and Wang.
Weinstein, Jack B. 1992. "A Trial Judge's Second Impression of the Federal Sentencing Guidelines." *Southern California Law Review* 66:357–66.

4
Beyond Metaphors:
Penal Reform As Net-Widening

THOMAS G. BLOMBERG

INTRODUCTION

Studies examining penal reforms since the 1970s have documented incremental patterns of increased social control despite the ostensible goals of these reforms to provide alternative, differentiated, or reduced social control. This finding of increased social control has been provided by measurements of sequential increases in the proportion of the base population subject to control before and after implementation of various penal reforms. Further, these reported increases in social control have been shown to be disproportionate to increases in population, arrests, or convictions. Notably absent from this literature have been studies reporting evidence seriously challenging the increased social control finding or evidence demonstrating any significant positive outcomes associated with these penal reforms.

The increased social control finding has been communicated in the literature through a series of metaphors, particularly net-widening, but including wider and stronger nets, dispersal of discipline, transcarceration, minimum-security society, maximum-security society, and now the new penology. These metaphors have been employed to characterize the recurrent theme in penal reforms over the last two decades, namely, the gap between goals and outcomes. Broader theoretical models like organizational convenience, professional interest, ideological contradiction, and political economy have been used to provide more generalized interpretations of the identified gaps between penal reform goals and outcomes. However, while these metaphorical characterizations and broader theoretical interpretations have been useful, they are often partial and overgeneralized. Specifically, the metaphors and associated theoretical interpretations do not convey the nuances of the penal reforms, their specific origins, their differences in implementation, their distinctive operational features, their potentially mixed outcomes, or the combined effects of broader influences in shaping penal reform processes.

In response to this shortcoming, several writers have argued for a different empirical and theoretical approach to study penal reform. For example, Matthews (1987) argues that an important point regarding metaphors like net-widening and the dispersal of discipline is that while there are inherent dangers associated with the unintended expansion of social control, attention must also be given to the simultaneous positive outcomes that can result from penal reforms. His point is that penal reforms involve complex processes that result in not only one outcome or result but rather several potentially mixed outcomes or results. As Matthews concludes:

> Making sense of these complex processes will require a more sophisticated theoretical approach than is realizable through overgeneralization, directionless statistical manipulation, and the kind of relentless pessimism which characterizes much of the literature. (Matthews 1987:356)

Cohen (1985) suggests that five theoretical models have dominated the literature concerning the goals and outcomes of penal reforms: progress, organizational convenience, ideological contradiction, professional interest, and political economy. Cohen argues that while each model can be emphasized for different purposes, ultimately all might be necessary to provide a compelling explanation of penal reform. Cohen claims that any satisfactory account of penal policy must sift through the various models and assign them relative explanatory weight. As Cohen states:

> Take the "simple" matter of net expansion. Even if this did not happen quite as planned, it is actually progressive for the net to widen if you believe that this is a way of doing more good to more people. It is also true that organizational feedback loops can explain exactly the way this expansion takes place. And this explanation is even more plausible if we consider the dominant vested interest of the people running these bureaucracies, namely to create a dependency on more people just like themselves. It is also true that contradictions in the ideologies of communities and state interventionism explain very well why expansion tends to take place. Finally, there are unmistakable tendencies in the political economy which simultaneously create more problematic, deviant and marginal groups as well as expand the size and range of methods to deal with them in an orderly way. (Cohen 1985:112–13)

The issue is how to move empirical and theoretical study of penal reform beyond the metaphors and theoretical overgeneralizations that have become increasingly subject to question, debate, and criticism. One suggestion, by Garland (1990), is to return to the empirically specific or concrete, to integrate and synthesize different theories in a way that approximates real-world objects and processes. Specific microstudies informed by the more general context would seem capable of responding to this particular suggestion. Moreover, the results of such microstudies could provide a number of wider implications for theory, for empirical research, and for penal policy.

This chapter reviews literature addressing the goals and outcomes of a constellation of penal reforms beginning with diversion in the 1970s and culminating with current intermediate punishment reforms. The review is intended to reveal some of the contributions and shortcomings of standard attempts (via metaphors and overgeneralization) to capture the "essence" of changes in social control associated with penal reforms. An alternative microapproach to penal reform study is discussed in detail, reflecting my previous study of several recent penal reforms. It is suggested that this microapproach is capable of identifying specific penal reform processes, the potentially mixed outcomes produced by these processes, and the more general contextual factors shaping these identified processes and outcomes. The chapter concludes that this research capability can provide the necessary empirical and theoretical connections from which meaningful predictions can be made about the problems and prospects of penal reforms.

STUDYING PENAL REFORM OUTCOMES

Considerable empirical interest in penal reform and social control began in the late 1970s. Initial studies were focused upon the social control outcomes produced by diversion programs. For example, several studies (Blomberg 1977; Klein 1979; Lemert 1981) reported on diversion's capacity to provide a supplemental rather than alternative function to previous penal practices. Specifically, these studies demonstrated that diversion practices were being centered upon youth and families that before diversion would not have been subject to any form of social control. This finding became communicated through the metaphor of net-widening or one of several related metaphors (e.g., wider or stronger nets, accelerated social control). Essentially, these metaphors were used to characterize the gap between diversion's formal goal and actual outcome related to social control. The patterned finding of increased social control was described by one of several metaphors and then explained through such theoretical models as organizational convenience, professional interest, ideological contradiction, or political economy. While the net-widening finding did not go unchallenged in the literature, no contradictory empirical evidence was provided by such net-widening critics as Binder and Geis (1984) or McMahon (1990).

For example, while ignoring net-widening's evidence and presenting no empirical evidence to support their claims, Binder and Geis (1984) concluded that concern over net-widening in diversion programs was without merit. They rhetorically suggested:

> [I]t has become fashionable within sociological criminology to condemn juvenile diversion. Participants in the condemnatory ritual identify each other as insiders by catchy words and phrases (like "widening the net"), and frequently substitute rhetoric for logic in their argumentation aimed both at gaining cultic recognition and winning over the unwary. (Binder and Geis 1984:624)

Additionally, while acknowledging net-widening's occurrence in community correctional reforms, McMahon argued:

> The concepts of "wider," "stronger," and "different," nets are effective in directing attention towards trends in the expansion and extension of penal control. However, these concepts also serve to direct attention away from any moderation of penal control which might have taken place. (McMahon 1990:144)

The 1980s rise of various get-tough-on-crime approaches resulted in several studies further utilizing the net-widening metaphor. The argument was that various get-tough strategies, like previous diversion and community corrections strategies, while promoted as alternatives to previous practices, were implemented as supplements and resulted in an expanded proportion of the base population subject to some form of social control. Thus, mandatory jail sentences for drunk drivers, flat or determinant sentencing, and stiffer penalties for drug offenders coupled with preexisting diversion, community, and traditional institutional strategies were found to cumulatively result in a larger proportion of the overall base population subject to some form of social control, thereby resulting in net-widening. For example, NCCD (1989), in a consideration of the social control impact of the get-tough war on drugs predicted that by 1994, the 1989 incarceration rate of 250 per 100,000 population would increase to 440 per 100,000, and when combined with the offender populations in community-based programs would result in not only more reliance on incarceration but greater social control over the base population. Similarly, other studies documented unprecedented increases in prison admissions and populations during the 1980s, which when considered in combination with the offender populations in diversion and community correctional programs, demonstrated increased proportions in the overall base population subject to some form of social control, again documenting net-widening (e.g., Hylton 1982; Blomberg 1987).

Beginning in the late 1980s, America's preoccupation with getting tough on crime became subject to challenge by a growing public demand for simultaneous protection from crime and higher taxes. The costs of building and operating prisons were being felt throughout the country as state correctional budgets represented the fastest growing component of state expenditures. In 1989 NCCD projected a 68 percent increase in the national inmate population, namely, 460,000 inmates by 1994. With an average prison cell construction cost of fifty thousand dollars, states would have to raise twenty-three billion dollars for prison construction. What emerged in response was the nationwide implementation of various intermediate punishment programs that were promoted as a means to provide less costly but still tough sanctions for offenders requiring more supervision than nominal probation but less than incarceration. Intermediate punishment included a range of punish and treat sanctions including intensive supervision, home confinement, electronic surveillance, daily reporting centers, work release, and numerous other private treatment services.

As with previous diversion and get-tough-on-crime studies, net-widening or some related metaphor resurfaced in several empirical assessments of the goals and outcomes of intermediate punishment. Again, the essential question being addressed in these assessments was whether intermediate punishment was differentiating or redistributing control away from prison or merely expanding the overall proportion of population subject to some form of social control. For example, we concluded that during the late 1980s, and despite the operation of a statewide Florida intermediate punishment program involving more than one hundred thousand offenders and their families, Florida's use of prisons experienced major increases disproportionate to the state's population and conviction increases (Blomberg, Bales, and Reed 1993). Further, in another study of a local intermediate punishment program, we documented not only net-widening but what we metaphorically termed the "piling up of sanctions" on participating offenders (Blomberg and Lucken 1994). Specifically we found, in support of net-widening, the jurisdiction's use of incarceration experienced substantial growth with simultaneous growth in the use of intermediate punishments disproportionate to the jurisdiction's increases in population and arrests. Moreover and beyond net-widening, it was shown that the piling up of intermediate sanctions on participating offenders was resulting in numerous violations of sentence conditions often resulting in incarceration followed by a recycling of the offender back through intermediate punishment. In effect, by piling up sanctions, the program was literally entangling offenders with multiple and simultaneous sanctions (probation, home confinement, chemical abuse treatment, impulse control treatment, etc.) often coupled with different and overlapping conditions and requirements resulting in frequent sentence violations, new jail sentences, and increased jail populations (see also Petersillia and Turner 1990).

Overall, these empirical depictions of the outcomes of various penal reforms, from the 1970s to the present, demonstrate increased social control despite the ostensible goal of these various reforms to result in alternative, differentiated, or reduced control. Further, these increases in penal control have been shown to be disproportionate to increases or changes in population, arrests, or convictions.

INTERPRETING PENAL REFORM OUTCOMES

Researchers attempting to interpret the gap between penal reform goals and outcomes have employed metaphors associated with the broader theoretical models previously mentioned. These metaphors and theoretical models have been used to conceptually capture the character and meaning of penal reforms as measured by specific social control outcome measures.

In a study of a juvenile diversion program, for example, I found that the outcomes of the program were in polar opposition to the formal goals of diversion. I reported that instead of diverting youth away from the formal court system, diversion actually expanded the numbers and proportion of the youth population and their families subject to social control. Moreover, because of this new social control and subsequent failure to fulfill associated court requirements, many of these new or so-called diverted youth and their siblings were accelerated into the court system through out-of-home placements. I employed the metaphor of "accelerated social control" to capture this particular diversion outcome and explained that this outcome was quite predictable given the organizational character of the juvenile court. I concluded:

> An essential question that emerges from this study's findings concerns how an apparent liberating concept becomes intentionally operationalized into juvenile court policy as family intervention, which results in more youth receiving some form of control. This question concerns the organizational transformation of a reform movement and necessitates consideration of the character of the juvenile court organization. In this study's attempt to specify the character of the court organization, several characteristics were identified. . . . These characteristics suggest that because the court operates under conditions of conflicting goals, ambiguous treatment technology, resource scarcity and operational uncertainty, it will respond to those programmatic opportunities perceived as compatible with the functional necessities, goals and practices of the court organization. Additionally, operational uncertainty predisposes the court to operationalize innovative programs to reinforce previous formal or informal court practices instead of significantly restructuring court operations. (Blomberg 1977:281)

While I interpreted diversion's accelerated social control outcome primarily through the organizational convenience model, elements of the ideological contradiction and professional interest models could have been connected to my interpretation as well. Specifically, diversion did indeed present the juvenile court with certain ideological contradictions and professional interest conflicts related to diversion's claim that the court system often did more harm to youth than good by mere contact and associated stigmatization. Moreover, if diversion's goals and outcomes corresponded, the juvenile court could easily have found itself without a clientele. Other studies addressing diversion's capacity to produce more instead of less control employing various metaphors and particular elements of organizational convenience, professional-ideological, or political-economic models include Klein (1979), Austin and Krisberg (1981), and Polk (1981).

In a later and more sweeping application, Lowman and Menzies (1986) employ the metaphor of transcarceration to capture not only penal reform outcomes but contemporary social control in general. The transcarceration metaphor is reflective of an instrumental or causal imagery between the political economy and the forms and levels of social control. This imagery assumes that contradictions in the political economy lead to increases in the proportion of surplus and/or superfluous population. According to Lowman and Menzies the existence of this growing surplus or superfluous population results in a need for an increasingly differentiated and coordinated penal and associated educational/welfare system ultimately producing increased social control over a larger proportion of the base population. Stated differently, the greater degree of contradiction in the political economy, the greater the proportion of surplus and/or superfluous population and the greater degree of penal and related system control over the population. With a rather confusing and overabundant use of metaphors and pessimistic overgeneralization, these authors claim:

> An understanding of transcarceration hinges on the notion that social control is no longer grounded in measures of exclusion, where legal subjects are relegated to invisible confines of total institutions; nor does it resolve itself into progressive practices of inclusion where deviance is supposedly repaired by reintroducing it to the community from which it sprang. While it does incorporate the concept of power dispersed throughout the "carceral archipelago," the transcarceral model must be more explicitly anchored in a political economy of penal authority than we find in Foucault's analysis. The abandonment of traditional analytic schema as a holistic dynamic—and in so doing stresses continuities among system components. Among these commonalties is the asymmetric arrangement of economic inclusion and exclusion that parallels and augments the operation of the coercive control system. (Lowman and Menzies 1986:107)

More recent studies have begun to employ new metaphors that incorporate several larger theoretical models in their attempts to capture what is being argued to be a transformation in contemporary penology, i.e., "postmodern penology" or "the new penology." Prominent among these new applications is Feeley and Simon (1992), who claim that today's penal system is indeed being transformed from the old penology, with emphasis on individual offenders, to the new penology or postmodern penology with emphasis on aggregate groupings of offenders. They contend that the major features of the new or postmodern penology are reflected in new discourses, goals, and techniques. The authors point out the new or postmodern penology metaphor is not meant to be a theory but rather a means to describe and capture some of the emerging features of penology in the 90s. Feeley and Simon summarize:

> The new penology argues that an important new language of penology is emerging. This new language, which has its counterparts in other areas of the law as well, shifts focus away from the traditional concerns of the criminal law and criminology, which have focused on the individual, and redirects it to actuarial consideration of aggregates. This shift has a number of important implications. It facilitates development of a vision or model of a new type of criminal process that embraces increased reliance on imprisonment and that merges concerns for surveillance and custody, that shifts away from a concern with punishing individuals to managing aggregates of dangerous groups. (Feeley and Simon 1992:449)

In response, Lemert (1993) claims that Feeley and Simon's argument that corrections is developing a new language and strategy aimed at increasing control over particular groups of offenders is not true in the case of probation. Lemert suggests probation's major practices in the nineties are largely unchanged from previous practices due to the deterioration in supervision that has occurred following patterned reductions in staff and major increases in caseloads. The result has been what Lemert terms "bankloading," an old practice with a new name that involves probation officers focusing upon serious cases while generally ignoring the remainder of their caseloads. Lemert concludes that Feeley and Simon's contention "that probation realizes the claims made for it as a part of a new penology or indeed whether its changes have been undertaken as the logical consequence of such penology must be doubted" (Lemert 1993:460).

The previous literature on penal reform and social control has provided several important findings and arguments. For example, it is clear from this literature that the goals and outcomes of penal reform are clearly not the same. Specifically, a salient outcome of various penal reforms over the past several decades has been increased control over a larger proportion of the population despite the formal goals of these reforms to provide alternative, differentiated, or reduced control. Yet, the literature has several important shortcomings. Specifically, is it accurate to describe all penal reforms as complete failures given the narrow empirical focus and overgeneralized interpretations that have characterized the prior literature? Are there no positive outcomes or results that have been produced from these various penal reforms? Moreover, is there a single explanatory model that accurately captures the meaning and consequences of these penal reform efforts? Or, are there a number of specific origins, operations, larger influences and relationships that together provide more meaningful description and explanation of penal reform as a complex and whole process capable of producing mixed outcomes?

TOWARD AN ALTERNATIVE APPROACH TO PENAL REFORM STUDY

Contemporary penology is an increasingly complex system continuously undergoing reform, refinement, and proliferation. The current penal system subsumes within its structure exploding prison and jail facilities, probation and parole services, and ever-enlarging systems of intermediate punishment. Moreover, most states have enacted crime victim bill-of-rights laws guaranteeing victims of crime the right to be notified, present, and heard at all phases of their assailant's legal and correctional hearings. Penal systems are now implementing these various crime victim functions and services.

These developments and others are necessitating more interagency activities between police, courts, corrections, and victim services. Further, each of these agencies is undergoing independent changes related to additional and often conflicting goals and practices. Moreover, accelerating public fear over crime and associated public demands for stronger action against criminals is fueling politicians to stake their individual claims that they are indeed "tougher" on crime than their political adversaries. In short, the name of the game is not to be smart or thoughtful about crime control policy but rather to be toughest on crime. Consequently, contemporary penology is an increasingly politicized system not easily described or interpreted.

Current intermediate punishment efforts provide an illustration of the need to employ several theoretical models and more comprehensive empirical designs to capture the full range of processes, outcomes, and meanings of penal reform. Authors like Lowman and Menzies (1986) or Feeley and Simon (1992) might interpret intermediate punishment as either the latest increment in the transcarceration movement or exemplary of the emerging new penology. But what do we know empirically about this particular penal reform movement? Empirically speaking, little is known about the precise origins, operational features, and potentially mixed outcomes of this particular reform. Yet, if the consequences and meaning of this strategy are to be established beyond social control metaphors and overgeneralization, an integrated empirical-theoretical approach that conceptualizes penal reform as an interrelated process involving origins, operations, and outcomes is necessary. Theoretically, this means that several theoretical models may be necessary to provide compelling interpretation of the origins, operations, outcomes, and associated interrelations of penal reform. Methodologically, this means a toolkit approach to data gathering will be required that seeks multiple items of information or data.

The origins of intermediate punishment, for example, have roots in a broader social context that is shaped by various intellectual, political, economic, and social influences. This broader social context has played a major role in shaping a particular idea and/or philosophical orientation upon which intermediate punishment's goals and operations are based, and from which outcomes are ultimately produced. But how does this broader social context lead to a particular penal reform philosophy, goals, and strategy? Who and/or what is salient in this evolutionary process? Put differently, which agencies, persons, and specific circumstances contribute to the origin, shape, philosophy and goals of a penal reform?

The empirical task is to identify contributors and processes that shape the origins of a particular penal reform. It is routinely announced in the literature that penal reforms do not originate out of a vacuum but reflect instead a variety of factors. With a few exceptions, however, this variety of factors and social context is seldom conveyed with any degree of specificity. However, documents, individuals, and proceedings can be identified and information can be collected that relates directly to contributing issues, problems, perspectives, concerns, beliefs, and processes that initiate and shape an idea and philosophy that, in the case of intermediate punishment, blurs punishment with treatment.

In a recent study of a major intermediate punishment program, we identified several contributing factors that shaped the origins and ultimate philosophy and goals of the program (Blomberg and Lucken 1994). Specifically, the concept "punish and treat" turned out to be welcomed by not only local key decision-makers ultimately responsible for developing the program but to the general local public as well. The official claims underlying intermediate punishment, namely, cost-effectiveness, punishment, and treatment, were well received by liberals and conservatives in and out of local government. This local jurisdiction, like numerous other local jurisdictions throughout the country, was experiencing lawsuits related to overcrowded jail conditions. Approximately one-third of all local jails in the United States have been under court orders to reduce overcrowding and improve jail conditions during the early 90s (Proband 1993). Moreover, much of this local jurisdiction's jail population increase was comprised of misdemeanor offenders. Intermediate punishment emerged as a way not only to reduce jail overcrowding and related lawsuits, which the local politicians were eager to achieve, but to deal more responsibly with the growing number of misdemeanor offenders in the jurisdiction. This response to misdemeanors was welcomed by local law enforcement, judicial, and penal personnel as well as interested citizens. Ultimately, a consolidation of jail and correctional services was approved with the underlying philosophy of a "continuum of care." This became the jurisdiction's intermediate punishment philosophy and we found that a number of local individuals were key to the development and implementation of this philosophy, including several local politicians, judges, the sheriff, and the program's director. However, the efforts of these key individuals must be understood in the context of local organizational mandates related to overcrowded jail conditions and ongoing lawsuits, increasing fiscal constraints as well as the associated public outcries for protection from crime and higher taxes. Intermediate punishment promised solutions to various problems and concerns; it was a responsive reform that an increasingly dissatisfied public, criminal justice professionals, and fiscally conservative minded politicians could collectively embrace.

The implementation of a penal reform philosophy initiates a series of events that shape and determine the operational practices and outcomes produced by the reform. Again, specific items of information are available that can be woven together to tell the reform's implementation and operational story. Central among these items of information are the thoughts and perspectives of the penal system actors. How do these actors perceive of the reform with regard to official versus unofficial goals and philosophy? Does the reform challenge or reinforce their dominant professional ideology and major organizational interests? Certainly the perceptions of program administrators, line staff, judges, and private agency personnel are central to the ultimate form characterizing the operations of a penal reform like intermediate punishment. Further, these perceptions can be described and measured. The task involves soliciting penal agency actors for their perspectives. When asked with interest, penal system actors will communicate not only their daily routines, problems, decisions, and practices, but the commonsense constructs and imagery upon which they base their everyday practices and decision-making. Additionally, program rules and prescribed practices are recorded in some form, providing researchers additional information about penal system practices.

For example, we found in our study of intermediate punishment, the program's major operational feature to be what we termed "the piling up of sanctions" (Blomberg and Lucken 1994). As we summarized:

> [I]n the split sentencing and/or "piling up of sanctions" process these programs become used as supplements to each other wherein an offender receives multiple sanctions. In this process, it is common for an offender to receive a period of incarceration to be followed by a term of probation, community

service, and/or a fine. When a period of incarceration and probation are imposed and the offender qualifies for work release or home confinement, the offender will be supervised simultaneously by a probation officer and work release counselor or home confinement officer. In these instances, offenders are not only supervised by two officers but are required to adhere to the conditions of individual program components. Furthermore, many offenders are serving terms of probation for both the state and county and are, therefore, subject to what are frequently overlapping conditions and requirements. (Blomberg and Lucken 1994:66)

By piling up sanctions, intermediate punishment program components are employed as supplements to each other, often resulting in offender surveillance and/or control that extends well beyond what would have been administered in the absence of intermediate punishment. However, from our interviews, we found that various intermediate punishment agency actors viewed the piling up of sanctions as both responsible and appropriate implementation of the explicit treatment and punishment philosophy of intermediate punishment.

The various actors interviewed constituted a diverse group with unique and often multiple interests. Nonetheless, whether interviewing jail staff, probation officers, program administrators, judges, or private treatment personnel, we found that these various agency actors shared several assumptions about how to deal with offenders. Specifically, they held several common offender expectations related to a "middle-class measuring rod" with regard to their view of what offenders should accomplish as part of their punishment and treatment. For full compliance with the requirements associated with intermediate punishment's piling up of sanctions, a level of competency and responsibility is required that is characteristic of middle-class law-abiding citizens with higher education, stronger community ties, and greater financial resources. However, the bulk of participating offenders in the intermediate punishment program did not possess the education, community ties, or financial resources that would facilitate their compliance with the various piling-up-of-sanctions requirements. Specifically, if the offender was employed, he or she might have the money to enroll in private treatment programs but no time to attend the required meetings each week. If unemployed, the offender had the time to attend meetings but was without the money required to participate. The piling-up-of-sanctions required offenders to use their limited resources over several often costly programs. The critical factors for satisfactory participation and completion of multiple programs and conditions, namely, money, transportation, and a sense of responsibility, were simply absent from most participating offenders.

While various sanctioning agents openly expressed awareness of these offender circumstances and obstacles, they did not excuse the offender from the consequences of their lawbreaking. Such offender circumstances were not viewed as unusual or deserving of special consideration. Rather, the general sanctioning agent perception was that strict enforcement of various program conditions and requirements was essential to redirecting the offender's behavior. To accommodate or sympathize with the offender's circumstances was considered inappropriate, too lenient, or enabling to the offender's life-style. These sanctioning agent perceptions and expectations coupled with offender characteristics and associated limited program participation capabilities set the stage for frequent offender violations of intermediate punishment's program requirements.

Explanation of intermediate punishment's piling-up-of-sanctions process involves elements of several theoretical models. For example, aspects of organizational convenience, professional interest, and ideological contradiction are relevant to understanding how and why this particular program practice emerged and came to characterize this program's operations. With regard to organizational convenience there are a number of organizational dynamics that contribute to this process. Private treatment agencies, for example, have a vested interest in both gaining clients and maintaining client contacts. This process is fundamental for the survival of these agencies, since their funding is determined by the number of offenders served and length of service. Moreover, various professional interests shape the piling-up-of-sanctions process, since various program sanctioning agents and private treatment staff hold what are often common views concerning the value and appropriateness of multiple punish-and-treat program services for offenders. Additionally, ideological contradictions are exemplified in intermediate punishment's punish-and-treat philosophy and goals that gain direct expression through the piling-up-of-sanctions process and resulting pattern of frequent offender violation of sentence requirements..

The origins and operations of penal reforms are ultimately measured in relation to outcomes. Typically, as demonstrated in the earlier review of prior research, only select aggregate quantitative data have been employed for outcome measures related to social control, but other items of qualitative data can provide more complete social control outcome measures. For example, to provide more comprehensive measurement of social control outcomes requires consideration of not only changes in proportion of population subject to control but description of the type and character of control being administered. Additionally, the length of time individuals are subject to control, description of the specific requirements and nature of control, and any follow-up consequences are all important considerations for any comprehensive and meaningful measurement and understanding of social control. Moreover, the perceptions of offenders and/or their family members concerning the character and consequences of social control are integral if the full range of penal reform and social control consequences is to be known. Further, and beyond social control measurements, other outcome measures should be sought concerning other possible results for offenders, families, communities, and penal agencies. The empirical task is to collect various measures that together provide a more comprehensive and accurate depiction of a penal reform's overall and potentially mixed outcomes.

In our study of intermediate punishment, for example, we found a number of negative outcomes associated with the piling-up-of-sanctions process, but we found several positive program outcomes as well. With regard to negative outcomes, there was a chain of events associated with this particular program practice. As mentioned previously, offenders involved in multiple vocational, education, and substance abuse programs with multiple demands and requirements were routinely found in noncompliance. This pattern of noncompliance resulted in return to court on violation of intermediate punishment conditions, often culminating in a jail sentence followed by a return to the same combination of intermediate punishment programs in which some offenders were recycled several times because of repeated sentence violations. Ultimately, intermediate punishment's piling up of sanctions led to increased demands for jail space and the jurisdiction found it necessary to expand its incarceration capacities initially by 300 beds and later by adding a 768-bed minimum security facility despite the goal of intermediate punishment to reduce reliance on incarceration. However, piling up sanctions was not detrimental to all offenders on intermediate punishment.

Concerning positive program outcomes, several findings warrant discussion. First, the intermediate punishment program included a work release component. The work release program selected all offenders from the jail population. While on work release the offenders were housed in a residential facility. A requirement of the program was for the offender to have a General Education Diploma (GED) before entering work release or earn a GED while in the program. All offenders selected for work release were either employed or quickly placed on jobs with assistance from the work release vocational counselors. The maximum term for offenders on this program was one year. Typically, offenders worked during the day and completed various counseling or chemical abuse treatment programs during the evenings. The offender's financial obligations, including child-support and restitution, were automatically deducted from their checks. Offenders with satisfactory work release performance could qualify for program release into the daily reporting program. In these instances the offenders would live at home, continue to work and be subject to automatic payroll deductions, and report daily to the daily reporting centers. Numerous offenders, employers, and program staff alike viewed work release as a successful program in terms of offender accountability, treatment, and vocational assistance.

The home confinement program component of intermediate punishment operated similarly to work release. Offenders were selected from the jail population and required to work and meet all financial obligations and participate in various other treatment programs deemed necessary. The program provided an alternative to jail with regular offender monitoring. Again, offenders, employers, and program personnel alike perceived of home confinement as a responsible alternative to jail that enabled offenders to participate in treatment, work, provide for their families, and meet other financial obligations.

In sum, the origins, operations, and outcomes of penal reform reflect an interrelated process that is shaped by a set of larger influences, circumstances, and contingencies. Any thoughtful consideration of the meaning and consequences of such a complex, interrelated, and whole process must necessarily be informed by a variety of empirical data and theoretical frames that, taken together, are capable of describing and interpreting the simultaneous problems, prospects, and meaning of penal reform.

SUMMARY AND DISCUSSION

This chapter has reviewed the tendency in penal reform literature to rely on metaphors and overgeneralization in attempting to characterize and interpret the recurrent disparity between penal reform goals and outcomes. Because of this narrow empirical focus and associated theoretical overgeneralization, numerous questions remain about the full range of consequences and meaning of penal reforms. As several writers have suggested, it is necessary to move beyond these narrowly conceived conceptualizations and to reconceptualize penal reform as a complex and whole system of action capable of producing different processes and outcomes, which are themselves shaped by several larger influences. This chapter has explored such an alternative conceptualization that views the origins, operations, and outcomes of penal reforms as an interrelated and whole process. Specific items of information or data sources have been identified as necessary to adequately describe the origins, operations, and outcome relationships of penal reform. Moreover, it has been argued that several larger theoretical models are necessary in any attempt to provide compelling interpretation of the meaning and consequences of penal reform. It is in this regard that Garland argues:

> A measure of abstraction is a necessary first step in the analysis of any complex phenomenon, and it is not unusual for a field of knowledge in its early stages of development to be characterized by competing abstractions and monocausal forms of explanation. But the ultimate objective of research must be to return to the concrete, to integrate and synthesize different abstractions in a way that simulates the overdetermination of real-world objects and approximates their complex wholeness. (1990:15)

Today, for the first time in U.S. history, the nation's state and federal prison population exceeds one million. According to a 1994 press release of the Bureau of Justice Statistics, this means that there are now approximately 389 prison inmates per 100,000 population compared to 187 prison inmates per 100,000 population in 1983. These prison figures do not include the approximately 440,000 individuals in jails either awaiting trial or serving short sentences. Moreover, given the recently passed Federal Crime Bill, which authorizes 7.9 billion dollars to assist states in expanding their prison capacities, it is clear that prison populations will continue their rapid explosion in the near future despite the fact that such increasing use of imprisonment is an irrational policy doomed for failure.

What, however, is the alternative? Are there alternatives to incarceration that offer something beyond net-widening and associated negative results? Can penal reform researchers provide concrete statements about what various alternatives to incarceration can and cannot do and for whom? Or will the proclamation that "nothing works" continue to set the stage for policy making in a research vacuum?

ACKNOWLEDGMENTS

I wish to thank Stanley Cohen, Sheldon L. Messinger, and Jerome H. Skolnick for helpful comments and suggestions.

REFERENCES

Austin, James and Barry Krisberg. 1981. "Wider, Stronger and Different Nets: The Dialectics of Criminal Justice Reform." *Journal of Research in Crime and Delinquency* 18(1):165–96.

Binder, Arnold and Gilbert Geis. 1984. "Ad Populum Argumentation in Criminology: Juvenile Diversion as Rhetoric." *Crime and Delinquency* 30(4):624–47.

Blomberg, Thomas G. 1977. "Diversion and Accelerated Social Control." *Journal of Criminal Law and Criminology* 68(2):274–82.

———. 1987. "Criminal Justice Reform and Social Control: Are We Becoming a Minimum Security Society?" Pp. 218–26 in *Transcarceration: Essays in the Sociology of Social Control*, edited by J. Lowman, R. J. Menzies and T. S. Palys. Aldershot, England: Gower.

Blomberg, Thomas G., William Bales, and Karen Reed. 1993. "Intermediate Punishment: Redistributing or Extending Social Control?" *Crime, Law and Social Change* 19:187–201.

Blomberg, Thomas G. and Karol Lucken. 1994. "Stacking the Deck by Piling Up

Sanctions: Is Intermediate Punishment Destined to Fail?" *Howard Journal* 33(1):62–80.
Cohen, Stanley. 1985. *Visions of Social Control.* Cambridge: Polity.
Feeley, Malcolm M. and Jonathan Simon. 1992. "The New Penology: Notes on the Emerging Strategy of Corrections and Its Implications." *Criminology* 30(4): 449–74.
Garland, David. 1990. *Punishment and Modern Society: A Study in Social Theory.* Oxford: Clarendon.
Hylton, John. 1982. "Rhetoric and Reality: A Critical Appraisal of Community Corrections Programmes." *Crime and Delinquency* 28(3):341–73.
Klein, Malcolm W. 1979. "Deinstitutionalization and Diversion of Juvenile Offenders: A Litany of Impediments." Pp. 145–201 in *Crime and Justice: An Annual Review of Research*, edited by Norval Morris and Michael Tonry. Chicago: University of Chicago Press.
Lemert, Edwin M. 1981. "Diversion in Juvenile Justice: What Hath Been Wrought." *Journal of Research in Crime and Delinquency* 18(1):34–46.
———. 1993. "Visions of Social Control: Probation Considered." *Crime and Delinquency* 39(4):447–61.
Lowman, John and Robert J. Menzies. 1986. "Out of the Fiscal Shadow: Carceral Trends in Canada and the United States." *Crime and Social Justice* 26:95–115.
Lowman, John, Robert J. Menzies, and T. S. Palys. 1987. *Transcarceration: Essays in the Sociology of Social Control.* Aldershot, England: Gower.
Matthews, Roger. 1987. "Decarceration and Social Control: Fantasies and Realities." Pp. 338–57 in *Transcarceration: Essays in the Sociology of Social Control*, edited by J. Lowman, R. J. Menzies, and T. S. Palys. Aldershot, England: Gower.
McMahon, Maeve. 1990. "Net-Widening: Vagaries of the Use of a Concept." *British Journal of Criminology* 30(2):121–49.
National Council on Crime and Delinquency. 1989. *The 1989 NCCD Prison Population Forecast: The Impact of the War on Drugs.* San Francisco: National Council on Crime and Delinquency.
Petersillia, Joan and Susan Turner. 1990. "Comparing Intensive and Regular Supervision for High Risk Probationers." *Crime and Delinquency* 36(1):87–111.
Polk, Kenneth. 1981. "Youth Services Bureaus: The Record and Prospects." Mimeo, University of Oregon, Eugene.
Proband, Stan C. 1993. "Jail Populations Up—Racial Disproportions Worse." *Overcrowded Times* 4(4):4.

5
Judicial Impact on Prison Reform

JAMES B. JACOBS

Beginning in the 1960s, federal courts started to become deeply immersed in institutional reform litigation involving schools, prisons, mental hospitals, and other institutions. Sweeping decisions in one case after another forced states to spend large sums of money to bring institutional conditions and practices up to minimum constitutional requirements and forced administrators to extend due process, rationalize their decisions, and limit their discretion. While such judicial activism had many champions and supporters, it also generated a great deal of criticism. Some critics objected to judicial efforts to reform institutions on grounds that federal courts lacked constitutional and political authority to play this kind of role, and that federal judges had usurped the authority that properly belongs to state legislators and executive branch officials. Other critics stressed the courts' lack of competence in fixing problems rooted in inadequate resource funding and malfunctioning bureaucracies. They warned that judicial intervention was as likely to make things worse as to improve them.

The most recent, and one of the most powerful, critiques of the role that courts have played in reform litigation is Gerald Rosenberg's *The Hollow Hope: Can Courts Bring About Social Change?* Professor Rosenberg, a legally trained political scientist on the University of Chicago faculty, has published an ambitious book that forcefully challenges the proposition that the federal courts, the Supreme Court in particular, have been successful in their efforts to produce social change. Rosenberg argues that courts have had a much more limited role in producing social change than is commonly thought. He sets out a formal thesis prescribing the necessary and sufficient conditions for courts to achieve social change, and attempts to support that thesis by examining empirical data and studies on social change in a number of contexts, particularly school desegregation and opportunities for abortion, but also including prison reforms.

Although Rosenberg (1991) deals with prison reform only in a relatively brief section, he raises important questions for American and foreign scholars trying to assess the capacity of courts to reform prisons. If courts have not been the primary impetus for prison reform in this quarter century, as Rosenberg seems to argue, then prison scholars are left to determine what is the force that drives prison reform.

Rosenberg sets out his thesis in very explicit terms. In brief, he argues that

> courts will generally not be effective producers of significant social reform for three [structural] reasons: the limited nature of constitutional rights, the lack of judicial independence and the judiciary's inability to develop appropriate policies and its lack of powers of implementation. (1991:10)

Rosenberg further argues that when "political, social and economic conditions have become supportive of change, courts can effectively produce significant social reform" (p. 3). However, Rosenberg suggests that court decisions are neither necessary nor sufficient for producing significant social reform.[1]

While Rosenberg does not rule out the possibility of judicially mandated reform, he is skeptical about the ability of courts to transform or even lead the way in transforming American institutions. Rosenberg's revisionist thesis is applied to the contexts of school desegregation and freedom of choice with respect to abortion. He finds that despite widespread belief that the Supreme Court's decision in *Brown v. Board of Education* [347 U.S. 483 (1954)] brought about school desegregation and that *Roe v. Wade* [419 U.S. 113 (1973)] expanded opportunities to obtain abortions, the Court's decisions actually were small (and by no means necessary) steps along the way to inevitable social reform. In other words, change would have occurred without the Supreme Court's intervention. In the context of school desegregation and abortion, the data that Rosenberg marshals in support of this revisionist viewpoint are quite impressive.

The purpose of this essay is to examine how well Rosenberg's thesis stands up when applied to prison reform. I take no position on the validity of his thesis when applied to other contexts, although I believe that my criticisms of his methodology might be applicable in those other contexts as well. I conclude that even if Rosenberg is right that the courts played only a limited role in bringing about school desegregation and opportunities for abortion, he is wrong when it comes to prison reform.

There are two key problems with the application of his thesis to prisons. The first problem is that Rosenberg fails to provide for the infinite variety of variables that can significantly impact prison reform litigation. The second problem is that there is an inadequate database from which to draw generalizations about the amount of prison reform and the extent to which it depends upon litigation and court interventions.

Unfortunately, Rosenberg addresses the issue of prison reform in only fifteen pages of his book, and the data that he presents in behalf of his thesis constitute only a fraction of the evidence that he brings forward in the school desegregation and abortion contexts. Equally unfortunate, in applying his thesis to prisons, he makes his argument far less well.

WHAT COUNTS AS SIGNIFICANT SOCIAL REFORM?

Rosenberg's thesis requires him first to consider whether there has been significant social reform in prisons. On that question, he says, "In sum, it appears that change has been uneven. Many of the worst conditions have been improved to at least minimal standards, but problems still abound" (1991:307). This is not enlightening; in fact, it is almost vacuous. One might safely offer the same "assessment" of any institution or social problem.

Many of the key terms in Rosenberg's analysis are vague or indeterminate (see Schuck 1993). The first term the reader must wrestle with is the dependent variable, "significant social reform." This term has both normative and positive components. First, Rosenberg should determine what counts as court-generated prison reform and how much of it exists. Then, he should determine which measurement (i.e., the sum total or average) of this court-generated prison reform qualifies as "significant."

Rosenberg fails to define "significant social reform." At points in his analysis, he equates "significant social reform" with "the stated goals" of the lawyers who bring institutional change litigation. Even assuming that the stated goals of prisoners' rights lawyers could be reliably ascertained and summed up (or averaged), this is a strange criterion. For instance, lawyers may have had unrealistic expectations when stating their litigation goals, may have stated the goals of their most vocal clients, or may have stated their goals in such a way so as to attract media attention or gain some tactical advantage. Surely it does not follow that if the activist lawyers' goals were only partially achieved, significant social reform has not occurred.

THE PROBLEMS IN ASSESSING THE SCOPE OF PRISON REFORM

The complexity and ambition of Rosenberg's project is mind-boggling. How can one "assess" the status of prison reform in several thousand prisons and jails throughout the United States? Likewise, how can one assess the impacts of twenty-five years of prisoners' rights litigation in all these diverse prisons and jails? There have been thousands of lawsuits, many hundreds of important ones, and hundreds of major decisions and consent decrees imposing wide-ranging reforms on various institutions and whole prison systems. Regrettably, this massive volume of legal activity has not been systematically transformed into a database; indeed, there have been only a few case studies of "judicial impacts" on prison reform and these themselves have been controversial (Dilulio 1990a).

Great epistemological and methodological problems cloud our ability to assess the overall status of prison reform in America. Rosenberg concludes that the extent of positive social change that has been achieved in prisons is debatable: "while some changes have been made, serious problems remain" (1991:306). Upon inspection, this "conclusion" does not respond to the question of whether significant social change has occurred. For example, massive social change may have occurred in Eastern Europe and an observer might still rightly conclude that "while some conditions have gotten better, some have gotten worse." One can rightly argue that all major social reform has some direct and indirect negative consequences.

Furthermore, in assessing the status of prison reform it is difficult to balance negative developments against positive achievements. For example, how can the deterioration in quality of food be weighed against enhancements of fundamental rights like freedom of speech and due process? Should the achievements of prison reform be discounted by increased risks of AIDS and tuberculosis in prisons and jails?

Rosenberg rightly notes that prison overcrowding has neutralized much prison reform. He argues that while judicial intervention in prisons has flowered, prisons have become more crowded and have suffered all of the strains and inconveniences that accompany crowding. However, it is inappropriate to conflate the significance of court-sponsored prison reform with negative developments unconnected to prisoners' rights litigation. Prison reform litigation does not produce prison crowding; in many cases it has ameliorated crowding through population caps, square footage requirements for cells, etc. Rather, prison crowding flows from tougher sentencing and law enforcement policies of legislatures, police, prosecutors, state trial courts, and parole boards.

Aside from the issue of crowding, Rosenberg is on the right track when he argues that a proper accounting for court-ordered prison reform must include the negative direct and indirect consequences of litigation, like the destabilizing effect on prison security occasioned by the implementation of certain changes. The expansion of prisoners' civil rights may, in some prisons, have led to the weakening of staff control and the breakdown of order (see Jacobs 1983; Dilulio 1990b).

In tracing the negative consequences of prisoners' rights litigation and court-ordered prison reform, we face another incredibly complicated methodological problem and again find ourselves befuddled by the absence of a database or a set of systematic case studies. What should be the "time frame" in assessing the positive and negative consequences of litigation-generated prison reform? At what point(s) in time after a court has mandated change should an observer make an assessment? Is six months after a judicial decree sufficient? Is it better to wait one year? Or five years?

Disentangling causes is a problem that goes to the core of Rosenberg's project. How can we be sure that court-ordered prison reform *caused* short-term, medium-term, or long-term deterioration of control? Rosenberg states that court-ordered prison reform has led to a decrease in safety and security in the prisons. To support this conclusion, he quotes a Texas inmate and a former member of the court-appointed special master's staff in *Ruiz* (the Texas prison case) who states, "contemporary wisdom in corrections is that despite more than a decade of close scrutiny and mandated reforms, many prisons are less safe than they were in the pre-reform days" (1991:307). The person quoted here may not be correct. However, even if he is correct, is the deterioration of prison safety directly (or even indirectly) attributable to prison litigation? Obviously, other independent variables are also at work, including an upsurge in violence in American society generally, deteriorating race relations, and gang activity. Might the inability of prison management to adapt to the new requirements of greater prisoners' rights also be counted as a "cause"?

Rosenberg's belief that prisons are less safe is debatable. Violence was a pervasive characteristic of prison life that existed well before the intervention of the courts. In fact, it may be one of the prime reasons for court intervention in the first place. Recall Chief Judge Henley's moving depiction of the violence in the Arkansas prison system that stirred him to hold that prison in violation of the Eighth Amendment:

> In a very real sense trusty guards have the power of life and death over other inmates. Some guards are doubtless men of good judgment; others are not. It is within the power of a trusty guard to murder another inmate with impunity, and the danger that such will be done is always clear and present. Very recently a gate guard killed another inmate "carelessly." One wonders. And there is evidence that recently a guard on night duty fired a shotgun into a crowded barracks because the inmates would not turn off the television set. In any event the rankers [ordinary inmates] live in deadly fear of the guards. [*Holt v. Sarver*, 309 F. Supp. 362 (D.C. Ark 1970)]

The opinions in such cases as *Ramos v. Lamm* [485 F. Supp. 881 (1972)] in Colorado, *Gates v. Collier* [349 F. Supp. 881 (1972)] in Mississippi, and *Ruiz v. Estelle* [503 F. Supp. 1265 (1980)] in Texas graphically describe the horrendous violence that triggered judicial intervention.[2] With respect to the Texas prisons, while some observers argue that the pre-*Ruiz* days were extremely violent with prisoners living under a reign of terror (Martin and

Eklund-Olson 1987), others remember the pre-*Ruiz* days as peaceful and orderly (Dilulio 1987). Moreover, while there seems to be a consensus that the Texas prisons experienced a period of destabilization and deterioration of control in the mid-1980s occasioned by inability or unwillingness to implement court-ordered reforms, some scholars foresee the reestablishment of control by the end of this decade (Eklund-Olson 1986; Eklund-Olson and Martin 1988).

ATTRIBUTING SOCIAL CHANGE IN PRISON TO LITIGATION AND COURTS

If it is accepted arguendo that significant social change has occurred, we must next examine whether it can be attributed to litigation and court intervention. Rosenberg finds that his overall thesis about the limited efficacy of courts in producing prison reform is confirmed. He argues that

> for change to occur as a result of litigation, reformers [had to] overcome the three constraints and then have present at least one of four [facilitating] conditions. With prison reform, courts overcame only one of the constraints entirely. In individual cases, other constraints were overcome. When this occurred, and when one of the conditions were present, meaningful change occurred. (1991:308)

Rosenberg argues that the presence or absence of conditions "explain both why change has been uneven and when it has occurred." Rosenberg argues political support was much more influential than litigation in creating prison change:

> [T]here is little evidence that prison reform litigators have put as much time, energy, and resources into political and social change as into litigation. Without that change, litigation will not be effective. Reliance on courts will not bring much change. The political change must be faced directly. Litigation, as the executive director of the ACLU's National Prison Project has come to understand, "is not, of course, the real answer." (pp. 313–14)

There is a tautological quality to this argument: where litigators and courts have been successful in implementing reform, it is because they have overcome impediments; but where they have been unsuccessful, they have not overcome impediments. Moreover, the tautology is compounded because the existence of insurmountable impediments is proved by the absence of change.

In attempting to account for the occurrence of significant social change in prison, it is hard to identify any causal variables that rival litigation. It is completely implausible to assign a key causal role to the political branches of government. While here and there governors and legislators sympathetic to prison reform may have appeared, political reality will always assign prison reform the lowest political priority. It is hard, if not impossible, to convince the citizenry that money should be invested to upgrade prison conditions rather than to upgrade schools, roads, health care, the state university, police, job training, and practically anything else. Even if politicians and prisoners are *not opposed in principle* to prison reform, and they often are, it is highly unlikely that they would serve as catalysts for change. Furthermore, no broad-based citizens movement in the 1960s and 1970s (or since) pushed for widespread prison reform.

The only other possible contender for chief causal agent in the occurrence of prison reform is the corrections establishment itself.[3] Prison reformers have worked within the system throughout American history, although ideas about what constitutes reform have varied and rarely correspond to the view of theorists and activists "outside" the system. It is possible that in the 1960s and 1970s, a new generation of prison officials sympathetic to a broad range of prison reforms appeared throughout the United States, and that they were able to obtain (independent of litigation threats) significant resources to implement their reform vision. However, I doubt that empirical evidence will support this hypothesis. Nevertheless, Rosenberg is right that in the late 1970s and 1980s some prison officials came to recognize that they could leverage litigation or the threat of litigation to obtain resources (especially more staff) and improvements.[4]

Arguably, Rosenberg's thesis does not withstand scrutiny in the case of prison reform. Prison reform is different than desegregation or abortion because there are no strong interest groups, supportive public opinion, or legislative or executive branch politics that press for expanding prisoners' rights or improving prison conditions. Prisons occupy a unique place among institutions targeted for reform by litigation precisely because of the lack of popular and political support for their reform. Clearly, courts did not simply and gently nudge along powerful, outside forces of change that were destined to make their mark. Courts became embroiled in prison reform despite strenuous claims by legislators that there was not enough money for implementation and claims by prison officials that the courts' orders would set off maelstroms.

TRACING CHANGE TO THE LOWER COURTS

The Supreme Court has been only minimally involved in judicial intervention in prison affairs. Certainly it has not played the pivotal role that it did in school desegregation and decriminalization of abortion. Of course, the

Court did hand down a few liberal decisions in the early 1970s that opened the door to prisoners' suits,[5] but no sooner was the door opened a crack than the Court began to force it closed. The Burger Court backed away from prisoners' rights suits very quickly, with Chief Justice Burger frequently urging deference to prison officials [*Hudson v. Palmer*, 468 U.S. 517 (1984); *Block v. Rutherford*, 468 U.S. 589 (1984)]. The *Wolf v. McDonald* [94 S.Ct. 2963 (1974)], *Estelle v. Gamble* [429 U.S. 97 (1976)], and *Bounds v. Smith* [430 US.Ct. 817 (1977)] decisions marked the watershed for prisoners' rights victories in the Supreme Court; since then, most cases that reached the Supreme Court resulted in victories for prison officials [e.g., example, *Bell v. Wolfish*, 441 U.S. 520 (1979); *Rhodes v. Chapman*, 452 U.S.337 (1981); *Hewitt v. Helms*, 459 U.S. 460 (1983); *Ponte v. Real*, 471 U.S. 491 (1985); *Whitley v. Albers*, 475 U.S. 312 (1986)].

In part, it is analytically difficult to apply Rosenberg's thesis to court-sponsored prison reform. Unlike school desegregation, where Rosenberg turned to the Supreme Court's decision in *Brown v. Board of Education*, or abortion, where he assessed the impact of the Supreme Court's decision in *Roe v. Wade*, Rosenberg does not and cannot focus on the impact of a particular Supreme Court decision or series of Supreme Court decisions in the area of prison reform. Most court-ordered prison reform has been accomplished by federal district courts after lengthy trials (and negotiated consent judgments) that have turned on specific conditions in one prison or prison system rather than on appellate court decisions announcing new constitutional principles. Thus, the most important (albeit not necessarily representative) prison cases are *Ruiz v. Estelle* [503 F. Supp. 1265 (S.D.Tex 1980)] in Texas, *Guthrie v. Evans* [93 F.R.D. 390 (S.D.Georgia 1981)] in Georgia, the "Tombs" [*Rhem v. Malcolm*, 389 F.Supp. 964 (S.D.N.Y. 1975)] litigation in New York City, and *Morales Feliciano v. Romero Barcelo*, in Puerto Rico [672 F.Supp. 591 (D. Puerto Rico 1986)].

As important, perhaps even more important, than *court-ordered* reform have been negotiated reforms entered into without a trial.[6] In many instances, the initiation of litigation or even the *threat* of litigation has produced significant prison reform. State officials may choose to settle because they wish to avoid the negative publicity of a trial or the risk of even more expensive court-ordered reforms.

In any event, the key question for Rosenberg is not why the courts stayed the course, but "why the change has been so uneven—why there was some change, but only some" (1991:307). This question is hard to understand. Is Rosenberg asking why some courts were receptive to prisoners' cases, while others were not? Or, why among those courts that were receptive to prisoners' claims, some courts were successful in reforming unconstitutional practices and conditions while others were not? Or is the question, why did judicial intervention succeed in dealing with some practices and conditions while failing to deal with others?

The fact that many district courts remained receptive to and actively involved in "totality of conditions suits," while the Supreme Court withdrew from the field, has never been adequately explained. I believe that the answer lies in the deplorable prison conditions, the superior lawyering skills of a highly specialized prisoners' rights bar, and the correspondingly poor quality of the state's representation in these cases.

WHAT ACCOUNTS FOR JUDICIAL SUCCESS AND FAILURE?

The question why, among courts that found in favor of prison reform, some were more successful at implementing change than others is intriguing and important. A satisfactory answer would require a strong empirical knowledge base, criteria for "success," and a coherent position on what time frame to use in carrying out the evaluation. Of course it would be well to remember that all prisons did not suffer from the same operational and physical deficiencies; thus, "success" would have to be defined differently in each case. Furthermore, different lawsuits asked for different relief, so it would be wrong to compare the achievements of a massive "totality of conditions" with the achievements of a more limited suit.

Assuming that we could adequately deal with the dependent variable "success" and with the time frame problem, empirical studies would be needed to identify independent variables that predict judicial success. A full-blown empirical study of cases in which judges wanted to achieve prison reform ought to focus on a number of independent variables, including resources, skills, and commitment of the prisoners' lawyers; the determination of the judge; whether the judge appointed a special master to supervise implementation of the decree; the special master's legal powers, resources, skills, commitment, and intelligence; the kinds of prison problems targeted for reform; the attitude of the prison's and prison department's officials toward reform, the attitude of the department's legal counsel toward reform, the attitude of the rank and file corrections officers toward reform; the attitude of the governor toward reform; the attitude of the legislative leadership and rank and file legislators toward reform; and the resources of the state. It is conceivable that all these variables could be scaled and entered into a regression analysis, but no such project has yet been undertaken.

Another factor that remains to be explained is the tremendously complex process by which courts obtain the support of prison officials. The strategies that judges and their special masters have used include the contempt power, publicly reprimanding prison officials, threatening to close down prisons, and persuading prison officials that reform is in their interest.

Rosenberg engages in a cursory reading of some limited descriptions or impressions of two or three prison cases and concludes that "[t]he active support of administrators and staff is required. And without the presence of factors external to the courts, that support will not be available" (1991:311). By "factors external to the courts," he apparently means political support for reform from the executive and legislative branches:

> Prison reform issues are essentially political, and prison reform is highly dependent upon the political process. When political leaders are willing to act, this constraint can be overcome. When they do nothing, or oppose court decisions, little change occurs. (p. 308)[7]

These observations seem sound as far as they go, but unfortunately they do not go very far. Court-ordered prison reform obviously cannot be achieved without cooperation from prison officials. If, in response to a court's prison reform decision, prison officials went on strike (or worse), no reform would occur (unless the court was able to remove the recalcitrant officials from their jobs and substitute compliant replacements).

Rosenberg himself notes that the constraint on a court's ability to achieve social change can be overcome by an alliance with prison officials who see an opportunity to leverage the court's decision to obtain more resources and other reforms that they themselves want. This point is well taken. Many prison officials have seen the velvet glove in the iron fist; in fact, some prison cases have resulted in something like collusion between prisoners' rights advocates and prison officials to obtain more resources from the legislature. Unfortunately, Rosenberg does not provide a formula for predicting when such collusions will occur and, if they occur, when they will be successful. What he provides is a truism: if prison officials support court-ordered reform, success will be more likely.

Another Rosenberg truism is that broad-scale prison reform cannot be achieved without some support from the executive and legislative branches. But without a full-scale empirical study, it is impossible to know how much variation there is from state to state in the process of obtaining fiscal support for court-ordered prison reform, or the different means courts have used to obtain the necessary funding. Whether access to funding ultimately depends upon the skill and commitment of the judge and the parties to the lawsuit or on the predisposition of the governor and legislative leadership is unknown. A study is needed to examine how judges have overcome political intransigence and resistance. Are there cases in which the courts have utterly failed to implement their decrees because no funds could ever be obtained?

CONCLUSION

In the context of prison reform, Rosenberg's thesis is not persuasive. At every point along the way, crucial terms have not been defined. Testing his thesis against empirical reality presents Herculean difficulties. What he means by "significant social reform" is unknown. Further, he lacks an adequate methodology to determine where "significant social reform" has occurred and how much can properly be attributed to courts. If courts have been the driving force behind reform, the process by which they have been able to enlist enough support to enforce their decrees remains shrouded in mystery.

Rosenberg's inquiry is overly ambitious. In a single volume, he seeks to prove with empirical evidence a complex thesis about the role of courts in producing social change in a number of massively complex contexts: schools, reproductive rights, environmental protection, and prisons, among others. He did not collect data or make observations himself, but summarized and synthesized the work of others. Therefore, his work can be no better than the underlying scholarship that he is reviewing. Unfortunately, at least in the context of prisons, the existing scholarship does not begin to address the vast amount of legal activity.

Finally, two thirds or more of the nation's prison systems have been operating, in whole or in part, under significant court decrees dealing with issues like disciplinary procedures and conditions, transfers, food services, ventilation, sewage, fire safety, recreation opportunities and facilities, lighting, cell size and assignments, guard training, and many more (*National Prison Project Journal* 1993). To anyone who has been part of or closely watched this legal activity, it seems naive to ask whether litigation has produced significant social change in prisons. Every prison has changed its practices and reconstructed parts of its physical plant as a direct consequence of prisoners' rights litigation. Construction, renovation, and rehabilitation of physical plants as required by court orders have led to huge expenditures in a number of states. Both Kentucky and Tennessee estimate the cost of court-ordered prison reform in excess of $250 million. Puerto Rico is currently engaged in a physical rehabilitation project estimated at $100 million. Since 1985, the Texas legislature has made biennial appropriations in excess of $1 billion for prison construction and renovation, much of which was precipitated by the massive *Ruiz* litigation. Florida estimates that it has spent $600 million in construction and compliance costs. North Carolina has had direct compliance costs of $200 million and, in 1991, presented plans for $400 million of new prison construction.

Against this tidal wave of apparent court-ordered prison reform, Rosenberg's revisionist view has little empirical support. I do not doubt that judicial intervention in prisons has been the most significant vehicle of prison reform in the latter quarter of the twentieth century. But why this development occurred, especially when the Supreme Court did not encourage it and no other formidable political and social forces were behind it, remains to be adequately explained. By the same token, much more needs to be known about *how* prison reform was implemented. No doubt the importance of lawyering skills, the personalities and politics of district court judges, and the stance and competency of prison administrators and staff will all turn out to be important.

In *The Hollow Hope*, Rosenberg has kept the issue alive. For those of us interested in writing the contemporary social history of the American prisons, it should serve to stimulate both more research and more theorizing.

ACKNOWLEDGMENTS

The author is very grateful for the extensive and insightful comments of Steve Martin and for the research and editing assistance of Jessica Henry.

NOTES

1. "They are not necessary because much reform takes place outside the judicial system and because courts lack independence. They are not sufficient because courts lack effective tools of implementation and require the existence of [at least one of several] particular conditions[:] a) Positive incentives are offered to induce compliance, b) Costs are imposed to induce compliance, c) Court decisions allow for market implementation or d) Administrators and officials crucial for implementation are willing to act and see court orders as a tool for leveraging additional resources or hiding behind. Without the presence of at least one of these conditions, court decisions will not produce significant social reform" (pp. 35–36).

2. See also *Feliciano v. Barcelo* [672 F. Supp. 591 (1986)] for a discussion of violence in Puerto Rican prisons.

3. Actually, riots are another possible causal factor for the occurrence of prison reform that are beyond the scope of this paper.

4. Prison officials in Texas routinely relied on "Ruiz Requirements" to justify their funding requests to the legislature. A former chairman of the Board of Corrections openly advocated including a certain level of staffing in the final settlement in order to ensure that the legislature would provide the funds necessary to operate the prison properly.

5. See *Wolf v. McDonald* [94 S.Ct. 2963 (1974)], *Johnson v. Avery* [89 S.Ct. 747 (1968)], and *Cruz v. Beto* [92 S.Ct. 1079 (1972)]. These decisions were devoted to civil rights. They did not require spending money or reorganizing prison administration. The really important prison reform cases were district court cases that did not flow from Supreme Court doctrine but from the judges' revulsion at squalid prison conditions.

6. For example, the states of Kansas, Nevada, New Mexico, and Texas have entered into consent decrees without there having been a trial.

7. Rosenberg goes on to note that political support for court-ordered prison

reform has been encouraged by the existence of the larger rights movement and prison violence.

REFERENCES

Dilulio, John J., Jr. 1987. *Governing Prisons: A Comparative Study of Correctional Management*. New York: Free Press.
———. 1990a. "The Old Regime and the Ruiz Revolution: The Impact of Judicial Intervention on Texas Prisons." Pp. 51–72 in *Courts, Corrections and the Constitution*, edited by John J. Dilulio, Jr. New York: Oxford University Press.
———. 1990b. *Courts, Corrections, and the Constitution: The Impact of Judicial Intervention on Prisons and Jails*. New York: Oxford University Press.
Eklund-Olson, Sheldon. 1986. "Crowding, Social Control, and Prison Violence: Evidence from the Post-Ruiz Years in Texas." *Law and Society Review* 20:389.
Eklund-Olson, Sheldon and Martin, Stephen J. 1988. "Organizational Compliance with Court-Ordered Reform." *Law and Society Review* 22:359.
Jacobs, James B. 1983. "The Prisoners' Rights Movement and Its Impacts." Pp. 33–60 in *New Perspectives on Prisons and Imprisonment*, edited by James B. Jacobs. Ithaca, NY: Cornell University Press.
Martin, Steven J. and Eklund-Olson, Sheldon. 1987. *Texas Prisons: The Walls Came Tumbling Down*. Austin: Texas Monthly Press.
National Prison Project. 1993. "Status Report: State Prisons and the Courts—January 1, 1992." *National Prison Project Journal* 8(1): (Winter).
Rosenberg, Gerald N. 1991. *The Hollow Hope: Can Courts Bring About Social Change?* Chicago: University of Chicago Press.
Schuck, Peter H. 1993. "Book Review: Public Law Litigation and Social Reform" (reviewing *The Hollow Hope*) *Yale Law Journal* 102:1763–86.

6
The Structural-Functional Perspective on Imprisonment

GRESHAM M. SYKES

I

The emergence of a structural-functional perspective on the prison, in the decades immediately following the end of World War II, can be explained in part by the particular interests, personal experiences, and intellectual training of those involved in penology in those years. I believe, however, that the temper of the time—the dominant intellectual fashions, the events in the headlines, the social and political trends of those years—also played a role, providing a spur for a particular kind of theorizing as well as a receptive audience. And pure chance, I think, had an influence as well, in the sense that quite fortuitous events led a number of people—many at the beginning of their academic careers—to immerse themselves in the study of punishment of criminal offenders, bringing a variety of new approaches to the issues. These notes, then, are a form of intellectual history, admittedly impressionistic, anecdotal, personal, and incomplete.

In my own case, for example, I was assigned the criminology course in my first year of teaching as an instructor at Princeton University although I knew almost nothing about the field, a kind of assignment of little concern apparently to sociology departments then and now. But I began learning what I could, one step ahead (often a misstep) of my students. I was appalled to find that textbooks in the field made almost no effort to examine what I would have thought to be basic issues, such as varying conceptions of crime, how and why society defined some behavior criminal, the meaning of crime from the viewpoint of the offender, and so on. The vast body of writing in the law (which I was dimly aware existed) was largely ignored, including the analysis of criminal intent that evidently played a large part in legal thought. And punishment was almost uniformly viewed as a barbarism, and ineffective to boot. A number of liberal sentiments, which I largely shared, seemed to have hardened into a set of cliches that closed off inquiry. But my experience in the army had persuaded me that, for better or for worse, people often became whatever they were assigned regardless of personal proclivities or skills, and I set about becoming a criminologist.

At Princeton in those days many classes were split between lectures and "precepts," or small groups meeting to discuss the lecture material. What was unusual was that the precepts were led not by graduate students but by faculty members, from junior instructors to senior professors. Enrollments in my criminology course began to go up sharply, with the result that the number of necessary precepts increased greatly, requiring more preceptors; and the sociology department persuaded Lloyd McKorkle, the warden of the New Jersey State Maximum Security Prison in the nearby city of Trenton, to meet with one of the discussion groups twice a week.

Lloyd and I became good friends, although I am sure he was more than a little bemused by my naivete and ignorance, and he urged me to make a closer study of the prison. The friendship had two important consequences. For one thing, Lloyd provided me with free and easy access to all parts of the prison, to both guards and inmates, and to the records of the institution. And in frequent, long conversations spread over a number of years, Lloyd and other prison officials provided intimate and detailed accounts of institutional life that proved invaluable.

Donald Cressey tells of a similar chance encounter with another Lloyd—Lloyd Ohlin, in his case—involving a missed connection after a meeting of the American Sociological Association in Urbana, and a shared ride to Chicago, leading to an invitation to study prisons in Wisconsin. Others seem to have had like experiences, in the sense that often seemingly whimsical, random, or accidental events led them into criminology and penology and the establishment of close and prolonged relationships with penal institutions. So much for the idea of an orderly, logical development of an intellectual career. But the important point is that these links with penal institutions produced detailed, intimate knowledge of prison life over a period of years, a knowledge that transcended what could be obtained through questionnaires or interviews, although these too played a part. And the knowledge was different, I think, from that obtained by being an official with an administrative role or being an inmate, although both have made important contributions to the literature of penology.

II

In the first half of this century, interest in the prison had taken six major forms.

1. Humanitarian concerns centered attention on the brutal and degrading conditions of confinement, and offered various programs of reform.
2. The prison was examined with an eye to the possibilities of rehabilitating the offender, with the deterrent effect of imprisonment largely discounted, as I have noted.
3. A good deal of anecdotal material was offered for public consumption, since tales of life behind bars seemed to feed an endless curiosity about the confinement of dangerous felons.
4. Linked to this anecdotal material, prisons were periodically subject to *exposés* detailing mismanagement, graft, and other forms of wrongdoing on the part of officials, with prison scandals serving as a convenient weapon for the party out of power.
5. Penal institutions served as a topic for historical investigations, although this interest remained limited until the shape of historical inquiries changed and "history from below" became more popular.
6. Finally there was a sociological concern with penal institutions—a concern often marked by a humanitarian impulse and utilitarian considerations of finding more effective means of rehabilitation, but laying claim to scientific objectivity and sociological relevance, and examining such things as patterns of socialization, status, and so on.

This sociological work provided an indispensable base for later studies, but with some notable exceptions it was mainly descriptive, an ethnography of the confined. Much of the theorizing centered on the question of "prisonization," or the process by which the individual acquired the values, norms, and attitudes of the inmate subculture, with less attention paid to the question of why the subculture existed in the first place. The diversity of inmate roles was made clear, but their relationship to one another and to the regime of the custodians remained relatively neglected.

After the end of World War II, however, American sociology began to change. Many of the changes were actually a flowering or a development of ideas produced in the 1930s and 1940s, ideas that had simply lain dormant or received little attention in a country preoccupied with war. In any event, research designs became much more elaborate and sophisticated, as did the statistical techniques for sample selection and the analysis of data. This push toward quantification was closely linked to the growth of federal funding for scientific research, with skills in quantification becoming an important qualification for securing funds, while at the same time large federal grants provided the resources that made more elaborate quantification possible. "Bigtime" research was becoming a notable feature of modern sociology. While some substantive areas fell out of fashion, others, such as stratification gained increasing attention. And in the area of theory, the ideas of Parsons and Merton, along with those of their disciples, rose into prominence.

Criminology and penology were inevitably influenced to some extent by these developments. As far as the study of the prison was concerned, however, quantitative research with large numbers of respondents and the precise measurement of variables remained relatively rare. The suspicion bordering on paranoia in the prison posed a major problem. It was extremely difficult and time-consuming to establish the trust necessary for the collection of reliable data by means of questionnaires and interviews, with both guards and inmates. Generally, empirical research on the prison continued to take the form of community studies or participant observation. But a way of looking at the prison, influenced by the ideas of Parsons and Merton, did become much more evident. First, the prison as a whole was taken as the object of study, a small-scale society or social system, with questions about the problems of continuity and order assuming major theoretical significance. Second, the parts of the system—the objectives of the custodial institution, the social and physical environment, the perceptions and social roles of guards and inmates, and so on—were seen as interrelated elements to be analyzed for their impact on one another and the system as a whole. Emphasis was placed not simply on the intended consequences of rules and behavior but on the unintended or latent outcomes as well. Third, the prison was seen as providing an opportunity for "middle-range" theorizing, with the special conditions of custodial institutions setting definite limits on generalization but offering the possibility of greater insights on the nature of totalitarian control. And fourth—and perhaps most important—the norms of both guards and inmates were seen as being significantly shaped by the system of power in which they played out their social roles. The existence of norms was not to be taken as a given, with commitment to those norms seen as a matter of socialization, enculturation, the transmission of culture, learning theory, differential association, and so on. Instead, the existence of norms was a problem to be solved, and the task was to analyze norms as a function of the social structure or social system in which individuals found themselves.

These themes were not original nor were they unique to the study of the prison. Albert Cohen, for example, in his book *Delinquent Boys*, had set forth a clear and powerful argument for the need to explore the origins of subcultures rather than merely to study the process of their acquisition, and had traced his ideas to Pitirim Sorokin's concern with the rise and fall of total systems. But the combination of these themes, the emphasis given to them, and the primary interest in the prison itself, rather than the effectiveness of the prison for rehabilitation, deterrence, or retribution, all brought something different to penology.

Two other things were important, I think, in the development of a changed perspective on imprisonment. First, there were some forty riots in eighteen months in American prisons, beginning in the early part of 1952.

Prisons obviously were not working very well, and public concern with the issue encouraged an academic interest. Thus, for example, funds were provided by the Social Science Research Council for a series of meetings, in 1956 and 1957, for a group of social scientists working in this area, leading to the publication of *Theoretical Studies in the Social Organization of the Prison* (Cloward 1960). Second, the 1950s saw an increased interest in systems of total power as more and more information about Nazi concentration camps became available. This factor acted in a very indirect fashion, I believe, and the analysis of concentration camps never became a part of American criminology in any full or systematic way. Nevertheless, reports on concentration camps became an important part of the intellectual climate, particularly through Bruno Bettelheim's "Individual and Mass Behavior in Extreme Situations" in 1943, and books such as Eugen Kogon's (1966) *The Theory and Practice of Hell* and Hannah Arendt's (1963) *Eichmann in Jerusalem*.

III

The structural-functional approach to the prison rarely concerned itself with precise definitions, conceptual elaboration, or the logical analysis of causal chains—or, indeed, the accumulation of a large mass of empirical data. Instead, I think its claim to attention rested on a set of basic insights that found a sympathetic audience:

1. It was recognized that prison, like any other complex social system persisting through time, could not be run by the use of force alone, that some degree of voluntary cooperation on the part of those who were ruled was necessary. The problem then was how this cooperation could be obtained.

2. The rewards and punishments legally available to the prison authorities were generally inadequate, as far as securing cooperation was concerned. Furthermore, the task of running the prison and securing cooperation was severely hampered by the fact that the prison was assigned objectives that were often contradictory or in conflict with one another. Thus, for example, efforts to rehabilitate inmates were frequently undone by the requirements of maintaining security and preventing disorder.

3. Some degree of cooperation could be obtained—and usually was— by a system of illegal or forbidden rewards, such as guards ignoring the infraction of prison rules by inmates. Prisoners were allowed to engage in various forms of deviant behavior—ostensibly of a minor sort—in exchange for a quiet institution. This pattern of the custodians breaking the rules for

the sake of peace and quiet was part of an extensive pattern of "corruption" based on friendship and the innocuous encroachment on the guards' duties on the part of inmates.

4. Imprisonment involved a set of deprivations that went far beyond the loss of liberty or material comfort. Prisoners were faced with a number of psychological threats to their self-conception or sense of worth, such as being reduced to childhood's dependence or being forced into homosexual liaisons.

5. Much of the behavior of inmates could be interpreted or understood as attempts, conscious or unconscious, to meet and counter the problems posed by the deprivations of prison life, including the potent threats to the ego. In later years, critics such as John Irwin (1970) would claim that the behavior patterns of inmates were rooted in a thieves' subculture, and much was made of an indigenous versus an imported model of the inmate social system. From the structural-functional perspective, however, the important issue was how the behavior of inmates was related to their present predicament rather than the possible influence of life before confinement. And although inmates' behavior was probably conditioned by prior criminal patterns, the crucial issue was how these general tendencies—such as the vaunted loyalty among thieves or the instrumental use of violence—might be reinforced or called into play the by the realities of prison life. (I think there was a common feeling that the inmate social system seen in prisons at the time would very likely come into existence almost without regard to inmates' criminal histories. I suppose this idea was based at least in part on assumptions about the power of totalitarian systems to shape behavior and the limited possibilities of dealing with the threats posed by imprisonment.)

6. It was claimed that the behavior patterns of inmates sprang from a set of values, attitudes, and beliefs that found expression in the so-called inmate code couched in prison argot. This code held forth a pattern of approved conduct, but as Shelly Messinger and I tried to make clear, it was an ideal rather than a description of how inmates behaved. It was argued that an important theoretical and empirical variable was to be found in the extent to which inmates actually did or did not conform to the inmate code with its demands for inmate solidarity, and this variation was likely to be a vital factor in determining the extent to which rehabilitation was possible in a prison setting.

These ideas came to be labeled "the structural-functional perspective on the prison," and I suppose that designation was appropriate, in the sense that interest in the prison centered on (1) the social structure of the prison as a whole, and (2) the ways in which beliefs, norms, and behavior of both inmates and guards functioned to maintain the prison as an ongoing system. The astonishing thing about prisons, from this viewpoint, was the fact that they didn't degenerate into perpetual chaos on the one hand, or, on the other, into the frozen order of masses of men locked in solitary confinement. Somehow, a social system, involving complex interaction, was kept going. It was precisely this fact, I think, that Shelly and I concentrated on in our discussion of the inmate beliefs and norms that we saw, not as an extension of the outlaw's code—a somewhat romantic notion, perhaps—but as an understandable response to the rigors of confinement, specifically addressed to the problems of prison life.

IV

As I look back on the development of these ideas some forty years after the fact, I still think they were a worthwhile innovation despite their limitations. Obviously, the nature of imprisonment has changed in a number of ways, such as the greatly increased balkanization of the inmate population along racial and ethnic lines described by James Jacobs (1983), court intervention in the legal powers of the custodians, shifts in the composition of the inmate population, and so on, and these changes must modify our view of the social system of the custodial institution. The neglect of race relations in the prisons in the 1950s is rather striking, and I think this was probably due to two things. First, the sociologists writing about the prison were almost exclusively white, and I suspect this helped to shape not only the range of their concerns, but also their ability to establish relationships of trust with black inmates. And second, there was an assumption that the social systems of black and white inmates—and their relationships with the power structure of the prison—were essentially the same. Along with this it was assumed that blacks and whites in prison frequently achieved a kind of modus vivendi, and, indeed, that the solidarity of inmates would, to some extent, override the antagonisms of race.

All this changed, of course, in the ensuing decades, and group conflict rather than inmate solidarity became a paramount feature of many custodial institutions. Not only did blacks and whites often move to violent confrontations, but so did bikers, different factions of Hispanics, political radicals, and others formed contesting alliances. Nonetheless, I believe the structural-functional perspective continues to provide a valid picture of the broad outlines of the nature of imprisonment in America today, with the recognition that inmate solidarity has fractured, in many institutions, along a variety of fault lines.

However, I must admit I am also struck by the fact that academic studies of the prison seem to have had little impact on public policy, and that in the last forty years or so the conditions of life in prison do not appear to have improved, and may indeed have grown worse. This may be due to the fact that theorizing about the prison has not led to a set of effective and politically feasible remedies. It is possible that remedies have been formulated and applied, but whatever changes have been introduced have been overwhelmed by vast increases in the rate of imprisonment and a variety of social conflicts arising outside the prison walls. But it is also possible that the problems of the prison are beyond the reach of the kind of social engineering usually envisioned by the social sciences—and it must be admitted that the social sciences have unquestionably suffered from an amazing hubris as far as their power to change social reality is concerned. I suppose this is another way of saying that when we try to analyze what happens in prison and consider possible reforms, we must take into account the politics of imprisonment no less than the internal dynamics of the prison social system. When all is said and done about rehabilitation, incapacitation, and deterrence, the prison remains an instrument of retribution. The public demand for retribution, finding expression in the political arena, cannot simply be dismissed as an irrelevant barbarism or the irrational goal of a misinformed public, and until we come to grips with this fact our understanding of the prison and our ability to introduce change are likely to remain inadequate.

REFERENCES

Arendt, Hanna. 1963. *Eichmann in Jerusalem: A Report on the Banality of Evil*. New York: Viking.
Bettelheim, Bruno. 1943. "Individual and Mass Behavior in Extreme Situations." *Journal of Abnormal and Social Psychology* 38:447–51.
Cloward, Richard, ed. 1960. *Theoretical Studies in the Social Organization of the Prison*. New York: Social Science Research Council.
Cohen, Albert K. 1955. *Delinquent Boys*. New York: Free Press.
Irwin, John. 1970. *The Felon*. Englewood Cliffs, NJ: Prentice-Hall.
Jacobs, James B. 1983. *New Perspectives on Prisons and Improvement*. Ithaca, NY: Cornell University Press.
Kogon, Eugene. 1966. *The Theory and Practice of Hell*. New York: Berkeley.

III

CRIMINAL JUSTICE:
Policing and Sentencing

Although prisons are scrutinized by researchers, practitioners, and inmates, they remain invisible to the public eye, except for the dramatic stories of riots and escapes and the routine stories of budgets and building programs. The public face of the criminal justice system is represented by the police and the courts. In the mass media and popular culture, this is where the drama of crime appears.

Research on public and private policing has been a major social scientific enterprise over the last two decades. Studies range from the ethnographies of police work to large-scale statistical evaluations of the impact of various forms of policing. Two chapters in this section cover developments in policing that have caught the attraction of scholars and the public alike. Egon Bittner, a pioneering contributor to the sociology of the police, looks in Chapter 7 at the appealing, but largely unclear notion of community policing. What does the demand for more policing entail? In Chapter 8, Gary Marx locates the apparently restricted methods of undercover policing in terms of wider changes in social control strategies. He takes this opportunity to reflect on his well-known 1988 book, *Undercover*, a detailed study of the methods and ethical implications of new technologies of covert policing. Any utilitarian claim for the success of "sting" operations or new forms of electronic surveillance must be located in a wider discussion about trust, secrecy, and deceit.

Debates about the aims of the criminal law in general and judicial sentencing in particular have always been dominated by the contrast between utilitarian and nonutilitarian rationales. The legal scholar Andrew von Hirsch has been a major figure in this debate for the last twenty years and is identified with the "back to justice" or "just deserts" model. In Chapter 9, he reflects on the attractions and criticisms of the principle of proportionality in sentencing. What is the influence of this model in the movement toward the fixed, determinate, or mandatory sentencing guidelines that are associated (causally or not) with increased rates of imprisonment?

7
Staffing and Training Problem-Oriented Police

EGON BITTNER

Over the course of the twentieth century, reform has been a virtually permanent and ubiquitous element in the structure of municipal policing in the United States. Of course, what was taken as constituting reform varied quite considerably over time and from place to place. A good deal of what was referred to as reform involved changes undertaken to satisfy partisan interests; other reforms were merely responses to local and passing urgencies, and some were merely spurious changes in appearance. Disregarding such variations, it is helpful to distinguish three phases in the reform of policing that are radically different in their substantive orientation—that is, in the perception of what was wrong, and what had to be done to correct it—and which are dynamically related, in that each provided the impetus for moving into the next. Thus, for example, the reformers in the third phase were not merely concerned with the state of policing they inherited from the reformers of the second phase, but were also polemically opposed to the reform aspirations of their predecessors. In each of the three phases, the reformers maintained that the changes they sought to bring about were sufficient to move policing to where it ought to be. But in the progression of time, the reformers changed from an unquestioned to a critical sense of certainty about their respective projects. We happen to believe that the changes in police practice and organization proposed in the most recent phase of reform are generally on the right track. But we also think that a problem of critical importance has not been adequately addressed. To be specific, we propose to discuss staffing, that is, the recruitment of appropriate personnel, for problem-oriented policing, a program formulated by Herman Goldstein, first in a paper published in 1979, then elaborated in other publications, and presently tested, refined, adapted, and adopted in several large police departments, in part or in totality. In order to make the argument, in particular, in order to show why merely raising entry standards from the high school diploma to the baccalaureate does not address staffing problems for problem-oriented policing adequately, we must discuss briefly the two earlier phases of reform, with special attention to their staffing arrangements.

During the first half of this century, the first phase of our story, changes in policing were closely tied to changes in municipal government generally. Civil service rules notwithstanding, access to and advancement in public employment were embedded in the political spoils system. Thus, the electoral victory that brought a new administration into city hall frequently led to a redistribution of power and benefits in the police departments. Since the electoral claims of the new administration included plans for changes that would improve government and public service, they provided the justification for the "shakeup" in the police department. And even though such changes were often enough simply rewards for political loyalty, electoral turnovers were as often preceded by scandals, and the changes in the police departments deserve consideration as reforms of sorts. While it is true that such changes left the prevailing structure of policing unchanged, that they occurred periodically played a part in preventing the police from becoming an independent force in the dynamics of local politics, in which the police was far more often a pawn than a player.

There is no evidence that the recruitment of personnel for the police followed carefully considered selection criteria. The chief officer was a political appointee who served at the pleasure of the mayor. His lieutenants (and it was, of course, always a *he*) were drawn from among "his people." The line personnel were recruited from among the segments of the population they were expected to police, namely, from among lower class "ethnics," which made it appear that in many cities being of Irish origin was a necessary, even if not a sufficient condition for being a police officer. Depending on their political strength, other ethnic groups have also gained entry into the ranks of the police. Being a police officer was viewed as a rather easily accessible alternative to a blue-collar occupation in public service or industry. No one thought that police work was an intellectually demanding way of making a living, that it might require technical training or skill, or that its performance would be coupled with concern for larger purposes or consequences. Instead, it was assumed that officers who relied on the street smarts one normally acquired in the circumstances of lower-class life would know what to do when their intervention was required to control undesirable behavior. It was also assumed that they would accept the control, and uncritically follow the orders of their superiors. Finally, it was expected that officers would avoid getting into trouble, especially of the sort that might embarrass their superiors. Staying out of trouble did not normally include avoiding the violation of the civil rights of troubled and troublesome people. Quite the contrary, one of the job qualifications was the capacity to impose physical restraint and punishment on those who were thought to require it, not, however, by any rule of law, but by commonsense perception of police sensibility. In sum, the recruitment policies of the police in the first half of this century reflected the view that anyone who had the stomach for it could be expected to be a competent police officer. Though one would not consider it a job qualification in the narrow sense, it might be mentioned that officers were expected to be constrained by a modest sense of public decency epitomized by the concept of "clean graft." Given the low wages officers earned, it was thought reasonable and morally acceptable that they should be free to accept and, if need be, extort gratuities from people who benefited from their service. But, as befits persons in low-grade occupations, they should be humble about it.

In the decade following World War II, the practice of newly elected mayors "bringing in their own people" to run their city's police department continued. But the trusted old ways produced new and unexpected results. Some of the newly appointed chiefs—for example, William Parker in Los Angeles, Stanley Schrotell in Cincinnati, Herbert Jenkins in Atlanta—set in motion an effort to terminate the process that brought them into positions of power, and with it the control city hall exercised over the details of police organization and practice. In those reformers' terminology, they sought to "professionalize" the police. They did not, however, have in mind analogizing police work with the practices and outlook of the traditional professions of divinity, law, and medicine. In fact, quite the opposite was their intention. While the traditional professions always stress the practitioners' independent judgment and responsibility, freedom from any form of supervisory control, and the critical use of complex knowledge and skill, the "professionalization" of the police involved the creation of tight organizational structures, the exercise of close bureaucratic control over line personnel, and an obsessive concern with rules and regulations. Beyond that, the ideal of professionalization entailed the recognition that police work executed a specific, and in the eyes of the reformers, nonpolitical mandate, namely, law enforcement. Law enforcement was seen as the defining social function of policing that needed to be attended to with the kind of sustained and methodical seriousness that was absent in the amateurish ways of the first half of the century. Practical considerations required the recognition that police officers had a good deal of discretionary freedom once they left the police station, and were routinely engaged in the unavoidable activities of peacekeeping that involved a large variety of interventions into urban life that had nothing to do with law enforcement, and were generally viewed as not real police work.

Quite clearly, the professionalization of the police gave the institution a definition of its function and the independence that it lacked before. Admittedly, the function was defined too narrowly. Still the reformers deserve credit for having set into motion efforts to make explicit what policing is all about and develop some proper ways of doing it. Compared to this, the policing of the first half of this century was amateurish. Because the professionalization of the police was a significant departure from the earlier sloth and indolence in policing, it is regrettable that recruitment norms retained the implication that police work is a low-grade occupation. In fact, it could be said that this view became more firmly established. While recruitment in the decades before World War II was haphazard and biased, more a function of history and circumstance than of rationally considered choice, the recruitment of professional police officers involved explicitly formulated selection criteria and thus conscious choice. What was in the past tacitly known was now openly acknowledged: police work was not for people with high aspirations. The ambitious among the recruits sought to move away from actual police work by joining the administrative structure of departments, through promotional exams. Many of those who remained in the ranks of line personnel became skilled practitioners dealing with complex and serious problems, but generally neither receiving, nor expecting recognition for their work.

As might be expected, recruitment into the professionalized department became a formalized procedure involving explicitly formulated criteria of selection and elaborate testing and background investigations. Initial appointments were provisional to further test the suitability of recruits. Furthermore, recruits were given a course of training in the police academy that, while not standardized in either content or duration, contained everywhere a very heavy dose of instruction concerning the internal rules and regulation of the department. Following graduation from the academy, recruits were entrusted to the guidance of seasoned officers who, more often than not, instructed the recruits to forget all they had been told in the academy.

While the recruitment procedures conveyed the impression of great care in the selection of suitable candidates, the acceptance of a high-school diploma as a condition of employment and the low caliber of the instruction in the academies clearly indicated that suitability did not include high levels of intellectual functioning. It was understood—and probably still is in most places—both inside and outside the police establishment, that police work relied primarily on common sense and an intuitive grasp of the distinction between right and wrong. If there was a need for analysis, it was to be done by management.

The professional police officers understanding of the nature of his (and it was still generally *his* rather than *her*) role in society and the underlying orientation of his occupational commitment was moralistic. In a sense, this expresses a correct understanding of the mission of the police, which is, after all, the social mechanism for holding people to proper conduct and for ensuring that persons who violate the norms of proper conduct receive their just deserts. But the dominant role of the perception of policing as a *moral* enterprise in the occupational outlook of officers tends to overshadow and diminish the concern for technical practicalities of having to cope with all forms of social deviance. The bright line of distinction that identifies evil tends to evoke unqualified condemnation of the sort that is ordinarily impatient with analysis. Thus, the moralistic attitude of the professional police officer is more compatible with efforts to overpower criminals than with trying to outwit them. That, in turn, favors officers who are impulsively courageous rather than resolutely prudent, and who feel justified in resorting to means that might otherwise be judged unacceptable legally or morally. All this projects a version of police work that can be performed adequately by persons with modest intellectual powers, provided they are of good moral character and are willing to accept a tightly regulated occupational environment. Indeed, given the reformers' preoccupation with organizational coherence and vertical control, it was not only unnecessary to recruit intellectually bright and inquisitive persons, but there would seem to be a positive advantage, from a management point of interest, to staff departments with persons who are not given to raising too many questions and who would be content to do what they are told. Chiefs who took seriously the mandate to police a city professionally would not want to have to do it by directing a bunch of geniuses with independent ideas.

It came to be accepted, both inside and outside the police establishment that police work was a lower-level civil service occupation, more or less on the same level of occupational prestige as industrial blue-collar work. While this view is still widely shared, together with all other ideas of professional policing, the lessons of the 1960s and 1970s have convinced many police executives that the original program of professionalization needed to be enriched, on the one hand by programs like "community relations," and on the other by the addition of some psychological consciousness-raising in the training of officers. In many instances this conviction was adopted in response to outside influences, especially from the Law Enforcement Assistance Administration, which as often as not came accompanied by financial incentives in the form of special project support. Interestingly, however, while management was willing to accept programs enriching police services, line personnel did not welcome them and often treated them as unwarranted impositions and unjustified changes in the terms of their employment. That is, the "cops" were quite willing to do what they were told, but they resisted changes that complicated their responsibilities, especially when they involved having to adopt attitudes and procedures that seemed to have the flavor of social work.

The latest phase of reform, problem-oriented policing, emerged in large measure as a reaction to the shortcomings of professional policing, just as the latter emerged in reaction to the shortcomings of its predecessor. While many things could be said to be wrong with professional policing as it emerged in the years following World War II, the shortcomings that were identified most often were (1) its excessive preoccupation with the management of internal departmental affairs, (2) the fragmented and largely reactive nature of police work, combined with an almost total lack of interest in the overall effects of the interventions, and (3) the isolation of the police in the communities they served. It must be emphasized that these features of policing are shortcomings only from a particular perspective. One could, after all, argue (leaving obligatory rhetorical pieties aside) that policing is essentially an emergency service whose function is to arrest untoward tendencies of all sorts, and leaving long-range care of the momentarily immobilized development to others. The police officer's responsibility, and interest, ends with the arrest of criminals; what to do with them is the function of the other parts of the criminal justice system. Similarly, the officer will prevent a family dispute from becoming violent, for the time being, but someone else will have to deal with the underlying problem. This sort of service is best rendered by maintaining a state of response readiness guaranteed by strong managerial control. Moreover, the necessary freedom of officers to act forcefully in the handling of emergencies might be impaired by relations of familiarity and trust with the very people they are supposed to restrain. Hence, the maintenance of distance between the police and the community is functionally efficient. But, of course—and this is the main point of the problem-oriented policing critique—this is an enormously ineffective way of doing police work, all the external appearances of snappy efficiency to the contrary notwithstanding. What is missing in professional policing is the effort to identify, analyze, and understand the problem complexes that create the need for police intervention in the first place; or, to put it differently, there is no interest in the analysis of the substantive problems with which officers are required to cope and, along with it, no interest in the general outcome of police work.

This is not the place to offer a detailed account of the practices and aims of problem-oriented policing. While a good deal has been written about it and some of it has been attempted in practice, much more of it is still being formulated and tried provisionally. It is probably much more than the most ambitious reform ever attempted in policing; it truly redefines the nature and purpose of police work in a fundamental way. In the past, and in many places still today, the police receive citizen complaints about vandalism, purse snatching, unruly youth, loud noise, assaults, shoplifting, and the like, and respond to them on a case-by-case basis. The problem is taken as defined in the complaint, and the solution—if the problem could be solved—is the arrest the miscreant or the abatement of the nuisance while the officers are on the scene. The occasional aggregation of certain complaints may give rise to the consideration of preventive strategies, e.g., by increasing the density of patrols. But this would be a managerial responsibility and the decision would be conveyed to the line personnel whose occupational horizon would remain limited to dealing with isolated incidents.

Contrary to this, to Problem Oriented Police officers, dealing with an incident is merely the beginning of their involvement with the problem. It leads to a program of inquiries and analyses that place the incident in context, may suggest possibilities of remedies that transcend the specific incident, may involve the engagement of resources outside the police, all undertaken—as needed—in consultation with associated officers. Of course, as in any other professional activity, this all becomes routinized in time and the process works in less ponderous ways than the description might imply. Two points must be stressed: (1) the initiative to engage in the inquiries and analyses of encountered problems is the occupational responsibility of the "street cops," and (2) the "street cops" are also authorized and expected to formulate remedial programs that may include the mobilization of resources outside the police.

Students of police work are aware of the existence of strong resistance among line personnel to any enlargement of responsibilities beyond what is sometimes called the "slam-bang" style of police work. But they have also noted the presence of officers who would be willing and could be trusted to undertake the enlarged responsibilities competently. Indeed, some of these officers practice problem-oriented policing informally and without acknowledgment. Now, it is not unreasonable to expect that starting with this cadre of imaginative and prudent officers one could slowly change from professional to problem-oriented policing. But it would seem more appropriate to try to institutionalize a redefinition of the meaning of police work to bring about a common understanding that the possession and exercise of analytical skills is a basic feature of the occupation. This will not be accomplished by merely liberating the inclinations and talents of some well-meaning officers who are now randomly distributed in police departments from stultifying administrative restrictions, nor by raising educational requirements of recruits in the hope of increasing the numbers of such officers in the future. Instead, it will be more appropriate to have the police follow the example of the other professions. That is, the police will need to institutionalize its training and recruitment in academic institutions in ways more or less analogous to how it is done in schools of education or social work. No doubt there will be voices urging that police work cannot be learned in the classroom. But this is also true of teaching and social work, and both professions require hefty doses of internship training for full acknowledgment of presumptive competence, as should be the case for the police. In fact, it would be necessary to retain a course of in-house training to acquaint recruits with local conditions of police practice.

The purpose of professional education is to provide students with the intellectual background and with habits of critical thought relevant to a field of practice, rather than with the ins and outs of local and timely problem-solving. Of course, there is a price to be paid by routing the recruitment and training of teachers and social workers through academic programs. It no doubt discourages some potentially fine teachers and social workers from joining the professions simply because they cannot face the stress of academic work, and there probably are other drawbacks. But on the whole this method has proven indispensable for the professions. While it is not always an unalloyed good, it does serve to ascertain that people who are entrusted with serious, important, and complex responsibilities are adequately prepared for them. They gain the understanding of their function in society that will enable them to act with confidence on their own initiative. Finally, even though it is not guaranteed, academic exercises are the method our society relies on for equipping persons with the mental endurance and the analytic inclination and aptitude for complex problem-solving demands.

There is another reason for creating professional schools of policing after the model of schools of education and schools of social work. Such institutions become centers of research and development in their respective areas. Thus progress in policing would no longer depend on desultory special projects—financed by grants from outside sources and under outside direction—but would acquire an intrinsic continuity and a natural affinity with practice.

We should mention in conclusion that while we argued strongly in favor of the establishment of credentialing schools of policing as preparation for entry into the occupation, our main point is to assert that the success of problem-oriented policing requires a different kind of police officer than was envisioned by the earlier proponents of professional policing. The academic institution is the means for the production of officers who, fully conscious of the nature, the seriousness, and importance of their role in society, will be able to identify, analyze, and address social problems—including crime—entrusted to their care.

8

Recent Developments in Undercover Policing[1]

GARY T. MARX

> She [jury member] was extremely liberal. She was a sociologist, and I don't like sociologists. They try to reason things out too much.
> —Florida Prosecutor (after losing case involving the undercover purchase of a 2 Live Crew album)

> I have no sympathy for those who are crybabies about the fact that police officers are selling to those who want to buy drugs. We use every legal means that we can. We want everybody to know that the next drug buy may be from a police officer.
> —Mayor Marion Barry, news conference, 1988

In recent decades social control has become more specialized and technical and, in many ways, more penetrating and intrusive. Cohen (1985) offers a good discussion of this. One manifestation is the expansion of undercover police practices as part of the rise of the new surveillance (computer dossiers, electronic location monitoring, drug and DNA testing, video and audio monitoring, etc.). The new surveillance tends to be differentiated from the old surveillance by at least ten major characteristics:

1. It transcends distance, darkness, and physical barriers.
2. It transcends time; its records can be easily stored, retrieved, combined, analyzed, and communicated.
3. It has low visibility or is invisible.
4. It is involuntary.
5. It is preventive.

6. It is capital- rather than labor-intensive.
7. It is decentralized and often involves self-policing.
8. It triggers a shift from targeting a specific suspect to categorical suspicion.
9. It is more intensive—probing beneath surfaces, discovering previously inaccessible information.
10. It is more extensive—covering an ever enlarging number of spatial, temporal, and functional areas.

In a previous work (*Undercover*; Marx 1988) I reported the results of an empirical inquiry into covert police practices. That study considered the changing nature of undercover practices; their history; factors responsible for their expansion and changing form; basic types and dimensions; ethical criteria by which the state's use of deception could be judged; intended and unintended consequences for targets, third parties, informers, and police; and policies for controlling them and the social issues raised by the general expansion of the new surveillance. Consistent with Shelley Messinger's approach to criminal justice phenomena, the study took a critical approach to this social control strategy and drew on a variety of historical, empirical, and theoretical sources.

F. Scott Fitzgerald's observation that "there are no second acts in American life" certainly applies to the fixity of a book in print. But persons of the pen have the luxury of reflecting on and updating the record elsewhere. In this chapter, I discuss some recent developments and research. I also consider some professional and personal questions that I was left with upon finishing this project.

The undercover tactic has continued to be used in imaginative, if sometimes questionable ways. Recent elaborations include game wardens using a lifelike target device "robo-deer" as a means of ensnaring poachers; anticrime decoys used to protect homosexuals and tourists in rented cars; stings in which postal authorities mail offers of illegal pornography and then arrest those who respond to their offer; the purchase and sale of endangered species such as Mexican red-kneed tarantulas or parts of species, such as the genitals of bears and walruses for which there is an Asian aphrodisiac market; and entering false information into computers to catch those illegally accessing systems. Reverse stings in which police sell rather than buy drugs have also increased in prominence.

After work on *Undercover* was finished in 1987, seven first-person accounts and a comprehensive model for practitioners appeared (LaBrecque 1987; Goddard and Levine 1988; Pistone and Brasco 1988; Murano and Hoffer 1990; Wansley and Stowers 1989; Wozencraft 1990; Rothmiller and Goldman 1992; Carter 1990). I approached these with curiosity: would they suggest important issues that I had left out or misinterpreted? While offering rich narratives and examples to supplement those in the book, they did not suggest the need for major revisions or extensions. In this sense I think they provide some external validation.[2]

Were I to revise the book today I would treat a number of additional topics beyond updating an ever-changing historical record.[3] But here I wish to merely update the book by reference to some recent developments and research.

In writing about any contemporary topic, one risks being out of date the minute the writing stops.[4] I recall the case of two political scientists whose book explaining how Lebanon was able to sustain a multiethnic democracy was published just as the Lebanese civil war started. While not in that league, *Undercover* was wrong in suggesting that the political misuses of covert means at the federal level appeared to be behind us.

The study documented the increased significance of undercover operations for criminal investigations. But it also reflected a belief that surveillance merely because of a person's legal political beliefs and actions was not likely to be a major problem. The FBI had responded to the abuses revealed during Watergate and the COINTEL programs by severely curtailing political surveillance and by developing restrictive guidelines. A new generation of agents seemed too principled, busy, and regulated to engage in the kinds of often illegal and immoral domestic political surveillance that characterized the 1960s and earlier periods. The undercover activity that had once been directed at persons who held unpopular beliefs was now directed at those engaged in white-collar and organized crime. Yet soon after the book was published, documents released under the Freedom of Information Act and congressional hearings revealed a massive spying campaign against critics of the administration's Central American policies (Gelbspan 1991).[5] Some of the CISPES (Committee in Solidarity with the People of El Salvador) investigation was illegal and much of it violated the bureau's own policies.

The bureau apologized for the investigation, acknowledged that mistakes were made, and sanctioned some agents. Yet because this investigation was not defined as domestic, it was possible to get around the guidelines that restrict domestic investigations. In addition, under a Reagan doctrine known as "active measures," a domestic group that criticized a U.S. policy that was also being criticized by the Soviet Union could be subject to surveillance. The spirit of the guidelines was also violated by delegating some functions to private groups that could take actions the government was prohibited from taking.

In considering covert means, there is an important distinction between criminal and political investigations. Because the latter rarely result in criminal prosecution and are governed by executive guidelines that can be (and have been) changed at will, they raise very different policy and oversight issues.

A schizoid response is called for, in which any enthusiasm one may have for the tactic when used for certain types of criminal investigation must be balanced by opposition when the tactic is used for political investigations. This is one of the paradoxes at the heart of covert means in a democratic society. In legitimating one use, we run the risk of increasing its use elsewhere.

UNDERCOVER UNDER THE COVERS: THE MAYOR BARRY CASE

Yet as the Mayor Marion Barry case suggests, separating the criminal from the political investigation can be difficult. The arrest and trial of former (and recently reelected) Washington, D.C., Mayor Marion Barry after he purchased drugs from an exgirlfriend raised a variety of ethical and policy issues involving police deception: Is it wise to focus scarce resources on occasional users rather than dealers? If a case for indictment cannot be made before a grand jury or before a judge for permission to search, wiretap, or bug, is it appropriate to move to an undercover temptation for which there is no legal minimum threshold? Was the grand jury used in a manipulative way to obtain a felony indictment (Barry's allegedly lying to it about cocaine use is a felony, while his possession of cocaine was only a misdemeanor). Was the effort to get Barry on a drug charge undertaken after earlier efforts to obtain direct evidence of corruption against him failed? Is it sound social policy to use the criminal law not for prosecution, but as a resource to negotiate (e.g., the prosecutor's hint that he would exchange leniency in return for the mayor's resignation)? Should special criteria be applied before a political figure becomes the target of an undercover investigation? What of the speculation that the highly visible prosecutor in the case had his own political aspirations? Is there a racial patterning to the selection of targets in recent sting operations or does the apparent pattern simply reflect greater black prominence in political life? Shouldn't the government try to block the flow of drugs rather than provide them? Should it have intervened after he purchased the drugs rather than letting him proceed to use them? What if he had suffered a heart attack or other serious health damage from the cocaine? Should the government be offering its citizens potentially toxic substances?

A particularly interesting question involves friendship and undercover investigations. When, if ever, is it appropriate to use friendship and the lure of sex as part of an investigation? This depends on the context (Marx 1992b). A typology can be created by combining dimensions of whether or not emotional intimacy and sexual intimacy are present. The most problematic law enforcement use of the tactic is "seduction" (faked emotional intimacy mixed with sexual intimacy). Five situations in which seduction most commonly occurs are (1) blackmail, (2) stigmatization and/or disruption, (3) general intelligence collection, (4) evidence or information collection for a prior offense, and (5) evidence collection for an anticipated offense.

NEW SUPPORTS

Undercover considered a number of material and legal resources that encouraged the use of covert tactics. Judicial rulings and legislation continue to encourage undercover investigations. In an Illinois case, the Supreme Court voted eight to one that the Miranda ruling was not required in prison settings. In this case, an undercover agent posing as a prisoner obtained a confession from a jailed suspect (although it was for a different crime than the one for which he was imprisoned; *Illinois v. Perkins*, 110 S. Ct. 2394, 1990). In another case the Court held that it is legal to rummage around in people's garbage.

But there were new legal restrictions as well. Thus a federal district judge in Phoenix issued a decision that limited the government's authority to send undercover personnel to secretly watch and record church gatherings. The Constitution bars the government from "unbridled and inappropriate covert activity" that is intended to abridge the First Amendment right of freedom of religion. However, a religious gathering can be infiltrated without a warrant if an agent is invited to participate in criminal activities. The ruling grew out of a case against Arizona churches that had offered sanctuary to illegal aliens from Central America. In the 1986 trial, ministers and priests, among others, were convicted of conspiracy and harboring aliens. The churches claimed they were offering refuge from political persecution. As part of the investigation, informers working for the Immigration and Naturalization Service attended church and recorded sermons (*New York Times*, 12 December 1990).

Another potential boost comes from what has been described by the Attorney General in several newspaper accounts as the "largest reallocation of FBI manpower in the bureau's history." This involved the 1992 shifting of 300 agents from cold war counterintelligence work to the investigation of gang violence and related crimes. Domestic criminal investigation involves a different ethos and methods than political counter-intelligence, but the clandestine cloak and dagger mentality and experience of these agents would seem likely to encourage covert means, whether directly or indirectly.

Congress increased the forfeiture authority of the Justice Department and Customs Service, extending it to pornography, money laundering, and espionage, and permitting the sharing of seized property with local law enforcement agencies. Between 1984 and 1994, there were more than 200,000 federal forfeitures alone worth $3.6 billion, and another $1.7 billion was expected (*Boulder Daily Camera*, Dec. 11, 1994). With this comes the danger of going after targets because of what the government stands to gain, rather than because of the seriousness of the offense or offender. In what hopefully will not become a national precedent, the small town of Helper, Utah is offering to help its police officers by giving them cash bonuses of

12% of any seized drug-related assets (*Law Enforcement News*, April 15, 1995). The feeding frenzy potential of such an incentive system is obvious, and personal use of such funds is prohibited at the federal level. Revenue raising and "maximizing profit for the government" can displace traditional criminal justice goals. There are also issues of justice and equity, since a civil court is involved, the standard is the "preponderance of evidence" rather than the more stringent "beyond a reasonable doubt." One need be neither charged with, nor found guilty of, a crime to have property seized by the government.

The funds available for informing have continued to increase. According to data provided by federal enforcement agencies, funds for informants went from forty-three million dollars in 1987 to sixty-three million dollars in 1989 (*Atlanta Journal-Constitution*, 31 March 1991). By 1995, this was approximately one hundred million dollars. A 1988 asset forfeiture law permits prosecutors to share up to 25 percent of seized assets with informants. In 1990, congressional legislation authorized paying "whistleblowers" up to fifty thousand dollars for information leading to the prosecution of savings-and-loan offenders.

One informant who had earned more than one million dollars in recent years (including five hundred thousand dollars from a single case in Kansas involving a marijuana ring he infiltrated) reports that he would like to be an undercover officer, "but cops just aren't paid enough" (*Atlanta Journal-Constitution* 31 March 1991). The implications of such incentives for informer abuses, as well as for the morale of the less handsomely rewarded police with whom they work, are worthy of study. Would the adversarial playing field be more level if defendants could also pay witnesses for testimony that results in their being found not guilty? In an adversarial setting where, under penalty of perjury laws, individuals swear to tell the truth, why is payment restricted only to the prosecution? Is justice better served by paying to find one guilty than to find one innocent?

These new financial incentives, along with the creation of mandatory life imprisonment or twenty-year minimum sentences, and the elimination of parole for certain drug offenses, has made it easier to attract informants.[6] A new (or expanded) class of superinformants has appeared.

This is also the case for weapons violations. In 1987, strict federal sentencing guidelines were adopted that mandate harsh penalties for weapons offenses. For example, a convicted felon found guilty of possessing a weapon faces up to ten years in prison. This has offered authorities a new resource to persuade those facing such charges to become informants. The definition of violent felon is rather broad and it permits holding a federal hammer over persons who in the past would have remained in state courts. It also increases the incentive authorities have to manage the environment so that felons are arrested in possession of weapons—in some cases as a result of being sold the weapon by an undercover agent (e.g., through the joint federal-local Achilles Task Force).

UNDERCOVER WORK AND DEVIANCE AMPLIFICATION

The conflict of goals between preventing crime and encouraging it in order to apprehend is nicely illustrated by a San Francisco officer. He is one of seventeen who patrol the streets in plainclothes looking for parking violators and meter jammers. He reports that his unit is effective because "if you have a uniformed officer there, no one is going to wipe off their tires" (*San Francisco Chronicle*, 13 April 1989). To which the skeptic might respond, "Isn't that what we want uniformed officers for—to prevent violations? Do we really want to encourage people to break the rules because we want them to think no one is there?" Underlying the officer's remark is the need to write citations in order to meet productivity goals. The unstated assumption here is, "We want to create a situation in which, because they never know whether or not a police officer is watching, persons won't wipe off their tires." This "myth of surveillance" comes with other costs, but it is believed to be more efficient than obtaining that result only when a uniformed officer is actually present. From a standpoint of empirical impact, we don't know if it is a myth.

The issue of the sometimes conflicting goals of preventing crimes and making arrests can also be seen in the case of Malcolm X's daughter, Quiblah Shabazz, who was accused of hiring a pretend hit man to avenge her father's death. When the informant was asked why he didn't try to discourage the plot, he said, "I'm supposed to sound like a murderer, remember? A hit man wouldn't agree to kill someone and then say it's wrong" (*Newsweek*, May 15, 1995). When a suspect is hesitant (e.g., Shabazz indicated that she was leery and wanted to put it on hold, and missed a planned meeting), should the informant respect this apparent withdrawal or ambivalent intent, or persist? In this case, 38 of 40 phone calls were initiated by the informant, and he appears to have done most of the talking on the tapes.

The issue of when undercover police should intervene to prevent a crime vs. letting it go on too long has continued to raise moral and practical questions. Thus in Dallas an undercover officer watched a woman being raped by a group he had infiltrated. He pretended to be sick to avoid participating. He stated, "You don't want to ruin your credibility" (*New York Times* 11 August 1989). Would he feel the same way if his wife, sister, or mother had been the victim?

In New York, police had prior information that a drug dealer planned to rob an undercover agent. They did not intervene to stop this and the agent was shot. Some critics within the department claimed that it should have been aborted. Dangers such as this are reflected in agent folktales. Question: What does an undercover agent do? Answer: He's like the kid they use down in Louisiana for alligator bait. They tie him to the end of a rope and he walks out into the swamp. All the kid can do is hope they jerk the rope back in time (Goddard and Levine 1988).

Police in a Long Island sting were criticized for permitting the illegal dumping of toxic waste to continue for what critics saw as an inordinate amount of time. Pollution was created in order to fight it. In a nonenforcement example in Boston, a drug informant was permitted to run an afterhours club in exchange for his cooperation. This led to neighborhood complaints about noise, disorder, and increased crime and to beliefs about the "police corruption" that permitted the place to flourish.

An inquiry in Los Angeles found that a nineteen-member special surveillance unit had often failed to prevent those it was watching from attacking people in armed robberies and burglaries. While in many cases they could have been arrested beforehand for lesser offenses or on existing arrest warrants, detectives waited for a violent felony to occur because that would make for a stronger case and a longer sentence. The department has now implemented a policy instructing officers to protect potential crime victims even if this jeopardizes an undercover investigation. It reads, "reverence for human life must always be the first priority when considering the extent to which a criminal incident is allowed to progress or deteriorate . . . during a stakeout or the surveillance of known criminals."

The unit has also been accused of dispensing punishment before trial. In a successful civil trial, a federal jury found the Los Angeles chief of police and nine officers in the surveillance unit liable for the death of three robbers and the wounding of a fourth. The suit accused the unit of being a "death squad" prone to shooting suspects instead of arresting them. In this case police had tracked the robbers for weeks. As the robbers entered their getaway car after holding up a restaurant, the officers opened fire, later claiming the suspects had pointed guns at them. The weapons turned out to be unloaded pellet guns.

The issue of intervention, as well as an example of unintended consequences from covert surveillance, can be seen in a St. Louis case. The FBI, hoping to record evidence of terrorist activities, planted listening devices in the apartment of a Palestinian-American. But instead it recorded the suspect's murder of his teenage daughter. An incriminating conversation ("Do you know that you are going to die tonight?") and the girl's screams as she begged her parents not to kill her) were captured by an automated listening device. The FBI surveillance unit was not staffed the night of the murder. It is not clear whether authorities could have intervened in time to prevent the murder at that time if they had been listening. However, there were earlier recordings of phone conversations in which the accused discussed various methods of getting rid of the daughter (*New York Times*, 28 October 1991).

Undercover mentions parking tickets given to unmarked vehicles as among the least of the unintended consequences that may occur, but gave no idea of its magnitude. In Boston in 1989, twenty thousand parking violations were dismissed as part of an agreement with agencies engaged in undercover law enforcement or investigative actions. One thousand of these were for the more serious "public safety violations" such as double-parking and parking by fire hydrants (*Boston Globe*, 14 February 1990).

The resources expended in an undercover operation can generate pressures to produce cases to justify the outlay. But when a sting goes awry the pressures may be even greater. In the largest misconduct award in New Hampshire's history, a physicist received a one-million-dollar court settlement. Police received a tip that thieves wanted for working a "diamond swap" at a chain store were to try again. A sting was set up and store personnel went along with the sting and handed over the jewels. Unfortunately the thieves then got away. Under enormous pressure police arrested an innocent man in spite of almost nothing to link him to the crime. In their determination to solve the case, police ignored evidence that would have cleared him and charges were not dropped until fourteen months later (*Boston Globe*, 8 December 1991).

Panamanian general Manuel Ortega appears to represent the ultimate in the intermeshing of cops and robbers. His defense claims that his drug and gun smuggling activities were undertaken with the tacit support of the United States, as part of its anticommunist activities. He worked with both the DEA and the Medellín drug cartel. He earned praise from the DEA for his cocaine seizures, which he then appears to have sold back to the cartel. He also sold it guns and provided photographs and addresses of DEA agents in Panama (*New York Times*, 24 November 1991).

In 1993 there were allegations that top officials of a CIA-funded Venezuelan antidrug unit smuggled several thousand pounds of cocaine into the United States. The CIA reportedly asked the DEA for permission "to let the dope walk" to facilitate intelligence gathering. The permission was denied but the shipment was still made. The chief of the antidrug unit acknowledged that he had run loads to the United States independently, but he said that this was done as a law enforcement technique. (*Washington Post*, 19 November 1993)

An example of unintended harm to innocent third parties can be seen in DEA officers putting 90 pounds of cocaine on a flight from Belize to Miami. When the plane stopped in Honduras, drug sniffing dogs discovered it. The three crew members and three passengers who knew nothing about the drugs were beaten and held in prison for 12 days. One would hope that the risks from loss of control over unaccompanied evidence in transit could have been anticipated in deciding whether or not to carry out the plan, and if carried out, that a contingency plan for failures would have been developed.

The fabrication of evidence and exploitative informers received renewed attention in a Los Angeles scandal involving jail house informers. An inmate demonstrated how he could fabricate the confessions of other inmates without ever having talked to them. Using the telephone and given only the name of a murder suspect, the inmate identified himself as a bail bondsman and was able to obtain information from official sources about the crime. He then called the bailiff at the jail where he was a prisoner and identified himself as a district attorney and ordered himself and the suspect transferred to a court for an interview. He could then say that he was with the suspect on the bus when he confessed. This would be admissible in court since authorities had not arranged it. The president of the Los Angeles Criminal Courts Bar Association, in commenting publicly on the revelations in the case, said, "All we've done is crack the egg here. The yoke will spill out all over the country."

A nice example of the symbolic and communicative aspects (and the potential for deflating official images) appeared in a speech given by President Bush on drug strategy from the Oval Office. The president dramatically held up a bag of crack purchased near the White House and said "I think it's great because it sent a message to the United States that even across from the White House they can sell drugs." Later it also sent a message about manipulation and image creation. It turned out that the seller had been lured to the cite by a DEA agent. He did not know where the White House was until the undercover agent who arranged the buy told him how to get there. There are also messages that boomerang with embarrassment. For example, a group of coast guardsmen photographed with the president congratulating them for a job well done against drug smugglers were later indicted themselves for smuggling and the picture ran a second time.

Barker and Carter (1989) suggest the lovely phrase "fluffing up the evidence," in describing a form of police lying. Undercover means nicely lend themselves to such activity. A police inspector in the Netherlands, in considering deception via omission, states, "we do try to keep things secret, but without lying about it. Sometimes it may seem like we put the judge on the wrong track, lay a mist over it" (Klerks 1995).

EFFECTS ON AGENTS

Undercover noted the unintended social and psychological costs that undercover work can have for its practitioners. Girodo (1991a) offers some systematic data on this in seeking to discover how personality traits interact with work situations to affect mental health and drug problems. He studied 271 federal undercover agents who volunteered (of 350 who were randomly asked). Self-reports of drug and alcohol abuse and disciplinary infractions were positively correlated with the extent of undercover experience. This is related to a prior research finding that accumulated experience in undercover assignments is associated with a variety of social and psychological problems. For example, in a related study Girodo (1991b) found undercover experience to be correlated with job dissatisfaction. But the effect of the undercover experience is mediated by the personality traits of the agent. Agents enter the corrupting undercover environment with varying patterns of character flaws and assets. Problem outcomes were most likely in those agents shown by personality tests to have either poor impulse control, neuroticism, or a desire for new experience. Agents assessed as having a "disciplined self-image" were at lesser risk.

A study by Farkas (1986) of undercover officers in Honolulu found that more than one-third reported negative changes in their social relations, stress over being with family and friends in public, and anxiety over being unable to discuss their work with those close to them. A study by Pogrebin and Poole (1993) of forty officers with undercover experience from diverse agencies illustrates these and related themes.

Among the implications of the above research is the need for greater vigilance the longer an operation goes on and the greater the accumulated undercover experience of an individual, and the importance of selecting *in* as well as selecting *out*.

Among the most tragic of unintended consequences involves the "friendly fire" shooting or assaults on undercover officers by other police unaware of who they are. In one such incident, a black officer holding a suspect at gunpoint in a New York subway station was shot by white officers who thought they had come upon a robbery. Following this, a black officers' association urged its members to refuse plainclothes assignments (*New York Times*, 19 November 1992).

STRATEGIES OF DECEPTION

As the work of Erving Goffman and others suggests, there is a generic structure to deceptive and manipulative interaction, regardless of the context. Consider, for example, the similarities between con men and undercover agents. There are parallels between agents and con men in the presentation of false selves and environments and in developmental stages, as one moves from the initial contact, to gaining confidence, to the action, to disclosure.

The "mark's" motivation to behave illegally is central to both con men and police (when undercover work does not involve entrapment or provocation). Con men say they do not steal: instead the mark literally thrusts a fat bankroll into their hand in hope of illicit gain. Compare the con man's belief, "You can't cheat an honest man," to Mel Weinberg's (the central figure in the Abscam case) observation that "a guy's either a crook, or he isn't. If he ain't a crook, he ain't gonna do anything illegal no matter what I offer him or tell him to do." In both cases such beliefs serve to neutralize cultural prohibitions against deception.

Some similar personality characteristics, or at least skills, may be shared by both—especially the ability to read human nature, to persuade and inspire confidence, and to think on one's feet. Maurer's (1974) appreciation of "the grand thinking, the unlimited gall, the sure touch, the high intelligence" of the best con artists such as Yellow Kid Weil also might characterize some legendary undercover agents.

The ironic and dramatic possibilities are indeed wonderful should a con man pretending to be a police official cross paths with an agent pretending to be a con man.

The deceptive ploy of using the media to create concern in suspects about a planned arrest in order to get them to talk without benefit of an attorney being present was illustrated by an FBI investigation of commodities dealers in Chicago. In what appears to be a careful strategy, information about the investigation was leaked in an apparently successful effort to scare potential defendants into cooperating. Authorities have much greater leeway and bluffing resources in questioning before an arrest is made than after it is. Apart from due process questions, this also appears to have damaged the reputation of persons who were never arrested (Protess 1989).

Jacobs (1992) has identified four modes of deception used by narcotics agents in one city: prior rehearsal, appearance manipulation, and verbal and physical diversion. He has also studied the counter to agents' efforts at dissimulation—the process by which targets try to discover whether someone is an agent (Jacobs 1993). His interviews with thirty-two heroin user-dealers suggests two major deception clues: trend discontinuity in which purchasers change their routine behavior (e.g., by bringing in a stranger or by significantly increasing the amount they seek to purchase) and illegitimate appearance and demeanor.

Irony could be the subtitle for any study of the intermeshing of social control with deviance (Marx 1981). To the many ironies and trade-offs discussed in *Undercover*, one can add the fact that a suspect's not knowing the true identity of an agent puts the agent at greater risk, although it is also a necessary condition for an effective investigation. In discussing the celebrated Florida Mi-Porn case (in which two agents posed as pornographers for several years) LaBrecque notes

> [T]hey pushed out of their consciousness their major fear: that if they made a mistake, their targets might kill them before they found out who they really were. . . . [T]here was safety in being discovered to be an FBI agent. (1987:)

In this case there is also irony in the fact that the devious appearance and nervousness which made Pat Livingston (alias Pat Salamone) such a good undercover agent worked against his credibility when he took the witness stand.

To enhance their credibility as drug users, agents may bring a variety of props such as a spoon and syringe to their encounters with drug sellers. Yet ironically this effort to appear real can lead the dealer to request that the agent then use the drugs on the spot as a condition for the sale (Jacobs 1992).

PRIVATE EYES

As part of the more general growth of the private security industry (related to public budget constraints) and continuing concerns over drugs and information leaks, private undercover operations have continued to gain in prominence. These vary from full-scale corporate espionage cases to the "personals"—background investigations requested by individuals. The pool of former government covert agents available for private sector work has continued to grow (including the central figure in the FBI's expanded use of undercover means).

Private investigators standing between a legal system that is not always good and clients who are not always bad have a unique vision and freedom. Neither cops nor crooks, their position can be powerful, even if fraught with moral ambiguity and temptation.

The Wackenhut Corporation's newly established special division for covert corporate investigations got off to a rocky start in 1990. It was hired by managers of the Trans Alaska Pipeline to investigate the loss of confidential company documents. But according to 1991 hearings held by the House Interior Committee, this escalated into a more questionable investigation of its critics. After six months and $290,000 the investigation was canceled (Committee 1991).

Highly trained investigators, sophisticated eavesdropping equipment, and a sting operation were used against a critic who passed on documents regarding environmental and safety problems to regulators and the news media. In an effort to discover his sources, agents set up a phony environmental organization to gain the target's confidence. He invited them to his home, where they stole documents from his desk, went through his garbage, and obtained his personal telephone records. In the logical, although not moral equivalent of government targeting the private sector, the agents also considered targeting Congressmen George Miller (the new chair of the House Interior Committee) in order to have him indicted for theft of corporate documents and to politically embarrass him.

One new specialty niche within the broader field is the ten to fifteen small firms that monitor activists concerned with social issues such as the environment, nuclear power, and animal rights. Their activities vary from simply using public materials to track persons and issues to undercover operations and infiltration.

Keeping track of protest movements is seen to be a wise thing to do for any business involved in sensitive work. This is a strand of the broad move toward strategic and anticipatory business planning. There is a perceived need for "intelligence" not only on markets and suppliers, but on rivals and critics.

The president of Perceptions International in Connecticut states, "[W]e look at the animal-rights movement in general." This includes certain "philosophical and tactical trends" of interest to clients (*Boston Globe*, 9 July 1989). One such client was U.S. Surgical Corporation, a group that was criticized for using anesthetized dogs to demonstrate its surgical staples. But the intelligence firm also gets specific. One of its employees infiltrated an animal-rights group and befriended a woman who was later arrested for planting a bomb in the parking lot of U.S. Surgical.

No-fault divorce laws have greatly reduced the use of private detectives for domestic investigations. But that is changing. Concern over sexually transmitted diseases and fraud have encouraged increased use of private detectives to investigate possible suitors. Some investigators actively seek out clients by placing adds directed toward singles, such as "Do you know who you're dating? Now more than ever it's important to know." One investigator notes, "[T]wenty years ago this was unheard of, but now we're getting as many single people as married" Women are much more likely to hire such investigators than are men. One investigator reports, "[T]here's nothing we can't get. It may not always be public record, but it can be obtained." Some ways of doing this—by watching targets, going through their garbage, subterfuge, or rewarding or coercing those entrusted with information. For $250, an Ohio company called Test-A-Mate even offers attractive female decoys who will test the loyalty of a partner. They find out where the target is likely to be and then sit near him, but won't speak unless spoken to first.

Individuals are also covertly watched not because of their uniqueness (as with the above), but because they are seen as representatives of more general social types. The latest development in market research is to use discrete "people-watchers." As one expert said, "[T]he best way to get an in-depth understanding of consumer values is to watch people buying and using products." Cultural anthropologists now observe and often videotape consumers in stores, shopping malls, and even their own homes.

Such techniques permit researchers to "get underneath the surface." The director of research for one large company states,

> [W]e look in the refrigerators, the kitchen cabinets and the closets. We ask people to show us their favorite things. We learn a lot more by looking around than we'd ever find out just asking people about their homes. Nothing is hidden from us.

Families that permit researchers to come into their homes presumably consent and are paid, but in large stores and shopping malls individuals are unlikely to be warned that they are being watched.[7]

HUMOR

As part of a study of cultural images and surveillance I have analyzed visual jokes and cartoons (Marx forthcoming). The names, props, and sets used in undercover investigations lend themselves to humor that is both intended and as a result of uncontrollable surprises. Some humor is in the use of words that have double meanings. As with a play, the audience knows what many of the actors do not. Other humor is like a situational comedy, at least for the agents and broader audience.

In Lincoln, Nebraska, wanted suspects were arrested when they came to collect a free pair of athletic shoes in return for filling out a survey. They had been sent an invitation to show up at the new Grabar Athletic footwear store: "a new concept for people on the run." *Gray Bar Hotel* is a slang term for jail. After the arrests the following sign was placed on the door: "Grabar Shoes closed. We'll catch you next time" (*Boston Globe*, 5 May 1989).

A marriage celebration in Michigan turned out to be a new form of the "shotgun wedding" in which the daughter of "fast Eddie Lang" was married by the "Reverend Billy Ray Hawk." The multiagency sting resulted in the arrest of sixteen unsuspecting guests who had previously been involved in drug deals with the groom, an undercover agent. Guests received matchbooks engraved, "Thank you for sharing our joy." When the band named SPOC (cops) played the song "I fought the Law and the Law Won," a police sergeant asked for the police in the audience to please stand up. Those who remained seated were arrested.

When suspects visited her house, undercover agent Kim Wozencraft frequently played "Everything You Do Will Come Back to You" and a song by Steely Dan with the lines "Agents of the law, luckless pedestrians, I know you're out there somewhere."

In New York City an operation using policewomen pretending to be prostitutes was called "Operation Losing Proposition."

There are also what can be called last laugh situations. For everyone who has ever seen an example of exceptionally bad driving behavior and wished that an officer was there, the following Boulder, Colorado case is heartwarming. In what is called a game of "road stalk," a young man in a Jeep followed another vehicle too closely with his headlights glaring. The other car turned, pulled over, and then turned again, and the tailing car stayed aggressively with its prey. The prey turned out to be a police officer in an unmarked car. The stalker was arrested for misdemeanor harassment.

In an ironic twist, a would-be car thief in a Lakeland, Florida, shopping mall broke into a police surveillance van while three officers were hiding in the back. One of the officers reported, "[I]t was hard to keep from laughing" as they watched the thief start the car (*Boston Globe*, 24 December 1990).

A 17 month sting directed at importers and sellers of illegal eavesdropping equipment in 40 "spy shops" seized pens, calculators, electronic power strips, and telephone jacks with hidden bugs. In a lovely irony which must have given a smile to those in the know, agents used sophisticated listening devices to document their transactions. To their chagrin, shop owners refrained from using the anti-bugging devices they also sell. While such devices have been illegal at least since 1968, this rare investigation was apparently triggered not by a desire to protect citizens' privacy, but to keep the devices out of the hands of drug dealers after a bug was found in a drug shipment which alerted smugglers to the discovery (*New York Times*, April 4, 1995).

While the humor may release tension, it may also be supportive of mistreatment of suspects. The use of deception makes it possible to view the deceived as a dupe. This can encourage cynicism and even contempt for the subject. This may make it easier to take and to justify questionable actions since they are directed at someone whose moral worth is already impugned and lessened by their being taken in.

GOOD QUOTES

Emerson wrote, "I hate quotations, tell me what you know," and playwright Tom Stoppard has said it is better to be quotable than to be honest. But such oppositions are not necessarily present. For instrumental and esthetic reasons, my study made extensive use of quotations. They can prepare the reader for what is to come, humanize abstractions, and serve as a shorthand for recalling longer arguments.

Quotes also help us grasp the phenomenology of investigations (an important topic for further research). For example, an experienced agent reports, "[T]he best undercover is exalted in what he's doing, he is loving it, it's almost a sexual thrill." Whatever the dangers (and perhaps because of them) undercover work can also be exciting and even addicting. Jack Katz (1988) has emphasized the "high" and the excitement of crime for some actors. The appeals of the subjective experience must be understood. Secret investigations can be highly engaging and offer a macho thrill involving the hunt, chase, and capture. There is a similar phenomenon for uniformed police.

The excitement also may apply to covert participation in illegal activities, apart from the chase aspects. Kim Wozencraft, in a semifictional account of her activities as an undercover narcotics agent reports:

I loved getting wired and staying out all night, staggering from bar to bar to private home, peeling hundred-dollar bills off my municipal bankroll to buy dope. Smoke it, snort it, swallow it, fix it, mix that dope, go up, go down, go sideways, go so fucking fast that your tongue can't keep up with the neurotransmitter Ping-Pong championship popping in your brain. (1990)

Among some of the better quotations I have encountered since the book's publication that illustrate particular themes:
On moral blurring and means-ends complexities:

What I do may not be reputable, but I am. In this town I'm the leper with the most fingers. (Jack Nicholson in *The Two Jakes*)
Some things are necessary evils. Some things are more evil than necessary. (John Le Carre, *The Russia House*)
Between two evils, I always pick the one I never tried before. (Mae West)
We are in a hell of a business. We do all the wrong things for the right reasons. (Burt Reynolds in *Hustle*)
I do my best to protect you and I may break a few rules, but I break them in your favor. (Raymond Chandler, *The Big Sleep*)
The greatest problem of any country is to deal with its enemies without becoming its enemies. (E. L. Doctorow, interview on public television,)
Send men that they may spy out the land of Canaan, which I give to the children of Israel; of every tribe of their fathers shall you send a man, every one a prince among them. (Numbers 13:1–2)
He who the sword of heaven will bear/ Should be as holy as severe. (William Shakespeare, *Measure for Measure*)
See yonder justice railing at you thief? Change places and handy, dandy, which is the justice and which the thief? (William Shakespeare, *King Lear*)
We do try to keep things secret, but without lying about it. Sometimes it may seem like we put the judge on the wrong track, lay a mist over it. (Police officer, in Klerks 1995)
I have always operated at two levels, a personal level and a political one. When the two have come in conflict I have had to put politics first. This conflict can be very painful. I don't like deceiving people, especially friends, and contrary to what others think, I feel very badly about it. But then decent soldiers feel badly about the necessity of killing in wartime. (P. Knightley, *The Master Spy: The Story of Kim Philby*)
You have to get rid of your conscience. You've got to have the mind-set that you're going to make every dime you can off your friends, neighbors, mother or pastor, if they are doing something illegal. (Informant, *Atlanta Journal Constitution*, 31 March 1991)
The simple truth is, I don't remember—period. (Ronald Reagan regarding the Iran-Contra affair,)
Every ship of state runs on a river of darkness. (Former CIA official)

On betrayal and its costs:

I played both roles, I was both sides. I comprehended their longing, I shared their needs and I despised us all. The difference between them and me was that I understood there was no difference. (John Le Carre)
I started to feel like an animal with one leg clamped in a trap. The options? stay and get skinned, or chew off a foot and drag your self into the forest, hope you don't bleed to death. (Kim Wozencraft, *Rush*)
[An agent states:] There are cases that you don't want to see come to an end because you don't want to arrest them. You like the people. You hate to see their lives ruined. You hate to think what are they going to think about you. . . . I can remember very distinctly going out and arresting these same people that had become my friends. I can't even talk about it now without getting emotional. (Pogrebin and Poole 1993)
There is no occupation that fails a man more than that of a secret agent. (Joseph Conrad, *The Secret Agent*)

On discretion in a covert role:

In the free-wheeling kind of undercover work we were doing, there was little supervision. We were guided by our own judgment and often free to pick and choose our targets, to make decisions outside the range of our authority. In a manner of speaking, we made up the rules as we went and played God, judge, and jury. And so I never made a case on Lloyd Quinn, for the simple reason that I liked the guy. (Wansley and Stowers, *FBI Undercover*)

On Different assessments of the consequences of the work:

I felt like a snail, spreading ooze in front of me so that I could slither ahead another inch or so, not really getting anywhere, just going for the sake of moving forward. (Kim Wozencraft, *Rush*)
Data protection means protection of criminals. (French police official, personal interview with author)
The country doesn't give much of a shit about bugging . . . most people around the country think it's probably routine, everybody's trying to bug everybody else, it's politics. (Richard Nixon, Watergate tapes)
The methods of intelligence services do not fit the moral standards of polite society anywhere. (Markus Wolf, East German Spymaster)
You know what I compare it [narcotics sweeps] to? The Dept. of Sanitation picks up our garbage every day. They know there's going to be more garbage tomorrow. Now, what would happen if they didn't? The city would be in chaos. It's the same thing with narcotics. We have to do these things. (Police official, *New York Times*, 25 December 1988)
They're [corrupt public officials] still out there. They're still dealing. It's a never-ending thing. We just don't have the manpower. The animals are running the zoo. (Prosecutor in Chicago judicial corruption case)

Its like squeezing Jell-o—it squirts out in other places. And we are squeezing the hell out of that Jell-o in the middle of the park [on displacement from a decoy operation]. (Los Angeles police officer)

On categorical searches:

To be sure, I can never be convinced that it would cause any harm to throw a cloth at a viper on which it can squirt its poison. [Vidocq in Savant (1956) in countering the argument that police-provided opportunities create crime] We wanted to find out if there was a problem. You never know until you go in to take a look. (County Sheriff regarding a broad sweep using drug-sniffing dogs of all ten thousand lockers and all cars within a one-block radius of the eight high schools in Tazwell County, Illinois; there was no problem with drugs. (*Village Voice*, 2 October 1990)

Another high school investigation also shows the public relations advantages of the tactic, whether or not anything is found. In this case, a fifty-thousand-dollar undercover investigation into drug use in a Colorado high school nabbed six students accused of peddling a few ounces of marijuana. A Sheriff's Department captain justified the operation by saying, "[W]e have reassured ourselves that there's not an immense problem in the school district here" (*Denver Post*, 19 May 1994). Regardless of its findings, the operation is also believed to send a strong deterrent message to students by putting them on notice that they can never be sure when such an operation is present.

On unintended consequences and the limitations of planning:

Some of [Sam] Spade's actions go beyond their intentions, some fall short, others boomerang on the actor. The point of all this is that actions hardly ever turn out to be what one expects them to be. Spade's wisdom consists in knowing that any action is, inherently, partly out of control, that actions must be herded or ridden but not programmed. The world changes actions, nullifying some, putting backspin on others. . . . The only detectives who know where their cases are going from the start do their work on prime time. (J. Thompson, *Gumshoe*)
For every smooth, well-orchestrated scam, however, there seemed always to be one that came straight out of an Abbott and Costello movie. In such cases, you learned to operate according to what came to be known as Grippi's Law. "If you fall in a fucking mud hole . . . check your back pocket real quick to see if maybe you caught a fish." (Wansley and Stowers, 1989)
You want to be as prepared as possible, even though that is somewhat impossible in this line of work. (Undercover narcotics agent, cited in Jacobs 1992)

On exiting from the undercover role:

I couldn't believe it was actually over. Snap. Just like that. . . . I had been [undercover] for a little over seven months. Now in the space of a few hours,

we were expected to slip back over to the other side, the straight world. . . . I felt cramped within the pale green cinderblock walls of the Vice Office, as though I had just returned from a long journey in a foreign land and was looking with new eyes at the customs of my native people. (Kim Wozencraft, *Rush*)
The investigation seemed to have a life of its own and I was caught up in the middle of a merry-go-round that I could not get off. (Pat Livingston, cited in LaBrecque 1987)

SECOND THOUGHTS AND ENDURING TENSIONS

Scholars such as those represented in this volume, who choose to work on criminal justice issues from a broad, interdisciplinary, qualitative, skeptical, and often critical perspective, generally have a more difficult time than their colleagues whose feet are squarely planted in a single discipline and who quantitatively pursue microlevel questions defined by funding agencies and criminal justice establishments.

In this section I shift from a consideration of substantive issues to some more personal issues. My study of covert practices was published in 1988. It moved from being a boomerang (with its recirculation between author, sponsor, and publisher) to being a missile. But alas, even missiles leave remnants. I did not part with the book easily, although I did so gladly.

Doing an interdisciplinary book on a broad topic that mixes social science with social criticism and is aimed at academics, practitioners, and the educated public is a recipe for angst, self-doubt, and role conflict.

I address eleven issues here that are more professional than substantive. These go beyond the specifics of the study and touch more general concerns. There are empirical or practical answers to some of the questions and, where there are not, I know that the tension between polarities can be positive. But that insight does not eliminate the discomfort. Knowledge is one thing and feelings another. I offer these concerns (stated in the form of questions) in the preliterate and psychoanalytic tribal tradition of exorcising ghosts and demons by identifying them, and because I know many colleagues share them.

1. Is it appropriate for social scientists whose legitimacy and traditions involve ordering microempirical measurements with systematic theory to study broad amorphous topics, such as privacy, deception, authenticity, liberty, autonomy, and justice in an interpretive fashion? Wouldn't it be better to start with just one question, replicate prior research, or test a few propositions using rigorous methods and quantitative data? Perhaps, but

when the topic has rarely been studied there is also a case for beginning by casting a broad net in the hope of stimulating more delineated studies. There is no correct answer to the recurring issues of forests, trees, and grasses. They are all there and are all important.

For social scientists trained in the positivist–happy times of the 1950s and 1960s, one risks (or at least imagines risking) peer rejection, a negative self-image, and guilt in not following the standard linear model of moving from questions to answers, and theories to systematic numerical tests. Yet the specificity and rigidity of this model did not feel right for the surveillance project. Instead I started with an interest in the phenomenon of deception by the state and a feeling that it was wrong, or at least risky as public policy. I began with an answer and looked for the questions. Some of the most important questions (how to balance the rights of the individual with the needs of the community) cannot be answered by empirical research. I also struggled with finding the right balance between description, classification, measurement, explanation, and prescription/proscription.

2. Even if one opts to focus on a broad topic, should it be approached from a multi- and interdisciplinary perspective, or from a narrower disciplinary base? Given the exploratory nature of my inquiry I sought whatever tools were available. But then as a nonspecialist one must confront the issues of poaching. I have chapters in areas in which my formal training goes no further than the sophomore introductory class (e.g., in history and in ethics) and I rely on secondary sources. Can/should we trespass with impunity/immunity in other professional vineyards if we like the look of their grapes? In trying to be all things to all people does one risk being nothing to anyone? Does a book need a disciplinary identity? Does breadth have to come at a cost of depth?

3. What does it mean to "understand" undercover police practices? What were the goals of my sociological inquiry? What does it mean to be interested in reasons as well as causes, in subjective experiences understood empathetically, as well as in more easily quantifiable objective factors? How can surveys and experiments be supplemented in the search for broad understanding? How can we make use of the "truths" of novelists and philosophers?[8] What role does wisdom play in the results of sociological research? How does prediction relate to "understanding"? How does understanding relate to judgment? What is the difference between a social scientist, a journalist, an essayist, and a novelist? What needs to be added to Robert Park's observation that sociology is "slow journalism"?

The strictly scientific part of being a sociologist neither satisfies my soul nor can it do justice intellectually or politically to the topics that I am interested in. I want my writing to be scientifically accurate and to reflect wisdom. I want to advance knowledge and also contribute to the quality of life. The research I have done on social control issues in the last two decades is not the work of an activist who starts committed to an end and selects data to push it forward, nor is it the artist's work of unbridled imagination where anything is possible. But it shares something with each of them. Can we have it multiple ways?

One way to combine these is through fictive social science scenarios (whether dystopian or utopian).[9] I think these should be as common in the tool kit of the social scientist as the ability to think conceptually or to analyze data. They can be a powerful form of communication, particularly for broader audiences. Yet they must be grounded by one's understanding of fact and social process.

In such writing the possible must be kept separate from the probable. But there is the interesting paradox that these are not necessarily independent. Given the power of scenarios, describing what is possible may effect the probability of its occurring by moving people to action. This lies behind George Orwell's observation that "I do not believe that the kind of society I describe necessarily will arrive, but I believe . . . that something resembling it could arrive" (cited in Crick 1980). Orwell was not making predictions, he was describing possibilities in the hope that this act could help avoid them.

4. Is it possible to balance social science and social criticism so that they are mutually supportive rather than corrosive? We need precision and passion. I don't want my concerns with civil liberties, inequality, and reform to distort my scientific observations—for both intellectual and practical reasons. Scientific understanding should not be sacrificed on the altar of commitment. Yet in this socially important area, I am more than the neutral scientist who just wants the facts (Marx 1972).

5. Can the same work make contributions to both social science and public policy? Must one choose between being an uncontaminated basic scientist seeking fundamental knowledge with little notion of how, when, where, or if it will be used; a hired gun seeking normatively based solutions to an applied problem someone else has defined; or a zealous, self-appointed social engineer–moral entrepreneur, peddling your own brand of expert truth and action?

How does and should knowledge relate to action? Do you have to know why in order to know how? Can academics, with their cross-case knowledge and tenure, who act as Monday morning quarterbacks with no responsibility for the consequences of the actions that practitioners must take, really have much to say that is useful?

6. Is it possible to write so that one's work is well received by both colleagues and the educated public? In trying to reach for (or at least not exclude) a general audience, one runs the risk of dilution and being labeled a popularizer or even a journalist. Books that are accessible are often suspect in the halls of academe. Yet the trappings of academic respectability— literature reviews, sophisticated techniques, jargon, the assumption of a

learned audience, and detached and spiritless writing—are hardly endearing to the average reader.

7. Was I taken in? In studying persons who are professional liars how far should I go in discounting what they say? Was I conned by some of the agents I interviewed? Aren't they in the best position to deceive an interviewer (described by one DEA agent as a "choir boy from M.I.T.")?

8. Between starting and finishing the book, my beliefs about the desirability of undercover tactics changed. Rather than seeing them as an unnecessary evil, I came to view their use in the United States under limited and controlled circumstances as a necessary evil. I gained excellent access to the FBI (something I would not have predicted from my days of Berkeley student activism). Does the change in my attitude say something about my openness and intellectual honesty in the face of a very complex situation, or was I co-opted? Had I come to that situation the madam warned the prostitute about: when one starts enjoying sex with the customers it's time to quit? At some level did I want to please and be liked by those sometimes heroic figures in almost white hats? Is the change partly a strategic ploy, since I want to affect the policy debate and know that a hostile polemic would likely preclude this? How can one balance and maintain a degree of respect/appreciation for our subjects and the sincerity of their beliefs, reciprocity (at least in so far as one doesn't harm them since they are giving something to us with little in return), with the need to be objective, to be faithful to our moral concerns, and not to be captured by our subjects?

9. How do you know when you are done? When do you let go? I stopped largely because of the sponsor's expectations, but could easily have spent several more years working on comparative international materials and on literary and film treatments. I was not quite ready to let go. But I know if I had worked on the book for several more years new topics would have appeared justifying further work, in an endless spiral. In finishing a book on a contemporary topic one risks being out of date as soon as the work is published. On the other hand partial information is better than none at all.

10. With respect to book reviews, was it possible to balance the cynicism of the sociology of knowledge perspective with the belief that there really are empirical and normative truths that transcend social settings?

While I am in this work primarily for the process, I can't claim the degree of disinterestedness or disdain that some artists have for critics (e.g., playwrights who report they never look at reviews). This partly reflects the tentativeness of the scholarly enterprise in which we must learn from each other and any one person is limited in what he or she knows (occupational norms require scholars to be less arrogant than artists).

The many reviews of the book have been fair and more laudatory than I anticipated. Yet I was not above applying a sociology of knowledge view in which a book review is often a Rorschach test revealing as much, or more, about the reviewer as about the book. This is not to suggest that reviewers are simply hapless captives of deterministic social forces. But about half the time I could predict at least some of a reviewers' responses by knowing their discipline and politics. Thus a law professor and a historian found things to criticize in the book's legal and historical sections, respectfully. A sociologist of organizations praised the chapter that dealt with bureaucracy and lamented the fact that the conceptual concerns of that chapter were not found throughout the book and he was impatient with the literary quotes. In contrast, an ethnographer was most critical of the bureaucracy chapter, finding it too abstract and lifeless. A conservative prosecutor accused me of losing my cool and exaggerating the dangers to civil liberties, while a radical criminologist faulted the book for failing to fully consider the macrosystem that leads American police to behave in the ways the book documents.

It is not news that opinions have social correlates. It does not follow from this that all views are necessarily equal, whether scientifically or morally, merely because they are socially situated and constructed. So are tunnels and bridges, but they show great variation in quality and usefulness. Yet awareness of the social construction of perspectives can be a salve for critical reviews, if also a bearer of humility for laudatory ones.

11. What obligations did I have to promote the book in order to have it be seen and reviewed beyond the confines of a few specialists and friends? Many in the university have a naive faith that if you do good work it will be noticed (as in the film *Field of Dreams* they assume that if you build it the audience will come). But this is life, not the movies. At its worst this optimistic view involves a conceit about how important the work we do is and how eager the outside world is for it. As graduate students in a meritocratic-appearing system, we are led to believe that the cream will rise to the top. If it doesn't, no matter, since virtue in scholarship is seen to be its own reward. Even in the American academic context, with only a hint of the genteel, scholarly aristocratic tradition, there is something a bit crass and self-serving about promoting your own ideas. Doing this risks contamination with the corrupt outside world.

The Twentieth Century Fund financed the study of undercover police and receives the royalties. I was glad to be finished and wanted to move on to other things. Yet I also felt a sense of responsibility to shape public debate. This was also consistent with the sponsor's interest in funding books that were accessible to a broad public and in having the results be widely disseminated.

I did not want the book's main impact to be taking up space in libraries and further depleting the rain forests. With more than fifty thousand books published each year in the United States it is rare that a book speaks for itself. I was not shy in calling the book to the attention of audiences whether colleagues, journal editors, journalists, policymakers, or bookstores.

Many reporters fell into one of two camps: either the devil's advocate, questioning my call for restraint in the face of serious crime problems, or the alarmist, demanding to know what needed to be done to stop the sky from falling. I enjoyed educating the former about means and ends relationships in a democracy and the latter about frames of reference. However, I was frustrated by the media's inability to see the difference between a sociologist and a social engineer.

There is a difference between helping to identify the right questions and having the right factual and then normative answers. Having the right questions is a first step. I think I have those and I have many of the factual answers, but I am far from the normative and policy answers. My initial concern was to identify the issues and encourage public discussion, and only secondarily to offer solutions. Indeed these topics are fascinating because there often are no solutions in the usual sense.

The mannered debates of the academy are very different from the raucous rhetoric of the radio talk show open to all callers. The ethic of many of the ideologues I encountered in publicizing the book on television and radio was one of simple expediency: say anything that will advance your case. The standards of logic, evidence, fairness, and civility that in principle characterize scientific debate were not much in evidence.

Nor did I enjoy having to fit what often should have been complex answers into the time, space, and sophistication limits of the media format in question. Reporters often ask good questions, but conditions rarely permit your giving good answers. It is frustrating to be told, "Come on, Professor, never mind all the qualifications and hedges, just answer the question yes or no" or "We only have a minute, can you give us a quick summary of the book?" When the story is complicated and ambiguous and there are no easy answers, as with the case of covert policing, the yes/no quick fixes that media questioners are after aren't there. In trying to fit into their format, you must either appear glib and inauthentic or indecisive and "academic." The latter is a surefire method for being edited out or not being asked back.

As the above suggests, I never felt fully comfortable marketing the book. I am more comfortable as a producer than a promoter, but books do not reach wider audiences on their own.

Yet in spite of these tensions there is a strong need for qualitative, interdisciplinary, and integrative approaches to broad topics of social importance. The softer social sciences residing between the humanities and the sciences are uniquely qualified for such inquiries. The building blocks of our highly specialized research endeavors must occasionally be brought together in an effort to see the broader landscape.

Comprehensive work on controversial topics takes time and scholarly independence. The Twentieth Century Fund was an ideal sponsor. I spent a decade working on the book and would not want to have been judged for tenure (or anything else) after only five years. The pressure to produce work quickly and to bring in research grants only on topics that established agencies want to fund can be highly dysfunctional.

There is no necessary opposition between policy and basic research, nor between writing for colleagues and the educated public. We need to search for wisdom, as well as knowledge. The former is impossible without the latter and the latter is pedantic and lifeless when divorced from the concrete details of everyday life and questions of value.

NOTES

1. This paper extends and revises Marx (1992c).
2. Of course, this is not to suggest that just because they are first-person accounts and seem believable they are necessarily correct. Proust's observation that his remembrances were a theory and not a record of the past may apply.
3. Were I to revise the book today, conceptually I would give greater attention to the literature on roles and role conflict and attenuation, identity inversion, situational stress, and con artists. The chapters on unintended consequences would be made more analytic and the book's policy chapter more closely tied to the earlier analysis. I would more fully differentiate between, and consider the different policies that may be required for, controlling infiltration into a constitutionally and/or traditionally protected zone, as against merely providing a public opportunity for a violation to be committed (e.g., as with fencing fronts and decoys). Empirically I would give more attention to comparative international questions, to images of surveillance in culture, to jail house informing [see Brown and Duffy (1991) for an Australian example], reverse stings, internal affairs units, private police, the use of sex in covert investigations, and the parallels between confidence men and undercover police. Some of these themes are treated in a special September 1992 issue of *Crime, Law and Social Change* devoted to covert policing. Marx (1987a, 1992a, 1992b) treats internal affairs units, private police, and sex as they involve undercover means. Fijnaut and Marx (1995, forthcoming) consider undercover means in Europe and across borders.
4. For example, units that were disbanded came back. Thus the San Diego Police Department's controversial undercover border patrol unit described by Joseph Wambaugh in *Lines and Shadows* was eliminated in 1978 after a scandal. It was reconstituted only to be abandoned again under similar circumstances. In 1989 it was recreated, although in a less aggressive mode.
5. Our understanding of the political uses more generally has been recently expanded by the good material in Powers (1987), Theoharis (1988), O'Reilly (1989), Keller (1990), and Churchill and Vander Wall (1990).
6. On the other hand, long mandatory sentences may have unintentionally made undercover work more dangerous. Some agents have suggested that suspects, feeling they have nothing to lose, will become more violent in an effort to avoid arrest.
7. Although one couple filed a suit against Nissan, claiming that a researcher who they let live in their home was spying on them to gain insight into how American families live. Nissan denied the charge, but did acknowledge that the researcher was engaged in a project to determine how Americans feel about cars (*New York Times*, 12 December 1989).

8. For a sensitive and insightful treatment of qualitative understanding see Eisner (1991).

9. My own modest efforts at such writing have been very satisfying and much more widely read than straight social science writing (Marx 1987b, 1990a).

REFERENCES

Barker, T. and D. Carter. 1989. "Fluffing Up the Evidence and Covering Your Ass: Two Facets of Police Lying." Paper presented at the annual meeting of the American Society of Criminology, Reno, Nevada.

Brown, D. and B. Duffy. 1991. "Privatizing the Police Verbal: The Growth Industry in Prison Informants." In *Travesty! Miscarriages of Justice*. Sydney: Academics for Justice.

Carter, D. 1990. *Law Enforcement Intelligence Operations*. East Lansing, MI: School of Criminal Justice.

Churchill, W. and J. Vander Wall. 1990. *Cointelpro Papers: Documents from the FBIs Secret Wars against Domestic Dissent*. Boston: South End.

Cohen, S. 1985. *Visions of Social Control*. Cambridge: Polity.

Committee on Interior and Insular Affairs. 1991. *Alaska Pipeline Service Company Covert Operation*. Washington DC: U.S. Government Office Printing Office.

Crick, R. 1980. *George Orwell: A Life*. London: Secker and Warburg.

Eisner, E. 1991. *The Enlightened Eye*. New York: MacMillan.

Fijnaut, C. and G. T. Marx. 1995. *Undercover: Police Surveillance in Comparative Perspective*. Rotterdam: Kulwer.

Farkas, G. 1986. "Stress in Undercover Policing." Pp. 433–40 in *Psychological Services for Law Enforcement*, edited by J. T. Reese and H. A. Goldstein. Washington, DC: U.S. Government Printing Office.

Gelbspan, R. 1991. *Break-Ins, Death Threats and the FBI*. Boston: South End.

Girodo, M. 1991a. "Drug Corruption in Undercover Agents: Measuring the Risk." *Behavioral Sciences and the Law* 9:361–70.

———. 1991b. "Personality, Job Stress, and Mental Health in Undercover Agents: A Structural Equation Analysis." *Journal of Social Behavior and Personality* 6:375–90.

Goddard, D. and M. Levine. 1988 *Undercover The Secret Lives of an Undercover Agent: The Story of DEA Agent Michael Levine*. New York: Random House.

Jacobs, B. 1992. "Undercover Deception Reconsidering Presentations of Self." *Journal of Contemporary Ethnography* 21(2).

———. 1993. "Undercover Deception Clues: A Case of Restrictive Deterrence." *Criminology* 31(2):281–99.

Katz, J. 1988. *The Seductions of Crime*. New York: Basic Books.

Keller, W. 1990. *The Liberals and J. Edgar Hoover*. Princeton, NJ: Princeton University Press.

Klerks, P. 1995. "Covert Policing in the Netherlands." In *Undercover: Police Surveillance in Comparative Perspective*, edited by C. Fijnaut and G. T. Marx. Rotterdam: Kulwer.

LaBrecque, R. 1987. *Lost Undercover: An FBI Agent's True Story*. New York: Dell.

Marx, G. 1972. *Muckraking Sociology*. New Brunswick, NJ: Transaction.

———. 1974. "Thoughts on a Neglected Category of Social Movement Participants: Agents Provocateurs and Informants." *American Journal of Sociology* 80(2).

———. 1981. "Stories of Social Control." *Social Problems* 23(3).

———. 1984. "Notes on the Discovery, Collection, and Assessment of Hidden and Dirty Data." Pp. 78–113 in *Studies in the Sociology of Social Problems*, edited by J. W. Schneider and J. I. Kitsuse. Norwood, NJ: Ablex.

———. 1987a. "The Interweaving of Public and Private Police in Undercover Work." Pp. 172–93 in *Private Policing*, edited by C. D. Shearing and P. C. Stenning. Newbury Park, CA: Sage.

———. 1987b. "Raising Your Hand Just Won't Do." *Los Angeles Times* 1 April.

———. 1988. *Undercover: Police Surveillance in America*. Berkeley: University of California Press.

———. 1990a. "The Case of the Omniscient Organization." *Harvard Business Review* (March-April).

———. 1990b. "Reflections on Academic Success and Failure: Making It, Forsaking It, Reshaping It." Pp. 260–84 in *Authors of Their Own Lives*, edited by B. Berger, Berkeley: University of California Press.

———. 1992a. "When the Guards Guard Themselves: Undercover Tactics Turned Inward." *Policing and Society* 2:151–72.

———. 1992b. "Under-the-Covers Undercover Investigations: Some Reflections on the State's Use of Sex and Deception in Law Enforcement." *Criminal Justice Ethics* 11(1):13–24.

———. 1992c. "Some Reflections on *Undercover*: Recent Developments and Enduring Issues." *Crime, Law and Social Change* 18:193–217, 1992.

———. forthcoming a. "Social Control Across Borders" in W. McDonald (ed.), *Transnational Organized Crime*.

———. forthcoming b. "Electric Eye in the Sky: Some Reflections on the New Surveillance in Popular Culture." In *New Technology, Surveillance and Social Control*, edited by D. Lyons and E. Zurick. Minneapolis: University of Minnesota Press.

Maurer, D. 1974. *American Confidence Man*. Springfield, IL: C. Thomas.

Murano V. with W. Hoffer. 1990. *Cop Hunter*. New York: Pocket Books.

O'Reilly, K. 1989. *Racial Manners: The FBI's Secret File on Black America, 1960–1972*. New York: Free Press.

Pistone, J. and Donnie Brasco. 1988. *My Undercover Life in the Mob*. New York: Dutton.

Pogrebin, M. and E. Poole. 1993. "Vice Isn't Nice: A Look at the Effects of Working Undercover." *Journal of Criminal Justice* 21:383–94.

Powers, R. 1987. *Secrecy and Power: The Life of J. Edgar Hoover*. New York: Free Press.

Protess, D. 1989. "Did the Press Play Prosecutor in Covering an FBI Sting?" *Columbia Journalism Review* (July/August).

Rothmiller, M. and I. Goldman. 1992. *L. A. Secret Police*. New York: Simon and Schuster.

Savant, J. 1956. *Le Proces de Vidocq*. Paris: de Romilly.

Theoharis, A. 1988. *The Boss: J. Edgar Hoover and the Great American Inquisition*. Philadelphia: Temple University Press.

Wansley, L. and C. Stowers. 1989. *FBI Undercover: The True Story of Special Agent "Mandrake."* New York: Pocket Books.

Wozencraft, K. 1990. *Rush*. New York: Ballantine Books.

9
THE FUTURE OF THE PROPORTIONATE SENTENCE

ANDREW von HIRSCH

The idea of the proportionate or "deserved" sentence has had considerable influence during the last two decades. In actual sentencing policy, that influence is not so widespread as sometimes has been supposed. In the United States, only a few jurisdictions—Oregon and Minnesota, for example—have relied on it in systematic fashion. In Europe, three jurisdictions—Finland in 1976, Sweden in 1988, and England and Wales in 1991—have adopted sentencing framework legislation that stresses explicitly the idea of proportionality.[1] But even where laws and policies have not changed so much, proportionalism has considerably altered thinking about punishment (see, e.g., Canadian Sentencing Commission 1986).

In previous writings,[2] I have tried to make out a substantive case for proportionate sentencing. Here, my interest will shift to political/ideological questions. What has made proportionalism an attractive idea? What concerns or worries does it generate that limit its potential attractiveness? What are the prospects of survival of the idea? My focus will be less on whether the idea is "right" on its merits, as on what the sources of its influence have been and whether that influence is likely to abide.

THE ATTRACTIONS OF PROPORTIONALISM

The Appeal to Fairness

Traditional preventively oriented penal theories—even if they purported to be humane—focused always on instrumental concerns: how a sentencing strategy can better protect *us* from the depredations of *them*, the criminals. Such an instrumental focus threatens unjust results: if the aim is prevention, why not do whatever works for that purpose? During the heyday of rehabilitation, that threat seemed muted—for the rehabilitative sentence was supposed to further the offender's interests as well as ours. But as faith declined in the identity of the offender's interests with those of the larger society, the potential oppressiveness of purely crime-preventive sentencing strategies has become more apparent.

Proportionalism gives notions of fairness a central role in penal theory. Proportionality of sentence rests on the idea that the penal censure expressed through the sanction should fairly reflect the degree of reprehensibleness (that is, the degree of harmfulness and culpability) of the actor's conduct [see, more fully, von Hirsch (1993:ch. 2), Duff (1995)]. This viewpoint helps deal with the tension over whether penal policy should favor societal interests or the interests of offenders. In a desert theory, the societal interest is expressed in the recognition that typical crimes (e.g., those of force and fraud) *are* wrongs, for which public condemnation through the criminal sanction is due. The individual's interest is protected through his entitlement to no severer a sanction than the degree of blameworthiness of the conduct would warrant, even if a harsher sentence would have better preventive effects.

It was fashionable for a time among social theorists to dismiss such fairness claims as facades, behind which social theories or practices are espoused for wholly ulterior reasons. I think this is a mistake. Granted, a theory or practice is unlikely to gain widespread adherence *merely* because of its claims to justice. But as David Garland elegantly argues (Garland 1990, ch. 10), sensibilities about humane or fair treatment of criminals have influenced attitudes about punishment, at least among some influential groups.

Proportionalism in punishment is sometimes characterized as a reversion to pre-Enlightenment notions: as returning to Old Testament conceptions of an eye for an eye, or "going back" to Kant. However, the desert rationale rests on the idea of *proportion* rather than harm-for-harm equivalence: penalties need not visit as much suffering as the harm done by offenses. A substantial deflation in overall penalty levels is permissible (indeed, desirable), so long as penalties are graded in the order of crimes' seriousness.[3] Kant, it should also be remembered, was not an Old Testament prophet but a major Enlightenment theorist. There always were two strands of Enlightenment thinking: one a consequentialist version, concerned with calibrating state responses to achieve certain desired social effects; the other, a version that sought to regulate state responses on the basis of certain moral imperatives or moral sentiments. Modern proportionalist theory does not rely on Kant's brief (and unsatisfactory) comments about punishment,[4] but on his larger moral assumptions that a person's claim to just treatment should take precedence over the achievement of collective societal aims.

Practical Guidance

Proportionalism has had the additional attraction of providing a degree of policy guidance: it suggests a way of scaling penalties. Traditional crime-preventative penal conceptions have in large part failed to offer such guidance.

Consider deterrence and rehabilitation. If one asks how sentences can be arrayed according to their supposed deterrent impact, the answer is indeterminate because not enough is known about the comparative marginal deterrent effects of different degrees of sentence severity. With rehabilitation, matters are scarcely better. To the extent treatment programs work at all, they succeed only for carefully selected subgroups of offenders. No "cure" is known, however, for routine cases of car theft, burglary, or robbery. There also is considerable difficulty translating rehabilitative concerns—which address programs of treatment—into the kind of decisions sentencers must make, about the type and duration of the sanction.[5]

What about incapacitation? It has been possible, for many years already, to make rough-and-ready forecasts about which offenders are the more likely to return to crime. That would seem to offer a practical alternative to desert-based scaling: namely, calibrating sentences according to offenders' degree of risk. Proposals of this kind have been made, most notably in the "selective incapacitation" schemes promoted by some conservative American penologists in the early 1980s (see, e.g., Wilson 1983:ch. 8). But there are ethical objections—for example, those concerning misclassification. Because predictions of dangerousness yield high false-positive rates, it is known that a substantial number of those classified as bad risks (and hence given longer sentences) would not offend were they to remain at liberty. A further drawback is the link to social class: many of the statistical indicia of risk are matters such as drug use, employment and school background, residential stability, and early offending. When these factors are relied upon in sentencing, lower-class offenders will tend to get the tougher sentences precisely in virtue of their class status.

There also are practical impediments. One is selective incapacitation's limited apparent effectiveness, when judged by its prospective impact on overall crime rates. Enthusiasm for selective incapacitation began to wane with the publication of a 1988 National Academy of Sciences report suggesting how small that net preventive impact might be (National Research Council 1986; von Hirsch 1988). The strategy also has potential for political embarrassment, because it presents itself as able to foretell who will and will not reoffend. This involves not only designating some offenders as dangerous, but designating others (convicted of similar crimes) as "better" risks—and giving the latter (comparatively) lower sentences. Because any prediction system yields false negatives as well as false positives, a significant number of those deemed good risks will commit serious new offenses anyway, and the sentencing authorities will seem responsible. It is thus not surprising that the major American sentencing guidelines systems have avoided explicit reliance on selective incapacitation. An actuarial, risk-oriented "new penology" is not about to take over sentencing policy[6], whatever its possible influence elsewhere.

A proportionalist sentencing theory provides fuller guidance on scaling matters: sentences are to be ranked in severity to reflect the comparative seriousness of crimes. Granted, there are problems. The theory gives less specific guidance (albeit still some) on how a penalty scale should be anchored. A theory for assessing crimes' comparative seriousness is only beginning to develop. There also are knotty conceptual questions about how much weight, if any, should be accorded prior convictions.[7] Nevertheless, grading is not an unmanageable task. The Minnesota and Oregon sentencing commissions, for example, anchored the penalty scale by reference to existing prison capacities—a practical choice based in part on the need to limit expenditures for building new prisons. Given this target, they were able to grade crimes in seriousness without great dissent, to assign a weight to the criminal record (a smaller weight in Oregon than Minnesota), and to construct presumptive sentence ranges on that basis.

Guidance for sentencers does not necessarily require numerical guidelines; it can be provided instead through statutory guiding principles, as Finland, Sweden, and most recently England and Wales have done. In England and Wales before 1991, courts were expected to develop a sentencing tariff on the basis of a not-very-well delineated rationale in which deterrence was supposed to carry considerable weight (Thomas 1979:14–17). The 1991 Criminal Justice Act furnishes a rationale, through its criterion that the gravity of the criminal act should primarily be determinative (see Ashworth 1992:chs. 4, 9, 10). It should be easier for courts to judge whether one crime is typically more serious than another than to decide the penalties for those crimes on the basis of their supposed deterrent effects.

Proportionalism can also be useful as an aid to implementing other practical sentencing aims. Consider a matter that has drawn so much recent interest: intermediate, noncustodial penalties. Such sanctions can successfully function as a substitute for imprisonment only if they are targeted to crimes of intermediate seriousness, rather than to lesser offenses, and if imprisonment may be used only sparingly as the penalty for those who breach the terms of their community sentences. A proportionalist sentencing rationale calls for observance of these policies: the sanctions, being of middle-level severity, are appropriate only for offenses of middling seriousness; and mere breaches of program conditions are not serious enough to deserve the severe sanction of imprisonment (see more fully, von Hirsch 1993:ch. 7). Crime prevention aims, by contrast, have greater difficulty supplying a workable basis for grading such penalties, and make it more difficult to limit the onerousness of breach penalties (pp. 64–68).

So far, my point is a modest one: that proportionality theory has a certain moral appeal, and helps scale penalties. The theory has not, however, generated the kind of broad consensus that supported rehabilitationism in earlier decades: substantial resistance to the idea continues. Some of the doubts have been raised by penal theorists and reformers who share proportionalists' ultimate aims of the fair and humane treatment of offenders, but worry about whether a desert theory can promote those aims. What, then, are the sources of disquiet?

MULTIPLE AIMS?

Proportionalism sets priorities among sentencing aims. A desert model assumes that it is more important to have proportionately ordered sanctions than to seek other objectives—say, incapacitating those deemed higher risks. This understandably evokes discomfort: why cannot one seek proportionality *and* pursue other desired ends, whether they be treatment, incapacitation, or something else?

While proportionalism involves priorities, it is not exclusive. In the 1970s in the United States, notions of proportionality came into prominence together with growing skepticism about the feasibility of effective treatment. However, the exclusion of treatment considerations is not presupposed. Treatments may be offered to imprisoned offenders within the duration of their deserved sentence. And where two noncustodial sanctions of approximately equivalent severity are available (say, a day-fine of so many days' earnings and intensive probation of a specified duration), desert constraints are not offended when one is chosen over the other on rehabilitative grounds (von Hirsch 1993, ch. 7). Indeed, the English sentencing reform act explicitly permits such selections to be made on grounds of which program might be more "suitable" to the offender (Wasik and Taylor 1994:57–59).

However, a pure desert model remains a constraining one: ulterior factors may be relied upon only where those do not significantly alter the comparative severity of penalties. Giving extra prison time to persons deemed high risks would breach the model's limits, for example. Why not, then, relax the model's constraints to allow greater scope to other, seemingly reasonable aspirations?

A possibility—sometimes referred to as a "modified" desert model—is to relax the constraints to a limited extent. Proportionality would ordinarily determine comparative punishment levels, but upward deviations would be permitted in case of extraordinarily harmful conduct or extraordinarily dangerous individuals. Or else deviations from the deserved sanction might ordinarily be permitted, but these would be restricted ones: say, a deviation of no more than 10 or 15 percent. These approaches still make desert the primary determinant of the ordering of penalties, but give some extra scope for ulterior aims. [For a fuller discussion of the structure and rationale of such "modified desert" schemes, see von Hirsch (1993:ch. 6).] Such schemes, however, remain significantly constraining. Especially dangerous offenders may be given extra prison time, but not the ordinary recidivist. A little extra leeway may be granted in choosing a noncustodial penalty suited to an offender's apparent treatment needs, but not much leeway.

Could more scope be given to nondesert considerations? In a mixed rationale, either desert will predominate or something else will. If—in the ordinary case—the seriousness of the current crime remains the primary determinant of the severity of the penalty, the system still is desert dominated. This has the attractions of which I have spoken: it seems fairer, and gives some useful guidance to decision-makers. Our limited knowledge of how to achieve preventive effects will also be no great obstacle: we do know something about treatment or risk in *some* situations, and when we do that may (to the requisite limited degree) affect the disposition. If ulterior aims are given still greater scope, however, that creates a system dominated by those aims. Desert then can serve only as a (much less important) outer limit. This reintroduces the difficulties of which I spoke earlier: those of apparent injustice, and insufficient practical guidance.

The writings of some of the proponents of "mixed" models reflect these difficulties. Norval Morris (1982, ch. 5) has long advocated what he calls "limiting retributivism." According to this view, desert would set only outer bounds on the severity of punishment, within which the sentence would be fixed on incapacitative or deterrence grounds. The difficulty is that he has never delineated the breadth of these bounds. If the limits are fairly narrow, then the scheme is akin to the modified-desert scheme just mentioned. If the limits are broad, then incapacitation and deterrence will chiefly determine penalties, with problems of which I already have spoken. As long as the character of the limits is unspecified, Morris's scheme remains indeterminate (more fully, see von Hirsch 1985:ch. 12).

Another variant that has been suggested is treating desert as only an *upper* constraint on punishment, below which sentences could be fixed on other grounds. That, however, leaves unresolved what those other grounds should be. Michael Tonry (1994b) speaks of "parsimony" as the basis for reducing sentences below what is deserved—but this would require an account of what categories of offenders should be entitled to such a more parsimonious disposition, and why so (see von Hirsch 1993:109–11). Treating desert as providing only upper limits poses the problem of what other conception sustains *any* level of punishment above zero. If crime prevention is invoked as the sustaining rationale, there reappears the problem of the poor guidance such rationales provide. There is also the additional hazard of a skewed ordering of penalties: what is to prevent those convicted of a lesser crime category from ordinarily receiving a penalty near that crime's applicable upper limit (say, because its perpetrators often reoffend) whereas a more serious offence is penalized much more leniently (say, because it occurs more infrequently)? To avoid such bizarre results, lower bounds based on the gravity of the crime need to be supplied. Perhaps these lower bounds may be "softer" than the upper limits, allowing departures below them to be made more readily (see von Hirsch 1994a:45–48). But this still would constitute some kind of modification of a desert theory—perhaps not so dissimilar to desert-based hybrids discussed above.

Tonry's proposal is motivated in part by concern for the deprived. Treating desert only as a ceiling, he hopes, will facilitate the giving of mitigated sentences to socially deprived offenders. However, mitigation might also be permissible under a desert model—to the extent it could be established that deprivation affects offenders' culpability (von Hirsch 1993:106–8). Granting wider scope to nondesert considerations will not necessarily aid such persons: to the extent those considerations are crime preventative, the deprived may be deemed higher risks and hence ineligible for lenient treatment. Moreover, extensive penalty reductions for deprived offenders are likely to encounter formidable political obstacles, irrespective of any theory.

JUSTIFYING PUNITIVENESS?

Proportionality and Punitiveness

Does proportionalism justify or lead to harsher sanctions? The idea of proportionality does not itself prescribe harsher punishments; indeed, it permits considerable reduction in sanction levels [see discussion above and von Hirsch (1993:chs. 5 and 10)]. Several of the jurisdictions that have relied on proportionality as guiding rationale have succeeded either in reducing penalty levels (as Finland has since 1976), or in limiting penalty increases (Sweden, Oregon, and albeit somewhat less successfully in recent years, Minnesota).[8] The systems calling for large penalty increases—for example, the U.S. Sentencing Commission's guideline scheme for federal crimes—tend explicitly or implicitly to reject the idea of proportionality (see, more fully, von Hirsch 1993:91–94).

But is this a sufficient answer? Even if proportionalism has no direct causal links to tougher sanctions, the theory does focus on penal deprivations. (Indeed, it is largely concerned with *how much* deprivation can be visited for various crimes.) Once we admit that punishment should be about "pain delivery," in Nils Christie's phrase, are we not legitimating the infliction of suffering? And once suffering is legitimized, what is to stop more from being inflicted?

It should be borne in mind, however, that a just-deserts theory does not need to be about pain delivery as an end in itself. It is only traditional retributivism that insists that deprivation is the only conceivably justified response to wrongdoing. Current desert theories—including R. A. Duff's (1986) and my own (von Hirsch 1993, ch. 2)—place much more emphasis on punishment's function of expressing *censure* for criminal acts. The shift to censure is important, because it permits significant reductions in punishment levels, so long as these adequately express blame for the conduct involved. Indeed, I have recently argued that high pain levels interfere with penal censure's moral functions: the higher overall penalty levels rise, the less the normative reasons for desistence supplied through penal censure will matter, and the more penal sanction becomes merely a system of threats (pp. 13, 41–45).

Proportionalism does call attention to the deprivations of punishment, by insisting that comparative sanction severities reflect the gravity of the conduct involved. However, insisting on this scrutiny might help induce greater awareness of the hurt one is visiting on the offender. Consider the sanction of probation. This was once considered not really a punishment at all, but as help to the offender. Benign as that "help" was supposed to be, it could be quite burdensome (involving, for example, residential custody in drug treatment facilities). Insisting on proportionality can make one aware of the pains involved in such a sentence.

Is this not too optimistic? Perhaps a greater awareness of the penal content of punishments will make the tender-hearted more careful about inflicting pain. But what of the uncompassionate—the proponents of law and order? Will they not utilize the greater awareness of punishments' severities precisely in order to advocate harsher sanctions?

Interestingly, however, today's law-and-order advocates have not flown retributivist colors. To the extent any theory is invoked, it is crime preventive and instrumentalist: what should count is not what criminals purportedly deserve, but how "decent, law-abiding citizens" can best be protected from victimization. Given this instrumentalist emphasis, it is not surprising that conservative penal theorists such as James Q. Wilson advocate deterrent- or incapacitation-based penal strategies, not those of desert (1983:ch. 8).

Indeed, desert theory has features that the penological right finds positively objectionable. Proportionalism, with its emphasis on the degree of gravity of the current offense, restricts the ability to impose markedly higher penalties on recidivists who are deemed greater risks. Moreover, the theory's emphasis on equity toward offenders is suspect: it is said that the penal system should pay more attention to protection of the law-abiding, and less attention to the rights of lawbreakers. Ernest van den Haag, one of today's most committedly right-wing penologists, exemplifies this way of thinking. In an earlier volume (van den Haag, 1975), he flirted with the idea of retribution: his book attempted to combine deterrence with desert to produce a policy of scaled, tough sentences. Soon thereafter, however, he became skeptical of desert as an undue limitation of the state's punitive power. Indeed, he now takes that skepticism to its logical conclusion, holding that an offender has *no* legitimate equity claims regarding the severity or character of his punishment, once he has voluntarily submitted himself to the risk of being punished through his decision to offend (van den Haag 1987).

Punitiveness and the Politics of Resentment

It is worth questioning, however, whether law-and-order initiatives are really designed to achieve *any* substantive policy objectives. Perhaps, the aim is not so much to prevent crime or punish as deserved, but rather to give expression to (and exploit) popular resentment of crime and criminals. Consider these well-known instances:

- In the 1988 presidential election campaign, George Bush made "toughness" the centerpiece of his campaign strategy. Most notable was his use of the Willie Horton case in the presidential debates: attacking his Democratic opponent for furloughing a black prisoner who went on to assault a white woman. Bush offered no specific recommendations on crime himself and, indeed, seemed little interested in the issue. What he was doing was appealing to public animus about crime and feelings about race.
- Once elected, Bush did put forward a crime "policy"—the so-called

war on drugs. It was claimed that harsh penalties would deter drug use (Office of National Drug Control Policy 1989). The effort did succeed in raising sanction levels spectacularly for drug crimes at both the federal and state levels. Judged as a policy initiative, the war on drugs has been a failure: it has not reduced lower-class drug consumption, but has badly aggravated prison overcrowding. But one wonders whether the initiative was ever meant to be judged by such policy-oriented standards. Perhaps the aim was simply to single out for harsh treatment a particularly unpopular group of offenders—lower-class (often black) drug dealers and users.

- In 1994, a number of U.S. jurisdictions enacted "three strikes and you're out" laws that would impose lifelong (or extremely lengthy) confinement upon the third conviction for a "violent" felony. The harshest of these measures, adopted in California, sweeps in much more than violent acts: intermediate, nonviolent offenses such as residential burglaries count as strikes, and the third offense may be *any* felony. As a result, someone convicted twice of burglary will receive nearly lifetime incarceration[9] on the subsequent theft of, say, a bicycle. On its merits, the legislation is scarcely credible—its main effect will be to incarcerate huge numbers of lesser repeat offenders for long periods. But perhaps the measure's point is political rather than programmatic. California's law was approved by popular initiative along with another striking instance of the politics of resentment: a measure that would bar medical care and schooling to illegal immigrants and their children.

- Beginning in 1993, the Conservative government of the United Kingdom began adopting strident law-and-order postures. The new home secretary, Michael Howard, announced a twenty-seven-point plan for toughening criminal policy. The points constituted a grab-bag of ideas ranging from restricting the right to silence in criminal trials to punishing those who interfere with fox hunting.[10] The new law-and-order rhetoric was accompanied by denunciation of a variety of other unpopular groups, such as single mothers and foreigners.

What is different about such initiatives is not that they involve political posturing (which politicians have always indulged in), but that substantive criminal policy objectives have been marginalized so much. [For the nonprogrammatic character of much mandatory-minimum legislation in much of the United States, see Tonry (1992).] Trying to blame such initiatives on this or that penological theory makes little sense, as law-and-order rhetoricians need no penal theory in order to advocate harsher responses. Doubtless, there is a kind of instrumental rationality involved: appeals to resentment can be the means for obtaining or maintaining political power.

But it is an instrumentalism that is far from criminologists' traditional concerns about the effectiveness of penal measures [on this theme, see also von Hirsch (1994b)].

Law-and-order politics, indeed, impede efforts to scale penalties proportionately to the seriousness of crimes. This is because the demand for tougher penalties tends to be opportunistic and nonsystematic. At any given moment, it is only selected types of crimes or criminals that attract public attention, and it is those crimes and criminals that are targeted for increased punishments. In recent decades, we have seen a veritable parade of crimes of the moment: drunken driving, child and spouse abuse, and drug dealing. As each of these species of specially disfavored conduct comes into the limelight, it is urged that it be punished with exemplary harshness—that is, out of all relation with the sanctions imposed on equally or more-serious conduct that is not so much in public consciousness. California's "three strikes" legislation, just referred to, is just the most dramatic example of such disproportionate sanctions.

In his article in the present volume, David Rothman charges that the liberal reform efforts of the 1970s—particularly the liberals' espousal of explicit guidance for sentencing decisions—were in part responsible for recent rises in punishment levels in the United States. He argues, essentially, that it was such reform efforts that legitimated restraints on sentencing discretion; that such restraints have since been used to increase penalties; and that in the absence of the reforms, sentencing would still be discretionary today, and hence not so easily escalated.

In actual fact, the chief vehicle for raising sentence levels throughout the United States has been the mandatory minimum sentence, which is in no sense a by-product of liberal reforms (see Tonry 1992). (The mandatory minimum was effectively initiated by the Rockefeller drug laws, which were adopted in New York at the outset of the 1970s—well before guidelines and comparable sentence-reform measures became influential[11]) Rothman's examples of the impact of sentencing guidelines are also highly selective. Of the four major sentencing guideline systems that have been in effect for some time in the United States, Rothman ignores the two (those of Oregon and Minnesota) that have had significant success in braking rises in imprisonment levels, and focuses on the one system that did significantly raise penalty levels (and indeed seems to have been designed to do so), namely, the federal system.

Rothman's thesis concerning the bad effects of the 1970s sentencing reforms would also imply, if correct, that jurisdictions resisting those reforms should have had greater success in keeping penalty levels from rising. But that has not been the case—as the experience of New York State plainly indicates. New York did not adopt sentencing guidelines (indeed, it considered and rejected them in the mid-1980s). Toughness on crime has been, however, a major theme in the state's politics. Not surprisingly, pressures for toughness have led to greatly raised penalty levels: prison populations in the state have more than doubled during the last decade alone.

Rothman's thesis rests on the assumption that the penological right can achieve its aims only by taking advantage of liberal reforms and turning them to its own purposes. If something goes amiss, it must be because liberals unwisely have espoused one particular kind of reform rather than another. This perspective, however, overestimates the extent to which progressive reformers control the criminal justice agenda. The politics of resentment have not needed liberal reforms to legitimate the quest for harsher punishment. The appeal is to the public's loathing of criminals, and the policy mechanisms can be quite varied—ranging from a policy of denouncing "lenient" judges to enactment of harsh habitual offender laws. "Three-strikes-and-you're-out" legislation is not a co-optation of some benevolently minded penal measure; it draws its force, instead, from popular images of habitually violent criminals and from sporting analogies.

"NEGATIVISM"

Another kind of worry about proportionalist sentencing theory has concerned its seeming negativism. It provides, at most, a fairer distribution of the pains of punishment. Positive benefits are not offered.

Rehabilitation purported to satisfy all interests: the citizenry would benefit through reduced recidivism, and the offender would gain through programs aimed at his needs. Whether rehabilitative programs in fact were so designed is doubtful: traditionally, their criterion of success has been whether recidivism is reduced; such a reduction helps *us* but does not necessarily aid the offender himself. Nevertheless, much of the rehabilitative ideal's attractiveness lay in its apparent commitment to "doing good."

With the decline of rehabilitationism as the dominant penal rationale, the desire for a happy ending has not disappeared. Another conception has been emerging: restorative justice. Crime is perceived as conflict. The response to crime should seek to resolve that conflict: to compensate the victim, give the perpetrator insight into the injuriousness of his conduct, and reassure other citizens.

I shall not attempt here to assess the merits of restorative-justice conceptions in any detail—a considerable literature already exists on this subject (see, e.g., van Ness 1993; Ashworth 1993; Ashworth and von Hirsch 1993; Zedner 1994). Suffice it to say that I am skeptical. Most crimes do not seem to me to be "conflicts" in any ordinary sense. I wonder whether "reassurance" of the citizenry can be made to amount to much more than crime control under a new name. Above all, I perceive in the literature of restorativism that fatal combination, once apparent in traditional rehabilitationism, of excessive ambitiousness about ends and insufficient specification of means and limits. The aims of restorativism are to compensate the victim *and* reintegrate the offender *and* repair bonds of community ruptured by the offense. However, the means—how exactly this felicitous combination of ends is to be achieved—are left sketchy, at best. And the limits on permissible intervention—to what degree the offender's rights may be intruded upon—are not delineated in comprehensible, principled fashion. And with this lack of specificity about means, limits, and amounts comes the familiar problem of insufficient guidance: it is difficult to know what kind of responses, to what kind of offenses and offenders, would and would not be appropriate under restorativism.[12]

Such skepticism, however, does not diminish the force of the desire for a more "positive" response to crime. If restorative justice fades because of its intrinsic problems and limitations of practical application, we can expect some other idea that purports to combine offender interests and societal interests. And, from those who find such ideas attractive, we can expect a continuing sense of discomfort with the "negativism" of the desert model.

THE PROSPECTS: UNITED STATES AND EUROPE

In what direction might thinking about sentencing policy go in the next decade? Predictions are hazardous, but let me venture some guesses. The prognosis is different in the United States than in some European jurisdictions, such as England and Sweden.

The United States

Historically, U.S. state and federal jurisdictions had the most fragmented sentencing systems of all: each judge had virtually untrammeled sentencing discretion, subject to no appellate review of his or her sentence. Thus an observer might have expected the greatest obstacle to change to be judges' reluctance to accept limitations on that discretion. Surprisingly, this has not been the case. Prescriptive sentencing standards designed to alter sentencing practice have been widely adopted: sentencing guidelines in a few jurisdictions, mandatory minimum sentences in many others. The judiciary has not been able or willing to block such initiatives—even though its discretion has thereby been restricted.

The major impediment to sentencing reform has, instead, been law-and-order politics. Testimony to the latter's vitality is the near trebling of America's prison population in recent decades. Illustrative is the U.S. Sentencing Commission's guidelines for the federal courts. The guidelines were written during a period (the mid-1980s) when Congress repeatedly enacted draconian mandatory minima for drug crimes. The commission—whose members were appointed by Ronald Reagan—considered its mandate chiefly to be one of raising sentencing levels, and raise them it certainly did: the guidelines were designed to halve the use of probation in federal cases. Desert was explicitly jettisoned as an aim, and not surprisingly so—since it would have interfered with the exemplary punishment of specially disfavored types of conduct (particularly, drug crimes).[13] The federal experience, because of its visibility, has had a considerable demoralizing effect. In the eyes of many observers, explicit systemwide sentencing reform has become identified with the harsh federal guidelines [see, e.g., Alschuler (1991); Rothman (Chapter 3 in this volume)].

The more interesting story of sentencing guidelines is unfolding, however, in the states—as is documented in a recent survey by Tonry (1994a). In some state jurisdictions, law-and-order pressures (while still significant) are less overwhelming than at the federal level, and fiscal concerns support efforts to limit the use of imprisonment. There, systemwide sentencing reform continues to be pursued, and notions of proportionality continue to be influential. An example is the Oregon sentencing guidelines, which took effect in 1989. The guidelines rely primarily on the gravity of the current offense, and restrict the weight given to the criminal record. Imprisonment tends to be limited to violent crimes: armed robbery draws a presumptive prison sentence on the first offense, but burglary (with certain exceptions) does not (see von Hirsch 1995). The standards, at least to date, have had considerable success in limiting the growth of prison populations.[14] Some other states having guidelines also have achieved (admittedly more modest) successes in slowing down the rate of increase in growth (see Tonry 1994a:171–74).

Explicit guidance schemes have likewise been helpful in promoting noncustodial penalties. In Phoenix, Arizona, for example, the Vera Institute of Justice has set up a day fines system targeted at certain classes of felony offenders. For qualifying offenders, the number of fine units for various crimes is prescribed in a schedule, and depends chiefly on the gravity of the instant offense.

Efforts such as those just described, however, are feasible only in jurisdictions in which demands for toughness do not overwhelm other policy concerns. And they have not attracted much attention in the media, or even (sadly) in academic writings.

England and Sweden

In Britain and some other Northern European countries such as Sweden, the idea of proportionality has achieved a different status. The English 1991 Criminal Justice Act makes proportionality the primary criterion for deciding the use of imprisonment and of noncustodial punishments. The 1988 Swedish sentencing law sets forth statutory principles that are comparable to England's in their general approach, but are more fully and carefully delineated (Jareborg 1995). In both countries, the idea of proportionality occupies center stage in the academic discussions.

Why so? One reason is that proportionalism fits traditional English and Scandinavian thinking better. Sentencers have long been accustomed to the idea of an informal sentencing tariff: of sentences graded roughly according to crimes' seriousness. The tariff was left to the courts to develop, its details were not well delineated, and it was unsupported by a coherent, articulated rationale. The new thinking changes this, insofar as it provides an explicit rationale and calls for express statutory guiding principles to encourage maintenance of proportionality. But the basic idea of graded penalties is not so unfamiliar.

The English 1991 Criminal Justice Act's proportionality requirements were also designed to help limit growth in prison populations—a growth that was seen as creating significant fiscal problems. By emphasizing the gravity of the current criminal act, it was hoped, courts would be discouraged from imposing prison sentences on repeated perpetrators of lesser property offenses. By emphasizing proportionality in the selection of intermediate punishments, courts would be encouraged to target noncustodial penalties of the more onerous sort at crimes of middle-level gravity, and not at minor crimes. Indeed, prison populations did drop off in the months immediately following the effective date of the Act (NACRO, no date). Sweden has always used noncustodial sentences (especially day fines) for the more routine property offenses and other lesser infractions, and the 1988 reform legislation was designed to regulate that use and to avoid any increase in imprisonment levels. [Immediately after the effective date of the Swedish act, a modest decline in imprisonment levels did occur, see Jareborg (1995).]

Recently, the atmosphere has changed in both countries. The U.K. government (as I mentioned earlier) has made a *volte-face* in its public position on imprisonment policy. Judges and magistrates seem to be responding to the government's recent appeals for more toughness, so that imprisonment levels (after an initial decline), are now rising to approach previous levels. However, it is still too early to tell how much further impact the government's campaign will have.[15] Its pronouncements on the need for more imprisonment have drawn criticism from influential politicians, judges, and correctional officials.

What remains uncertain is the English judiciary's willingness to take seriously the principles set forth in the act. The Court of Appeal has already somewhat diluted the act's requirement that criminal conduct must be "serious" in order to warrant imprisonment, by holding that the conduct's prevalence and its supposed need for deterrence are elements of seriousness. Some recent decisions have recently treated fairly routine thefts as "serious" enough to warrant confinement.[16] Whether the court is willing to brake further erosions of the act's standards remains to be seen. However, the court is beginning to discuss concepts such as proportionality in its opinions, suggesting that the 1991 act is having at least some impact on judges' thinking.

In judging the English developments, a certain realism is advisable. The rate of prison commitments is likely to continue to rise and fall with the political mood—so that the present increases are scarcely surprising. What matters is the magnitude of any increase. If England can avoid drastic escalation in sanction levels of the kind that have accompanied American-style law and order, and if the 1991 act helps even modestly in discouraging prison use for lesser infractions and in making sentencing decisions more reasoned ones, then something positive will have been achieved.

Sweden also has witnessed a change of government policy. The 1991 elections were won by a conservative party that made its election slogan "Put criminals inside so you can go outside." That government (which held office for the next three years[17]) secured enactment of a postponement of parole eligibility from one-half to two-thirds for most prison sentences, which can be expected to add to prison populations (see von Hirsch 1993:101–2; Jareborg 1995). However, the government did not succeed in altering the basic principles set forth in the sentencing law. Judicial nullification is also less of a problem: the Swedish judiciary has a tradition of taking statutory formulations of policy seriously—and indeed, of examining and relying upon the legislative history of such provisions.

In conclusion, we can expect that proportionalism will continue to exercise influence on sentencing policy—although the degree of that influence will vary considerably among jurisdictions. One reason for that influence has been discussed at length already: the theory's usefulness as a practical way of scaling penalties. The other reason is the apparent insufficiency of known alternative conceptions. Punishment is deeply rooted enough as an institution to make a wholesale shift to a different (say, restorative) paradigm unlikely. And as long as punishment is the prevailing response, it will continue to seem practically and morally problematic to distribute sanctions chiefly on grounds other than the degree of reprehensibleness of the conduct.

The claim I am making, however, is a conditional one: that *to the extent* penological theory shapes sentencing policy at all, proportionalism will have continuing influence. Many jurisdictions will continue having no explicit guiding rationale at all—that is, they will leave sentencing in large part to judicial discretion, limited only by a variety of ad hoc precedents and rules. Certain jurisdictions that have moved cautiously toward systematic sentencing guidance might also revert to wide discretion and ad hoc responses—a result that (unfortunately) is not beyond the bounds of possibility in England. Still more troublesome a threat is law-and-order politics. To the extent such politics prevail, the achievement of proportionate penal responses must suffer—as will any kind of effort at rationality in sentencing policy. There is hope for sensible and decent penal measures only in places where the politics of resentment can be resisted, at least to a degree.

ACKNOWLEDGMENTS

My main debt in writing this article is to Sheldon L. Messinger, from whom I learned so much over the years about sentencing policy and its politics. I am grateful also for comments supplied by Andrew Ashworth, Estella Baker, Stanley Cohen, David Garland, and Lucia Zedner.

NOTES

1. For a description of these three systems, see for Finland, Lappi-Seppälä (1992); for Sweden, Jareborg (1995); and for England, Ashworth (1992).
2. See von Hirsch (1976), von Hirsch (1985), von Hirsch (1993).
3. For arguments favoring a deflation of sanction levels in fixing the penalty scale's anchoring points, see von Hirsch (1993:ch. 5).
4. For the difficulties in ascertaining Kant's penal views, see e.g., Murphy (1987).
5. For the issues relating to deterrence and rehabilitation as the basis for sentence, see von Hirsch and Ashworth (1992:chs. 1 and 2).
6. The term *new penology* is taken from Feeley and Simon (1992), who assert that an actuarial, risk-oriented penal practice has recently been developing—and

cite selective incapacitation as an example. However, such actuarial forecasting schemes have had surprisingly small impact on sentencing policy. There could be more scope for risk prediction in paroling policy, and Simon (1993) asserts that parole revocation policy in California has become strongly risk driven. Simon's study describes practices, however, that might be interpreted somewhat differently. He notes, for example, that the California parole authorities almost automatically reimprison offenders who have been arrested for new crimes (Ch. 7). Such an automatic revocation policy suggests, however, that the authorities are more concerned with avoiding exposure to potential public criticism then they are with trying to identify which parolees actually represent substantial risks to public safety.

7. I shall not go into these issues here, as each of them has been discussed elsewhere [for anchoring points, see von Hirsch (1993:ch. 5); for crime-seriousness, von Hirsch (1993:ch. 4) and von Hirsch and Jareborg (1991); for prior record, Wasik (1987), von Hirsch (1985:ch. 7), and von Hirsch (1991).

8. For the Swedish experience see Jareborg (1995); for that of Oregon and Minnesota, see von Hirsch (1994a), Frase (1995), and von Hirsch (1995).

9. The specified penalty is twenty-five years to life, with only 20 percent off for good behavior.

10. Several of these proposals, including restrictions on the right to silence and provisions on fox hunting, became law as part of the Criminal Justice and Public Order Act of 1994.

11. The Rockefeller drug laws took effect in September 1973. Most of the reformist literature on guidance for sentencing, such as *Doing Justice* (von Hirsch 1976), did not appear until middecade. The first sentencing commission guidelines, those of Minnesota, were written still later: Minnesota's standards took effect in 1980.

12. There is today, and will continue to be, a variety of programmatic experiments influenced by ideas of restorative justice—most notably, victim-offender mediation schemes. Such experiments, however, are usually backed by the possibility of recourse to traditional punishment—a recourse that can be invoked, for example, for more serious offenses or for offenders refusing to cooperate with restorative schemes. Such recourse would no longer be possible, if restorative justice were really to become (as its proponents urge) a new paradigm replacing punishment.

13. For analyses of the federal sentencing guidelines, see von Hirsch (1989), Doob (1995), and Roberts (1994).

14. However, a popular initiative approved during the 1994 elections created mandatory minima for a number of violent offenses, which are likely to add somewhat to the prison population. Minnesota, on the other hand, may be going in the opposite direction—toward modest penalty reductions. A proposal by the Sentencing Guidelines Commission, made in late 1994 at the prompting of the legislature, would reduce the sentence levels for a number of crimes—including some drug and property crimes. Whether the proposal survives remains to be seen.

15. In 1993, the Conservative government did succeed in having repealed one provision of the 1991 Criminal Justice Act that restricted reliance on prior criminality in deciding sentence, and in replacing it with vaguer language. It remains to be seen how the courts will respond to this change. [For an argument why the new language

still should significantly restrict the use of prior criminal history, see Wasik and von Hirsch (1994).]
16. For a discussion and critique of these Court of Appeal cases, see Ashworth (1994).
17. The conservative coalition lost to the Social Democrats in September 1994.

REFERENCES

Alschuler, Albert. 1991. "The Failure of Sentencing Guidelines: A Plea for Less Aggregation." *University of Chicago Law Review* 58:901–51.
Ashworth, Andrew. 1992. *Sentencing and Criminal Justice*. London: Weidenfeld & Nicholson.
———. 1993. "Some Doubts about Restorative Justice." *Criminal Law Forum* 4:277–99.
———. 1994. Editorial. *Criminal Law Review*:153–55.
Ashworth, Andrew and Andrew von Hirsch. 1993. "Desert and the Three R's." *Current Issues in Criminal Justice* 5:9–12.
Canadian Sentencing Commission. 1986. *Sentencing Reform: A Canadian Approach*. Ottawa: Canadian Government Publishing Centre.
Doob, Anthony. 1995. "The United States Sentencing Commission Guidelines." In *The Politics of Sentencing Reform*, edited by R. Morgan and C. Clarkson. Oxford: Oxford University Press.
Duff, R. A. 1986. *Trials and Punishments*. Cambridge: Cambridge University Press.
———. 1995. "Penal Communications: Recent Work in the Philosophy of Punishment." *Crime and Justice: A Review of Research* 20:(forthcoming).
Feeley, Malcolm and Jonathan Simon. 1992. "The New Penology: Notes on the Emerging Strategy of Corrections and Its Implications." *Criminology* 30: 449–74.
Frase, Richard. 1995. "Sentencing Guidelines in Minnesota and Other American States: A Progress Report." In *The Politics of Sentencing Reform*, edited by R. Morgan and C. Clarkson. Oxford: Oxford University Press.
Garland, David. 1990. *Punishment and Modern Society*. Oxford: Oxford University Press.
Jareborg, Nils. 1995. "The Swedish Sentencing Reform." In *The Politics of Sentencing Reform*, edited by R. Morgan and C. Clarkson. Oxford: Oxford University Press.
Lappi-Seppälä, Tapio. 1992. "Penal Policy and Sentencing in Finland." *Canadian Journal of Law and Jurisprudence* 5:95–120.
Morris, Norval. 1982. *Madness and the Criminal Law*. Chicago: University of Chicago Press.
Murphy, Jeffrie G. 1987. "Does Kant Have a Theory of Punishment?" *Columbia Law Review* 87:509–32.
NACRO. No date. "The Criminal Justice Act 1991: Its Impact on Sentencing." London: National Association for the Care and Resettlement of Offenders.

National Research Council, Panel on Research on Criminal Careers. 1986. *Report.* In *Criminal Careers and "Career Criminals,"* vol. 1, edited by A. Blumstein, J. Cohen, J. Roth, and C. Visher. Washington, DC: National Academy Press.

Office of National Drug Control Policy. 1989. *National Drug Control Policy.* Washington, DC: Government Printing Office.

Roberts, Julian. 1994. "The Role of the Criminal Record in the Federal Sentencing Guidelines." *Criminal Justice Ethics* 13(1):21–30.

Simon, Jonathan. 1993. *Poor Discipline: Parole and the Social Control of the Underclass, 1890–1990.* Chicago: University of Chicago Press.

Thomas, D.A. 1979. *Principles of Sentencing.* London: Heinemann.

Tonry, Michael. 1992. "Mandatory Penalties." *Crime and Justice: A Review of Research* 16:243–73.

———. 1994a. "Sentencing Commissions and Their Guidelines." *Crime and Justice: A Review of Research* 17:137–95.

———. 1994b. "Proportionality, Interchangeability, and Intermediate Punishments." Pp. 59–83 in *Penal Theory and Penal Practice,* edited by R. Dobash, R. Dobash, R. A. Duff, and S. Marshall. Manchester: Manchester University Press.

van den Haag, Ernest. 1975. *Punishing Criminals: Concerning a Very Old and Painful Question.* New York: Basic Books.

———. 1987. "Punishment: Desert and Control." *Michigan Law Review* 85:1250–60.

Van Ness, Daniel. 1993. "New Wine and Old Wineskins: Four Challenges to Restorative Justice." *Criminal Law Forum* 4:251–76, 301–6.

von Hirsch, Andrew. 1976. *Doing Justice: The Choice of Punishments.* New York: Hill & Wang.

———. 1985. *Past or Future Crimes: Dangerousness and Deservedness in the Sentencing of Criminals.* New Brunswick, NJ: Rutgers University Press.

———. 1988. "Selective Incapacitation Reexamined: The National Academy of Sciences' Report on Criminal Careers and 'Career Criminals.'" *Criminal Justice Ethics* 7(1):19–35.

———. 1989. "Federal Guidelines: Do They Provide Principled Guidance?" *American Criminal Law Review* 27:367–90.

———. 1991. "Criminal Record Rides Again." *Criminal Justice Ethics* 10(2):2, 55–57.

———. 1993. *Censure and Sanctions.* Oxford: Oxford University Press.

———. 1994a. "Sentencing Guidelines and Penal Aims in Minnesota." *Criminal Justice Ethics* 13(1):39–49.

———. 1994b. "The Logic of Prison Growth" (review essay on N. Christie). *Modern Law Review* 57:476–82.

———. 1995. "Proportionality and Parsimony in U.S. Sentencing Guidelines: The Minnesota and Oregon Standards." In *The Politics of Sentencing Reform,* edited by R. Morgan and C. Clarkson. Oxford: Oxford University Press.

von Hirsch, Andrew and Andrew Ashworth (eds.). 1992. *Principled Sentencing.* Boston: Northeastern University Press.

von Hirsch, Andrew and Nils Jareborg. 1991. "Gauging Criminal Harm: A Living-Standard Analysis." *Oxford Journal of Legal Studies* 11:1–38.
Wasik, Martin. 1987. "Guidance, Guidelines, and Criminal Record." Pp. 105–25 in *Sentencing Reform: Guidance or Guidelines?* edited by M. Wasik and K. Pease. Manchester: Manchester University Press.
Wasik, Martin and Robert Taylor. 1994. *Blackstone's Guide to the Criminal Justice Act 1991*, rev. ed. London: Blackstone.
Wasik, Martin and Andrew von Hirsch. 1994. "Section 29 Revised: Previous Convictions in Sentencing." *Criminal Law Review*:409–18.
Wilson, James Q. 1983. *Thinking About Crime*, rev. ed. New York: Basic Books.
Zedner, Lucia. 1994. "Reparation and Retribution: Are They Reconcilable?" *Modern Law Review* 57:228–50.

IV
SOCIAL CONTROL:
Changing Strategies and Meanings

Besides being wider in scope than the fields of criminology or criminal justice studies, the rubric of social control also frees scholars from the constraints of policy relevance. Very practical matters can be studied—how courts reach decisions, what goes on in prisons, how drug laws are enforced—but from the luxurious vantage point of long-term contemplation. The social control literature has always been historically informed: sensitive to changes and trends, obsessed with either discovering the new or recovering the old.

These themes are explicitly addressed in the first two chapters of this section. In Chapter 10, Jonathan Simon and Malcolm Feeley summarize their much-discussed 1992 paper, which depicted the emergence of a "new penology." They then ask why there appears to be so little congruence between the internal professional-academic discourse and wider public opinion. This paper explicitly connects the terrain of criminal justice with wider political concerns in American society. In Chapter 11, David Garland, the author of major theoretical works in the sociology of punishment, is more skeptical about what is "new." He moves to a broader sociological canvas—the much-proclaimed era of postmodern society—only to find the residues of modernism in penal practice.

From the 1970s onward, feminist theories and movements have made a major impact on law and the social sciences. In the study of crime and punishment, feminist work has moved beyond showing the distorting results of leaving half the population out of the deviance control equation, to showing how the social control of women points to more general issues. Pat Carlen, a leading student of women criminals and prisoners in Britain, comes from this second phase of work. Her Chapter 12 is as much about the social control of women as about the general dichotomies that run through all strategies and meanings of social control: formal/informal, public/private, and exclusion/inclusion.

In a different way, Chapter 13 by David Matza and Patricia Morgan also launches from the specific to the general. No contemplation of crime control systems would be complete without paying attention to the subject of drug control. Societies have numbly accepted the major government resources devoted to the "war against drugs," its costs in human misery, and its impact on the administration of criminal justice (accounting for some two-thirds of the entire prison population). But are these social consequences inevitable? The allusion to Prohibition in Matza and Morgan's subtitle is not just a historical reference to the failed American experiment with controlling alcohol use, but an invitation to think about the whole logic of social control based on prohibition.

10
True Crime:
The New Penology and Public Discourse on Crime

JONATHAN SIMON and MALCOLM M. FEELEY

INTRODUCTION

One of the enduring themes in Sheldon L. Messinger's scholarship has attended to the internal ideologies through which the penal apparatus defines its own capacities and limits (see, e.g., Messinger 1969; Messinger and Berk 1987). It was in the spirit of that work (if not with Messinger's customary rigor) that in "The New Penology: Notes on the Emerging Strategy of Corrections and Its Implications" (Feeley and Simon 1992), we identified three emerging features of the criminal process that together we termed the *new penology*. This paper expands on these developments, and explores one of the anomalous results, the growing gulf between penology[1] and public discourse about crime and crime policy.[2] We begin by reviewing the central elements of these three features of penology, and then explore the growing disjuncture between public discourse, which remains anchored in the old penology, and professional discourse, which reflects the new penology.

Distinctive Features of the New Penology and
Their Implications

Discourses. The discourses of modern punishment have varied widely over time, from the language of religion and economics to psychology and social work, and more recently sociology. Despite significant differences among them, each of these discourses portrays crime primarily as a relationship between individuals and their communities. In contrast, we have argued, the language of the new penology is anchored in the discourse of systems analysis and operations research. It conceives of crime as a systemic phenomenon and crime policy as a problem of actuarial risk management. While traditional divisions within the penal field, like that between academics and professionals, remain relevant, the dispersal of new penology discourses cuts across this and many other traditional divides.

Objectives. The objectives of modern punishment have also varied over time. Early eighteenth-century reformers stressed certainty and proportionality of sanctions as a way of steering people away from crime. Nineteenth-century reformers developed penitentiaries for the purpose of reforming wayward souls. And in the early twentieth century, Progressive reformers produced a high modernist version of both these latter objectives, which aimed at adjusting the individual offender in his community. Our purpose here is not to argue that these objectives were achieved, but that as objectives they were widely *shared* by intellectuals, criminal justice policy makers, and the "public," that there was—at least in broad outline—something of a consensus about objectives among the various interested communities.

In contrast, the new penology reveals a shift away from the objective of transforming individuals. It embraces a new objective: risk management and the management of the system itself. To twist David Rothman's (1980) enduring phrase out of shape, in the new penology *convenience* has become the primary form of *conscience*.

Techniques. Modern penology has experimented with a host of techniques, ranging from the silent system in the new prisons of the 1830s, to heavy reliance on imprisonment in the late nineteenth century, to the invention of the indeterminate sentence, juvenile justice, parole, and probation in the Progressive Era (Rothman 1971, 1980; Simon 1993). Many recent innovations in technique build on this heritage. Boot camps, for example, are defended in moral terms reminiscent of the justification of the silent isolation in the cell 160 years ago. And intensive probation and parole seek in some ways to do with new technologies (electronic surveillance and drug testing) what Progressives sought to do through good casework.

Although we acknowledge that institutions are always in flux, in our earlier article we argued that these changes identified above, which have emerged over the last thirty or so years, represent the beginning of "a marked break with the past." The new penology represents an emerging new paradigm of thought and institutional practice.[3]

Theory as Map

This thesis has sparked vigorous debate. Some suggest our argument is merely a reformulation of long-standing dichotomies and debates over, say, clinical vs. quantitative prediction (Meehl 1954), or another version of the due process vs. crime control models (Packer 1968), or conscience vs. convenience (Rothman 1971, 1980). Others have pointed to earlier antecedents and argued that what we claim as new is in fact old (police have long engaged in "surveillance," public officials have long sought to "control" the "dangerous classes," and the like). Still others claim that we have missed the essential continuities between older and newer methods of punishment in general, and point to current penal practices and proposals and discourse in order to substantiate their position (Garland 1994).

We have found these criticisms helpful; they have forced us to broaden our inquiry, rethink the core features of our ideas, and probe what may be discontinuities between our analytic categories and reality. Still, we believe that the new penology provides a useful analytic grid in which to interpret the emerging set of practices, discourses, and objectives in the criminal process. This new formation (and not our interpretation of it) offers a way of thinking about and working within the criminal process that has important, if as yet unclear implications.

However, we are writing a history of the present. Our aim is not to describe a *completed* historical change. Rather our objective is to establish useful associations among different aspects of the contemporary penal landscape in order to reveal features that are not visible if examined one at a time. Thus the historical weakness of our "model" is not likely to prove fatal if it nevertheless serves as a heuristic device for interpreting emerging changes in discourse and practice.[4] For us the relevant questions are: Does the analytic grid suggested by the new penology help link, and therefore interpret, a variety of new practices? Does it provide a means for imposing even quasi-coherence on a wide variety of disparate new practices? Does it help identify emerging strategies or possibilities for strategic action within the present situation?[5]

Scholarship is, of course, populated by many would-be Moseses who point to perceived new Promised Lands only to find that they are mirages that evaporate upon closer inspection. Perhaps the new penology is such a mirage (although it is certainly no Promised Land). But the task at hand is to see if it is useful in interpreting emerging new ideas and practices.

In this paper we want to extend our analysis (and open ourselves further to the possibility of failure) by exploring one important but troublesome feature of the present situation in penality that we only touched on in our earlier article. Here we examine the new penology in terms of its relationship to the public discourse about crime and punishment. To state the point as sharply as possible at the outset: Why has the success of the new penology among insiders and specialists in criminal justice not been followed by a commensurate influence on public discourse?

Although there has always been a gap between professional and public discourse, this gap has not always been so great, and at times an agreement between scholars, reformers, and public opinion leaders has facilitated significant reforms. For example, during the Progressive Era, which we consider below, the media, political leaders, and criminal justice professionals shared common assumptions and a mutual interest in diagnosing problems and presenting reforms. Ideas like the indeterminate sentence and juvenile justice were lauded not only by professionals in their journals, but in the writings of journalists and crusading community leaders, who drew on professional penology to offer the public compelling portraits of crime and programs to deal with it.

Of course, there have always been policies and institutions that have been greeted skeptically by the public (e.g., parole), and there have been periods of widespread criticism of corrections and the criminal process. Still, these criticisms must be seen in the context of a broader influence of penology through narratives of crime and its control that helped guide institutional innovation and helped foster a reserve of political legitimacy for crime policies even in periods of strain.

An essential ingredient in that earlier relationship in the Progressive Era is a set of representations of crime and criminals that link "scientific" theories and popular treatments of the problem.[6] Like "the recidivist," who has haunted the public imagination for over a century, the best of these representations allowed professional discourses, practices, and objectives to be inserted in the political process. That is, professional representations helped shape public understanding and pubic debate about crime and crime policy.

What seems striking today is the virtual absence of successful new representations of crime. Current penology provides neither policies that succeed nor words that succeed (Edelman 1977). It not only does not "solve" the crime problem, it does not even provide reassurances that something significant is being done. Indeed the successful advancement of a new program for managing crime and criminals must be accompanied by a compelling account of the crime problem, its measure, and what can be done about it (Simon 1993).[7] As David Garland has argued, penality provides an inevitable cultural and narrative side (Garland 1990). If so, one function of policy discourse is to provide a culturally satisfying account of social problems, and assurances that they are "being taken care of." To date, however, the new penology has not provided such a compelling or culturally satisfying story about crime and how to deal with it. It has not (yet) succeeded in producing a viable *truth about crime*. Instead contemporary policy discourse is a recirculation of older representations, which do not fit very well within the language or concepts of the new penology. Indeed the representations produced by the new penology probably heighten anxiety about crime, since they focus on system management and offer no compelling moral vision through which to define problems. Indeed they often call attention to the problems of the system itself.

THE NEW PENOLOGY AND THE PROBLEM OF PUBLIC OPINION

In the United States, it is generally conceded that public opinion, stoked by "moral entrepreneurs," drives much public policy, crime policy included (Gusfield 1963; Scheingold 1991). Thus "moral panics" and strong pressures to "do something" are often thought to be the proximate causes of increases in sentence severity, increases in prison size and population, additional mandatory minimum sentences, calls for reintroduction of the death penalty, "three strikes and you're out" laws, and the like (Hall, Critcher, Jefferson, Clarke, and Roberts 1979; Scheingold 1991; Gordon 1990; Currie 1987). Still, the programs of insiders—their discourses, techniques, and objectives—have always had a relationship to such moral panics.

The Secret of Life of Experts

The rapid penetration of the new penology among insiders would lead one to expect to see a parallel development in public discourse of crime. Yet public discourse during this period has been rooted in fear, moralism, individualism, and the belief in the efficacy of punishment that has long been the hallmark of public rhetoric about crime in the United States, and not the language of the new penology. As we observed in our 1992 article, "[t]he new penology is found among criminal justice practitioners and the research community. However, it certainly has not (yet) emerged as a hegemonic strategy for crime and crime policy" (Feeley and Simon 1992:451).

Surely it is no surprise that public discourse about crime differs from expert discourse—the two diverge in most areas of policy. In virtually every aspect of public policy, public discourse stresses values and emotional appeals, while expert discourse emphasizes operational questions that public discourse ignores. Being attentive to these distinctions illuminates the process of policy formation and implementation, as David J. Rothman's (1980) seminal analysis of "conscience" and "convenience" in the Progressive Era revealed. But the same analysis makes clear that the key to mobilizing resources and power for policy institutions is the ability of players in both professional and public discourse to formulate common, or at least complementary, positions.

As Murray Edelman (1967, 1977) has argued, one of the major functions of discourse about public policies, and indeed the policies themselves, is to present a coherent "understanding" of a social problem that provides a satisfactory diagnosis and a comforting solution. In Edelman's phrase, words can succeed even though policies fail (1977), i.e., images generated by public policies can create a sense of confidence that problems are being attended to even when little or no concrete progress is made. This is true in the criminal process as well. As David Garland has observed:

the success of the penal-welfare strategy—a success which has allowed its persistence for nearly a century—is not, then, the reform of offenders or the prevention of crime. It is its ability to administer and manage criminality in an efficient and extensive manner while portraying that process in terms which make it acceptable to the public and penal agents alike. (1985:260)

If Edelman and Garland are correct, then one function of penology is to provide a reassuring account of crime policy. This does not necessarily mean a reassuring lullaby, but a sense of coherence and a seriousness of purpose. For instance, our confidence in medicine, while sullied by debates over the quality and cost of care, is rather high, even though many of us will die sooner than we think we ought to. We know that medicine sometimes fails, but still there is a consensus—shared both by the medical community and the public at large—that the basic account medicine gives about health (though not perhaps its delivery system) is good enough. There is no crisis in the *concept* of medicine.[8]

Indeed, most puzzling of all about the present discourse on crime policy is that the penal system has grown dramatically over the last decade and a half despite the failure of the insider discourse to influence public discourse in ways that it did in earlier eras. Americans responding to surveys show no greater confidence in their criminal justice institutions than they did twenty years ago; despite this, during the past twenty years they have voted for politicians who have promised and delivered a massive expansion (U.S. Department of Justice, Bureau of Justice Statistics 1992a:96–7).

Professionals at the Plate

This gap between insiders and the public—or, put another way, the failure of the new penology to influence popular discourse—was highlighted in 1994 by the rapid success across the United States of a variety of "three-strikes-and-you're-out" laws, measures that impose life sentences for repeat offenders.[9] The attachment of the baseball slogan[10] to the longstanding idea of life sentences for repeat offenders was conceived by Mike Reynolds, a Southern California businessman whose daughter was brutally murdered by a man with a long string of prior convictions. The movement (if it can be called that) received massive press attention in 1991 after another murder, that of Polly Klaas of Sonoma County, California, an elementary school student whose kidnapping from her own home during a slumber party and subsequent slaying horrified people across the nation.

The basic pitch was that a lot of violent crimes were committed by a handful of repeat offenders who continued to receive light sentences, and that it made sense to crack down on them.[11] Within months of the Klaas murder a number of states and the federal government had embraced some version of a three-strikes law.[12] Although some police officials and prosecutors tended to support these measures, many criminal justice insiders—policy intellectuals and administrators—opposed them. Many of these opponents pointed out that these new laws required either massive tax increases and/or huge shifts in funds away from other public programs, such as education and welfare.[13]

This spate of three-strikes laws, as well as other types of mandatory sentences, can easily be characterized as mindless "spending sprees" or "throwing money at a problem" without likelihood of benefit. Indeed, such spending for crime control is probably as good a case as one can find for the proposition that government spending may make people worse off than if they were simply given an equal amount of money to spend themselves. Despite all this, such counterarguments, even when advanced by "credible" spokespeople like police chiefs and prison wardens, have not even risen to the volume of a whisper in *public* discourse about crime and corrections. Indeed public officials cannot easily raise such concerns without running the risk of being labeled "soft on crime" and thus committing political suicide.

To take but one example, California—a state staggering from budget crisis to budget crisis, and the birthplace of the taxpayers' revolts of the 1970s—recently enacted an extreme version of the three-strikes-and-you're-out legislation. Indeed state legislators clambered over each other to proclaim support of the toughest of four bills that had been introduced. And once adopted, this law was quickly signed by the governor with ceremony. The voices of professionals who questioned its wisdom were all but drowned out by the chorus of supporters. This sweeping version of the three-strikes bill was embraced with near unanimity by state legislators, despite the state's acute fiscal crisis and despite the fact that the state's own corrections department estimated the action would nearly double its exiting two-billion-dollar budget by 2004.

Fear Itself

One possible explanation for the lack of influence of experts on public discourse about crime is fear itself. If the public has gotten itself truly worked up about crime, the public will support intensifying efforts even if they are skeptical that the efforts are really all that good. In times of fear, people may retreat to the most traditional responses. Although imprisonment was once revolutionary, it has become our traditional punishment of choice. Indeed, it is all but synonymous with punishment. So even if the public is skeptical about the efficacy of imprisonment, it may be that it is seen as the only alternative and thus worth investing in despite reservations.

If this interpretation is correct, the questions are: What accounts for such intense fear? And what accounts for the dramatic increase in fear in recent years? Shifts in levels of fear of crime are not well-understood, and the answers to such questions are both complex and incomplete.[14] But one important piece of the puzzle is well-charted if not well-understood: the intensity of public concern with crime is not directly or strongly related to the magnitude of crime. Indeed in recent years, concern about crime has increased despite a decline in overall rates of victimization (U.S. Department of Justice, Bureau of Justice Statistics 1993b:11). To be sure, some groups have experienced significant increases; young people from twelve to fifteen years of age, for example, experienced a 34 percent increase in violent crime victimizations during the 1980s (U.S. Department of Justice, Bureau of Justice Statistics 1992b:11). And citizens of our poorest inner-city neighborhoods, in particular young African-American males, have experienced significant increases in violence over the past decade. Still, the groundswell of support for more and more punitive crime measures in recent years has come after a decade of steady or declining crime rates for suburban middle-class whites, that segment of the population from which the strongest support for new get-tough measures comes. Why is this group, which in other respects seems relatively insensitive to the well-being of people in communities distanced from themselves by poverty and race, and which is otherwise so skeptical of increases in government expenditures, so responsive to threats that in an objective sense affect them less now than at any time in recent memory? And why, when they generally resist increased government spending, are they willing to support vast new expenditures for crime control measures of dubious efficacy?

Fear by itself is an inherently unsatisfying explanation for the formation of recent crime policy. Indeed, it is difficult to explain the fear itself, in its own right. And the very lack of any clear correspondence between objective risk and fear suggests that discourse, including the discourse of crime and penality, must be a fundamental input to fear itself, along with factors such as neighborhood disorder (Skogan 1990), economic anxiety, and changes in racial demographics (Jackson 1989).

Thus we face the issue: much crime policy, and certainly much public discourse about crime policy, is framed in traditional terms that do *not* reflect the new penology. Furthermore, unlike earlier eras in which they took an active role in articulating and shaping public opinion on crime policy, criminal justice professionals are now on the fringes. Their discourse—expressed in varying degrees in terms of the new penology—has barely penetrated and has not even begun to shape public debate. And when upon occasion the discourse is heard, it is usually ignored, resented, or ridiculed. Or it is rephrased within the language of the old penology. Penal reform has never proceeded by advancing proven solutions for crime.

But at times it has succeeded in producing culturally satisfying accounts that have gained widespread public acceptance, and have legitimated crime policy and helped shape its formulation. The language of the new penology has not done even this.

PROGRESSIVE PENOLOGY AND ITS REPRESENTATIONS

It is, of course, problematic to divide history into precise periods. History flows continuously, and it is impossible to provide a wholly convincing account of why it should be broken up into distinct periods. Still, it is useful to distinguish three eras in American history during which "professional" penology succeeded in capturing the public imagination: the Jacksonian era (1830s), the Progressive Era (1880–1920), and the postwar era (1944–1973). Each era was characterized by the emergence of new and powerful representations of crime and its solutions which understood crime policy as a quest for national destiny. There is rich historical work on the first two of these eras, both for the United States (Rothman 1971; Melossi and Pavarini 1981; Rafter 1990) and parallel movements in Europe (Foucault 1977; Ignatieff 1978). However, the postwar era is just now beginning to be the subject of scholarly analysis (Cohen 1985; Scheingold 1991; Walker 1993; Simon 1993).

It is not our purpose to summarize this work here, but we do want to emphasize one of its central lessons: penal reform has a politics, a politics of cultural imagery and national identity (Scheingold 1991), just as much as it has a politics of coalitions built on conscience and convenience (Rothman 1980). Below we briefly survey the cultural imagery of the Progressive Era, and contrast it with the imagery of the current era. This contrast is useful, we think, because the scope of the Progressives' success was great and their institutional legacy remains potent today.

Progressive Representations of Crime

There is broad agreement that the last two decades of the nineteenth century and the first two decades of the twentieth constituted a distinctive period of self-conscious social reforms, both in the United States, where the period is known as the Progressive Era, and in Europe, where the foundations for the modern welfare state were laid.[15] One measure of the success of the Progressives' agenda is that it developed representations that captured the essence of its policies and as well permeated and affected popular discourse. David Rothman (1980) has identified three of its most successful representations, and argued that their popularity helped facilitate acceptance of its criminal justice reform policies. They are the ideas of (1) a "delinquency area," (2) the "individual" delinquent, and (3) the "born criminal." We explore the significance of each.

Delinquency Areas. One of the most enduring representations of the crime problem to emerge from Progressive penology was the criminogenic neighborhood. If one had to give a name to the picture that was drawn, it might be "delinquency area," a phrase coined by Chicago School sociologists and Progressive intellectuals Robert Park and Ernest Burgess, who used it to describe certain urban neighborhoods with different waves of ethnic composition and high levels of crime (Shaw 1929). This was more than just a theory about crime causation, although it borrowed and extended environmental theories of criminogenesis that extend back into the nineteenth century. This potent representation centered on the *ghetto* or *slum*, which at the turn of the century was just beginning to be viewed as an endemic feature of American cities swollen as they were with new immigrants from Southern and Eastern Europe. The representation was of an infected environment physically shaped by pathological forces (brought over from Southern and Eastern Europe in part), which in turn reinfected its denizens.

Although frightening, this representation was also optimistic. As Rothman observes:

> The problem was manageable: it could be located spatially in the ghetto and it could be solved, given the right programs. The bad news all related to the immigrant slums. The good news was that the rest of American society was strong, prosperous, and stable. (1980:52)

In addition to the social scientists who coined the expression delinquency area, journalists, novelists, and politicians all borrowed the image to make their own cases for national action. This idea—and the solution it implied—came to shape public perception of both the diagnosis of the problem of crime and its solution. The goal was to inoculate the new immigrant, to educate him, to turn him into a new American, and thus to remove and to immunize him from the diseases of the delinquency areas.

Individual Delinquents. A second important metaphor Rothman (1980) identifies is that of the "individual delinquent." In his conception (the term comes from the title of an important book by William Healy (1915), which David Rothman sees as a near-perfect exemplar of Progressive penality), the criminal is understood as the product of a specific developmental history that leads to deviance and eventually lawbreaking (Rothman 1980:55; Simon 1994). Popular acceptance of this notion helped facilitate support for new programs that would diagnose and treat individuals with abnormalities in order to transform them into healthy productive citizens.

Born Criminals. A third metaphor used in Progressive criminology was the "born criminal." This idea was first expounded by the Italian criminologist Cesare Lombroso to capture an inherently and permanently crime-prone individual, but it gained its deepest following in the United States (Rothman 1980), where it was used successfully to justify lengthy prison terms. Through education, a new community of immigrants could be taught to lose the bad habits of the Old World. Through treatment, the pathologies of the maladjusted individual could be cured. But for the born criminal, a lengthy prison term was the only solution. This representation of the born criminal was not an isolated concept. It was compatible with the then-powerful eugenic movement, which was so concerned about the racial makeup of the United States. Lengthy indeterminate sentences for born criminals promised to interrupt the biological reproduction of a criminal class.

Each of these three representations of crime was closely matched with prototypical stories that reformers used to describe problems and promote new programs. Each borrowed from the discourses of medicine, social work, and the emerging human sciences. Each implied a diagnosis of a problem as well as a solution to it. As Rothman (1980) pointed out, these representations accommodated a host of different stories about crime. The criminal, as victim of the rotten environment could receive the necessary change of conditions so that he could escape a criminal life. The criminal, as psychologically maladjusted, could be treated and cured. And the biologically doomed born criminal could be locked away for life. The widespread appeal and acceptance of these representations go a long way toward explaining the successes of the Progressive reformers.[16]

Each of these Progressive ideas was anchored in a belief in individualization. Each built upon earlier eighteenth-century penal reforms that also celebrated the individual in their press for uniform and transparent penalties (Ignatieff 1978; Garland 1985). And each reinforced reliance on the prison, which marked the individual as the central target of sanctions with its cellular structure and policies of penitent isolation and regimes of silence. However, these Progressive ideas reformulated the functions of the prison. As Garland (1985) has suggested, the eighteenth-century prisoner was conceived of as a black box, targeted, but not necessarily penetrated by penal ideologies. The distinctive contribution of the Progressives was that they penetrated the black box and in so doing endowed the criminal offender with social and psychological features—educatable, treatable, and at times incurable. With imprisonment, they sought to counteract the influences of a bad environment, correct the maladjusted psyche, and when necessary, permanently incarcerate the incorrigible. Such strategies required a strong and positive defense of discretion and a belief in professional expertise (Rothman 1980). Progressive penology vigorously sought both, and for the most part obtained them. The representations advanced by its professionals were widely embraced by the politicians and the public, and the policies that flowed from them were also embraced.

Progressive penology also implied distinct methodologies and epistemologies, and they too were embraced. One of the most important methods in these new sciences was case analysis: a potpourri of observation and interview developed in social work and medicine. Another was the ethnographic community study made famous by the Chicago school sociologists whose environmental accounts of crime constituted a plausible account of invisible networks of norms that shape life in definable communities. A third was the statistical study of inmates and parolees, also pioneered by Chicago sociologists, which measured recidivism and thus provided a basis for determining the success or failure of new rehabilitative techniques.

This epistemic base for Progressive penology was critical to winning support from the influential class of college-educated journalists and professionals who helped shape public opinion. The new human sciences represented modernity, and in their own way were representations of power that had great cultural resonance for the new professional class that emerged as a major force in American institutions in the early twentieth century.

What Worked?

David J. Rothman (1980), David Garland (1985), and others have documented the ideological success of Progressives in the United States and like-minded reformers in Europe, both in generating a compelling account of crime and punishment and in effecting a successful agenda for action. Both these scholars have shown how reform proposals were carefully crafted to reflect the distinct concerns of quite different factions within reform coalitions and to blur their many differences. Yet many ideological systems, ranging from Marxism-Leninism to Hare Krishna, have offered coherence and practical application without becoming successful programs of institutional power. A distinctive feature of Progressive penology was that it not only provided a more-or-less coherent view, it was also successful in shaping public discourse about crime, and thus crime policy itself. This was the result of how the discourse of shared aspirations and ideas appealed to different segments of the public. The Progressive alliance in the United States, and its equivalent in Europe, were based on class, religion, and social status (Hofstader 1955). Two factors seem particularly important in light of our concern with the contemporary situation and the new penology: the rise of the working class, and the use of penality to emphasize a form of nationalism based on the problem of the social.

Normalizing the Working Classes. While the Jacksonians formulated their penology largely out of repugnance for the urban poor whose ranks had been growing since colonial days (Dumm 1987), the Progressives responded to the rising tide of working-class political power. This new power was expressed in labor militancy and in the voting power of the white working class.[17] Historians have long stressed the roots of the Progressive movement: its humanistic principles and its basis in the growing power of the working class, and the interaction of the two. But the two are not exclusive of one another. U.S. Progressives and similarly situated Europeans recognized the task of creating social institutions capable of granting the working classes a measure of stability and a tangible (if limited) sense of entitlement to solutions to their problems from the government. In penology, as Garland (1985) emphasizes, Progressive reforms were from the outset understood as part of the formulation of a comprehensive system of social welfare, one that sought to separate the "social" from "socialism" and one that brought about a modus vivendi between classes based on a system of social welfare and not socialism. A whole set of measures aimed at securing the worker at work—rudimentary health and safety regulations, liability law reforms, worker's compensation, and the like—were adopted in the first two decades of the twentieth century. Progressive penal reform was but one component of this comprehensive agenda, and flowed directly from its central premises.

Penology and Nationalism. Since Durkheim (1947), students of social control have argued that crime and crime policy foster social solidarity, that the process of creating deviance and labeling the deviant reinforces social solidarity (Erickson 1966). Yet Durkheim and his followers took such social response to crime as a manifestation of an underlying natural reality, the *collective conscience.* More recently, a number of historians and political scientists have reformulated this understanding of crime and identified a variety of collective identities that can be reinforced by representations of crime and criminality (Hall et al. 1979; Garland 1990; Scheingold 1991).

In his recent study of Southeast Asia, Ben Anderson (1986) has explored the unifying power of nationalism, showing how it helps construct "imaginary communities" and reinforce group solidarity. He argues that in contrast to other forms of collective identification, especially race, nationalism is a powerful unifying force. While nationalist regimes have fomented great violence, nationalist movements also stress art, literature, and other forms of positive self-expression in ways that foster an intense sense of unity (Anderson 1986:146–50).

Others have shown how crime and crime policy can play a role in fostering nationalism and hence collective solidarity. Social historians in both the United States and Europe have long pointed out how crime—as well as other social problems—was something that not only affected individual citizens, but threatened the very well-being of the nation as well. Indeed, some argued that it revealed deep truths about the nation's flaws and potential. The combination of the latter two themes—the challenge of crime and the sources of national salvation—offered a compelling vision of national destiny that captured the public imagination and was expressed in a wide variety of forms.

Marie-Christine Leps (1992) has pursued this theme in her study of popular culture and criminology in the late nineteenth century. She argues that crime policy and public perceptions of crime are important means of mobilizing concern around the problem of national identity:

> The exclusion of the criminal served not only to contain certain segments of the population, but also, more importantly, to discern the limits of a consensual "we", identified with "the people of the nation" or that well known character, "the public." (p. 69)

She then goes on to argue that depictions of crime in novels, newspapers, and more recently television have been a powerful instrument for reinforcing national identity and national investment in social control (p. 141). Novelistic and journalistic accounts of crime are especially potent, she suggests, because they are freed from the methodological rigors of "scientific" discourse, and allow the valorization of norms to reach intense and explicit heights not easily available in works of social science. She illustrates this with accounts of journalistic responses to the Jack the Ripper murders in London in the late 1880s (1992:116–30). French papers characterized the crimes as an English phenomenon, and contrasted the security and order of the French to the vulnerable and bumbling Brits. The English press focused on the killings as a phenomenon of Whitechapel, an urban slum whose infamous "rookeries"—streets of crowded lodging houses—were deemed among the most dangerous in the city. The stories combined journalistic retelling of criminological account, with moralizing about the community and the victims.

Such accounts can also smooth out underlying ideological tensions in criminology, with their clashing notions of determinism and free will. For instance, French novelist Rosny Aine blended environmental and hereditary accounts in his description of the slums, while at the same time emphasizing the role of agency in his narrative (1992). Freed from the mandate to reconcile competing and contradictory meanings, imaginative literature can even heighten the features of both views simultaneously:

> Discourse on "criminal man" served not only to generate and restrain a "residuum", but also to produce a consensual community defined by its difference from, and opposition to, criminality. National education systems and the new, mass-produced press would further articulate the place and voice of "the public", usually defined in terms of "the nation." (p. 221)

Although scholars of Progressive politics have not focused extensively on the cultural side of penal reform, some have identified a distinct national dimension to crime and penal reform policies.[18] For instance, they show that in both the United States and the United Kingdom, reformers were deeply concerned with the threat immigration posed for a coherent national identity (Painter 1987; Rothman 1980; Garland 1985). Crime was one of many pathologies spawned by the poverty and ignorance of immigrants. But, as we noted earlier, even though the Progressives embraced this view, they were also confident that the virtues of American political culture would not only be saved, but could be harnessed to attack these pathologies and absorb the immigrants into their new culture (Rothman 1980).

RETOOLING PROGRESSIVE PENOLOGY: THE GREAT SOCIETY AND CRIME

After World War II, the Progressive penal agenda was revived, but with a number of new features. Progressive politicians like California's Earl Warren returned to attack the problems of crime, but they were able to do so with a level of funding and a degree of public confidence that was unprecedented (Simon 1993). And in the 1950s and 1960s, penological discourse became even more sociologically informed (Cloward and Ohlin 1960). As in the Progressive Era, criminological ideas became the locus for a mobilization of experts, politicians, and journalists, and many of the earlier representations reappeared in a guise, as discourse continued to reflect advances in the social sciences and technological developments.

Rebel without a Cause. One of the important new postwar representations was the "juvenile delinquent." This figure was a *child* of the nineteenth century whom the Progressives raised to almost a master paradigm for penality (Rothman 1980). By the 1950s, both sociology and popular culture had transformed his basic valorization. On the movie screen James Dean gave the delinquent a sexiness that had been absent from the child who had sat on Judge Ben Lindsey's knee during the early decades of the century (Rothman 1980). And the sociologist Howard Becker (1963) and other labeling theorists provided a strikingly positive view of the delinquent as an existential actor, as they traced the influence of the criminal process in generating negative attributes associated with delinquents (Lemert 1967; Matza 1964). And Richard Cloward and Lloyd Ohlin's *Delinquency and Opportunity: A Theory of Delinquent Gangs* (1960) helped connect the new juvenile delinquent to the Kennedy liberalism, which was looking for appealing and safe strategies of social intervention (Lehman 1991:119).

The System. In his important book *Taming the System*, Samuel Walker

(1993) has argued that the most enduring contribution of the criminal justice reform movement of the 1960s (symbolized by the President's Commission on Law Enforcement and the Administration of Justice, widely known as the President's Crime Commission) was the successful promotion of the idea of the criminal justice *system*. Fostered by earlier work undertaken at the American Bar Foundation and sponsored by the Ford Foundation in the 1950s, this effort to "tame the system" by controlling discretion, improving efficiency, and thinking "systemically," he argues, represents a watershed in thinking about the criminal process, and led to a host of new controls on police behavior, pretrial detention, and sentencing. There is no doubt that Walker is correct: he has identified a profound change in thinking about crime and the problems of crime.[19] In our original article we suggested that this trend was a central feature of the new penology, and linked it to another feature of the new penology, the move from an individualized criminal process to an actuarial system. Walker's analysis captures some of this shift, and reveals how potent this new idea of a system became. And he is correct to insist that this is the central organizing metaphor for thinking about crime and crime policies since the 1960s.

However, he fails to explore the full implications of the idea or to locate it in broader context. The idea of the criminal justice *system* is in fact much more radical and far-reaching than Walker intimates. It not only constituted a new approach in thinking about the long-standing problems of discrimination and arbitrariness, it also represented a significant break with Progressive penology. It sought to "tame discretion" to cope with these problems. But discretion—the exercise of professional judgment—was also at the heart of Progressives' clinical models of individualized penality. Under Progressive penology, discretion was part of the solution to the problem: discretionary authority to make important clinical judgments was delegated to trained professionals. But under the systems approach, discretion became *the* problem, something to be restricted.

In contrast, the *problem* of discretion became one of the most successful representations of crime and punishment that was produced in the 1960s and 1970s. Both the Right and the Left mobilized to produce a number of ideologically distinct representations associated with discretion. While these concerns never did achieve mass public appeal, they did influence journalists and political elites, who joined together in support of a number of new efforts, such as determinate sentencing, bail guidelines, and stricter rules governing police (Walker 1993), in the name of curbing unbridled discretion. But, as we have argued, this concern also ushered in a diminished appreciation of rights and individualized judgments of all sorts. The criminal justice system and the twin problems of the nonsystem and unregulated discretion that it made visible represented a significant break with Progressive penology. After all, discretion was at the heart of the Progressives' clinical model of individualized penality. In contrast, discretion is a central problem for the new penology in its quest for system rationality.

Crime in a Free Society. The Reports of the President's Commission on Law Enforcement and the Administration of Justice mark the transition from the old Progressive penology to the new. They represent the high-water mark of traditional thinking about crime and crime policy, even as they ushered in systems thinking and the new penology. The commission's Task Force reports on Corrections, Juvenile Justice, and Narcotics summarized traditional liberal thinking and contained recommendations to promote increased adversarial proceedings, expanded individualized treatment alternatives in corrections, and increased discretion to divert arrestees from the criminal process, recommendations that are in many respects at odds with a drive to "tame the system" by restricting discretion. However, the Task Force Report on Science and Technology (1967b), and to a lesser extent the Task Force Report on Courts (1967a), as well as the commission's summary volume, *The Challenge of Crime in a Free Society*, represented a new future. They promoted the idea of the criminal justice *system*, and in so doing established a grammar for the new penology. Thus while some task force reports proposed to "cure," "treat," and humanely "punish," others emphasized process and the need to transform the nonsystem into an effectively managed system.

In retrospect, it was as if some of the task force reports contained unintentional obituaries for the ideas of rehabilitation, decriminalization, and the idea of discretion itself, while others contained birth announcements for the new systems thinking. The new prevailed: systems analysis came to crime. Operations research came to replace sociology as the frame of reference. The language of rights gave way to the language of administration. The quest for individual-focused justice was superseded by a concern with the management of risk-segregated populations. The new penology was born. No doubt we overstate. The old language did not wither away, and the new language did not emerge over night, let alone immediately translate into new institutionalized practices. The basic outlines of Progressive penology remained in force throughout the 1960s, but an important new language and perspective—and an emerging set of practices—did grow up side by side with the old.

THE NEW PENOLOGY AND ITS REPRESENTATIONS

The history of penality in the 1960s is now only beginning to be written. Those who offer cultural analysis of the present are necessarily parasitical on such work, and the emergence of the new penology in this period requires a far more detailed and contextualized analysis.[20] Still it is possible to see in the victory of the "system" and its logics over those of "delinquency" a decisive step away from Progressive penology. The new discourses and practices showcased in the reports of the crime commission, and widely embraced since, have fundamentally transformed the thinking and work of academics and criminal justice professionals.

But this new discourse has not become the language of the public, the media, or the politicians. Instead, it has created a chasm between those professionals and academics who have embraced it and those politicians and the public who have not. This development has not only created a gap between these two sets of communities, it has contributed to increased ambivalence among the public. For many, criminal justice agencies—the "system" itself—is now seen as the problem, and confidence in the criminal process has plummeted. This gap stands in marked contrast to the consensus and shared confidence among academics, professionals, the media, and opinion makers during the Progressive Era.

The Failed Representations of the New Penology

In our previous work we examined several programs that exemplified the new penology, including such programs as selective incapacitation, preventive detention, and drug courier profiles. Below we revisit some of these programs in order to explore their cultural links with public discourse about crime.

Career Criminals and Criminal Careers. The idea of the "career criminal" is one of the most appealing representations proffered by the new penology. It offers a picture of the crime problem as rooted in the conduct of a small and specifiable subpopulation. Moreover, it promises that measures aimed at such offenders will lower crime with better management, and without the need for massive new programs or funds or even significant changes in crime-fighting strategies. In their two-volume compendium for the National Research Council, *Career Criminals and Criminal Careers*, Alfred Blumstein and Jacqueline Cohen (1981) review recent research on this topic. Their study documents the emerging importance of these new ideas about crime and criminals. The "career criminal" is, of course, the contemporary cousin of the older "habitual offender" and the "born criminal," but this most recent offspring is also quite different. The career criminal represents a shift away from a eugenic-based explanation of crime, or any other type of sociological explanation that seeks to identify the causes of crime. Instead, it is agnostic about the causes of crime; it is preoccupied not with an explanation of crime as a prelude to diagnosis and response, but with the identification of high-risk offenders in order to incapacitate and manage.

The new and distinctive feature of the concept of career criminal is that it purports to show that a small handful of people account for a vast share of all crime. Its policy implications are obvious: it is possible to achieve both crime control and fiscal restraint by incapacitating high-rate offenders. The new criminal career research is overwhelmingly actuarial and managerial. Its aim is to identify patterns of behavior in whole cohorts in order to promote public safety by incapacitating high-risk offenders for lengthy periods.[22] In contrast, earlier research on the professional or habitual criminal e.g., Sutherland's *The Professional Thief* (1937) and Irwin's *The Felon* (1970) was undertaken with the aim of "understanding" offenders as a first diagnostic step toward treatment or deterrence.

This idea has entered public discourse. In the 1970s, the U.S. Department of Justice launched a major campaign of pilot grants and research to convince local police and prosecutors to concentrate on career criminals. In 1987, the United States Sentencing Commission cited career criminals as deserving of special targeting of resources. And more recently, the idea received widespread attention in the media and in political discourse in connection with the spate of "three-strikes-and-you're-out" laws adopted by a number of states. In California, for instance, supporters of "three-strikes" legislation to imprison violent repeat offenders for life repeatedly invoked the term "career criminal" and repeatedly cited Wolfgang's work (Wolfgang et al. 1972).

Although one of the most promising of representations offered by the new penology, the concept of career criminal still has not permeated public discourse. Its most radical version, the selective incapacitation approach put forward by the Rand Corporation's Peter Greenwood (1982), has been a political nonstarter. Its image of a dangerous predatory offender is popular, but the idea of selectively targeting a small group of high-risk offenders is not. In the California legislative battle over "three strikes," for instance, a moderate bill that would have focused on "predatory career criminals" lost out to a much more inclusive version that included all those—high risk or not—with "three strikes," and thus greatly expanded the scope and cost of the new policies.

The Underclass. The concept of the underclass is not new. Nor was it coined by criminologists or even first used within penological discourse (Wilson 1987; Katz et al. 1992). Yet in recent years it has been revised and widely embraced, both within criminology and in broader public discourse, as a metaphor that captures the idea of a permanent subpopulation that is dangerous and in need of management. Elsewhere we have argued that it is a convenient term to convey the idea of a group of persons permanently trapped in poverty and social marginality, and who pose a high danger risk for society (Feeley and Simon 1992). The idea invites an aggregate response. Techniques like preventive detention and drug courier profiles are coherent risk management strategies directed at such a population.[22]

The exploration of the relationship between disorder and fear of crime developed by Wilson and Kelling (1982), Skogan (1990), and others, is another effort to develop a coherent response to the underclass. In some ways this work is an extension of the older environmental studies of crime, especially the social disorganization perspective of the Chicago school. Crime is understood as a product of fears generated both directly by underclass behavior (broken windows) or indirectly by concerns that the neighborhood is changing and becoming more underclass.

This picture of crime suggests a number of policy responses. One is to attack the disorder, no doubt because it is more visible and routine than criminal behavior. Another is that the fear of crime is itself a cause of crime, and thus crime can be attacked successfully by measures that bolster confidence. Such ideas have gained considerable popular acceptance. A number of new mayors, including New York's Rudolph Giuliani, have adopted programs that attack visible traits of disorder, such as begging, public drunkenness, and windshield washing, arguing that they are effective crime-fighting measures.

Perhaps the strongest policy manifestation of this idea is "community policing" (Skolnick and Bayley 1986), the idea that the focus of policing should shift from making arrests to addressing community fears of disorder by being more responsive to community calls for maintaining order. This policy draws on nostalgic representations of earlier American communities (Scheingold 1991), but it also fits within the strategies of the new penology to the extent that it aims at establishing managerial control over disorderly populations. The 1994 Federal Crime Act may be an indication of the strength of public acceptance of this form of controlling the underclass; it provided funding for one hundred thousand new police officers. Although supporters are vague as to what these police will do, the act was defended in terms of the values of community policing.

A variety of other "new" programs such as "intensive" parole and probation and boot camps also tie into the belief (Petersilia 1987; Feeley and Simon 1992) that there is an entire class that is no longer capable of maintaining basic order among its members, and needs police and other agents of the state to intervene not just to deal with crime, but to maintain order. Yet despite some limited successes, none of these programs has emerged as an alternative to traditional sanctions.

Drugs and Drug Testing. During the 1980s, for reasons largely independent of penology, drugs became the central focus for a political response to crime. Both Presidents Reagan and Bush saw illegal drug use as signifying a deep moral decline in certain portions of American society, and mounted the moral equivalent of war on it, and spectacular media coverage of the violence associated with drugs helped build a public conception of drugs as a catalyst for violence. Furthermore, research has revealed the presence of drugs among a high proportion of arrestees, and this in turn has contributed to a continuous expansion of penalties for drug possession and tests for drug use. In light of all this, extraordinarily harsh sentences for drug use and widespread reliance on drug testing have come to be seen as sensible strategies to protect public safety (Gordon 1994).

But even though drug use is identified as a reliable indicator of membership in a high-risk population, efforts to construct penal strategies to control drugs have not been embraced by the public. Although the 1994 Federal Crime Act does provide some funding for drug treatment programs, to date the response to drugs remains largely punitive.

Part of the problem lies in the distinctive way in which the new penology views drugs. The old penology understood drug use as an explanation for why some individuals became criminals, and thus it provided a story about how to control crime. In contrast, the new penology regards drug use in risk management terms as an indicator of dangerousness. To the extent that the public also views drugs primarily as a measure of risk, evidence revealing high levels of drug use among arrestees may only solidify a belief in the need to manage a permanent high-risk underclass rather than punish use or treat users.

What Doesn't Work

The representations produced by the new penology are not without some resonance in public discourse. They are heard in state and national debates about crime policy, but they are typically minor themes. The 1994 Crime Act included several measures that embody new penology themes about career criminals, the underclass, and drugs, but they were eclipsed by much larger programs that stressed harsher punishments and more police. Appeals to new penology themes like "punishing smart" were subordinated to appeals to popular public fixations like capital punishment.

The limitations of the new penology reflect in part changes in the structure of public discourse itself. Four factors are particularly important:

1. *The growth of the system.* The bigger the system becomes, the more attention and noise are generated by the internal concerns of managing the system itself. Thus as the system has grown, professionals and academics alike have turned their attention to the ever-expanding management prob-

lems. Throughout the 1980s, large corrections systems in California and Texas were swamped by the tasks of finding bed space, hiring new staff, and building new prisons to accommodate the mushrooming prison population. Systems management helped them cope with this crisis.

2. *The popularization of crime politics.* The politics of reform in the Progressive Era was largely a politics of elites. Apart from occasional highly salient issues (e.g., Prohibition and the Mann Act), transformations in the objectives and techniques of punishment were rarely the subject of broad public debate. Even in legislative bodies there was little substantive political debate; most of the key conflicts were sorted out in the process of program formation internal to elite professional groups (Garland 1985). However, since the 1950s crime policy has been an integral part of general political debate in popular forums and in the electoral process, a phenomenon that intensified in the 1980s (Scheingold 1991; Simon 1993).[23]

Although crime is a potent ideological issue in modern societies (Hall et al. 1979), until recently its most popularized forms remained somewhat removed from the actual formation of penal institutions.[24] However, as penal reform questions come into the full play of electoral politics, ideological appeals triumph over either cultural influence or system effect.

3. *The general crisis of governmental power.* In the early twentieth century, the problem of crime constituted a powerful reason to expand the role of government in fostering welfare in order to integrate marginal members of society into the mainstream. But by the end of the century it has become the opposite. The new penology divorces crime policy from concern with social welfare.[25] Increasingly, crime policy is conceived of as a process for classification and management of populations ranked by risk; in need of segregation, not integration. Indeed this new direction may reflect what E. J. Dionne, Jr. calls "the decline of a 'politics of remedy'" (1991:17):

> Since the 1960s, the key to winning elections has been to reopen the same divisive issues over and over again. The issues themselves are not reargued. No new light is shed. Rather, old resentments and angers are stirred up in an effort to get voters to cast yet one more ballot of angry protest. Political consultants have been truly ingenious in figuring out endless creative ways of tapping into popular anger about crime. (p. 16)

4. *Crime as a national problem.* Stuart Scheingold (1991) has argued that in recent years, crime and punishment have become increasingly defined as "national" problems, and that this tendency exacerbates the emotionalism already endemic to discussions of crime. Local crime politics are more pragmatic because local public figures have to cope more directly with the problems of managing the policies that are put into place, and they have to answer for failure. However, we think that it is more than the distance involved in national politics that has changed. Progressive dis-

course also defined crime as an issue of national significance, but it reflected elite fears and aspirations. Today national discourse on crime is populist and centered on fear. Moreover, the nationalism of the Progressive Era was expansive and at least partially (if grudgingly) inclusive of the new immigrants. Today's national crime discourse is defensive and exclusive. Some observers have noted important changes at the molecular level in which voters are appealed to politically, from a system of group loyalties based in part on locality to an abstract politics in which the individual is both isolated and attached to the nation as an abstraction (Simon 1987; Dionne 1991):

> [In the past] political loyalties were reinforced by other forms of group solidarity. Now, insofar as voters identify with groups, it is often with abstract national groups rather than concrete local ones. An Italian machinist in a Detroit suburb may identify himself more with his fellow gun owners than with his ethnic group, his neighborhood, or his fellow workers. (Dionne 1991:17)

All of these developments need to be seen in a much richer context than we have provided. Structural economic change, demography, and the spatial distribution of economic and political power are all involved in shaping the receptivity of public discourse to penology (Hall et al. 1979; Scheingold 1991; Gordon 1990). A rich literature has also documented the role of the media in the last several decades (and earlier) in polarizing public discourse on crime along ideological lines (Cohen and Young 1973; Hall et al. 1979; Ericson et al. 1987, 1991; Barak 1994). At present we want to hold such issues in the background, and concentrate instead on the internal features of the new penology, which contribute to its cultural sterility.[26]

CONCLUSION: THE NEW PENOLOGY AND ITS DISCONTENTS

Our aim here is not to criticize the formalism of the new penology or to romanticize the more successful representations of earlier eras. Rather it is to explore some of the implications of the failures of the new penology to provide a satisfactory *account* of crime, or, in Murray Edelman's terms, to provide us with a set of "words that succeed" even if the policies fail.

In our original article, we argued that the new penology is more than just a set of ideas, or an integrated system of practices (Feeley and Simon 1992). Rather, it is an interpretive construct that we as observers cast over a complex set of ideologies and practices in order to help identify and interpret emerging relationships among them. Neither deep structure nor mentality, the new penology offers room for maneuver and adaptation. The question is: can it provide a successful set of narratives to guide public discourse, and will it contribute to the acceptance of a new type of crime policy? To date, we have argued that it has not. Although it forms an important basis for professional and academic discourse about crime and crime policy, the new penology has not (yet) permeated public and political discourse. Public discussion of crime remains rooted in the moralism of the old penology. In this article we have explored why this is the case, why professional and academic discourse has not become public discourse as well. In doing so we have identified and begun to diagnose what may be a fatal weakness in the new penology, i.e., its failure to articulate representations of crime and its control that resonate with the public, and to explore why this is the case. We summarize the central features of these weaknesses below.

The Endurance of Volitional Theories

One possible explanation for the difficulties of the new penology in penetrating public discourse is the general distaste of the public for discourses that emphasize social and institutional circumstances and ignore *willful* individuals. As Stuart Scheingold (1991) has observed, "volitional" theories of crime have long dominated both professional and public discourse about crime, and in contrast, "structural" accounts of crime, which seek to understand crime in terms of social conditions and social structures rather than individual acts of volition, are virtually absent in American policy discussions. The policy implications of these two perspectives are strikingly different. Volitional theories imply alteration of factors that affect calculating individuals. Structural analysis of crime tells us that the causes, and hence most important factors contributing to crime, lie outside the purview of the criminal process, and thus we should attack them if we really want to reduce crime.

Although structural analysis has some support in scholarly circles (Currie 1987), it has not even gained a precarious foothold in public discussions of crime. No doubt one important reason for this failure is that Americans are firmly anchored in a tradition of individualism and skepticism about authority. Indeed, almost all American policy discourse—both public and professional—is expressed in language that emphasizes volitional and eschews structural analysis.

The new penology may fail for this same reason. Although, in the dichotomy between volitional and structural that Scheingold presents us with, the new penology is not fully structural, it does fall some place between these two modes of thinking. It is not fully structural, in that it remains focused on crime. However, it does shift attention away from affecting individual behavior to managing aggregates. Still this is not structural, in that it does not propose to move outside the criminal process to affect criminal activity. Nor is it visionary; it does not depend upon the transformation of individuals or of society. Rather it seeks a more efficient and a more strategic management of dangerousness. Above all, it does not embrace traditional volitional notions of crime and criminality, and thus it remains somewhat distinct from established public and political discourse. Although it has come to be the language of choice among many academics and professionals, to date it has not caught on with the public.

The Cultural Failings of the New Penology

Although the new penology has bolstered rationality and accountability in decision-making that has led to a number of improvements, its limited successes may be irrelevant to the more fundamental task of government, which is to provide the public with a sense of security. Moreover, its emphasis on system efficiency and management rather than outcome may have undermined public confidence in the criminal process. The focus on the system has exposed the nonsystem, and thus fostered the belief that justice is the problem.

From the struggle against widespread use of capital and corporal punishment in the eighteenth and nineteenth centuries to the Progressive establishment of a separate juvenile justice process, the development of parole and probation, and other similar measures, new forms of penality have always had to deal with the traditional cultural meaning associated with crime and punishment. As Garland (1990), following Elias (1982), Spierenberg (1984), and others, has argued, these developments eventually came to be seen as part of a "civilizing process" by which Western societies have steadily denounced public displays of violence and pleasure in the suffering of others. But at the same time these techniques and discourses have produced their own cultural effects (Garland 1990). As we argued above, one dimension of the Progressive effort was the production of potent representations of crime that achieved broad resonance in public discourse (see also Garland 1990). While these representations were very much rooted in the new human sciences and other modernist cultural developments, they also reached back to and incorporated much of the cultural meaning invested in the figure of the criminal by early and premodern society. Progressive penology transformed this figure of the dangerous felon into a site of humanity, and thereby channeled the investment of new cultural meanings. The apparent failure of the old Progressive penology to sustain itself in the last several decades should not lead us to assume that the immense "deposits of power" (Cohen 1985) left behind no longer have any resonance or power.[27] Indeed one weakness of the new penology is its failure to tap into these layers of meaning (and hence power) associated with the figure of the criminal and the Progressives' strategies for coping with crime.

Although the new penology has offered some representations by which to understand its central concerns—underclass, the funnel of justice, system—these terms do not dissolve or rechannel the representations of the old penology. Nor are the new representations, as were those of the Progressives, easily compatible with the moralism and individualism of the American national character. Thus despite its substantial development during the past thirty years, the new penology has not provided a widespread and popular account of the truth of crime.

One reason for this is surely the very blindness of the new penology to the cultural effects of penality itself. The systems logic that pervades the new penology is based squarely on a denial of the very specialness of crime. It assumes that the problems of penality are no different than the problems of managing other types of large systems, whether they be transportation networks or military logistics. It fails to appreciate that the "irrational" division of the world through categories is near the heart of any adequate definition of culture (Douglas 1966), and as a consequence it fails to provide satisfying cultural representations of crime and the criminal.

Another problem is the failure of the new penology to address public discourse at all. The tendency of penal practices to generate their own internal expert discourse has been developing for a long time.[28] The Jacksonians and the Progressives had their own versions of specialized discourse, with a definite secular trend toward less overlap with popular discourses (like religion). Still, we think the new penology represents a quantum leap toward a technical and internal discourse that cannot offer plausible and culturally satisfying accounts of crime and its control.

While the new penology is formally neutral as to the specific objectives of the criminal process, its tendency to translate all issues into system flow questions ultimately influences the normative effects of penality. As Garland notes:

> The internal regimes of most modern prisons are remarkably deficient in "moral tone" and rarely adopt any serious attempt to instil virtue or morality beyond the basic demands of obedience and discipline. (1990:261)

No doubt this reflects the long-term failure (and autocritique) that Foucault noted in modern punishment. Substantive studies of modern penal institutions (Messinger et al. 1987; Jacobs 1978; Rafter 1990; Simon 1993) have all documented the gap between the programmatic aspirations behind the institutions and the reality of practice.

Our current practices are even further removed. This is consistent with the political triumphs of incapacitation and deterrence, and the decline of the rehabilitative ideal. But the lines of causation may be more complex. The new penology produces representations of the system that facilitate objectives like deterrence (which demands only efficiently produced punishment) and incapacitation. The traditional appeal of modern penal reformers has been to emphasize the humanity of offenders and the cruelty of current penal practices. The new penology not only has trouble recognizing the cultural investment in the figure of the criminal, it has trouble with the concept of humanity.

The Stakes

What is at stake in this failure of the new penology to successfully address the public's need for effective representations of crime? One thing is that many of the values that have come to seem like enduring values of modernity may be jeopardized. One place where we part from Garland is his implicit assumption that the direction of cultural change is one-way (1990). Garland tries to read the present support for severe and violent punishments as the product of contradictions within the modernist framework of penology (distancing the public tends to undercut the empathy with a fellow human) rather than as signs of a fundamental rupture. The very concept of a "civilizing process," with its roots via Freud in nineteenth-century evolutionism, imports a model of progress to history. We want to close this essay with the concern that the process is far from irreversible (indeed it may not be helpful to use such metaphors with their inherent implication of progress and regress).

The continued endurance of support for the death penalty in the United States suggests more than a small bump on the road to renouncing public violence. Garland (1990), following Zimring and Hawkins (1986), suggests that residual support for the death penalty is in line with European states where abolition preceded significant changes in public opinion. But recent polling data suggests that the death penalty now commands overwhelming and growing support. It will not do to blame this on the pathology of American politics (although those are plenty) because the death penalty as a cultural production has come to be a determinant of that politics.[29]

The recent spectacle of massive public support for the flogging of an American boy in Singapore for the crime of spray-painting a public wall also suggests that a renewal of corporal punishment as a routine feature of penality is not out of the question. We also see strong political pressure to eliminate or curb many of the victories won by the prisoners' rights movement in its struggle for more humane living conditions in prisons.[30]

Although the language of the new penology has become commonplace, and important components of the new penology are now reflected in successful legislative programs, there is little evidence that the new penology has created a coherent narrative that can provide an appealing account of the truth about crime and crime policy. Although some techniques and strategies emerging from the new penology seem to resonate momentarily in public discourse, the rhetoric of recent debates about crime reveal that the public remains firmly anchored to an account of crime and punishment associated with the old penology—individualistic, moralistic, and volitional.

In this chapter, we have tried to point out a problem rather than formulate solutions, but we do not want to end on a note of despair. As we have stressed throughout, the new penology is not a fixed entity but an evolving formation of knowledge and power. In comparison to past formations, this one has failed to influence public discourse in ways that are critical to sustaining a sense of security and optimism in the crime policy debate. But its future is not fixed or inevitable. Perhaps the first step is to recognize the cultural role of penology. But once the new penology begins to do that in a self-conscious way it will already be something else.

ACKNOWLEDGMENTS

We wish to thank Stan Cohen and Tom Blomberg for helpful comments on an earlier draft, and Professor Feeley also wishes to thank the Institute for Advanced Studies, Hebrew University, for support while he was working on this project.

NOTES

1. By penology, we mean the discourses and practices generated by all of us who pose as professionals in the realm of the exercise of the power to punish. That includes staff at various levels of our correctional agencies as well as those of us who produce knowledge about the correctional system and how it is functioning. We want to include not only theories of corrections in the high-minded academic sense, but the whole universe of insider communication in speech, memos, articles, conference papers, etc., the words we use, the images and metaphors we employ, our excuses, and our aspirations. This definition brings together groups that have often been at odds, e.g., academics versus professionals or custodial professionals versus treatment professionals. Such a conflation ignores real differences and does so at the risk of overstating the structural features of the situation. We feel the risk is warranted for several reasons. First, because when seen as an important domain of cultural production the combined effects of penal discourses may be quite different than the intentions of particular adversaries within penology. Second, because the new penology itself is characterized by a considerable convergence between different factions.

2. By public discourse we mean the talk about crime and how it should be responded to, generated by the media, professional politicians, and community lead-

ers of various sorts: those whose words and thoughts become public in the sense of widely promulgated. Of course, ordinary citizens also produce discourse about crime but it only becomes public when it is framed by the media (whether in a letter to the editor or a feature story that collects quotes about how ordinary people feel), by politicians and leaders, and to some extent by social scientists.

3. As we stressed in our *Criminology* article, the distinction between discourses, techniques, and objectives is for analytic purposes only (we don't assume the world comes carved up into such pieces). Any particular practice, e.g., house arrest with electronic monitoring, may draw on and support a variety of discourses; it may deploy any number of new and old techniques; it may be aimed at any number of objectives (explicit or implicit).

4. The late Michel Foucault sometimes described his researches that way, and while we do not lay claim to his powers of observation or description, we share his sense that those of us who comment on contemporary affairs must use the tools of historians without necessarily accepting their self-imposed disciplinary standards.

5. We could be appropriately criticized for ignoring the role of agency in favor of a highly abstract rendering of contemporary debates in penality. We follow Garland in pointing out: "This notion of strategy refers to a pattern or logic inscribed within a network of apparatuses which operate in loose co-ordination around a series of common or complementary objectives. . . . Such strategies are not the results of a single battle plan, drawn up in advance, but are rather the outcome of a complex and fragmented process of struggle within which the calculations of individuals and agencies play a crucial, but by no means controlling, part" (1985: 208).

6. The role of metaphors in the operation of law more generally has been explored by Steven L. Winter (1989).

7. As David Garland puts it: "New sanctions or practices had to be argued for effectively in the political domain and had to be capable of being represented within the legitimate discourses that overlay penal relations and represented them to the public" (1985:171).

8. The Clintons' effort to make their critique of the current medical paradigm, with its emphasis on specialists and extreme procedures, part of the health care debate seems to have found relatively little resonance with the press or the public.

9. Within less than six months the slogan moved from a citizen initiative in California to President Clinton's 1994 State of the Union address.

10. Along with Silvio Berlusconi's use of the soccer slogan *"Forza Italia"* for his right-wing political party, the three-strikes appeal requires political scientists to think more about sports and politics than they have in recent years.

11. In fact there is considerable reason to doubt the accuracy or relevance of this fact. Under most current state laws a person with a history of distinct violent crimes and convicted of a violent felony would face a lengthy term. Two factors seem to have played a role in focusing public concern on this problem. Richard Allen, the accused killer of Polly Klaas, had served a brief term for an earlier conviction for armed robbery. In fact, Allen was the beneficiary of a brief window of relatively

lenient sentences in the original determinate sentence act of 1977, and the process of ratcheting up sentences that began almost immediately after. The other factor is the role of "good time credits" sometimes forced by court-ordered caps in diminishing time served to release well under the facial value of sentences for serious crimes (of course, the facial value has been grossly inflated over the last decade in most states).

12. The statutes vary widely. Some do no more than provide a new label for the already long sentences for repeat offenders. Others, however, provide for dramatically increased sentences for repeat offenders.

13. For an insightful analysis of the potential for criminologists to influence the news media, see Barak (1994).

14. Considering that the formal study of fear of crime as a sociological phenomenon is so young, it has made impressive advances.

15. For purposes of convenience we use the term Progressive Era and Progressives to characterize these developments both in the United States and in Great Britain. For general discussions of politics and society in the Progressive Era see Hofstadter (1955), Weibe (1967), and Painter (1987).

16. In his somewhat parallel study of penological policies in the United Kingdom, David Garland (1985) has also identified a set of representations that served to provide satisfying accounts of crime and justify new crime policies. The representations he identifies as most salient are: violence—crime as war of absolute destruction; crime as diseases; and crime as degeneracy.

17. Garland (1985) shows that the expansion of working-class franchise (itself a concession to rising social power) was a prime concern behind the effort to reform penality.

18. Garland (1990) has since argued forcefully for a cultural reading of penal history, an argument that has significantly shaped our thinking on the matter.

19. This shift may be symbolized by the shift in iconography in the criminal process; the flow chart of the funnel of justice that was published as a centerfold in the commission's Task Force Report on Science and Technology has subsequently come to replace the traditional representation of justice as a blindfolded woman holding a set of scales. American criminal justice texts published in the past twenty five years, for example, are more likely to reprint the commission's funnel of justice chart than a representation of justice. The commission's reports are in sharp contrast with those of its predecessor, the Wickersham Commission, which issued its findings in 1931. The latter's reports emphasized corruption and lack of proper qualifications for personnel—failings of individuals—and not systemic factors.

20. See Simon (1993) for an attempt to provide such for the practices of parole supervision.

21. Wolfgang, Figlio, and Selli's famous study of crime among Philadelphia boys, *Delinquency in a Birth Cohort* (1972), is perhaps the single most influential example of this approach. Contrast that with William Healy's *The Individual Delinquent* (1915).

22. A sign of this is a recent federal district court opinion that upheld the use of a drug courier profile even though it disproportionately targeted African-Americans for questioning. The district court reasoned that the use of a racial classification was justified by the government's compelling interest in controlling drug trafficking and

the close relationship between the drug dealing industry and the poverty and unemployment that are endemic in many African American communities. See *United States v. Travis* 837 F. Supp. 1386 (E.D. Ky. 1993).

23. As late as the determinate sentence movement in the mid-1970s, crime policy unfolded with only moderate levels of public attention.

24. For a long time the division between substantive criminal laws, which focused on the acts sanctioned in court, and the practice of police and corrections on either side of the court, sheltered penal strategies from the glare of most public debates.

25. The debate over the 1994 crime bill serves as a measure of this shift. Liberals have introduced a number of economic development and community investment programs under the guise of crime "prevention." It remains far from clear, however, that the public which welcomed the massive spending measure was very conscious of the prevention aspects. The idea of prevention as a mandate for more government is the last thing the Democratic party wants to defend at this point. Indeed, the measure is being in part funded through reductions in federal employment.

26. Garland points out that once we acknowledge that penality is both a product of culture and a determinant of it we must abandon any mechanical accounts of causation (1990:249).

27. In a recent paper, Simon (1994) has analyzed the play of just such deposits of power in the figure of the criminal and human being in one of the most significant public documents of recent times, i.e., the Warren Commission Report.

28. Garland suggests usefully that it may be traced to the very movement toward privatizing the act of punishment in the eighteenth century (1990).

29. Representative Newt Gingrich of Georgia, the fiery Republican leader in the House, noted to a reporter that the death penalty was a key component in a process of forming a new right-wing ruling majority in the United States.

30. An especially disturbing trend is the willingness of some politicians to balk at court ordered caps on the assumption that public demand for punishment will overwhelm judicial willingness to enforce liberal precedents in the Eighth Amendment area.

REFERENCES

Anderson, Benedict. 1986. *Imagined Communities: Reflections on the Origin and Spread of Nationalism*, rev. ed. London: Verso.
Barak, Gregg. 1994. *Media, Process, and the Social Construction of Crime: Studies in Newsmaking Criminology*. New York: Garland.
Becker, Howard S. 1963. *Outsiders: Studies in the Sociology of Deviance*. Glencoe, IL: Free Press.
Blumstein, Alfred and Jacqueline Cohen. 1981. *Career Criminals and Criminal Careers*.
Cohen, Stanley. 1985. *Visions of Social Control*. New York: Polity.
Cohen, Stanley and Jock Young. 1973. *The Manufacture of News: Social Problems, Deviance and the Mass Media*. London: Constable.

Cloward, Richard and Lloyd Ohlin. 1960. *Delinquency and Opportunity: A Theory of Delinquent Gangs*. Glencoe, IL: Free Press.
Currie, Elliot. 1987. *Confronting Crime*. New York: Pantheon.
Dionne, E. J., Jr. 1991. *Why Americans Hate Politics*. New York: Touchstone.
Douglas, Mary. 1966. *Purity and Danger: An Analysis of the Concepts of Pollution and Taboo*. London: RKP.
Dumm, Thomas. 1987. *Democracy and Punishment: Disciplinary Origins of the United States*. Madison: University of Wisconsin Press.
Durkheim, Emile. [1893] 1947. *The Division of Labor in Society*. Glencoe, IL: Free Press.
Edelman, Murray. 1967. *The Symbolic Uses of Politics*. Champaign-Urbana: University of Illinois Press.
———. 1977. *Words That Succeed and Policies That Fail*. New York: Academic Press.
Elias, Norbert. 1982. *The Civilizing Process*, translated by Edmund Jephcott. New York: Pantheon.
Erickson, Kai. 1966. *Wayward Pilgrims: A Study in the Sociology of Deviance*. New York: John Wiley.
Ericson, Richard V., Patricia M. Baranek, and Janet B. L. Chan. 1987. *Visualizing Deviance: A Study of News Organizations*. Toronto: University of Toronto Press.
Ericson, Richard V., et al. 1991. *Representing Order: Crime, Law, and Justice in the News Media*. Toronto: University of Toronto Press.
Feeley, Malcolm M. and Jonathan Simon. 1994. "The New Penology: Notes on the Emerging Strategy of Corrections and Its Implications." *Criminology* 30: 449–74.
———. 1995. "Actuarial Justice: Power/Knowledge in Contemporary Criminal Justice." Pp. 173–201 in *The Futures of Criminology*, David Nelken. London: Sage.
Foucault, Michel. 1977. *Discipline and Punish: The Birth of the Prison*, translated by Alan Sheridan. New York: Random House.
Garland, David. 1985. *Punishment and Welfare: A History of Penal Strategies*. Brookfield, VT: Gower.
———. 1990. *Punishment and Modern Society: A Study in Social Theory*. Chicago: University of Chicago Press.
Gordon, Diana R. 1990. *The Justice Juggernaut: Fighting Street Crime, Controlling Citizens*. New Brunswick, NJ: Rutgers University Press.
———. 1994. *The Return of the Dangerous Classes: Drug Prohibition and Policy Politics*. New York: Norton.
Greenwood, Peter, with Alan Abrahmse. 1982. *Selective Incapacitation*. Santa Monica: Rand Corporation.
Gusfield, Joseph. 1963. *The Symbolic Crusade: Status Politics and the American Temperance Movement*. Urbana: University of Illinois Press.
Hall, Stuart and Chas Critcher, Tony Jefferson, John Clarke, and Brian Roberts. 1979. *Policing the Crisis: Mugging, the State, and Law and Order*. London: MacMillan.

Healy, William. 1915. *The Individual Delinquent: A Text-Book of Diagnosis and Prognosis for All Concerned in Understanding Offenders*. Boston: Little Brown.
Hofstader, Richard. 1955. *The Age of Reform*. New York: Vintage.
Ignatieff, Michael. 1978. *A Just Measure of Pain: The Penitentiary in the Industrial Revolution*. London: Penguin.
Irwin, John. 1970. *The Felon*. Berkeley: University of California Press.
Jackson, Pamela Irving. 1989. *Minority Group Threat, Crime, and Policing: Social Context and Social Control*. New York: Praeger.
Jacobs, James. 1978. *Stateville: The Penitentiary in Mass Society*. Chicago: University of Chicago Press.
Katz, Michael, ed. 1992. *The Underclass Debate: Views from History*. Princeton, NJ: Princeton University Press.
Lehman, Nicholas. 1991. *The Promised Land*. New York: Basic Books.
Lemert, Edwin M. 1967. *Human Deviance, Social Problems, and Social Control*. Englewood Cliffs, NJ: Prentice Hall.
Leps, Marie-Christine. 1992. *Apprehending the Criminal: The Production of Deviance in 19th Century Discourse*. Durham, NC: Duke University Press.
Matza, David. 1964. *Delinquency and Drift*. Berkeley: University of California.
Meehl, Paul. 1954. *Clinical Versus Actuarial Prediction*. Minneapolis: University of Minnesota Press.
Melossi, Dario and Massimo Pavarini. 1981. *The Prison and the Factory: Origins of the Penitentiary System*. Totowa NJ: MacMillan.
Messinger, Sheldon. 1969. *Strategies of Control*. Ph.D. thesis, University of California, Los Angeles.
Messinger, Sheldon L. and Richard A. Berk. 1987. "Review Essay: Dangerous People." *Criminology* 25:767–81.
Packer, Herbert. 1968. *The Limits of the Criminal Sanction*. Stanford, CA: Stanford University Press.
Painter, Nell Irvin. 1987. *Standing at Armageddon: The United States 1877–1919*. New York: Norton.
Petersilia, Joan. 1987. *Expanding Options for Criminal Sentencing*. Santa Monica, CA: Rand Corporation.
President's Commission on Law Enforcement and Administration of Justice. 1967. *The Challenge of Crime in a Free Society*. Washington, DC: USGPO.
Rafter, Nicole. 1990. *Partial Justice: Women, Prisons and Social Control*. New Brunswick, NJ: Rutgers University Press.
Rothman, David J. 1971. *The Discovery of the Asylum: Social Order and Disorder in the New Republic*. Toronto: Little Brown.
———. 1980. *Conscience and Convenience: The Asylum and its Alternatives in Progressive America*. Toronto: Little Brown.
Scheingold, Stuart A. 1991. *The Politics of Street Crime: Criminal Process and Cultural Obsession*. Philadelphia: Temple University Press.
Shaw, Clifford. 1929. *Delinquency Areas: A Study of the Geographical Distribution of School Truants, Juvenile Delinquents, and Adult Offenders in Chicago*. Chicago: University of Chicago Press.

Simon, Jonathan. 1987. "The Rise of Risk: Insurance, Law and the State," *Socialist Review* 95:61–89.

———. 1993. *Poor Discipline: Parole and the Social Control of the Underclass, 1890–1990*. Chicago: University of Chicago Press.

———. 1994. "Ghost in the Disciplinary Machine: Lee Harvey Oswald, Life-History, and the Truth of Crime." 1994 American Sociological Association Meetings, Los Angeles, CA.

Skogan, Wesley G. 1990. *Disorder and Decline: Crime and the Spiral of Decay in American Neighborhoods*. New York: Free Press.

Skolnick, Jerome and David A. Bayley. 1986. *The New Blue Line*. New York: Free Press.

Spierenberg, Pieter. 1984. *The Spectacle of Suffering: Executions and the Evolution of Repression: From a Preindustrial Metropolis to the European Experience*. Cambridge: Cambridge University Press.

Sutherland, Edwin H. 1937. *The Professional Thief*. Chicago: University of Chicago Press.

Task Force on the Administration of Justice. 1967a. *Task Force Report: The Courts*. Washington, DC: USGPO.

Task Force on the Administration of Justice. 1967b. *Task Force Report: Science and Technology*. Washington, DC: USGPO.

Task Force on the Courts of the President's Commission on Law Enforcement and Administration Justice. 1967. *Task Force Report; Science and Technology*. Washington, DC: USGPO.

U.S. Department of Justice, Bureau of Justice Statistics. 1992a. *Sourcebook of Criminal Justice Statistics, 1992*. Washington, DC: USGPO.

U.S. Department of Justice, Bureau of Justice Statistics. 1992b. *Criminal Victimization in the United States*. Washington, DC: USGPO.

United States Sentencing Commission. 1987. *Sentencing Guidelines: Preliminary Draft*. Wilmette, IL: Callaghan.

Walker, Samuel. 1993. *Taming the System: The Control of Discretion in Criminal Justice: 1950–1990*. New York: Oxford University Press.

Wiebe, Robert H. 1967. *The Search for Order, 1877–1920*. New York: Hill & Wang.

Wilson, James Q. and George Kelling. 1982. "Broken Windows." *Atlantic Monthly* March, pp. 29–38.

Wilson, William J. 1987. *The Truly Disadvantaged: The Inner City, the Underclass, and Public Policy*. Chicago: University of Chicago Press.

Winter, Steven L. 1989. Transcendental Nonsense, Metaphoric Reasoning, and the Cognitive Stakes for Law. *University of Pennsylvania Law Review* 137:1105–1237.

Wolfgang, Marvin E., Robert Figlio, and Thorsten Sellin. 1972. *Delinquency in a Birth Cohort*. Chicago: University of Chicago Press.

Zimring, Franklin E. and Gordon Hawkins. 1986. *Capital Punishment and the American Agenda*. Cambridge: Cambridge University Press.

11
Penal Modernism and Postmodernism

DAVID GARLAND

One of the most harmful habits in contemporary thought is the analysis of the present as being precisely, in history, a present of rupture, of high point, of completion, or of a returning dawn. The solemnity with which everyone who engages in philosophical discourse reflects on his own time strikes me as a flaw. . . . I think we should have the modesty to say to ourselves that . . . the time we live in is not *the* unique or fundamental irruptive point in history where everything is completed and begun again. . . . [O]n the other hand, the time we live in is very interesting; it needs to be analysed and broken down, and that we would do well to ask ourselves, "What is the nature of our present?"
—Michel Foucault, "Structuralism and Poststructuralism"

INTRODUCTION

There is a widespread sense today that contemporary penality is undergoing some kind of transformation. Until quite recently, accounts of contemporary penal transformations tended to be quite narrow in their focus and quite modest in their claims. In the last year or two, however, a new and stronger thesis is beginning to emerge; one that is much broader in its scope and much deeper in its implications. The new suggestion is that the penal realm, like other areas of social and cultural life, is becoming in some sense "postmodern," and that this historic shift forms the broad explanatory framework within which the diverse trends of contemporary penality can best be understood.

Postmodernism is, of course, very old news in cultural studies, social theory, and some branches of philosophy, where the term has been a hot topic of debate for the last fifteen years. Once the term *postmodern* escaped from the lexicon of artistic styles into broader debates about the nature of contemporary experience, it rapidly become a kind of catchall adjective to describe the various intellectual and political predicaments of an age in which foundational claims (in respect of knowledge, value, truth, and so on) are viewed as "mere" conventions.[1] Now, a decade and a half later, when the word has begun to lose its initial incendiary appeal, and has started to settle down as a more or less defined position in a number of well-worn debates, it has at last reached the distant shores of criminology and penology, where its precise implications have yet to be worked out.

The importation of modish intellectual terms is often dismissed as the product of an academic fashion industry, driven by the marketing strategies of publishers and the status concerns of writers who hope to impress by their taste in terminology. But it is also the case that writers who are seeking to develop new perspectives in their field do so using the language and concerns of contemporary intellectual life. Consequently, the appearance of the vocabulary of postmodernism in this latest field is liable to produce original insights and radical perspectives as well as the slavish repetition of fashionable postures developed elsewhere. One can only judge the matter in terms of the substantive analyses actually produced, and seek to avoid the polarized "love it or hate it" response that the mere mention of the term *postmodernism* now frequently provokes.

The claim that penality is becoming postmodern takes a number of forms and has been put forward by a number of writers, but the precise meaning of the claim is still rather inchoate. Writers such as Stanley Cohen (1990) and Jan van Dijk (1989) have used the term *postmodern* to refer to certain aspects of contemporary criminological discourse. Others such as Carol Smart (1990), Alison Young (forthcoming), and John-Paul Brodeur (1993) have proposed postmodernism as an intellectual and political stance relevant to thinking about crime and punishment (and especially to thinking about that thinking). Robert Reiner (1992) has discussed the problems of policing what he terms a "postmodern society." However the postmodernist thesis has been put forward in its strongest form by Jonathan Simon, first of all in an article entitled "The New Penology" [coauthored with Malcolm Feeley (Feeley and Simon 1992)] and more recently in his 1993 book *Poor Discipline*, where he titles one chapter "Penal Postmodernism: Power without Narrative" and explicitly raises the question "Are we postmodern?" (see also Simon 1991; Howe 1994; Schwartz and Friedrichs 1994; Henry and Milovanovic 1994).

A common feature of these references to the postmodern is that they all have something of a *gestural* character. Their use of the term evokes a whole range of new attitudes, discourses, and practices, against the broad background of a new social and cultural configuration, but the precise meaning of the postmodern *in criminology or penology* is rarely specified in any detail. Even Simon's writings, which are by far the most substantive and interesting, are disappointingly thin when it comes to a positive characterization of what is postmodern about the present. (He is much better on what has become problematic about the modernist past.)

Since most readers of criminological theory have some understanding of what postmodernism has come to mean in other fields, it has been possible to use the term in an ill-defined way and yet still succeed in communicating something (though that something is often very imprecise). At a minimum, the suggestion is that penality now increasingly exhibits certain new characteristics, which are distinguishable from those of the recent past (i.e., from "penal modernity") and which resemble the kinds of postmodern phenomena that analysts have identified elsewhere in contemporary culture and society. The task of specifying precisely what the postmodern elements of penality might be is an important exercise that has not yet been undertaken. I hope that the analyses developed in the following pages may succeed in provoking further work in this direction.

If the notion of a postmodern penality could be shown to be a plausible description of the present this would have a far-reaching significance. It would, for example, imply that the sociology of modernity was an increasingly inappropriate framework for understanding punishment and penal history. Our interpretation of penality would no longer be set within the long-term processes of rationalization, differentiation, commodification, and civilization that the sociology of modernity has established as the configurational setting in which modern penal institutions developed (see Garland 1990). Recent work by sociologists and historians of punishment has extended that analysis of modernity into the field of penality and described the contours of "the modern" in this area of social life: such work would cease to be a history of the present and become instead the history of a past that is now disappearing before our eyes.

The coming of postmodernity might also suggest that the *politics* of penality—with its characteristic conflicts, interest groups, structural constraints, cultural sensibilities, etc.—are no longer as we have come to understand them. The plausibility of current political objectives, the appropriateness of particular values, the possibility of desired social arrangements, and the viability of specific reform strategies would all be put in question if we have indeed entered upon a new historical era in which the assumptions of modernity no longer hold.

Following a discussion of the issues and an extended attempt to set out a postmodern interpretation of current penal trends, my argument will be that the concept of the postmodern is not particularly persuasive or powerful as a means of understanding contemporary penal developments. I will suggest instead that the various changes taking place are better understood in terms of concepts derived from the sociology of modernity, and I will briefly sketch out an analysis that attempts to make such an interpretation. My claim will be that these changes are the outcome of certain long-term modernizing dynamics operating in combination with a set of conjunctural political and cultural shifts. To the extent that important changes have occurred—and indeed they have—these need to be understood at a level of specificity that is less global and less world-historic than the notion of postmodernity tends to imply. They need to be understood in relation to the specific social and penal settings in which they occur—globalizing tendencies have not altogether erased the importance of national differences in this respect, as comparative research has shown (e.g., Downes 1988)—and in relation to the shifting political and professional balances of power in these locales.

That I come to a negative conclusion on the question of postmodern penality does not, I think, make the discussion of these matters any less valuable. The attempt to come to terms with the idea of the postmodern in social and cultural studies has had the immense value of sharpening our sense of the historical and cultural configuration in which we live. In debating the postmodern, social theorists have improved our understanding of modernity and the ways in which it is and is not subject to change. The discussion now under way in respect of penality has the potential to do the same in this corner of social inquiry.

PENAL MODERNITY

The concept of the postmodern (and its derivatives, postmodernism and postmodernity) is, of course, defined in terms of a contrast with the modern (and with modernism and modernity), although the precise referents of these generic terms will vary according to the field in which they operate. The contrasts between the modern and the postmodern in the conventions that govern the production and reception of artistic, architectural or literary works are rather different from the contrasts drawn by sociologists between modern and postmodern social forms, cultural experiences, or political interventions. Consequently, it is necessary to begin by describing how terms such as modern and modernism have come to be used in the sociology of punishment and penal history. In setting out the key features of penal modernity I also provide a basis from which to gauge the extent to which current trends depart from the modern configuration.

The modern system for managing, supervising, and punishing violators of the criminal law is a specialized differentiated one, formally independent of other normative systems, and increasingly distinct from other forms of legal regulation. It is largely state controlled and administered by professional bureaucracies that exercise legally sanctioned powers over individual offenders, utilizing institutions and sanctions specially designed for that purpose. Historical work makes it clear that these modern arrangements were put in place comparatively recently, and in fact the movement toward system differentiation and professionalization continues today. In that respect, modernity is best thought of as a dynamic and continuing historical process rather than a static social type.

As the nation-state gradually wrestled control of the power to punish away from competing secular and spiritual authorities and concentrated it in the institutions of criminal justice, so too did the forms of punishment take on their distinctive modern character. The traditional repertoire of corporal and symbolic punishments, carried out in public, together with banishment and exile and public works, slowly gave way to the deprivation of liberty, the use of institutional enclosures, and a quiet penal discipline that took place largely behind the scenes.

The prison and the reformatory have come to be seen as the characteristic inventions of the nineteenth century, although it is probably more accurate to regard that period as the point at which such institutions became the standard and accepted response to crime. In fact, penal institutions based on work and reformatory discipline had been evolving in Europe since the mid-sixteenth century, and may be regarded as one of the institutional features of the early modern social landscape that began to emerge in Europe at that time (Spierenburg 1991; Beattie 1986). Similarly, monetary penalties slowly became a standardized means of punishing offenders. Fines payable to the state came to replace the traditional practice of private restitutive settlements between the parties, and, with the monetarization of the economy, it gradually became possible to use the fine to punish the mass of common offenders and not just the wealthy minority. To this penal repertoire, the twentieth century added a lighter, more dispersed network of supervisory practices, variously known as probation, suspended sentences, parole, or community supervision. In the perspective of the long term, these were new forms of punishment and control, adapted to the conditions of modernity, and substituting for traditional modes of control, which had become either ineffective or intolerable.

These new institutions emerged correlatively with groups of functionaries that, over time, became increasingly differentiated and professionalized, developing distinctive identities, ideologies, and interests. And alongside this developing industry there emerged a profession of criminologists whose task it was to supply the new forms of knowledge upon which the system increasingly depends: knowledge about individual offenders and their antecedents, but also the reflexive, self-monitoring knowledge that has become such a necessary aspect of all modern institutions. Modern organizations strive to become transparent to themselves, scrutinizing their own practices, tracing their own effects, and it is this reflexive function—rather than their more ambitious efforts to uncover the causes of crime—that increasingly provides criminologists with their professional raison d'être.

THE CULTURE OF MODERN PENALITY

The apparatus of modern penality has, over the past two centuries and more, slowly displaced the penal arrangements of traditional society. Where traces of these remain, as with the death penalty, their forms and representations have been thoroughly "modernized."[2] For most of that two-hundred-year period, a powerful reforming tradition of Enlightenment rationalism has been the leading current of penal culture. Against the "harsh" methods and "terroristic" objectives of absolutist penal regimes, this liberal reforming movement counterposed utility, rationality, the rights of man, and the rule of law. Punishments were to be regulated by law and by reason, carefully calibrated to ensure the maximum effect from the minimum of pain, put to good use rather than striking out destructively and at random. From Montesquieu, Voltaire, and Beccaria to Howard, Bentham, and Mill, punishments were to be rationally administered and made positive in their results. According to this way of thinking, punishment should be preventative. It should deter, reform, and, if necessary, restrain. Hence, it should be measured, parsimonious, temperate, not destructive of the offender's capacities, and not neglectful of his or her rights. A reformed criminal law was to be the first step toward realizing this liberal program. The well-run penitentiary would be its showpiece institution. The fine, especially the modern system of adjusted installments and day-fines, would be its most authentic expression.

From around the 1890s a different cultural theme began to emerge in the penal realm. This new current was a legitimate child of Enlightenment tradition; indeed, in many ways it was the highest expression of that tradition's rationalist and utilitarian ambitions. But the new current opposed itself to the penological program of Beccaria and Bentham and viewed itself as an antidote to that program rather than a development of it. This new approach is usually known as the treatment model, correctionalism, or else the rehabilitative ideal, and is closely associated with the new science of criminology (or "criminological positivism" as the latter is often termed). I think, however, that these terms tend to narrow the phenomenon, reducing a whole way of thinking and acting to the particular forms of policy to which it gave rise. I would prefer to describe the new approach as a new penal rationality that might best be known as *penological modernism*. This term will, I hope, capture the scope and historic importance of this new approach, as well as suggest the links between this specifically penal culture and the trends that dominated other areas of cultural and intellectual life from the 1890s onward. It describes not just a particular policy but a whole style of reasoning, together with the broad program of criminological thought and penological action to which it gave rise.

Penological modernism took the Enlightenment rationalist framework to its logical conclusion and, in so doing, threw out many of its liberal principles and assumptions about how to govern the social realm. Punishment in general, and retributive punishment in particular, is viewed by modernists as an irrational disutility, a remnant of premodern traditions based upon emotion, instinct, and superstition. Even the liberal principles of proportionality and uniformity are tainted by archaic thinking. The proper management of crime and criminals requires individualized, corrective measures adapted to the specific case or the particular problem. To this end, one needs expert knowledge, scientific research, and flexible instruments of intervention, as well as a willingness to regulate aspects of life that had previously been deemed beyond the reach of government. The normative system of law must give way to that of science. Punishment must be replaced by treatment. Good government and social utility should become the overriding aims of criminal justice.

For penal modernism, the phenomena of crime are symptoms of deeper problems. They speak of maladjusted individuals and social pathologies. Good government can address these underlying problems, given the proper know-how and the political will. Penality need no longer be a tragic realm in which bad things happen. In this new reforming culture, knowledge, transparency, the understanding of action, and the in-depth control of conduct become the key considerations. Moral concerns give way to technical issues. The more complex and layered image of psychological man, with its social determinants and precarious stability, replaces the robust rational hedonist that Bentham had described. Welfarism and social defense, in-depth knowledge and in-depth intervention, individual investigation, and customized treatment regimes are the hallmarks of the modernist program.

It seems to me that this program can properly be described as modernist in respect of its technicist, social engineering, positivist style; because of its statism and its explicit linking of penality with distinctively modern strategies of rule; because of its utter confidence that human reason can penetrate to the essential truth of social conditions, making them fully amenable to social control; and above all because the criminologists and reformers of the early twentieth century were self-consciously aligning themselves with the culture of scientific modernism that they saw all around them. It is also modernist in that it reflects the interests and experience of key actors and social groups who owe their existence to the new functional positions that emerged in the modern system. Penal modernism is the product and working ideology of the new professional groupings in the modern penal system, the new class of criminological experts and knowledge professionals who increasingly challenged the hold that lawyers and moralists once had on this field.

From the 1890s onward, penal modernism increasingly became the leading *critical* discourse in the penal realm, and was widely supported by criminologists, psychiatrists, social workers, and penal reformers. During the course of the twentieth century, this critical vision began to make a serious impression, as social inquiries, reformatory regimes, individual classification, and indeterminate sentences became routine aspects of the system. The practical success of the new movement was always uneven and rarely satisfied its most enthusiastic proponents. There was always resistance to its efforts, either from the liberal legalism of the Enlightenment tradition, which insisted upon proportionality and just deserts, or else from an older, premodern tradition, which saw punishment either as an important end in itself or else as a necessary manifestation of sovereign power. But the modernist movement did succeed in transforming the character of penality to some extent and it was able to do so because the ideologies and interests of the new penal professionals articulated smoothly with the developing strategies of rule of the welfare state (see Garland 1985). "Reform," "rehabilitation," "treatment and training," "the best interests of the child"—all of these objectives meshed effectively with the ideological stress upon universal citizenship and social integration that characterized social politics in the postwar period. So too did the concern to utilize science for social purposes and to extend the capacity of the state to govern more and more aspects of individual and social life.

Above all, the modernist reformers succeeded in the establishment of a new apparatus of investigation, assessment, record-keeping, classification, and prediction. And while this apparatus was initially justified in the name of rehabilitation and welfarism, its uses were not, and are not, restricted to those of that particular version of the modernist program. Penal modernism insists upon an apparatus of investigation, upon expert authority, upon self-reflexive, rationalized practices, and upon a utilitarian, rationalist orientation. But the substantive ends to which this apparatus is put remain indeterminate. It is, and always has been, an apparatus capable of supporting strategies other than the rehabilitative, correctionalist one that accompanied its construction.

The politics of penal modernism are deeply ambivalent. They depend upon the ideological orientation of those who staff the institutions, and upon the political and legal context in which they operate. They can range from the Fabian reformism that has dominated British criminology and the British social work establishment to the crude authoritarianism of many fascist and communist regimes. Moreover, one cannot read off the effects of these programs from the declared objectives of the reformers' programs, as critical analyses sometimes do, since these aims have frequently been undermined or transformed in the process of implementation (cf. Rothman 1980; Allen 1981). Like the Enlightenment tradition from which it stems, penal modernism is capable of progressive and humane applications, but also of reactionary and dehumanizing ones.

Much of the revisionist penal history of the last twenty-five years has been concerned to bring the repressive aspect of the Enlightenment to our attention, sometimes in a very dramatic and disconcerting way. As we will see, the relatively rapid transformation of modernism from being a critical, reforming program, to being an element of the established regime and the focus of a newly critical self-consciousness, is one of the causes of what I have elsewhere termed the current "crisis of penal modernism" (Garland 1990:7). The question to be addressed is whether that crisis is a terminal one, which now points to the death of modernism and the emergence of a postmodern penality, or whether it will be recuperated in a modernism that survives despite its chronic weaknesses and self-doubt. To better approach that question, we need to consider the accounts of penal change that are currently in circulation. As we will see, the postmodern thesis does not deny these existing accounts, so much as subsume them within a broader characterization of penal and social change.

THEORIES OF TRANSFORMATION

One of the most interesting characteristics of commentary on penality today is that everyone agrees the field is changing, and in fundamental ways. However, there is surprisingly little agreement about the precise nature of this transformation, or about the causes that are bringing it about.

Francis Allen (1981) has described the "decline of the rehabilitative ideal" during the 1970s, and has attributed this ideological shift to a series of converging circumstances, including the failure of correctional efforts, abuses of implementation, and a changed cultural climate in which value consensus and faith in state institutions are no longer widespread. Others have taken up this story and described the subsequent movement toward determinate sentencing laws that took place in the United States and elsewhere, as well as the broader influence of the just-deserts model upon sentencing, prison regimes, and even probation practice (see von Hirsch 1983; Bottoms and Preston 1980; Hudson 1987; Cavadino and Dignan 1992).

While acknowledging the ideological changes noted by Allen, sociologists such as Andrew Scull and Stanley Cohen have identified the expansion of "community corrections" as the major developmental tendency. Scull (1977) initially suggested there had been a shift from custody to community prompted by fiscal considerations and the critique of "total institutions," but later acknowledged that "decarceration" was less evident in the penal sphere than it was in the control of treatment of the mentally ill (see Scull 1984). Cohen (1985) argued that, despite the apparent intentions of reformers, no transfer of the penal population from institutional confinement to community supervision had actually occurred, but rather that there had been an overall expansion in "the net of penal control," with both prisons and community "alternatives" undergoing a massive expansion and elaboration (see also Gordon 1991; Marx 1988). Cohen's net-widening thesis has been very influential, among practitioners as well as academics, but it has been recently been subjected to criticism. Maeve McMahon (1990) has questioned the empirical and methodological basis of Cohen's claim, suggesting that some of the evidence for the proposition may be unreliable and pointing to the fact that policymakers and practitioners have begun to take steps to prevent the occurrence of this unintended consequence.[3] Tony Bottoms (1983) has also argued that the most significant development of the last twenty years is not the expansion of the net of penal control, and certainly not "the dispersal of discipline" in any Foucauldian sense, but rather the increased use of sanctions such as the fine, compensation, and suspended sentences, which involve little in the way of "normalization." Bottoms places this development in parallel with a trend toward more severe custodial sentencing for offenders who are deemed to be "dangerous," and suggests that this "bifurcated" penal strategy is designed to deal with two different populations of offender. For those offenders who are viewed as largely self-controlled and integrated into mainstream society through work, family, respectability, and so on, a light form of penalty is all that is required. For those offenders who are deemed more marginal or more threatening, the emphasis continues to be upon punitive discipline and incapacitation.

Bottoms is also one of several commentators (see also Peters 1988; Feeley and Simon 1992; Tuck 1991) who have pointed to the growth of what he terms "managerialism" in the penal system—a new and pronounced concern with system management, resource allocation, cost-benefit considerations, and organizational efficiency. This theme is given its fullest elaboration by Malcolm Feeley and Jonathan Simon (1992), who argue that the managerial approach forms a part of a "new penology," which is beginning to emerge as an important framework of thought and action.

According to Feeley and Simon, the social-psychological criminology of the mid–twentieth century—and the normalizing, rehabilitative penal practice that it supported—is now being displaced by a framework that no longer focuses upon the individual offender and no longer aims to produce behavioral change. Instead, the new approach addresses itself to aggregate populations and large groups of offenders, which it seeks to manage by reference to actuarial inferences from statistical data sets. The calculation of risks is now a matter of viewing each individual as a member of a calculable group, whose profile can be derived from actuarial tables compiled from large-scale data sets that condense the details of large numbers of offenders, rather than seeking to develop a direct clinical knowledge of the particular individual. The primary goal of prediction is now to ensure the proper allocation of resources and the efficient management of risk, not to secure the best treatment for the purpose of individual reform.

As Simon discovered in his own research, field workers in probation and parole (at least in parts of the United States) are ceasing to be social work counsellors and are becoming risk management technicians, whose task it is to monitor offenders by means of urinalysis and electronic checks, measuring them the whole time against an actuarial profile of high and low risk. Professional, clinical discretion is increasingly limited by centralized system monitoring in which the key decision is whether to return the offender to custody or not. And where returning a client to court was previously regarded as a failure to rehabilitate, it is now seen as an index of the efficient and effective management of risk (see Simon 1993).

For Feeley and Simon, this new penology is the outcome of a number of forces. The resource pressures upon penal systems, the failures of penal-welfare strategies, the logic of modern power-knowledge, the decline of industrial work, the erosion of the community resources and solidarities upon which the old penology relied, and the willingness of governments to accept the existence of an underclass that is to be contained and controlled without any serious prospect of integration into the social and economic mainstream all combine to render the old penology archaic and produce conditions in which the new one can thrive.

One of the characteristics of this new penology is that criminological discourse becomes more statistical, more actuarial, ever more concerned with aggregate groups and populations, and decreasingly interested in the individual offender as a clinical case. This point registers one aspect of a broader shift that has affected criminological thinking since the 1970s. Starting with the influential work of James Q.Wilson in the United States, and of Ron Clarke in the United Kingdom, the idea of the offender as a maladapted or undersocialized individual with a criminal disposition has been challenged by a conception of the offender as a rational economic actor. This new pragmatic approach argues that, whatever the truth of the matter, offenders can, for policy purposes, be regarded as if they are fully rational agents, responding to incentives and disincentives, seizing opportunities where they exist, and desisting from crime wherever situational deterrents or preventatives are set in place. The criminal is thus viewed as a kind of consumer, though one who must be repelled rather than seduced (see Wilson 1983; Clarke 1983; Cornish and Clarke 1986; Mayhew, Clarke, Sturman, and Hough 1976; Felson 1994).

A similar emphasis on the rational, "responsible" actor now features in, of all places, the policy statements of prison regimes, which declare that the prisoner must be viewed as a customer who is capable of making choices and must be "made to take responsibility" for such things as sentence planning and personal development (Scottish Prison Service 1990). It has echoes as well in the philosophy of punishment, which has also undergone significant shifts in the last two decades. Here one sees a forceful reemergence of a deontological discourse, emphasizing the autonomy of the individual but also the necessity of punishment as a social duty and thus an end in itself. The intellectual focus is now much more upon *retribution*—whether as a Kantian requirement of justice or as a means of communicating community values. Utilitarian argument and reformative purposes have given way to an emphasis upon desert, denunciation, and punishment (see Duff and Garland 1994). And although much of this retributive theorizing emerged as a liberal reaction to the excesses of the therapeutic state, the new respectability it has lent to "punishment" would seem to have encouraged more punitive government discourses and policies (see Home Office 1988). What was originally intended as a liberal critique of modernist reasoning in favor of classic Enlightenment restraints has been taken up by a more punitive antimodernism, which emphasizes the importance of punishment as a symbol of sovereign power and social authority.

A POSTMODERN PENALITY?

We have, then, a cluster of historical theses. Each one highlights a transforming dynamic, each draws distinctions between a before and an after, and each characterizes the present as somehow different from the arrangements that prevailed in the past. Penality is variously described, in effect, as "postrehabilitative," "postdisciplinary," "postcriminological," "postindustrial," "postutilitarian." No wonder that the term *postmodern* so easily suggests itself to many analysts as a way of summing up the present. Penality is a social field in flux. It is eclectic; host to a hotchpotch of different discourses and programs; devoid of any coherent, overall direction. The fleeting, fragmentary, recursive quality of postmodern culture seems to have displaced what was once a strong sense of penality's historic mission and progressive reforming program. One of the few constant themes to emerge is a negative one, namely, that all of these diverse developments tend to define themselves in opposition to the framework of penal modernism.

Postmodern is the term that most readily suggests itself as a way of characterizing—however vaguely—the dynamics and discontents of the present. And as we have seen, postmodernism is beginning to enter the discourse as a shorthand, catchall term that conveys the sense of one era ending and another getting under way. But despite the attractions of this way of conceiving things—particularly its implication that nothing is settled and that the future of penality is once more "up for grabs"—there is reason to avoid the casual use of such powerful terms, especially if their tendency is to overstate the novelty of the present and to imply a qualitative break with the past. In the pages that follow, I have sought to go beyond the fragmentary suggestions made by other commentators, and to set out a more elaborated account of postmodernity in the penal realm. This account is my attempt to explore the possibility that the phenomena and developments described as postmodern in the wider sociological and philosophical literature might have a number of direct analogies in the field of penality. Other theorists may subsequently construct a different and more persuasive account, in which case my conclusions will need to be revised. However, I have sought to make the postmodernist case in its strongest form, given my own, no doubt limited, understanding of both the literature of postmodernism and the contemporary character of penal developments.

What follows, then, is an inventory of postmodern sightings in the penal field—glimpses of what might conceivably be postmodern phenomena, whether these be forms of consciousness, discursive formations, or policies and practices. First, I will present these observations in a way that highlights their postmodern affiliations. Thereafter I will consider whether this is the most plausible way of interpreting them.

Most strikingly, one can point to a collapse of the grand narrative of penal reform and penal progress as a characteristic sign of the postmodern.[4] In the penal context, this collapse has a number of aspects. The Enlightenment ideal of a rational, utilitarian penal policy has been subjected to a thoroughgoing critique. Revisionist histories have changed our relationship to the Enlightenment project. Where we once saw the advance of reason and humanity, we now see a darker side. The monstrous aspects of modernity— its disciplines, its dehumanization, its well-administered Holocausts—are now never far from our thoughts when considering policies of "correctional intervention" or "social defence"(see Foucault 1977; Christie 1993; Bauman 1989). This disavowal of Enlightenment rationalism is most forcefully expressed in contemporary reactions to the treatment or rehabilitative model, or, more broadly, to what I have termed penal modernism. The modernist project is now regarded not just as a failure, but as a positive danger—an intrusive, authoritarian program, blind to the importance of individual autonomy and human worth. After a century of tirelessly pursuing the modernist vision, criminologists and penologists now increasingly distance themselves from its aims.

The intellectual climate and penal policy culture of the 1970s and 1980s took on a disillusioned, cynical, nihilistic character. For the first time in two hundred years there was no guiding vision, no coherent philosophy of progress. Instead, there was the sense of the exhaustion of a tradition, the end of an era. The view that "nothing works" quickly became widespread, particularly among academics, and even the most optimistic of practitioners lacked general solutions. The best one could hope for became small-scale, local initiatives with a markedly low level of ambition (see Palmer 1992). The broad consensus of the correctionalist era quickly fragmented, and in its place there emerged an eclectic mixture of competing perspectives and politics. The old paradigm was dead, but no new one rose up to replace it. The leading historian of the age of penal progress—Sir Leon Radzinowicz—set his judgment on the new era, when he gave his review of recent history the title "Penal Regressions" (Radzinowicz 1991).

In criminological discourse, and indeed in crime control policies, there is evidence of what one might term a shift from depth to surface.[5] It was an article of faith for criminological modernism that crime is a symptom of deeper psychological and social problems that must be investigated and treated; that the truth of crime lay deep in the offender's biography and circumstances. Nowadays prominent criminologists are losing interest in criminological depth, and indeed, in criminological truth (cf. Wilson 1983; Clarke 1983). Pragmatic considerations prompt a return to surface phenomena—to choices and opportunities and rational calculations. Whatever one thinks about causation, offenders can be treated "as if" they are free, rational, responsible individuals, responsive to penalties and prices. Crime can be addressed by manipulating situations rather than changing dispositions. The fact that such policies do not address the "root causes" or deep-lying problems is not perceived as a failing. Pragmatic considerations prefer available, manipulable surface to hard-to-reach depth. In any case, the critique of the treatment model has made in-depth approaches problematic in principle as well as in practice. In these perspectives, the category of the criminal shifts from deep subject to shallow opportunist, from psychological man to situational actor, from a specific individual with a history that has to be explored to a universalized decision-maker whose behavior can be statistically predicted.

These shallow conceptions of the offender, though important for policy, are by no means the only current conceptions. Indeed, the criminological field has never been more diverse, fragmented, and eclectic (see Ericson and Carriere 1994). Genetic, neurological, and biological perspectives that were once considered archaic are now back in the repertoire (see Nelkin 1995) as are econometric models, so that there is hardly any human science approach that is not present in the criminological domain. The field is divided into dozens of competing perspectives, none of which can claim to be the orthodox position. This endemic eclecticism and pluralism has given rise to a sense that the "truth" of crime is unattainable. All that we have is a repertoire of accounts that can be selectively drawn upon depending on one's purposes. The self-conscious sense that truth-claims, in this field, are merely strategic rhetorics—that one describes offenders in ways that suit one's purposes rather as lawyers do in court—echoes a broader sense that postmodern pragmatism has replaced modernist hopes of scientific objectivity.

The relativization (and thus the abolition) of criminological truth has its parallel in the relativization of morals in the penal realm. Despite its claim to be a form of social hygiene or social medicine, the rehabilitative approach confidently endorsed a definite moral code with which offenders were to be realigned. Values such as work, respectability, domesticity, sociability, and self-knowledge were at least as important in the process as respect for law or the prevention of recidivism. The postmodern decline of moral codes and the erosion of state authority have destroyed the easy moral confidence upon which rehabilitation was based. Using the penal process to impose values upon inmates and clients is now viewed as morally suspect. The moral authority of the system is contested and uncertain. The idea of a mainstream moral community into which offenders must be integrated appears dangerously outmoded in the age of multiculturalism, moral disestablishment, and the deification of "difference."

Crime-control has likewise become increasingly amoral or demoralized. Policies such as situational crime prevention, target-hardening, and general deterrence seek to manage criminal risks, not to reform criminal attitudes. Similarly, the displacement of rehabilitation by just deserts and incapacitation makes punishment a matter of costs and constraints, not moral education. Punishment becomes a system of inputs and outputs, risks and resources, and the impact of moral sentiments (whether these are compassionate or punitive) are viewed by the professionals as a kind of unwanted noise in the system.[6]

Systems of crime-control have become increasingly self-referential and self-serving, increasingly "autopoietic."[7] The aim is no longer to respond to external social demands for the control of crime and the reform of offenders. Instead the aim is to develop an immunity from outside demands of this kind by setting up internal aims and self-generated criteria of success. If the system cannot influence crime rates, then perhaps it can at least control punishment rates. If it fails in its social task, perhaps it needs to redefine its mission in terms of goals it can achieve—hence the focus on system management, new performance indicators, and the repeated refrain that police and prisons cannot control crime by themselves.

The waning of penal modernism, and the widespread cynicism about penality's capacity to produce real social benefits, has been accompanied by a much more explicit commercialization of the penal process. The monetary costs of doing justice are no longer a background consideration. Instead they are foregrounded and explicitly made part of the process. They become a value consideration on the same plane as other values (such as justice and humanity) and in direct competition with them. So, for example, the British police were recently advised by the government's Audit Commission to classify reported offenses into those which would be investigated and those which would not, in order to avoid wasting resources on inquiries that are likely to be fruitless (reported in the *Manchester Guardian* 20 September 1993).

In much the same way, crime control and punishment have become much more explicitly politicized. Issues that were once a matter for expert discretion—such as sentencing decisions, regime design, and the content of supervision—are no longer left to the professionals and their established canon of accepted practices. Instead these have become the subject of political debate and public controversy. The widespread fear of crime and the sense of urban insecurity have prompted politicians to reclaim the issue and to make it a core symbol in debates about social order and political authority (see Scheingold 1991; Hall, Critcher, Jefferson, Clarke, and Roberts 1978). And in these debates, the findings of criminologists and the common sense of penal functionaries are not regarded as authoritative.

Finally, one might mention the tendency of philosophical writing in this area to focus more and more upon the signs and symbols of punishment. The new philosophical work privileges the expressive over the instrumental, characterizing punishment not as a form of violence or material deprivation, but as a special form of communication. Punishment is increasingly seen as a system of signs and images, a semiotic conductor, a way of "saying things with walls" (see Duff and Garland 1994). At a time when theorists of postmodernity are increasingly intent on rethinking the social world as an economy of signs, an information society, a universe of free-floating images and *simulacra* (cf. Baudrillard 1983), we begin to see the materiality of punishment dissolved into one more set of ethereal signs and representations.

THE PERSISTENCE OF THE MODERN

The collapse of grand narratives and Enlightenment ideals, the preference for surface over depth, the fragmentation of discourse and moral code, the self-conscious pragmatism and eclecticism, the waning of affect and of a sense of history, the dominance of signs and images, the turn to nihilism, localism, commercialism, politicization.[8] These are, of course, the well-known thematics and motifs of the postmodern, and the fact that penality can be represented in these terms indicates that the thesis of an emerging postmodernity has a certain plausibility.

Such a thesis would have considerable appeal. If penal trends could be shown to be local instances or analogs of broader social and cultural trends, then this might provide a powerful means of explaining the causes and character of the contemporary penal changes. Explaining the particular by reference to the general, the penal by reference to the social and cultural, is, after all, a favored explanatory trope in the sociology of punishment. Similarly, it would be a nice paradox (and sociologists are notoriously susceptible to paradoxical accounts) if a system that is often seen as archaic, uncivilized, even premodern, were to be shown to be at the forefront of cultural and social change. But despite these attractions, I want to argue that the developments that are affecting contemporary penality are occurring *within* the contours of modernity and modernism, rather than representing some kind of break with them. Therefore, if the notion of the postmodern implies such a break, as I believe it does, if it involves a movement beyond the contours of the modern into some new and distinctive social and cultural configuration, then it would be misleading to talk of a postmodern penality in any empirically descriptive sense.[9] I will argue that we should think instead in terms of a penality that has entered a phase of "high modernity" (cf. Giddens 1990) or, as I might less elegantly put it, a self-conscious and hence self-doubting phase of modernity. Such descriptions place the phenomena within the long-term processes of modernization, which I will argue to be their proper analytical location, and suggest the continued relevance of the sociology of modernity as a framework for their explanation.

I would argue, against my own effort to represent penality as postmodern —and, by implication, against other attempts to do the same—that the postmodernist interpretation is undermined by three interrelated problems: first of all, the indeterminacy and ambiguity of some of the key concepts involved; second, the fact that certain purportedly postmodern characteristics are actually typical of modernity rather than distinct from it; third, that the thesis of a distinctive postmodern social configuration depends upon a caricature of modernity and its sociological referents.

Some of these "postmodern sightings" fail to carry much evidentiary weight because the motifs of postmodern identification are so abstract and empirically indeterminate that facts can easily be made to fit. For example, claims about the decline of grand narratives could have been made at any time in history. Grand narratives are always collapsing, only to be replaced by others. (Ironically enough, postmodernism has become such an all-encompassing account of historical and cultural change that *it* is often presented as if it were a candidate for such a status, to the embarrassment of theorists like Lyotard, who are thus caught in a contradiction.) *Penal modernism*—like the modernisms that prevailed in architecture, or art, or literature—has always had its critics and dissenters, just as the rationalism of the Enlightenment has long been challenged by romantics, conservatives, and traditionalists of all kinds. As I argued above, the narrative of penal modernism was always compromised and challenged by these alternative narratives. Today, opposition to modernism still takes the dual form of a liberal "just deserts" critique, and a more conservative drive toward a form of punitiveness that operates as an archaic symbol of sovereignty. All that has changed is the balance of power in the struggle to define what punishment should mean. And even then, the basic Enlightenment notion that punishment should be made to be useful—that it should aim to control crime and reform criminals—continues to be the central assumption of most penal policy, despite the skepticism of academic critics. Moreover, although the critique of penal modernism has clearly had an international impact, it is by no means clear that the "decline of rehabilitation" or the "critique of positivist criminology" has meant the same thing in different national contexts.

Other aspects of my account suffer from a similar imprecision and looseness of fit. Metaphors of surface and depth are just that—metaphors—which are too vague and too loose in their application to be very useful analytical tools. This is especially true when such terms are applied to discursive fields where they have no settled meaning or controlled connotations. In the field of aesthetics, the concepts of surface and depth are well defined and capable of precise and well-understood usage. But when one uses these terms out of context, they become metaphors rather than concepts, and can be used to gloss very different phenomena with spurious and superficial resemblances. Criminology's supposed relinquishment of "depth" and new concentration upon "surface" is probably a gloss of this kind, which simplifies a complex discursive phenomenon and overstates the resemblances between developments in criminology and broader cultural trends. We should remind ourselves, for instance, that J. Q. Wilson is also the author of *Crime and Human Nature: The Definitive Study of the Causes of Crime* (Wilson and Herrnstein 1985), which suggests that the concern for etiological inquiry has not entirely faded. Similarly, we should note that perhaps the most influential criminological work of the 1980s and early 1990s was that of Travis Hirschi and his co-workers, whose concern is precisely to produce a general theory of crime (see Gottfredson and Hirschi 1990). We should also remember that the rejection of causal inquiry in favor of a more pragmatic type of analysis is no new development of the 1970s and 1980s. In the immediate postwar period, at the height of enthusiasm for penal modernism and "positivist" criminology, leading figures, such as Walter Reckless, Mannheim and Wilkins, and Leon Radzinowicz all argued for the pragmatic, administrative approach that J. Q. Wilson is now assumed to have invented (see Garland 1994). More importantly, the depth/surface distinction breaks down when one recalls that, however familiar they have become, notions such as reason and the calculation of economic interest involve a definite psychology and conceptions of subjectivity that are hardly behaviorist. And to describe rational choice criminology as postmodern would be to suggest that neoclassical economics and Benthamite utilitarianism must also be included in postmodernism.

There are, at present, interesting changes taking place in the ways in which the figure of "the criminal" is represented in official and policy-oriented criminology. These changes are important and are influenced by wider political and ideological trends, as well as by pragmatic considerations. (The now-popular image of the offender as situationally induced actor seems closer to the modern figure of the consumer than to the Enlightenment ideal of the rational man.) But changing styles of criminological representation are just glossed over and explained away if we take them to be merely one more example of a general stylistic shift that first occurred in architecture and aesthetics and now purportedly defines the whole cultural domain.

Similar points can be made about criminology's eclecticism, which I would claim is a constitutive part of the discipline, rather than a new development (see Garland 1994; Ericson and Carriere, 1994), and about the demoralization of policy, commercialism, politicization, and so on. Each of these claims is easier to assert than to demonstrate, because they all rely upon a version of the past (and of the present) that derives from critical purposes rather than from historical research. It may be the case that commercial and political concerns have become more prominent recently, if the contrast is with the immediate past, but a longer-term comparison would show no great change in this respect (see Rusche and Kirchheimer 1968; Wiener 1990). And alongside the "demoralization" of some policy developments one would have to place the "remoralization" of penal measures, which has been a theme of recent governmental rhetoric in both the United States and the United Kingdom. To assert the coming of postmodernity in the penal realm is to rely upon spurious contrasts and pseudohistorical periodizations. As an interpretation it depends upon our willingness to accept very simplified accounts of how things used to be as a basis for differentiating how they are today (cf. Calhoun 1993).

If the concept of the postmodern does not advance our understanding of contemporary trends in penality, what will? In the remainder of this paper I present a number of points that suggest that the rumblings of contemporary change need to be placed within a long-term process of modernity and modernization, rather than mistaken for signs of a great postmodern upheaval. And to the extent that institutional changes and shifts of direction are occurring, these should be attributed to political forces that are local, contingent, and reversible, rather than to the stirrings of a new historical epoch (cf. O'Malley 1991). Precisely because the changes affecting contemporary penality do not involve a break with the broad sociohistoric configuration of modernity, any analysis of these developments will have to proceed at a much lower and more concrete level of analysis.

The first thing to notice is that the *apparatus* of penal practice is not undergoing any major change of form or any radical shift of emphasis. When we move from the rather impressionistic analysis of discourse to the more quantifiable examination of institutional practice, we do not see the same glimmers of a major realignment. Imprisonment, supervision, and monetary penalties continue to be the mainstay of penal practice, and there is no sign that any one of these sectors will soon disappear or that a new one will emerge to augment them. There are, of course, new technologies of surveillance, new forms of custody, and new financial sanctions (see Gordon 1991; Marx 1988). And the balance between the different sectors is continually shifting as the whole system expands in an uneven and usually unplanned way. But this is not an era in which new institutions and practices are being legislated into existence. It is not, in that sense, comparable with the late eighteenth century or with the period between the 1890s and the First World War. If the apparatus of penality is changing, it is in its objectives and orientation, not in its institutional forms.

Once in place, the infrastructure of penality attains a certain resilience and inertia, and major changes in that apparatus tend to occur slowly and against a great deal of resistance. But these institutions and practices are always capable of being deployed in a number of different ways and supporting quite distinct strategies, so that change at the level of strategy can be much more rapid and much more frequent. Thus, for example, the procedures of examination, assessment, and classification—which were gradually introduced during the course of the twentieth century as part of the strategy of penal-welfarism (see Garland 1985)—were not suddenly dismantled when the policy of rehabilitation fell into disrepute. On the contrary, they were simply put to different uses, such as measuring security risk or crime career profiles. Consequently, the normalizing apparatus continues to grow more extensive and more sophisticated, even if the aims that guide it now seem somewhat different (see Cohen 1985).

Similarly, the professional groups that staff the penal apparatus are essentially the same ones that have been developing throughout the twentieth century, albeit that each individual sector has expanded and differentiated, and the balance of power between and within groups has been subject to frequent change. The working patterns and official objectives of probation officers, prison governors, parole agents, and others are currently undergoing important changes, partly in response to new social environments, partly at the behest of political masters with specific agendas (see Simon 1993;

Hudson 1993). But there is nothing to suggest the diminishing importance of the utilitarian forms of knowledge and knowledge-based intervention that have come to define modern penality and the contribution that these professional groups make to it. Nor is it clear that the forces bringing about these changes are identical on either side of the Atlantic. [Compare the analyses in Rees and Hall-Williams (1989) with those of Simon (1993).]

The rise of managerialism in the penal sphere is a new and important development, and analysts such as Feeley and Simon have made a valuable contribution by highlighting this trend and its potential consequences. But managerialism is a phenomenon that is largely explicable in terms of the dynamics of organizational growth and the new possibilities for control generated by advances in information technology. Organizational sociology, building largely upon the work of Max Weber, has long since charted this developmental tendency and identified its operation in a variety of organizational settings (see Heydebrand 1979; Heydebrand and Seron 1990). Far from being a postmodern phenomenon, the penal system is only now, somewhat belatedly, experiencing a form of management that has long been taken for granted elsewhere.

This is not to downplay the significance of these changes. Recent government initiatives accelerate this tendency by imposing strict auditing mechanisms and fiscal controls, and by requiring criminal justice agencies to monitor their performance by reference to government-specified criteria. These initiatives change the balance of power between field staff and management, subject agencies to closer governmental control, and bring about changes in the day-to-day activities of the organization and its treatment of offenders. But however significant these changes may prove to be, they fall squarely within the analytical framework of modernity rather than postmodernity.

I think the same may be said about Feeley and Simon's claim that an actuarial style of analysis is replacing the older concern for an in-depth, reformative knowledge of the individual offender (Feeley and Simon 1992). I am not convinced that this development is either as novel or as extensive as they suggest. A focus upon the differential risks posed by classes and categories, a notion of criminality as an aggregate phenomenon, and a concern to manage populations were all characteristic of the eugenics movement at the turn of the century, a movement that influenced both criminological discourse and penal policy at that time (see Garland 1985). And even today with all the clamor about career criminals and actuarial prediction, this remains a rather marginal aspect of penal *practice*, particularly outside the United States. [As Diana Gordon suggests, sometimes "the more hotly debated the policy shift, the fewer people it directly affects" (1991:34).] But even if we grant that some such shift is beginning to occur, it would be entirely in keeping with the administrative logic of modern management, and suggests the deepening importance of modernist practices rather than their supersession by something quite different.

The "decline of the rehabilitative ideal" and the "crisis of penal modernism" also need to be understood as something other than the end of an era, or one more example of the collapse of grand narrative. To begin with, the critique of penal modernism has not made it possible to think and act in ways that are postmodernist. As I noted above, the leading alternative to penal modernism is actually an Enlightenment liberalism, which is also committed to making punishment useful, but is unwilling to abandon individual rights or the rule of law in pursuit of utilitarian goals. At most, one might say that an antimodernist moralism has been resurgent since the 1970s, pressing for punishment as a ritualistic end in itself. But as I have argued at length elsewhere, modern penality has always been characterized by this struggle between the modern and the antimodern: "[T]here are two contrasting visions at work in contemporary criminal justice—the passionate, morally-toned desire to punish and the administrative, rationalistic, normalizing concern to manage. These visions clash in many important respects, but both are deeply embedded within the [modern] social practice of punishing" (Garland 1990:180).

Nor has this critique produced a lasting mood of nihilism or an abandonment of all Enlightenment ambition. Its true that a certain 1970s literature made heavy use of the rhetoric of reaction (Hirschman 1991), claiming that the correctionalist approach produced perverse results, or was altogether futile, or jeopardized the very values that it claimed to support. But this moment of intransigent opposition quickly gave way to a more positive policy climate (see Palmer 1992). The past two decades have witnessed a positive deluge of new schemes for making punishment useful again: whether through deterrence, or incapacitation, or denunciation, or punishment in the community, or through some revised form of rehabilitation. Rather than seeing the development of a postmodern consciousness on the part of penal agents, we see instead the beginnings of yet another version of a project that, in its general orientation, would be familiar to penal reformers from any time in the last two centuries.

As for the claim that the modernist penal project cannot prosper in an age of multiculturalism and moral disestablishment—that it depends upon some kind of value consensus that once existed but is now no more—this seems to misunderstand the way that normalizing practices actually work. Normalizing strategies do not require a public moral consensus because they delegate the specification of norms and values to professional agencies that develop these in the context of their local practices. Such a strategy is, in fact, characteristically found in pluralistic societies where moral standards are contested, because in these settings, more traditional sources of moral authority have been undermined and replaced by the kind of behavioral expert promoted by modernist penal policy. Typically, these experts seek to adjust conduct in pragmatic and adaptive ways, rather than to preach a moral code, and it is precisely this reliance upon "floating norms" and upon mutual, pragmatic adjustment that is best suited to modern society. The modernist penal project is not defeated by the fact of moral diversity—it was actually designed to deal with it (see Donzelot 1979). And while the critique of rehabilitation may have exposed the covert moralizing of penal professionals, it has done little to interrupt their task of seeking to impress different standards of conduct upon individual offenders.

The age of penal modernism is not yet over. Nor is penal modernity about to fade. Instead, what we have been witnessing since the late 1960s is the transformation of penal modernism from being a critical, reforming program to being itself a part of the fabric of modern penality, and hence a target for other critical, reforming movements. With this shift, one sees the closing of a long period of naive enthusiasm and optimism regarding the modernist project and the emergence of a more mature, more informed, more ambivalent understanding of what it entails. Modernism has come to understand itself better, and to appreciate that the program of modernist penality has serious limitations and is riven with a deep moral ambiguity.

This process of disillusionment and adjustment was always destined to happen. So long as modernism was a critical, reforming program, battling against a more traditional penal establishment, the likelihood of achieving successful results could be grossly overstated. Even when the system slowly began to adopt modernist practices, and the new experts and professionals struggled to lay claim to their new territory, it still made political sense to talk up the potential of this new approach. But the fact is that *reflexivity* is a crucial part of modern institutions, and as the penal system gradually modernized its approach, so too did it develop procedures for monitoring its own practices and examining their outcomes. Indeed, the new discipline of academic criminology made this monitoring and evaluating process a central part of its raison d'être, and put the scrutiny of penal practice onto a new, scientific, footing. The ironic result was that penal agencies soon learned about their own limitations and have had to face up to their failures. The accumulation of negative evidence, especially by the 1970s, has prompted these organizations to adjust to their failures—either by changing their practices, or, more usually, by altering their declared objectives and the terms by which they ask to be judged. One sees this process not just in relation to penal rehabilitation—though this has been the most dramatic example—but also, in the United Kingdom, to policing and to the government's overall policies of crime control.

This process may also help us to explain a number of important trends that are often noted but have not yet been theorized or explained in sociological terms. These include the growth of mediation and reparation schemes, the increased use of diversion, and especially the reemergence of the victim as a more active and more valued participant in the penal process.[10] To some extent, these developments might be described as a kind of controlled disinvestment by the state of certain minor aspects of criminal justice: a willingness, often prompted by resource constraints, to allow other parties into what had become a state monopoly. Similar considerations may well be involved in the development of a small commercial sector in the prison industry, and of the much larger private security industry. The new emphasis upon enlisting the help of the community in policing and preventing crime—through neighborhood watch, multi-agency policing, target hardening, etc.—might also be viewed as a de facto breakup of an unsuccessful state monopoly and an attempt to enlist the aid of civil society in the business of crime control.

Precisely because modern institutions are self-reflexive and self-monitoring, they are necessarily also self-critical and self-reforming. Foucault singled out the prison and made a scandal of the fact that this institution is always in crisis and always undergoing reform. But he might more accurately have noted that *all* modern institutions share this characteristic, be they schools, or hospitals, or even government itself. All modern institutions are forced to constantly reinvent themselves because they are all increasingly caught in the tyranny of self-knowledge. Only unrealized programs and their reforming supporters can enjoy the luxury of unchallenged optimism.

The relative (and perhaps temporary) decline of the rehabilitative ideal and of research on the causes of crime does not signal the collapse of grand narratives nor the dawn of postmodernism in the penal realm. It is merely the historical moment when a program of government has become sufficiently established to allow its limitations and unintended consequences to be made clearly visible. As it happens, that moment of institutional disillusionment coincided with a powerful shift in the political orientation of several Western governments, with the result that penal organizations have been more vulnerable to external political pressures than they might otherwise have been. Indeed, if one were writing a history of penality's present, it is probably here that one would begin. But that is another story, and one that takes as its central theme the distinctively *modern* arrangement whereby strategies of punishment are articulated with strategies of rule.

To tell that story is to engage the issues with greater empirical specificity and more finely grained analytical instruments. Temporary and reversible conjunctural shifts must be distinguished from long-term structural transformations, just as changes in discursive style and emphasis must be distinguished from more profound transformations in the problematics and rationalities that structure criminological discourse and penal policy. The rapid changes manifest at the level of government representations and rhetoric must not be mistaken for alterations in working practices and professional ideologies, nor should it be assumed that the discrediting of a particular vocabulary (such as "rehabilitation") means that the practices that it once described have altogether disappeared. The relatively fixed infrastructure of penal techniques and apparatuses must be viewed separately from the more mobile strategies that determine aims and priorities and dictate how penal resources are deployed. The distribution of activity between penal agencies, shifts in power between professional groups, the relative and absolute rates of sanctioning, the forms adopted by penal measures, and their instrumental and symbolic functioning are all analytically distinct questions requiring quite different methodologies and data if they are to be properly addressed and answered. And analyses that wish to make international generalizations must ensure that they rest upon solid comparative analysis, rather than the looseness and ambiguity of catchall conceptual terms. These more modest and more mundane forms of analysis may have less intellectual cachet than the high-flown theory of the modernity/postmodernity debate. But they are liable, in the end, to be of more assistance in the struggle to understand the present.

ACKNOWLEDGMENTS

I am grateful to the following friends and colleagues for their help with this paper: Colin Bell, Tony Bottoms, Stanley Cohen, James B. Jacobs, Russell Keat, Jonathan Simon, and Andrew von Hirsch.

NOTES

1. Philip Yenawine provides a good description of the artistic postmodern: "This term is used to reflect the diversity of styles and mediums that proliferated beginning in the 1970's, mostly reactive to modernism. . . . It is usefully defined by a set of contrasts. Where modernism was seen as elemental and formal, Post-Modern art is often ornamental, even to the point of excess. While modernists attempted to throw off the past and strove for individual innovations, Post-Modernists appropriated liberally from the past, putting old information into new contexts. Post-Modern art is blatantly emblematic and eclectic, collecting imagery, techniques, and ideas from diverse sources, some recent, some far back in history. Where modernism tried to invent universal languages that captured the "now" and were self-evidently "true" (and therefore readable by people everywhere), Post-Modernists tend to be realistic about the fact that understanding modernism helped create an elite of experts and that Post-Modernism is also difficult for many people. While modernism was metaphoric, sometimes hermetic, and enthusiastic about the potential of the times, Post-Modernists are more likely to be socially engaged in a direct sense, often skeptical, critical, and/or overtly political. While modernists tended to create signature styles and usually stuck to a single medium, Post-Modernists often change from one style to another, from one medium to another, and/or combine mediums in bold and fear-

less ways. . . . While modernism tenets proclaimed a hegemony that established an artistic mainstream, Post-Modernist eclecticism embraces great diversity, welcoming artists and styles which were relegated to modernism's margins"(Yenawine 1991:153–54). Jean-Francois Lyotard gives a definition of the term's broader use: "[T]he word *postmodern* . . . designates the state of our culture following the transformations which, since the end of the 19th century, have altered the game rules for science, literature and the arts. . . . Simplifying to the extreme, I define *postmodern* as incredulity toward metanarratives" (Lyotard 1984:xxiii–xxiv).

2. Thus although the death penalty is still employed by some modern Western states (see Hood 1989), it is nowadays represented as a technical, quasi-medical operation, which seeks to sanitize the violence involved, deny the gruesome bodily aspects of the killing, and turn the event into a symbol rather than a spectacle (see Garland 1990:ch. 10).

3. There seems little doubt that the size of the population undergoing some form of penal control has markedly increased. The question at issue is whether this expansion can be explained by the fact of higher rates of crime, or whether the development of "alternative" sanctions has played a part in bringing about the overall expansion.

4. Compare Lyotard: "Simplifying to the extreme, I define *postmodern* as incredulity toward metanarratives" (1984:xxiv).

5. Compare Jameson: "[T]he emergence of a new kind of flatness or depthlessness, a new kind of superficiality in the most literal sense [is] perhaps the supreme formal feature of all postmodernisms" (1991:59). See also Harvey (1989).

6. This is not true of all the advocates of just deserts: von Hirsch (1993) argues for a policy that combines proportionate sanctioning with moral censure.

7. Simon (1993:248) gives this as an example of contemporary penality's postmodern character. On autopoiesis, see Teubner (1992).

8. One might extend the list by referring to the tendency of current penal policy to "quote" from the penal styles of the past, producing a kind of pastiche effect, in which older practices are revived not because they are functional, but because they evoke the sense of a past era. Jonathan Simon (1993:248) refers to this as "nostalgia" and cites the current popularity of boot camps in the United States as an example.

9. The notion of a postmodern penality could certainly be used as a normative concept, or as a kind of utopian desideratum for the future. My discussion here is limited to its use as a sociological description.

10. At present, these developments have the character of radical innovations on the margins of criminal justice. Were they to develop into mainstream characteristics of the system they might well entail an important break with the structures of penal modernity.

REFERENCES

Allen, F. A. 1981. *The Decline of the Rehabilitative Ideal*. New Haven, CT: Yale University Press.

Baudrillard, J. 1983. *Simulations*. New York: Semiotext(e).
Bauman, Z. 1989. *Modernity and the Holocaust*. Cambridge: Polity.
Beattie, J. 1986. *Crime and the Courts in England 1660–1800*. Princeton, NJ: Princeton University Press.
Bottoms, A. E. 1983. "Neglected Features of Contemporary Penal Systems." Pp. 166–202 in *The Power to Punish*, edited by D. Garland and P. Young. London: Heinemann.
Bottoms, A. E. and R. Preston, eds. 1980. *The Coming Penal Crisis*. Edinburgh: Scottish Academic Press.
Brodeur, J.-P. 1993. "La Pensee Postmoderne et la Criminologie." *Criminologie* 26(1):73–121.
Calhoun, C. 1993. "Postmodernism as Pseudohistory." *Theory, Culture and Society* 10:75–96.
Cavadino, M. and J. Dignan. 1992. *The Penal System: An Introduction*. London: Sage.
Christie, N. 1993. *Crime Control as Industry*. London: Routledge.
Clarke, R. V. 1983. "Situational Crime Prevention: Its Theoretical Basis and Practical Scope." *Crime and Justice: An Annual Review of Research* 4:225–56, edited by M. Tonry and N. Morris.
Cohen, S. 1985. *Visions of Social Control*. Cambridge: Polity.
———. 1990. "Intellectual Scepticism and Political Commitment: The Case of Radical Criminology." Bonger Institute, University of Amsterdam.
Cornish, D. and R. V. Clarke, eds. 1986. *The Reasoning Criminal*. New York: Springer-Verlag.
Donzelot, J. 1979. *The Policing of Families: Welfare Versus the State*. London: Hutchinson.
Downes, D. 1988. *Contrasts in Tolerance: Post-war Penal Policy in the Netherlands and England and Wales*. Oxford: Clarendon Press.
Duff, R. A. and D. Garland. 1994. "Thinking about Punishment." Pp. 1–43 in *A Reader on Punishment*, edited by R. A. Duff and D. Garland. Oxford: Clarendon.
Ericson, R. V. and Carriere, K. D. 1994. "The Fragmentation of Criminology." Pp. 89–109 in *The Futures of Criminology*, edited by D. Nelken. London: Sage.
Feeley, M. and J. Simon. 1992. "The New Penology." *Criminology* 39(4):449–74.
Felson, M. 1994. *Crime and Everyday Life*. London: Pine Forge.
Foucault, M. 1977. *Discipline and Punish: The Birth of the Prison*. London: Allen Unwin.
———. 1983. "Structuralism and Post-Structuralism: An Interview with Michel Foucault" (with G. Raulet) *Telos* 55(Spring):195–211.
Garland, D. 1985. *Punishment and Welfare: A History of Penal Strategies*. Aldershot: Gower.
———. 1990. *Punishment and Modern Society: A Study in Social Theory*. Oxford: Clarendon Press.
———. 1994. "Of Crimes and Criminals: The Development of Criminology in Britain." Pp. 17–68 in *The Oxford Handbook of Criminology*, edited by M. Maguire, R. Morgan, and R. Reiner. Oxford: Clarendon.

Giddens, A. 1990. *The Consequences of Modernity*. Cambridge: Polity.
Gordon, D. 1991. *The Justice Juggernaut: Combatting Street Crime, Controlling Citizens*. New Brunswick, NJ: Rutgers University Press.
Gottfredson, M. and T. Hirschi. 1990. *A General Theory of Crime*. Stanford, CA: Stanford University Press.
Hall, S., C. Critcher, T. Jefferson, J. Clarke, and B. Roberts. 1978. *Policing the Crisis: Mugging, the State, and Law and Order*. London: MacMillan.
Harvey, D. 1989. *The Condition of Postmodernity*. London: Routledge.
Henry, S. and D. Milovanovic. 1994. "The Constitution of Constitutive Criminology: A Postmodern Approach to Criminological Theory." Pp. 110–83 in *The Future of Criminology*, edited by D. Nelken. London: Sage.
Heydebrand, W. 1979. "The Technocratic Administration of Justice." *Research in Law and Society* 2:29–64.
Heydebrand, W. and C. Seron. 1990. *Rationalizing Justice: The Political Economy of the Federal District Courts*. Albany, NY: SUNY Press.
Hirschman, A. 1991. *The Rhetoric of Reaction*. Cambridge, MA: Harvard University Press.
Home Office. 1988. *Punishment, Justice and the Community*. London: HMSO.
Hood, R. 1989. *The Death Penalty: A World-Wide Perspective*. Oxford: Clarendon.
Howe, A. 1994. *Punish and Critique*. London: Routledge.
Hudson, B. A. 1987. *Justice Through Punishment: A Critique of the 'Justice' Model of Corrections*. Basingstoke: MacMillan.
———. 1993. *Penal Policy and Social Justice*. Basingstoke: MacMillan.
Jameson, F. 1991. *Postmodernism, or the Cultural Logic of Late Capitalism*. London: Verso.
Lyotard, J.-F. 1984. *The Postmodern Condition: A Report on Knowledge*. Manchester: Manchester University Press.
Marx, G. 1988. *Undercover: Police Surveillance in America*. Berkeley: University of California Press.
Mayhew, P., R. V. Clarke, A. Sturman, and J. M. Hough. 1976. *Crime as Opportunity*. Home Office Research Study No. 34, London, HMSO.
McMahon M. 1990. "Netwidening: Vagaries in the use of a Concept." *British Journal of Criminology* 30(2):121–49.
Nelkin, D. 1995. *The Power of the Gene*. New York: Basic Books.
O'Malley, P. 1991. "After Discipline? Crime Prevention, the Strong State and a Free Market." Unpublished manuscript.
Palmer, T. 1992. *The Re-emergence of Correctional Intervention*. London: Sage.
Peters, A. 1988. "Main Currents in Criminal Law Theory." Pp. 19–36 in *Criminal Law in Action*, edited by J. J. M. van Dijk. Deventer: Kluwer.
Radzinowicz, Sir L. 1991. "Penal Regressions." *Cambridge Law Journal* 50(930):422–44.
Rees, H. and E. Hall-Williams. 1989. *Punishment, Custody and the Community*. London: L.S.E.
Reiner, R. 1992. "Policing a Postmodern Society." *Modern Law Review* 55:761–81.
Rothman, D. 1980. *Conscience and Convenience: The Asylum and its Alternatives in Progressive America*. Boston: Little Brown.

Rusche, G. and O. Kirchheimer. 1968. *Punishment and Social Structure.* New York: Russell and Russell.
Scheingold, S. 1991. *The Politics of Street Crime.* Philadelphia: Temple University Press.
Scwartz, M. D. and D. O. Friedrichs. 1994. "Postmodern Thought and Criminological Discontent: New Metaphors for Understanding Violence." *Criminology* 32(2):221–46.
Scottish Prison Service. 1990. *Opportunity and Responsibility: Developing New Approaches to the Management of the Long Term Prison System in Scotland.* Edinburgh: Author.
Scull, A. 1977. *Decarceration: Community Treatment and the Deviant—A Radical View.* Englewood, NJ: Prentice Hall.
———. 1984. "Afterword 1983." Pp. 161–89 in *Decarceration*, 2nd ed. Cambridge: Polity.
Simon, J. 1991. "Doing Time: Postmodernity and the Crisis of Penal Reform." Unpublished manuscript.
———. 1993. *Poor Discipline: Parole and the Social Control of the Underclass, 1890–1990.* Chicago: University of Chicago Press.
Smart, C. 1990. "Feminist Approaches to Criminology or Postmodern Woman Meets Atavistic Man." Pp. 70–84 in *Feminist Perspectives in Criminology*, edited by L. Gelsthorpe and A. Morris. Milton Keynes: Open University Press.
Spierenburg, P. 1991. *The Prison Experience: Disciplinary Institutions and Their Inmates in Early Modern Europe.* New Brunswick, NJ: Rutgers University Press.
Teubner, G. 1992. *Law as an Autopoietic System.* Oxford: Blackwell.
Tuck, M. 1991. "Community and the Criminal Justice System." *Policy Studies* 12(3):22–37.
van Dijk, J. J. M. 1989. "Penal Sanctions and the Process of Civilization." Pp. 191–204 in *International Annals of Criminology*, Vol. 27. Liege.
von Hirsch, A. 1983. "Recent Trends in American Sentencing Theory." *Maryland Law Review* 42(6):6–36.
———. 1993. *Censure and Sanctions.* Oxford: Clarendon.
Wiener, M. 1990. *Reconstructing the Criminal.* Cambridge: Cambridge University Press.
Wilson, J. Q. 1983. *Thinking About Crime*, 2nd ed. New York: Basic Books.
Wilson, J. Q. and R. J. Herrnstein. 1985. *Crime and Human Nature: The Definitive Study of the Causes of Crime.* New York: Simon and Schuster.
Yenawine, P. 1991. *How to Look at Modern Art.* New York: Harry N. Abrams.
Young, A. Forthcoming. *Postmodern Criminology.* London: Routledge.

12
Virginia, Criminology, and the Antisocial Control of Women

PAT CARLEN

INTRODUCTION

> I thought how unpleasant it is to be locked out; and I thought how it is worse perhaps to be locked in. (Virginia Woolf [1929] 1989:24)

In 1938, nine years after the publication of her much acclaimed *A Room of One's Own*, Virginia Woolf published *Three Guineas* ([1938] 1986). It was a book that discomforted some of her family and friends, and it predictably provoked the wrath and derision of her enemies (see Bell 1984; Nicolson 1980). For unlike the playful and elegant *Room of One's Own*, which brings an incisive humor to the exposition and analysis of women's inequitable educational opportunities, *Three Guineas* is a passionate and scathing polemic making sustained and condemnatory comparisons between masculinism and militarism, between patriarchy and fascism. I had just finished reading it for the first time when I was asked to write an article on women and social control. And it seemed to me, as I alternately mulled over the meanings of social control, and the political conundrum posed in *Three Guineas*, that distinguishing between social control and antisocial control might be a useful way of thinking about both Virginia's conundrum and the similar puzzle confronting campaigners intent on remedying the wrongs done to women within the criminal justice system. I refer to the dilemma faced by all excluded and oppressed peoples: the question of how they can best penetrate an exclusionary and oppressive structure without their revolutionary objectives being nullified through incorporation into the (thereby strengthened) oppressive structure in question.

The rest of this essay is divided into four parts. The first outlines Virginia's inclusion/exclusion conundrum and discusses its relevance to "justice for women" campaigns by criminologists. The second examines the concepts of social and antisocial control before going on to discuss their theoretical capacity to inform analysis of the exclusionary and inclusionary modes of social and antisocial control experienced by women. The third (and largest) part argues that the informal and antisocial control of women is constituted within exclusionary and inclusionary practices that both preempt and buttress women's (relatively infrequent) criminalization and imprisonment. Then, by way of conclusion, the fourth part returns to Virginia's conundrum and asks, What is to be done?

VIRGINIA'S CONUNDRUM: AND ITS RELEVANCE TO CRIMINOLOGY

Three Guineas was conceived as a sequel to *A Room of One's Own,* but it was written in very different circumstances. In 1937 the threat of fascist aggression haunted Europe; in July of that year, when Virginia Woolf was in the middle of writing *Three Guineas,* her nephew Julian Bell was killed in Spain, driving an ambulance for the noncombatant organization Spanish Medical Aid. In *Three Guineas* the author rages at the futility and waste of war; at men's love of uniforms and the seeming continuum between patriarchal mores, militarism, and fascism; and at a societal hypocrisy that, while publicly idolizing women as daughters, wives, and mothers, ruthlessly excluded them from all the public institutions wherein they might be better equipped to contest the aggression and bellicosity of men. The savagery of the ridicule heaped on men and their exclusive and exclusionary institutions may even today startle any reader expecting to find in *Three Guineas* the urbanity of style that characterizes *A Room.* Yet the two books have themes in common: both lay emphasis on the extraordinary feat of (anti-) social control whereby women are both included in and excluded from societies that accord them heavy responsibilities without similarly according them powers and privileges; and both develop this theme to a greater degree (in *A Room*) or lesser degree (in *Three Guineas*) by detailing women's exclusion from the level of educational opportunity allowed to men. In *Three Guineas,* however, two other concerns are given equal space: questions about the similarities between patriarchy and fascism, and questions about the possibilities of women entering, and being empowered by, male-dominated institutions, without acquiescing in (and thereby strengthening) the antisocial practices of supremacy and domination fashioned by men to preserve patriarchal social relations.

But what, you may well ask, has all this to do with present-day analyses of the social control of women, of contemporary campaigns for justice for women within the criminal justice system? A great deal. For Virginia Woolf's concerns of the 1930s can be translated into the following distinctly criminological questions of the 1990s:

1. What are the relationships between social justice for women and criminal justice for women?
2. How does the informal antisocial control of women (physical, institutional, and ideological) preempt and buttress women's relatively infrequent criminalization and imprisonment?
3. How can analyses of the informal antisocial control of women inform criminal justice campaigns without initiating nonprogressive changes that merely result in (a) more women being dealt with by the criminal courts without any diminution of the antisocial controls brought to bear on them both within and without the criminal justice system; and (b) a concomitant strengthening of the sexist, racist and class-biased nature of the formal justice systems?

SOCIAL CONTROL AND ANTISOCIAL CONTROL

Social control is a vacuous term. Unless closely defined it can imply meanings that range from any type of constraint on individual action— through a "conspiracy theory" which implies that in capitalist, or patriarchal or communist or fascist, etc., societies every social practice is "really" part of a totalizing "social control" process, whatever other ends it might appear to serve—to a very narrow conception that refers only to the state's formal apparatuses for crime control and the regulation of other officially prohibited behaviors. For my purpose here—that of analyzing the different types of controls experienced by women—I shall use the following definitions:

- Social control: a generic term for a variety of benign institutionalized practices designed to set limits to individual action in the interests of the collectivity's proclaimed ideals of social and criminal justice as instanced in law and dominant ideologies.
- Antisocial control: a generic term for a variety of malign institutionalized practices that may *either* set limits to individual action by favoring one set of citizens at the expense of another so as to subvert equal-opportunities ideologies in relation to gender, race, and class (or

other social groupings); or (in societies without equal-opportunities ideologies) set limits to individual action in ways that are antisocial because they atrophy an individual's social contribution and do so on the grounds of either biological attributes or exploitative social relations.

The advantage of these formal definitions when analyzing the main modes of controlling women, both within and without social and criminal justice systems, is at least threefold. First, they help avoid libertarian implications that all social control is a bad thing. Second, they help avoid the circularity of conspiracy-type theories, which imply that as a majority of legal and other state bureaucracies have traditionally been dominated by men, *all* their laws, rules, and practices must necessarily be always and already in the interests of men and against those of women (see Cousins 1978, 1980). And third, they allow the same substantive practices to be theorized differently according to the differing combinations of economic, ideological, and political conditions in which they are realized. Thus, for instance (and to illustrate all three foregoing points), the contemporary ideology of child-centeredness encapsulated in the phrase *good parenting* might be seen as a positively benign form of social control when actualized in a society where all have equal opportunities and responsibilities to be good parents. But it may equally be seen as being a very antisocial form of control in societies where some parents are always-already prevented from being good parents by their adverse economic circumstances; or in societies where responsibility for good parenting falls systematically upon mothers rather than fathers (or vice versa). In the former example, good parenting ideology may be seen as being a form of antisocial control because it includes under its "ideal" rule those who are in fact excluded from it by their "real" circumstances; in the latter example, it may be construed as being an antisocial control because it subverts a society's equal-opportunities rhetoric. In conventional criminological terms, of course, the anomie experienced by those concomitantly included under a rule, and excluded from the conditions necessary to its fulfillment, is a frequent precursor (if not cause) of crime; and the poverty-stricken women who have perennially justified their stealing or soliciting by claiming, "It was only done to feed my kids," are usually seen to have a point (though not one strong enough to absolve them from guilt and its subsequent punishment).

Now let's use these definitions and the ensuing discussion of them to inform an analytic overview of the main ways in which the informal anti- (and ante-) social control of women has both preempted and buttressed their more formal (but relatively infrequent) control by the police, courts, and prisons, as well as by other regulatory agencies, such as mental hospitals and welfare bureaucracies.

WOMEN: IN AND OUT OF CONTROL

During the last two decades there has been a much more sustained focus upon the control of women by formal and informal means than there had been prior to the mid-1970s. [For a comparative perspective on the search for a feminist jurisprudence see Boyle, Bertrand, Lacerte-Lamontagne, and Shamai (1985) for Canada, Dahl (1987) for Norway, MacKinnon (1987) and Fineman and Thomadsen (1991) for the United States, Redcar (1990) and Grbich (1991) for Australia;, and Smart (1989) for England.] Dominant constructs informing analyses of the control of women have been those relating to control via the politicoeconomic institutions of family, marriage and welfare; control via the economic systems and ideological structures of patriarchy; control via the ideologies of femininity and the menace and effects of masculinist discourses; and, more formally, the sexist, racist, and class-biased control of women in the criminal justice and penal systems. In overviewing the different dimensions of the antisocial control of women, I shall be arguing that they all emanate from the power of one fundamental ideological mechanism for keeping women "in their place": the fracturing of women's subjectivities within complex and contradictory discourses that insist on women's essential "power for good" (femininity) at the same time as engendering social relationships wherein discourses of femininity are incorporated into "Other" discourses ("masculism"; Brittan 1989:4) justifying a close ideological and physical control of women's biological, emotional, and intellectual powers. Anne Worrall has described the anguish of being always and already Other:

> Women. . .are always-already *not men*. Femininity is constructed on the site vacated by masculinity, and this absence of maleness is manifested in two opposing sets of expectations (Eichenbaum and Orbach 1983). On the one hand, femininity is characterized by self-control and independence. Being a normal woman means coping, caring.. . .On the other hand, femininity is characterized by lack of control and dependence. Being a normal woman means needing protection (Hutter and Williams 1981). It means being childlike, incapable, fragile and capricious.. . .[T]he centrality to the construction of femininity of the dilemma of having to be both "in control" and "out of control" poses a routine problem. (Worrall 1981:3, 8; cf. Chesler 1974; Allen 1987)

For women then, the Kafkaesque anterooms of the criminal courts are to be found in the simultaneity of the inclusionary and exclusionary devices of the antisocial family, the antisocial state, and the antisocial practices and discourses of men's violence, *mens rea*, men's rule, and male menace. Given the strength and elasticity of these informal controls, it is not surprising that the formal system of control has seldom to be invoked against women; nor that, when women are on trial, the courts are doubly punitive toward those who are seen already to have eluded or violated informal gender controls. Theorists have focused on informal controls when analyzing the (anti-) social control of women, and it is to three dimensions of these antecedent controls that we will now turn before examining the formal control of women by the courts, prisons, and other regulatory agencies.[1]

Women: In and Out of the Antisocial Family

The strength of the best studies analyzing the social control of white, Western women within the politicoeconomic institution of the family lies first in their historical specificity even though, alas, their *cultural* specificity is too often glossed over. Second, it inheres in a thoroughgoing materialism that, in prioritizing analyses of the social conditions in which women's physical and economic control is accomplished, at the same time is also able to facilitate explanation of the modes of control wherein their *subjective* coercion is achieved. A good example of this type of study is that of Ehrenreich and English, which was published in 1979 and entitled *For Her Own Good*. Subtitled *150 Years of the Experts' Advice to Women*, the book shows how nineteenth- and early twentieth-century experts controlled women (and taught middle-class "ladies" how to control working-class "housewives") via an attractive mix of rationalist and romanticist discourses that both objectified women's sexuality in the service of men and denied them their independence for the "good of the family." [See Smart (1992) for a collection of feminist historical essays on the regulation of marriage, motherhood, and sexuality.] As Zedner, also writing on women in Victorian England, has stressed, "[A]lthough women gained considerable power within the limited sphere of their influence, in order to protect their own purity they were admonished to leave the house as little as possible" (1991:14).

The woman "simply by being a model of chastity, altruism and morality was supposed to induce men to raise themselves to her level of virtue" (pp. 17–18). While discriminatory laws relating to public life, education, and the professions combined to keep middle-class women in their place (see Sachs and Wilson 1978), the interrelated institutions of marriage, wage labor, and prostitution kept working-class wives and daughters in theirs. For, though poverty-stricken women might have reason enough to be oft-tempted to rebel against man or master, they had equal reason to fear that no destiny other than prostitution would be the fate of anyone foolhardy enough to risk being cast out "characterless" by either husband or employer. Thus, historically, women have been expected to subject themselves first and perennially to the family—in obedience to the rhetoric that "good mothers make good families make good societies." Then, contradictorily but simultaneously, they have been expected to accept and be regulated by an alternative but equally powerful ideology: that the family itself must forever be at the service of the military, the markets, and the Man.

Women: In and Out of the Antisocial State

But did women ever have *so* much power within the home? If one examines closely the public/private distinction (*public* referring to the worlds of work, war and state; *private* to those of family, intimate relationships, etc.) it is easy to establish that the "privacy of the home" ideology has functioned primarily to allow all kinds of physical and sexual abuses to proceed unchecked on the patriarchal assumption that a "man's home is his castle." Moreover, even when domestic violence has not been lacerating families from within, war and poverty have been routinely destroying them from without. British women have twice this century been called upon to encourage their men to go to war, *and* to leave their children in order that they themselves might go out to work for the war machine. The wars over, women have then been required to give up their jobs to the men, being reminded that their first priority is *of course* with their children once more— until the next time (Woolf [1938] 1986:161–63)! However, by the end of the 1940s, it was already being realized that regular war and poverty cycles might no longer be depended upon to discipline families sufficiently to meet the needs of markets. So the agents of state welfare control made their debuts. Physically, they policed the homes of the poor via their social workers (Wilson 1977). Ideologically, they interpellated mothers of all classes via the "psy" and "expert" pedagogies of "good parenting" and "child centred familiness" (Donzelot 1979; Meyer 1977; Hall, Critcher, Jefferson, Clarke, and Roberts 1978; Rose 1989). Nowadays, women who either cannot or will not pay obeisance to *all* of these opposed ideologies (women who, as one might put it more figuratively, refuse to keep so many balls in the air at once) are likely to be made examples of—by the media, by welfare regulation, or by the courts. Two striking examples from the last decade have been the Greenham Common (antiwar) women; and, most recently, unmarried mothers on welfare.

The founding of the women's anticruise missile camp at Greenham Common in 1981 started a women's movement for peace that achieved worldwide acclaim. Its members braved hard weather conditions, separation from families and friends, media derision, arrest, and in some cases imprisonment. And for over a decade "they were vilified by some of the British tabloids—as dirty lesbians, soviet stooges, [and] irresponsible wives and mothers" (Coote and Campbell 1987:50). In the long tradition of punitive obloquy directed at women who attempt to link feminism and pacifism:

> The women of Greenham Common came in for a particularly nasty brand of misogynist reporting, which characterized them as dirty violent scroungers who were probably in the pay of Moscow. Worse still, the homophobic press invariably described them as lesbians in such a way as to denigrate all lesbians, and by association all Greenham women. (p. 280)

The media's pillorying of unmarried mothers on welfare has, in the 1990s, been sparked off both by the work of conservative American "underclass" theorist Charles Murray (1984, 1990) and by a British media-inspired scare about persistent young criminals. According to Murray, "underclass" poor are found in neighborhoods containing high numbers of fatherless families reared by unmarried mothers. Having been reared by "permissive" mothers, and a "supportive" welfare state, underclass young men are supposed to refuse to work and engage in violent crime. This interlinking of welfare dependency, single parenthood, undisciplined children, and crime in an unbroken causal chain also coincides with two other 1990s concerns: with real doubts about the actual success and future redistributionist potential of Western welfare systems; and (in Britain at least) with a conservative backlash against feminist struggles for increased female dependence from male-related domesticity. The imagery used by Murray and other underclass theorists is one of disease and infection, a continuation of a long tradition in which misogyny has combined with exploitative class relationships to ensure that "undeserving" poor women have been represented both in life and literature as being especially invidious bearers of social and moral contagion. On the war fronts they have been stigmatized as venereally diseased prostitutes weakening the physical strength of the British army. In the property stakes, they have (like Dumas's *Lady of the Camellias*, 1986) been represented as sexual adventurers threatening class structures by bringing the contagion of the gutter right into the heart of bourgeois society. Murray's solution to "his" problem would involve a "ghettoization" of underclass families into separate neighborhoods. Governmental responses to increases in single parenthood have included increased regulation of women on welfare (see Cook 1988) and, more recently, threats to develop new policies to "deter" women from choosing to rear children apart from men.

Greenham women took seriously the social values of protecting and nurturing children by rejecting militarism. Single mothers on welfare take seriously their duties to their children—but without embracing male-related domesticity and thereby testing the limits to welfarism in an increasingly illiberal welfare state. For their pains (and for opposing militarism and bucking market morality) they are repeatedly subject to exclusionary and antisocial control measures, antecedent to their regulation (or not) by more formal measures.

Women: In and Out of Men's Violence,
Men's Rea, Men's Rule, Male Menace—and an
Antisocial Masculism

The antisocial regulation of women has always been as much physical as ideological. Physical exclusion from public space, public institutions, and workplaces has primarily been managed via law, economy, and tradition. Sexual and physical regulation within the home and on the streets has been via either threatened or actual male violence and the peculiar mix of gender ideologies that engender such violence and facilitate its persistence (Adler 1989; Dobash and Dobash 1979; Dworkin 1981; Radford and Russell 1992). Additionally, in the second half of the twentieth century, a further subjection of women has been achieved: by harnessing media and markets in a double targeting of women's bodies as new sites of anxiety and guilt— about body weight, personal appearance, and sexuality (Coward 1984; McRobbie 1991). For women unable to cope, there have been the (overprescribed) tranquillizers (Iles 1986) and the (oversubscribed) mental hospitals (Chesler 1974; Sim 1990). When men and women have been locked in courtroom battles, again and again the judicial concept of *mens rea* has operated only to reflect an empiricist rationality based on men's worldly experiences, not women's (see Carlen 1993, and below). As Arthur Brittan has succinctly put it, "the ideology that justifies and naturalizes male domination" is "masculism" (1989:4). And masculism is already antisocial because "masculism as an ideology universalizes 'man' as the 'maker' of history. . . . Man is the 'subject' of history. . . . But what this history has glossed and ignored is the systematic objectification of women by men" (p. 174). Drawing the same parallels between masculism and fascism that Virginia Woolf insisted upon, Brittan quotes Thewelweit, who noted:

> What fascism promised men was the reintegration of their hostile components under tolerable conditions, dominance of the hostile 'female' element within themselves. This explains why the word 'boundaries' in fascist parlance, refers primarily to the boundaries of the body. (Thewelweit 1987, quoted in Brittan 1989:frontispiece)

In the next section it will be argued that the British criminal justice system is inseminated by a masculism that in denoting crime a male preserve, objectifies women who have dared to be other than Other. Such objectification of women within the criminal justice and penal systems is antisocial in that it is one of the two main causes of the liberal state's failure to take seriously the crimes of both men and women. At the boundaries of law— and always calling it into question—today's marketeering and militia men are much more violent and ruthless than they ever were in the 1930s.

Women: In and Out of the Courts, Prisons, and Other Regulatory Agencies

The majority of British women who go to prison are sentenced not according to the seriousness of their crimes but primarily according to the courts' assessment of them as wives, mothers, and daughters (Worrall 1981; Farrington and Morris 1983; Carlen 1983; Dominelli 1984). Yet the moment of sentence is only the end-point of a series of class-, race-, and gender-biased negotiations, the outcomes of which make criminal women either more or less vulnerable to acquiring the gender-deviant bad characters that result in them receiving harsher sentences than either men or their more conventional sisters. To understand gender biases in criminal justice, it is not advisable to only look at sentencing patterns, but also to detail the ways in which unconventional, troublesome, or criminal women are discriminated against from the time when they first come to the attention of the state's regulatory agencies.

Since the 1940s when the welfare state ideal was premised on the right to the relief of need, the practice of social work in England and elsewhere has focused on the policing of families in general (Donzelot 1979; Meyer 1977; Carrington 1993), and the pedagogic regulation of women in particular (Wilson 1977). In exchange for material assistance, twentieth-century women, especially working-class mothers, have been subjected to an increase of that tutelary supervision (Donzelot 1979) that their predecessors suffered at the hands of late-nineteenth- and early-twentieth-century middle-class charity organizations (Ehrenreich and English 1979). Most women who end up in penal custody, however, have come into contact with social workers at a much earlier stage, as a result of being taken into the residential care of a local authority.

In court, girls in care are viewed by sentencers as already being out of their proper place (that is, the family) and are therefore likely to be dealt with more harshly. Further escalation up the tariff of penalties occurs for a variety of reasons, not the least of them being that the range of facilities for young women is much narrower than that for young men (Gelsthorpe 1989). Of particular relevance to gender discrimination along the care/custody axis are the following findings: of Webb (1984) that girls are made subject to supervision orders for less serious offenses than those committed by boys; of Dominelli (1984) that courts are biased against giving women community service orders; of Milham, Bullock, and Hosie (1978) that several children, particularly girls, can find themselves stranded in (secure) remand provision that has no long-term program; and of Fisher and Wilson, who found that female residents of a probation hostel "tended to have less serious criminal records than the males" (1982:137). Walker (1985) has argued that even much probation practice is biased against the interests of female clients. Housing research suggests that women leaving institutions suffer disproportionately from the shortage of rented housing for single people (Department of the Environment 1982; Austerberry and Watson 1983; Greve 1991:17). Mixed noncustodial programs and hostels for offenders are seldom suitable for women who have young children or who have previously suffered sexual or physical abuse from men (Carlen 1990). Women-only programs and hostels, or ones making provision for mothers and children, are almost nonexistent. In any case, some older women who have been in care are so vehemently against further contact with social workers that they choose to go to prison rather than agree to a renewal of supervision under a noncustodial order (Carlen 1988). However, even by the police, courts, and prisons, offending women are more likely to be viewed as gender-deviant females than lawbreaking citizens.

Although there is statistical evidence to support claims that at least some female offenders in England are treated more leniently than men by both the police and the courts (Home Office 1985), official figures indicate that convicted women are guilty of less serious crimes than men and, when given a custodial sentence, are more likely to be imprisoned for a minor crime of theft than for any more serious offense (Seear and Player 1986, cf. Daubeney 1988). Even when women are *victims* of crime, police (and other criminal justice personnel) routinely treat them as offenders. This is especially so in cases of rape (Adler 1989); the sexual abuse of adolescent girls (Carlen and Wardhaugh 1991; Morgan and Zedner 1992); and domestic violence (Dobash and Dobash 1979). Conversely, women found guilty of serious crimes are much more likely to receive noncustodial sentences than males convicted of similar offenses (Allen 1987). How can such sentencing patterns be explained?

A small proportion of women lawbreakers are imprisoned because their crimes are either so outrageous or inexplicable that they would most likely be locked up in any country, whatever its political creed. But, as I claimed earlier, the majority of women in British prisons have been sentenced not primarily according to the seriousness of their crimes but more according to the courts' assessment of them as wives, mothers, and daughters. If they are young and their parents or state guardians believe them to be beyond control, if they are single, divorced, or separated from their husbands, or if their children are in residential care, they are more likely to go to prison than women who, though their crimes might be more serious, are living more conventional family lives. Black female offenders, because they experience racism in regard to employment and welfare policies, are even more likely to be in the categories at risk. Frequently, they are further disadvantaged by a racist stereotyping that portrays them as excessively promiscuous and/or aggressive. Even when the nature of their crimes or their personal circumstances do not make convicted women prone to imprisonment, there are other factors at work that push them nearer the custodial than the noncustodial end of the tariff.

These include:

- The inability of many criminal justice personnel to "make sense" of their female clients, whom they often perceive as being less rational and more devious than their male clients (see Worrall 1990).
- The courtroom domination by the metaphor of the "reasonable man,"

which can bias the logic of the proceedings against women. [For example, the questioning of rape victims or women on charges of carrying offensive weapons or assaulting males is frequently based on moralistic assumptions about what *moral* women *should* do when threatened with rape or attack that are quite opposed to what *reasonable* women with prior experience of male violence actually do; Chambers and Millar (1987), Adler (1987), Carlen and Worrall (1987).]

- The relative scarcity of suitable noncustodial programs and hostels for women (as compared with those for men), which results in either probation officers being reluctant to recommend mixed programs and hostels for women who have already suffered male violence or other abuse; or women in mixed schemes failing to complete their orders and thus being made more vulnerable to harsher sentences if they should reoffend.
- The general paucity of child care provision, which makes attendance at noncustodial schemes impossible for mothers with young children.
- The tendency of some report writers to recommend custody for pregnant women on the grounds that their material circumstances are so poor that their babies will be better off in prison (Carlen 1990).

Sentencing practices and criminological and popular theories that have repeatedly implied that women criminals and prisoners are either mad, masculine, menopausal, or maladjusted (to conventional female roles) have resulted not only in it being denied that they are real women, real criminals, and real prisoners, but also in claims that women's prisons are not real prisons (Carlen 1983). Nothing could be further from the truth.

Education, work, and leisure opportunities in many of the women's prisons in Britain, Canada, Australia, and the United States are limited, and disciplinary regimes are rigid. The disproportionate numbers of discipline charges leveled against female as compared with male prisoners in Britain result both from regimes that aggravate and multiply the problems that many women already have when they go to prison, and from discriminatory social ideologies that demand higher standards of behavior from women than from men. Moreover, many women in British prisons have felt that prison doctors have been particularly unsympathetic about their gynecological problems and the many nervous ailments related to their present domestic circumstances and/or their previous sociobiographies as daughters, wives, and/or mothers (cf Bertrand 1985).

A number of ideologies constantly undermine attempts to diminish the deprivations and barbarities suffered by female prisoners:

- *The numbers game*: The most frequently expressed explanation of

inadequacies in custodial provision for women is that as there are relatively few female prisoners it would be uneconomical to provide the range of penal facilities available to males. (The relatively *small* number of women prisoners has also always been used to justify the imprisonment of women far from their homes.)
- *Women's prisons must be real prisons*: Although women's prison regimes have constantly been adapted to the so-called special disciplinary needs of women—i.e., their "need" (as deviating women) to be feminized, medicalized, domesticized, and infantilized (Carlen 1983)—the overriding ideological notion that women prisoners should not be better off than their male counterparts has in England resulted in a concomitant demand that pregnancy, motherhood, and other physical and emotional states related to female biology should not result in women prisoners having special privileges. As a consequence, especially high behavioral standards are expected of pregnant prisoners and inmates in mother and baby units. Allowing imprisoned mothers to have their babies with them or even to receive visits from their children is seen as a privilege, not a right; and the question of continued access to their children is routinely used as another disciplinary weapon in the armory of controls available to the administrators of the women's prisons.
- *The main concerns of women prisoners relate to personal relationships*: The ideology that women are essentially creatures living primarily according to their emotions and dependent upon personal relationships to give meaning to their lives has not only been responsible for the dependency-inducing domesticity inherent in penal regimes for women, it has also increased that dependency by not taking women's employment needs seriously. Too often, the refrain that women are more concerned about personal relationships becomes a self-fulfilling prophecy. Ill-equipped to provide for themselves, many released women prisoners go back to an unsatisfactory (or even dangerous or destructive) relationship in order to get a roof over their heads or, maybe, just a bed for the night.

In England women constitute only 4 percent of the prison population. Feeley and Little (1991) have suggested that the relatively small proportions of women in prison in most Western countries has come about as the informal controls on women have strengthened and tightened. Certainly recent reports suggest that when women appear in the criminal courts they are often treated as out of place, out of mind, and out of order. Accordingly, the judicial and penal response to them is fashioned not only by an assumption that they may have transgressed the law of the land. There is also a deeper fear: that they have violated a gender lore that insists (1) that crime is a male activity; (2) that the criminal justice system should operate according to a masculism that universalizes male experiences and needs as the essential yardstick for the computation of guilt and innocence; (3) that "decent" women should never be in a position where they can become victims of male crime; (4) that, even if not always desirable, male violence is a natural and inevitable component of social life; and (5) that as women criminals and female crime victims are not real women, real criminals, real prisoners or real victims of crime, no special attention need be paid to the plight of women in (but always-already out of) the criminal justice system.

WHAT IS TO BE DONE?

So back to Virginia's conundrum: as translated into a gender problem about criminal justice, the question is, How can the criminal justice system be made more user-friendly for women? The short answer is that it cannot be—not without a massive change in present mores in relation to male violence and masculinist principles of (anti-) social (dis-) organization. The reasons are twofold. First, whatever liberal changes are made in the courts [and in recent years some important changes in British judicial attitudes toward women *have* occurred (Kennedy 1992)] the contemporary daily diet of media violence routinely and effectively elevates the rule of male violence above the rule of state law. And if this seems an extreme statement, try to conjure up a picture of *women* engaged in military maneuvers or dramatization involving gun law/lore. It is difficult. Rather, you will find that

> another picture has imposed itself upon the foreground. It is the figure of a man; some say, others deny, that he is Man himself, the quintessence of virility, the perfect type of which all the others are imperfect adumbrations. He is a man certainly. His eyes are glazed; his eyes glare. His body, which is braced in an unnatural position, is tightly cased in a uniform. Upon the breast of that uniform are sewn several medals and other mystic symbols. He is called in German or Italian Führer or Duce; in our own language Tyrant or Dictator. And behind him lie ruined houses and dead bodies—men, women and children. (Woolf [1938] 1986:162)

Arguably, more so in the 1990s than in the 1930s! In the 1990s, however, unlike the 1930s, this celebration of worldwide male violence can be relayed to our homes nightly. For not only are TV audiences around the world injected with a round-the-clock imagery of uniformed males killing each other on the world's battlefields, such "news" is routinely supplemented by cosier (and "sexier") "entertainment" comprising domestic dramas in which *men* star as adepts at gun (and other types of) violence.

But second, and much more important, criminal justice reforms are only of indirect relevance to women because the greater (and most effective) part of the antisocial control of women is not accomplished by the criminal justice system at all.[2] It is effected informally and antisocially: by the threat and reality of male violence and the continuing exclusion of women from the corridors of power.

Let us, therefore, translate Virginia's conundrum into a broader question of what is to be done about the informal and antisocial control of women. The analyses of this paper suggest some radical answers. Generally, it seems that women should refuse and resist all antisocial controls in the form of gender constraints imposed by masculism. In specific and substantive terms this would at the least involve supporting a variety of household forms other than those of the conventional family type; refusing to countenance all types of militarism, nationalism, racism, and class exploitation; and resisting all attacks on women's bodies whether they be by men of violence, media sexual objectification, or marketeering cosmetic and diet "laws." The argument is that, by destroying the informal antisocial controls on women, we may simultaneously refashion the formal controls, re-forming them to be nondiscriminatory and thereby fully social. Then, and not till then, may we have a chance of meeting Virginia's challenge (see Woolf [1938] 1986:78): To cease to be victims of patriarchy, without becoming champions of capitalism.

NOTES

1. As I have argued elsewhere (Carlen 1993) I am not committed to always privileging gender in explanations of women's oppression; in many specific instances it would be more appropriate to privilege racism or class exploitation. In this essay, however, I do privilege gender.

2. Similarly, the criminal justice system is not the major locus of social control for men. However, men's informal control *qua* men is accomplished via inclusionary *social* control devices such as work and public associations (though, of course, some men also experience an antisocial control via the exclusionary structures of racism and class oppression).

REFERENCES

Adler, Z. 1989. *Rape on Trial*. London: Routledge and Kegan Paul.
Allen, H. 1987. *Justice Unbalanced*. Buckingham: Open University Press.

Austerberry, H. and S. Watson. 1983. *Women On The Margins*. London: City University Housing Research Group.
Bell, A. O., ed. 1984. *The Diary of Virginia Woolf,* Volume 5, 1936–1941. London: Hogarth.
Bertrand, M. 1985. "Minimum and Non-Custodial Sentence." In *A Feminist Review of Criminal Law*, edited by C. Boyle et al. Ottawa: Ministry of Supply and Services.
Boyle, C., M. Bertrand, C. Lacerte-Lamontagne, and R. Shamai. 1985. *A Feminist Review of Criminal Law*. Ottawa: Minister of Supply and Services.
Brittan, A. 1989. *Masculinity and Power*. Oxford, Blackwell.
Carlen, P. 1983. *Women's Imprisonment*. London: Routledge and Kegan Paul.
———. 1988. *Women, Crime and Poverty*. Buckingham: Open University Press.
———. 1990. *Alternatives to Women's Imprisonment*. Buckingham: Open University Press.
———. 1993. "Gender, Class, Racism, and Criminal Justice." Pp. 134–44 in *Inequality, Crime and Social Control*, edited by G. Bridges and M. Myers. Toronto: Westview.
Carlen, P. and J. Wardhaugh. 1991. "Locking Up Our Daughters." In *Social Work and Social Welfare Yearbook 3*, edited by P. Carter, T. Jeffs, and K. Smith. Buckingham: Open University Press.
Carlen, P. and A. Worrall. 1987. *Gender, Crime and Justice*. Buckingham: Open University Press.
Carrington, K. 1993. *Offending Girls: Sex, Youth and Justice*. Sydney: Allen and Unwin.
Chambers, G. and A. Millar. 1987. "Proving Sexual Assault." Pp. 58–80 in *Gender Crime and Justice*, edited by P. Carlen and A. Worrall. Buckingham: Open University Press.
Chesler, P. 1974. *Women and Madness*. London: Allen Lane.
Cook, D. 1988. *Rich Law, Poor Law*. Buckingham: Open University Press.
Coote, A. and B. Campbell. 1987. *Sweet Freedom*, 2nd ed. Oxford: Basil Blackwell.
Cousins, M. 1978. "Material Arguments and Feminism." *m/f* 2.
———. 1980. "Men's Rea." Pp. 109–22 in *Radical Issues in Criminology*, edited by P. Carlen and M. Collison. Oxford: Martin Robertson.
Coward, R. 1984. *Female Desire*. London: Paladin.
Dahl, T. S. 1987. *Women's Law: An Introduction to Feminist Jurisprudence*. Oslo: Norwegian University Press.
Daubeney, D. 1988. *Taking Responsibility. Report of The Standing Committee on Justice and Solicitor General on its Review of Sentencing, Conditional Release and Related Aspects of Corrections*. Ottawa: Supply and Services, Canada.
Department of the Environment. 1982. *Single Homeless*. London: HMSO.
Dobash, R. and R. Dobash. 1979. *Violence Against Wives*. London: Open Books.
Dominelli, L. 1984. "Differential Justice: Domestic Labour, Community Service and Female Offenders." *Probation Journal*. 3.3:100–3.
Donzelot, J. 1979. *The Policing of Families*. London: Hutchinson.
Dumas, A. 1986. *La Dame Aux Camélias*. Oxford: Penguin.
Dworkin, A. 1981. *Pornography: Men Possessing Women*. London: Women's Press.

Ehrenreich, B. and D. English. 1979. *For Her Own Good*. London: Pluto Press.
Eichenbaum, L. and S. Orbach. 1983. *What Do Women Want?* London: Michael Joseph.
Farrington, D. and A. Morris. 1983. "Do Magistrates Discriminate Against Men?" *Justice of The Peace*, 17 September: 601–03.
Feeley, M. and D. Little. 1991. "The Vanishing Female: The Decline of Women in the Criminal Process, 1687–1912." *Law and Society Review* 25(4).
Fineman, M. and N. Thomadsen, eds. 1991. *At the Boundaries of Law*. New York: Routledge.
Fisher, R. and C. Wilson. 1982. *Authority or Freedom?* Aldershot: Gower.
Gelsthorpe, L. 1989. *Sexism and The Female Offender*. Aldershot: Gower.
Grbich, J. 1991. "The Body in Legal Theory." Pp. 61–76 in *At the Boundaries of Law*, edited by M. Fineman and N. Thomadsen. New York: Routledge.
Greve, J. 1991. *Homelessness in Britain*. York: Rowntree Trust.
Hall, S., C. Critcher, T. Jefferson, J. Clarke, and B. Roberts. 1978. *Policing the Crisis*. London: Macmillan.
Home Office. 1985. *Criminal Statistics England and Wales 1984*. London: HMSO.
Hutter, B. and G. Williams. 1981. *Controlling Women*. London: Croom Helm.
Iles, C. 1986. *Patriarchal Therapeutism*. Doctoral thesis, Kent University.
Kennedy, H. 1992. *Eve Was Framed*. London, Chatto and Windus.
MacKinnon, C. 1987. "Feminism, Marxism, Method and the State: Toward Feminist Jurisprudence." In *Feminism and Methodology*, edited by S. Harding. Buckingham: Open University Press.
McRobbie, A. 1991. *Feminism and Youth Culture*. London, Macmillan.
Meyer, P. 1977. *The Child and The State*. Cambridge: Cambridge University Press.
Milham, S., R. Bullock, and K. Hosie. 1978. *Authority or Freedom?* Aldershot: Gower.
Morgan, J. and L. Zedner. 1992. *Child Victims of Crime*. Oxford: Clarendon.
Murray, C. 1984. *Losing Ground: American Social Policy 1950–1980*. New York: Basic Books.
———. 1990. *The Emerging British Underclass*. London: Institute of Economic Affairs.
Nicolson, N. 1980. *Leave The Letters Till We're Dead: The Letters of Virginia Woolf 1936–1941*. London: Hogarth.
Radford, J. and D. Russell, eds. 1992. *Femicide*. Buckingham: Open University Press.
Redcar, R., ed. 1990. *Dissenting Opinions*. Sydney: Allen and Unwin.
Rose, N. 1989. *Governing The Soul*. London: Routledge.
Sachs, A. and J. Wilson. 1978. *Sexism and The Law*. Oxford: Martin Robertson.
Seear, N. and E. Player. 1986. *Women in The Penal System*. London: Howard League.
Sim, J. 1990. *Medical Power in Prisons*. Buckingham: Open University Press.
Smart, C. 1989. *Feminism and The Power of Law*. London: Routledge.
———, ed. 1992. *Regulating Womanhood*. London: Routledge.
Thewelweit, K. 1987. *Male Fantasies*. Cambridge: Polity.

Walker, H. 1985. "Women's Issues in Probation Practice." In *Working With Offenders*, edited by H. Walker and B. Beaumont. London: Macmillan.
Webb, D. 1984. "More on Gender and Justice: Girl Offenders on Supervision." *Sociology* 3:367–81.
Wilson, E. 1977. *Women and The Welfare State*. London: Tavistock.
Woolf, V. [1938] 1986. *Three Guineas*. London: Hogarth.
———. [1929] 1989. *A Room of One's Own*. London: Grafton.
Worrall, A. 1981. "Out of Place: Female Offenders in Court." *Probation Journal* 28:90–93.
———. 1990. *Offending Women*. London: Routledge.
Zedner, L. 1991. *Women, Crime and Custody in Victorian England*. Oxford: Clarendon.

13
Controlling Drug Use:
The Great Prohibition

DAVID MATZA and PATRICIA MORGAN

INTRODUCTION

Next to the now-defunct Russian Revolution, Prohibition was the twentieth century's greatest social engineering project, suffering some of the same defects, but still alive despite a widely shared sense of basic failure. The Great Prohibition has shifted from alcohol to psychoactive drugs as the main substance controlled by penal sanction; users of both alcohol and drugs have been subjected to prohibition this century. After eighty years of governmental effort to enforce the Great Prohibition, prevention of drug use remains an unachieved and elusive goal. The main effect of Prohibition was to magnify the private problems of individual persons using alcohol or drugs. Prohibition created a large, public domain devoted to restriction and punishment. If Paul Johnson's *Modern Times* (Johnson 1983) delivered a definitive call for freedom from the clutches of socialist and welfare state experiments at social engineering, Michael Woodiwiss delivers a similar critique to prohibitions in the United States, 1900–1987:

> U.S. prohibition laws have not succeeded. Instead of solving the problems of excessive, drinking, gambling and drug-taking, the laws themselves caused the devastation and termination of countless lives, exacerbated street crime, fostered successful organized crime, nullified or corrupted the law enforcement and criminal justice systems and reduced civil liberties. America's moral crusade has two faces. The rhetoric was righteous, but the reality only highlighted an unlimited capacity for lies, hypocrisy and illegal enrichment. The American people have been the victim of a successful double-cross. (1988:229)

The Great Prohibition did not succeed in controlling alcohol or drug use just as Communism did not succeed in controlling exploitation or economic failure. The difficulties in controlling use have been attributed to greed, to the corruption of authority, to the nature of addiction or dependency, to the role of alcohol or drugs in forming the basis for a way of life or "subculture" in modern society, or to the individual or collective quest for alteration of consciousness (Fingarette 1988; Weil 1972; Reinarman 1983). Whether because of the particular hold of especially demanding substances, or as simply a sign of popular products, effective demand for illegal drugs persists. The mark of the social engineering mentality is to imagine that the reason for failure has been an insufficient effort at law enforcement. Thus the failure in prohibition is thought by its proponents to require an ever greater and greater enforcement.

To understand the history of prohibition, we must separate the intentions from the consequences of meaningful actions, as well as grasping the difference between prohibiting and actually controlling drug use. Moreover, we must include in the social history the changing identities and labels attached to various drugs and users throughout the period. Such an approach leads to the interpretation that public policy toward drugs and alcohol in the United States has gone through cycles utilizing various combinations of public, social, and individual control, depending less perhaps on the inherent danger of any particular substance than on changing social, economic, and political factors. Simply put, social science has provided mounting evidence revealing that these cycles of control and prohibition have not been framed by uniform normative or problem criteria (Helmer 1975; Reinarman 1983; Duster 1970; Cohen 1985). Rather than any inherent standard of danger or harm, different rationales have been employed concerning the use of tobacco, alcohol, heroin, marijuana, and other psychoactive substances. This is most clear when examining separately "intentions" for control and the "consequences" of control for these various substances over time.

In other words, it is not clear—given the known facts of the relative deadliness and the relative danger of tobacco, alcohol, and the psychoactives—why tobacco has been allowed from colonial times to today, why alcohol is ranked second in the scale of danger presumed by law as indicated by a rescinded twenty-five year prohibition, and why psychoactives have been more or less prohibited since between the last quarter of the last century and the first third of this century. The inherency thesis that the judgments reflect the inherent dangers of the substances is difficult to take seriously because of the great deadliness associated with tobacco and the high levels of deadliness and danger associated with alcohol. It would be difficult to show that the psychoactives come anywhere near the levels of the two main comparable substances. Thus, the conferral thesis seems preferable to the inherency thesis, which would suggest that the revealed scale of American law is either irrational or haphazard. The scale of American law is to rate tobacco lowest and psychoactives highest in dangerousness. The inferences of such a revealed or presumed scale are not to prohibit tobacco from colonial to contemporary times, to subject alcohol to a twenty-five year period of prohibition, and to prohibit psychoactives for a much longer though variable period: opiates and cocaine the longest, marijuana since the thirties, and others for shorter periods. The legal treatment of these related matters of tobacco, alcohol, and psychoactives seems better explained in terms of political, social, and economic factors, including ignorance, than by the principle of rationality usually expected in modern law, according to Weber.

The discussion of whether tobacco or marijuana and whether psychoactives or alcohol are more inherently dangerous has yielded no definitive result. To repeat, uniform normative or problem criteria have not been used in framing the discussion.

In this chapter the cycles of prohibition and control are discussed within two broad historical frameworks. The first outlines the process marking the shift from individual to social control taking place in the last half of the nineteenth and the first half of the twentieth century. The second examines how multiple labels of drug and alcohol problems identified as addiction, abuse, and dependency in the late twentieth century promoted a shift back toward selectively applied individual control.

FROM INDIVIDUAL TO SOCIAL CONTROL

The road to contemporary drug prohibition stemmed from the discovery of linking concepts of addiction and loss of control with the use of alcohol in the early part of the nineteenth century. Levine describes how alcohol was transformed from the "good creature of God" in colonial America to "demon rum" by the mid–nineteenth century. Levine notes the positive definition of alcohol before the onset of the Victorian nineteenth century:

> All liquor was regarded as good and healthy; alcohol was tonic, medicine, stimulant and relaxant. It was drunk at all hours of the day and night, by men and women of all social classes, and it was routinely given to children. . . . Puritan ministers praised alcohol but denounced drunkenness as a sinful and willful misuse of the "Good Creature." Most colonials, however, regarded drunkenness as unproblematic and unsurprising; drunkenness was seen as the natural, normal and harmless result of drinking. (Levine 1984:110)

Beginning in the late eighteenth century, Dr. Benjamin Rush led physicians to turn away from colonial notions that drinking was good and Puritan reservations that drunkenness was a willful and sinful choice, a choice distinguishable from mere drinking. Rush argued that regular drinkers became addicted, experiencing "uncontrollable, overwhelming and irresistible desires for drink . . . what today is referred to as loss of control" (Levine 1984:110; see also Levine 1980; Wilkerson 1966; Rorabaugh 1979). The concern with individual drunkenness grew during the first third of the nineteenth century into a middle-class-elite movement promoting "temperance," then defined as abstinence from distilled liquor and moderation in the use of beer and wine. Industrialization, urbanization, and the influx of immigrant workers transformed the meaning and activities of temperance into a broad social movement, which defined alcohol in general as the basic cause of various social problems. In this emerging ideology—what was to become prohibitionism—alcohol took the place of urbanization, industrialization, and immigration as the basic cause of the social problems; the movement to control drinking changed from temperance to prohibition. The conception of the problem became generalized: if individual drunkenness caused the loss of self-control, societal drinking led to the loss of social control.

By the end of the nineteenth century, alcohol became a major scapegoat for the perceived breakdown in social order. Increasing crime, prostitution, poverty, and the supposed degeneracy of "the undeserving poor" were caused by alcohol, according to the growing number of adherents to Prohibitionism. Alcohol became the symbol for the Protestant middle classes of the breakdown in the older, agrarian society (Gusfield 1963). The enemy of social order became the greed of the liquor industrialists and the local saloon, as well as the working-class people who frequented saloons. The evaluation of alcohol was transformed from an earlier focus upon the problems of individual drunkenness to the belief that social control was undermined by drinking in general.

Subsequently, drugs, typically used by immigrant groups, were drawn into the pattern defined by the prohibition of alcohol. Opiates had first been available in many forms and were used medicinally and as tonics and stimulants, following the earlier pattern of alcohol use. Some of the most common medicinal substances used by middle-class Americans, such as laudanum, came under attack (Duster 1970). Prohibitions began against the mainly Chinese immigrants' practice of smoking opium. Influenced by the newly formed American Medical Association, which wished to gain control over the dispensing of drugs, federal policy proceeded by 1915, under the Harrison Act, to drive users underground. By 1926, users of proscribed narcotics had become defined as "criminal addicts" (Helmer 1975).

An intolerance to substances has seemed highly correlated with an intolerance toward ethnic groups or social classes using the substances. Many studies have revealed that drug and alcohol control in the United States has been aimed specifically at disadvantaged populations for reasons of political expediency, cultural advantage, or economic and social control (Becker 1963; Duster 1970; Helmer 1975; Himmelstein 1983; Morgan, Wallach, and Buchanan 1988; Reinarman 1983; Trebach 1987).

The transition from tolerance and enthusiasm to intolerance for alcohol in the United States was repeated in the response to opium, cocaine, heroin, marijuana, methamphetamines, psychedelics, and other substances. Temperance served as a midpoint in the reaction against the initial celebration, pointing to moderation instead of total restriction. Whether the accumulation of experience among users or the perception of an association of use with negative effects by nonusers played a greater role in the cycle from tolerance to intolerance is a matter of continuing dispute. Probably internal factors played a smaller role than external opinions in moving public opinion from positive to negative evaluations. A better understanding of the cyclic character of the societal response is possible if we consider the second framework, which has occurred only in the case of alcohol, after the end of Prohibition in 1933. An example of Durkheim's organic solidarity developed in the transition from the prohibition of alcohol to a selectively applied individual control.

INDIVIDUALIZING SOCIAL CONTROL

Following the end of Prohibition, no clear policy emerged until the end of the war. Initially, government and the relegalized alcohol industry joined forces in sustaining the legitimacy of alcohol production and consumption. The remnants of the Prohibition movement pointed to the continuing problems of alcohol use. Certain federal agencies and some Prohibitionist opinion began to shift the focus to marijuana as a problematic substance. Alcoholics Anonymous (AA) formed in the middle thirties but made little headway at first, and formulations of the nature of "alcoholism" were not clearly set. By the middle-forties, Alcoholics Anonymous had attracted the attention of some members of the medical community who had favored the establishment of a medical definition of alcoholism as a disease.

The emergent synthesis of a medical model and an Alcoholics Anonymous approach received critical support from the alcohol beverage industry, which was still engaged in a holding action against Prohibitionist critics of Roosevelt's New Deal liberal alcohol policy. The alcohol industry funded some of the early research on the disease of alcoholism and was represented in organizations espousing the Alcoholics Anonymous viewpoint politically. By the late forties, Alcoholics Anonymous had attained national recognition as manifested by an address by President Truman to a national AA convention.

By the beginning of the postwar era, several tendencies combined to result in the new pattern of societal response to alcohol use. Despite subsequent change and variation, a relatively stable and functional mix emerged. Social control of alcohol use became individualized. On the one hand, a tolerant attitude, supported and pictured in mass advertising, favored the development of what came to be known as social drinking; on the other hand, a concept of the "alcoholic" was fixed upon a small proportion of problematic drinkers and attributed to individual differences in the capacity to manage alcohol (Moore and Gersten 1981).

The medical model of heavy drinking and problem drinking culminated in the "alcoholic." Addicted to alcohol, the alcoholic suffered from loss of control, manifested characteristic traits of belligerence, poor work habits, and, at the extreme, suffered loss of memory and other dysfunctional traits. Alcoholics were perceived within the disease category of the medical perspective. Alcoholics Anonymous promulgated the medical concept that the alcoholic was addicted to alcohol, but AA also developed a distinctive approach to treatment that differed somewhat from the strict medical model, but worked easily with it. The medical model and the Alcoholics Anonymous approach, based upon frequent meetings, group support, and individual sponsorship by veteran members, complemented each other.

Medical facilities specializing in the treatment of alcoholics began to utilize AA meetings and personnel within the treatment programs and referred persons to local AA groups at the end of treatment. There has been significant dispute regarding the effectiveness of the AA treatment model, especially with regard to whether control must be total instead of partial once one has been deemed an alcoholic. For our purposes, however, the important matter is not such disputes but the emergence of the joint Alcoholics Anonymous—medical model as part of the prevailing policy "beyond the shadow of prohibition." This functional mix is part of the cycle in the societal reaction to alcohol, and represents the key development of the post-Prohibition period. The question whether this last part of the cycle could be applied to drug users in addition to alcoholics has already been answered affirmatively by AA organizations. Separate Narcotics Anonymous groups exist, but at the same time many drug-users attend Alcoholics Anonymous meetings. Little distinction is made with regard to the nature of the problem and the approach to rehabilitation.

While the labeling of someone as addict or alcoholic can harbor a punitive or degrading implication, it is equally important to recognize that the current mix of societal reaction to alcohol moves back partially to the tolerance of the earlier periods. Most drinkers are tolerated as social or normal. Heavy or problem drinkers come at a certain point to be regarded as alcoholic addicts. Such persons are regarded as problematic alcoholics, but they are not usually imprisoned. The current functional mix of public policy toward alcohol is to that extent an individualization of social control.

Aided by government agencies, including law-enforcement, the alcohol industry promoted the mixture of tolerance for social drinking and a medical-organizational model for treating anonymous alcoholic addicts. State and federal agencies were lobbied to develop a "public health" approach. Clearly, such programs served the interest of the alcohol industry by providing an alternative to the demands of temperance or prohibitionist organizations pushing for greater social control of drinking. The function of an addiction concept is to imply that only a small minority of people using alcohol—or some other drug—suffer the negative consequences of losing control over the degree or the consequences of use. The great majority are assumed able to drink normally and socially. The deviance of the alcoholic is medicalized (Conrad and Schneider 1980; Morgan 1988). To the extent that social scientists and medical specialists affirm the concept of addiction, the consumption of alcohol may function within the limits of social tolerance. Such is the mix that currently guides public policy beyond the shadow of prohibition (Moore and Gersten 1981). Whether the mix is a good one is a matter of opinion; nevertheless, the current mix has been remarkably stable. The mix has been able to withstand and adapt to the increasing concern with the disastrous effects of drunk driving or the alleged increase in teenage drinking. The distinction between normal and addicted use seems generally established socially as well as professionally with regard to the drug of alcohol.

Many problems remain in applying the functional mix to a technological society where some people drive after drinking, or even drink while driving cars or locomotives or while operating cranes or office computers. A current dispute regarding the tolerable alcohol level in the legal definition of drunk driving illustrates the continuing conflicts of interest and viewpoint between the American Beverage Institute, a trade organization for restaurants and other businesses that sell alcohol, and citizen's groups wishing to make the standard for legal driving more rigorous. Mothers Against Drunk Driving (MADD) opposes the American Beverage Institute's attempt to maintain the .10 percent level of blood alcohol as the permissible standard for driving under the influence of alcohol. Many state legislatures are moving to lower the level to .08 percent in defining the level of social drinking permissible when driving. The importance of this debate is clear. Aside from the personal slant of whether Candy Lightner has betrayed MADD (which she founded and headed) by becoming a main lobbyist for the American Beverage Institute, the issue speaks to a critical matter in the definition of social drinking, and indicates that matters of social control and penal sanction maintain their relevance long after the abolition of the general prohibition of alcohol (*San Francisco Chronicle*, 15 January 1994).

CONTROL OF PATHOLOGY: ADDICTION, ABUSE, AND DEPENDENCY

Addiction is the basic English language term referring to the illness of use. Other terms stand in opposition to the implications of the addiction concept, soften or revise the meaning, mimic, repeat, or shift the meaning of this much abused term. To figure the meaning of addiction, one must contemplate the background from which addiction stands out. As in the case of alcohol, addiction takes its meaning in contrast with normal, social use. This background meaning is lost or buried in the case of illegal drugs, since the law does not brook a social usage once an activity is deemed illegal. But in the world of customary users and the social circles in which users work and play, a distinction can be made between social or recreational users and users for whom use is problematic. The legal context of prohibition makes the term *addiction* too broad, for there is an inclination to regard any illegal use of drugs as an addiction. It is for this reason that a legalistic approach quickly develops an intolerance to the addiction concept: Drug use is better regarded as an abuse.

Once considered an individual instance of deviation from a customary notion of normal use, the heavy user may thus be defined in a variety of ways (Smart 1974). Whether the objective judgment of experts, or as subjective judgments apparent in the world of users, the evaluations proceed in several directions. The most common definitions are medical and moral. Most words used in recent history to refer to the 10 to 15 percent of problem users have been overweighted and thus subjected to unwarranted criticism. Each concept has implied or insinuated an explanation of the overuse as well as a meaning, or definition of the usual indications or correlations of the higher than normal degree of drug taking. The first and most persistent term, *addiction*, follows the medical definition begun by Benjamin Rush at the turn of the nineteenth century. The addiction concept refers to a pressing of need because the body's appetites are changed by the chronic use of a particular substance. The body likes the feeling associated with the drug and proceeds from wanting some to needing more than was anticipated at the outset. As the body's tolerance to the substance increases, the person needs more and more to obtain the sought-after feeling. In the event of withdrawal, the body becomes ill or feels bad because of being deprived of the substance. Alfred Lindesmith's (1947) rendition of this concept suggested that if persons did not define an association between withdrawal and the ill effects, the chances of escaping a self-concept as addict might be maximized.

Objections to the addiction concept came from many sources. The allegedly unpleasant symptoms or ill effects of withdrawal varied significantly among differing substances and users. The failure to find an effective treatment adversely affected the acceptance of a medical concept of addiction.

Two of the most professionally endorsed drug treatments of drug addiction—heroin and methadone—proved less than successful, managing only to substitute one strong drug for another. Furthermore, addiction was held by some critics to imply a sense of nonresponsibility. As in the case of mental illness, addiction seemed to imply an excuse or a rationalization for harmful actions or illegal behavior. Because addiction had been found wanting as a basic concept for grasping the phenomenon of "overuse," abuse emerged gradually as a rival idea.[1]

Soon after the widespread increase in drug use during the sixties and early seventies, the concept of drug abuse began to take on a distinctive meaning. More moralistic than medical, the increased popularity of the abuse concept mirrored a negative national reaction to the widespread enthusiasm and popularity of the drug culture. The meaning of abuse and the associated explanation of drug-taking followed two roads, one minimalist and short-lived, the other broader and still prominent.

The minimalist concept of drug abuse referred to the misuse of drugs. Drugs were meant to be taken as treatment for illness, not for pleasure or religious experience or sensual gratification or recreational release. This meaning was widespread among medical professionals, but never quite caught on with the general population. Many countercultural exponents and social scientists challenged the premise that drugs in their nature were to be used only as treatment for illness. Moreover, the increasingly large population opposed to the drug culture thought misuse was too limited a meaning for the concept of drug abuse.

Abuse, in the broader conception of drug abuse, implies more: that drug abuse is taking advantage and is immoral, and that it is justifiable to condemn it and make it illegal. Drug abuse—like sexual abuse or physical abuse—is taking advantage of, an exploitation of close family members and other members of society. People who use drugs, regardless of the amount or patterns of use, were deemed immoral, hedonistic, bending the normative order to their own advantage and for their own pleasure. Culturally, the best symbol of the abuse concept was with reference to athletes who used drugs to enhance their performance. Seeking enhanced performance, pleasure, strength, energy, or alteration of consciousness was endowed with a deviant meaning and intention. Achieving social goals by means of drugs was deviant, abusive.

The explanation provided for drug taking by the abuse concept is that it is rational, willful. The explanation of addiction is involuntary; the user is captured, controlled by the substance. An abuse is an unfair means to obtain conventional ends. Since conventional means are provided, public opinion is offended by the cutting of corners, the unfair edge, presumed to motivate users of illegal substances.

To a certain extent, the disagreement between the concepts of addiction and abuse has been resolved by a division of attribution. Members of some groups are more likely to be thought of as addictive when coming to the notice of authorities, whereas members of other groups may be assumed abusive. Such attributions of illness and deviation may be further confounded by internal group preferences regarding designation. Middle-class youth and adults may prefer being seen as sick or addicted, rather than deviant and abusive, whereas members of underclass subcultures may prefer the deviant role to attributions of illness or addiction. Such a division of attribution would be consistent with Klein's (1983) observation that being ill and against the law make up two sides of the same coin.

The dispute between the ideas of addiction and abuse has also been mediated by a third alternative. Between addiction and abuse, dependency is usually regarded as the meekest of concepts when applied to drug or alcohol use. Yet precisely because the concept implies neither the medical disease of addiction nor the judgmental moralism of abuse, many practitioners and professionals fall back on a notion of dependency when working with or referring to problematic users of chemical substances. Though dependency is often considered a psychological concept, dependency also has social, economic, and political meanings. The individual meaning of dependency of psychology is augmented by the social meaning of persons dependent on welfare, the economic meaning of dependent nations before they became developing nations, and a political meaning, as in Albert Memmi's (1984) definition of dependency as a state of being dominated. Dependency implies a state of neediness that is not based in either an organic reduction to addiction or the moral outrage of abusiveness. Dependency does not imply a specific explanation of overuse, but remains open-ended. Psychological, social, economic, and political sciences have utilized the concept of dependency, and have often developed ideas of overcoming the state through programmatic aid, political action, or self-help organizations. Given the present state of knowledge regarding the nature of the heavy use of drugs and the societal capacity to control overuse, dependency, the weakest of the most popular conceptions, would seem the wisest choice. Being referred to as being dependent on drugs is slightly less insulting than being called addicted or being held guilty of drug abuse; it is also in most cases probably a more accurate appraisal of the extent of neediness.

When seen from the standpoint of abstinence or withdrawal, the several concepts referring to problematic use appear less competitive. Complementary meanings emerge for what academically or externally, appear as rival concepts struggling to account for the phenomenon. There is no reason to favor one concept over another when behavior, or feelings associated with each, appear during the experience of withdrawal. When the concepts are seen alongside each other, instead of as alternatives, we are forced as analysts or as participants to sharpen the meaning of each concept, so as to remove the overlap that passes unnoticed from the external perspective.

CONCLUSION: CONTROLLING DRUG USE

The idea that persons can achieve a greater self- and social control over drug use in prison is perhaps the greatest single harm committed by the social engineering mentality in the United States. The idea that prison can help someone overcome drugs is one of those ideas that deserves being compared to using the concentration camp to help people not be bourgeois deviationists, or mentally ill. As the Great Prohibition nears the end of its century, the imprisonment of users of prohibited substances should be reconsidered. "Sooner or later," said Walter Lippman "the American people will have to make up their minds either to bring their legislative ideals down to a point where they square with human nature or they will have to establish an administrative despotism strong enough to start enforcing their moral ideals. They cannot much longer defy the devil with a wooden sword" (quoted in Woodiwiss 1988 [from Walter Lippman, "The Underworld as Servant," Forum, January-February, 1931]).

The policy of imprisoning drug takers has had long-term, permanent effects, most of which have ranged from the sad and bad to the vicious and criminal. Rehabilitation has not been aided by enforced confinement. The drug traffic has continued to flow in and out of prison. People who stop using typically return when out of prison. Prisoners who need drugs (which will now include tobacco in some prisons) and are without money are constrained to obtain drugs by nonmonetary means.

When a person is dependent on drugs, the proper goal for the individual or society is freedom from the necessity to use. To be free of this neediness upon drugs ranging from legal coffee, tobacco, and alcohol, to illegal marijuana, cocaine, and heroin, may mean either consuming in the conventional manner of the social drinker or to stop entirely in the manner of the anonymous, recovering exalcoholic. This is the functional mix that defines the public policy in the society beyond Prohibition. In either event, the aim is to achieve a freedom from a reliance upon a particular substance. Social drinkers are drinkers who have not been discredited by their incapacity to imbibe in a controlled manner. They are assumed to be not reliant upon drinking. Addicted, abusive, or dependent drug takers are labeled persons whose use has led to problematic life circumstances, ranging from arrest or unemployment to divorce or social isolation. To use coercion to impose upon such a person the capacity to be free of a dependency seems the cruelest of hoaxes, the most senseless of punishments. To liken the social control of social work intervention, or even mandatory treatment, to the policy of penal sanction seems a bit insensitive to commonly understood differences of degree. The paradox of controlling drug use is the necessity for freedom, but this does not mean that communities may not insist on some measures of intervention when persons become known or labeled as problematic users. Thus, freedom from the use of drugs may prove a more difficult project than the once celebrated freedom to use.

The possibility of penal sanction for using drugs or alcohol does not end with the end of prohibition. Social control is moved from the simple matter of which substances to prohibit to questions of medical or social work intervention for persons labeled addictive, abusive, or dependent. Penal sanctions in the form of imprisonment for drunk or drugged driving remain; corporations, universities, and government bureaus may require drug testing and fire employees discovered to be drinking or using drugs. Such a shift in focus defines the offense more specifically, but still maintains the expectation of sobriety in driving, working, and other major social roles. Such a complicated mix of attitudes and definitions involves many compromises, apparent inconsistencies, and a political deferring to lobbies, interests, and professional expertise. Whether the functional mix that defines the complex state of social control of alcohol is preferable to the prohibition of psychoactive drugs is the major question of current social policy. Perhaps the dispute between those who support the current prohibition and those favoring legalization of drugs will benefit from the reminder that alcohol remains the model of Prohibitionist policy. After the Great Prohibition upon alcohol, social control over the use of alcohol was maintained, though in changed form. Penal sanctions were specified to deal with the dangerous or deadly consequences of drinking, rather than drinking itself. Whether currently prohibited drugs can be expected to follow a similar course is a difficult question to answer. A current reading of public opinion would probably indicate a greater likelihood for the prohibition of tobacco than for the legalization of marijuana. In either event, specialists in the field of drugs and alcohol will continue to profit from continuing research and treatment of afflicted persons.

NOTES

1. Many thanks to Gresham Sykes for a critical response to an earlier draft of this article that discussed addiction but neglected the concept of abuse.

REFERENCES

Becker, H. 1963. *Outsiders: Studies in the Sociology of Deviance*. Glencoe, IL: Free Press.
Cohen, S. 1985. *Visions of Social Control: Crime, Punishment and Classification*. Cambridge: Polity.
Conrad, P. and J. Schneider. 1980. *Deviance and Medicalization*. St. Louis: C. V. Mosby.

Duster, T. 1970. *The Legislation of Morality*. New York: Free Press.
Fingarette, H. 1988. *Heavy Drinking: The Myth of Alcoholism as a Disease*. Berkeley: University of California Press.
Gusfield, J. 1963. *Symbolic Crusade: Status Politics and the American Temperance Movement*, Urbana: University of Illinois Press.
Helmer, J. 1975. *Drugs and Minority Oppression*. New York: Seabury Press.
Himmelstein, J. 1983. *The Strange Career of Marihuana*. Westport, CT: Greenwood.
Johnson, P. 1983. *Modern Times*. New York: Harper and Row.
Klein, D. 1983. "Ill and Against the Law: The Social and Medical Control of Heroin." *Journal of Drug Issues* 13(1):31–56.
Levine, H. G. 1980. "The Discovery of Addiction: Changing Conceptions of Habitual Drunkenness in America." *Journal of Studies on Alcohol* 39:143–74.
———. 1984. "The Alcohol Problem in America: From Temperance to Alcoholism." *British Journal of Addiction* 79:109–19.
Lindesmith, A. R. 1947. *Opiate Addiction*. Evanston, IL: Principia.
Memmi, A. 1984. *Dependence*. Boston: Beacon.
Moore, M. and D. Gersten, eds. 1981. *Alcohol and Public Policy: Beyond The Shadow of Prohibition*. Washington, DC: National Academy Press.
Morgan, P. 1988. "Power, Politics and Public Health: The Political Power of the Alcohol Beverage Industry." *Journal of Public Health Policy* 9(2).
Morgan, P., L. Wallach, and D. Buchanan. 1988. "Waging Drug Wars: Prevention Strategy or Politics as Usual." *Drugs and Society* 3:99–124.
Reinarman, C. 1983. "Constraint, Autonomy and State Policy: Notes toward a Theory of Controls on Consciousness Alteration." *Journal of Drug Issues* 13(1):9–30.
Rorabaugh, W. J. 1979. *The Alcoholic Republic*. New York: Oxford University Press.
Smart, R. 1974. "Addiction, Dependency, Abuse or Use: Which Are We Studying with Epidemiology?" In *Drug Use: Epidemiological and Sociological Approaches*, edited by E. Josephson and E. E. Carroll. New York: Wiley.
Trebach, A. 1987. *The Great Drug War*. New York: MacMillan.
Weil, A. 1972. *The Natural Mind*. Boston: Houghton Mifflin.
Wilkerson, A. 1966. *A History of the Concept of Alcoholism as a Disease*. Doctoral dissertation, University of Pennsylvania.
Woodiwiss, M. Crimes. 1988. *Crusades and Corruption: Prohibitions in the United States, 1900–1987*. Totowa, NJ: Barnes and Noble.

V
MEASURING CRIME AND CONTROL

The line of sociological work on social control, as represented by the chapters in Part IV, relies mainly on historical and qualitative sources. Images are picked up from trends and patterns that extend backward for decades and are projected forward into the future.

At some point however—as Messinger's studies of changes in the Californian correctional system show—these trends need grounding in the detailed statistical record of what the system actually does. Social control is not an abstract process; it leaves behind measurable traces of its operations. At the descriptive level, we need raw information about what is done to what number of people over what time. At the more complicated evaluative level, we need reliable data to assess the impact of all these operations.

The two chapters in this section are both concerned with measurement. In Chapter 14, Richard Berk (a regular statistical collaborator with Messinger) and his colleague David Freedman consider some of the methodological problems in measuring the impact of penal policy. Can the natural science model of experimental group/control group be adapted to evaluating particular programs? In Chapter 15, Alfred Blumstein, who has pioneered the use of systems theory to study the criminal justice process, uses the measurable variable of imprisonment rates to examine the "stability-of-punishment" hypothesis. Whether or not some internal adjustment mechanism ever operated to stabilize amounts of punishment—Messinger and others have been skeptical of this hypothesis—Blumstein's characterization of the correctional system as being "out of control" clearly points to the breakdown of such internal regulation. His analysis of these statistics invites a theoretical debate, but also public concern about where these trends are leading.

14
Statistical Assumptions as Empirical Commitments

RICHARD A. BERK and DAVID A. FREEDMAN

INTRODUCTION

Researchers who study punishment and social control, like those who study other social phenomena, typically seek to generalize their findings from the data they have to some larger context: in statistical jargon, they generalize from a sample to a population. Generalizations are one important product of empirical inquiry. Of course, the process by which the data are selected introduces uncertainty. Indeed, any given dataset is but one of a very large number that could have been studied. If the dataset had been different, the statistical summaries would have been different, and so would the conclusions, at least by a little.

How do we calibrate the uncertainty introduced by data collection? Nowadays, this question has become quite salient, and it is routinely answered using well-known methods of statistical inference, with standard errors, t-tests, and p-values, culminating in the "tabular asterisks" of Meehl (1978). These conventional answers, however, turn out to depend critically on certain rather restrictive assumptions, for instance, random sampling.[1]

When the data are generated by random sampling from a clearly defined population, and when the goal is to estimate population parameters from sample statistics, statistical inference can be relatively straightforward. The usual textbook formulas apply; tests of statistical significance and confidence intervals follow.

If the random-sampling assumptions do not apply, or the parameters are not clearly defined, or the inferences are to a population that is only vaguely defined, the calibration of uncertainty offered by contemporary statistical technique is in turn rather questionable.[2] Thus, investigators who use conventional statistical technique turn out to be making, explicitly or implicitly, quite restrictive behavioral assumptions about their data collection process. By using apparently familiar arithmetic, they have made substantial empirical commitments; the research enterprise may be distorted by statistical technique, not helped. At least, that is our thesis, which we will develop in the pages that follow.

Random sampling is hardly universal in contemporary studies of punishment and social control. More typically, perhaps, the data in hand are simply the data most readily available (e.g., Gross and Mauro 1989; MacKenzie 1991; Nagin and Paternoster 1993; Berk and Campbell 1993). For instance, information on the use of prison "good time" may come from one prison in a certain state. Records on police use of force may be available only for encounters in which a suspect requires medical attention. Prosecutors' charging decisions may be documented only after the resolution of a law suit.

"Convenience samples" of this sort are not random samples. Still, researchers may quite properly be worried about replicability. The generic concern is the same as for random sampling: if the study were repeated, the results would be different. What, then, can be said about the results obtained? For example, if the study of police use of force were repeated, it is almost certain that the sample statistics would change. What can be concluded, therefore, from the statistics?

These questions are natural, but may be answerable only in certain contexts. The moment that conventional statistical inferences are made from convenience samples, substantive assumptions are made about how the social world operates. Conventional statistical inferences (e.g., formulas for the standard error of the mean or t-tests) depend on the assumption of random sampling. This is not a matter of debate or opinion; it is a matter of mathematical necessity.[3] When applied to convenience samples, the random-sampling assumption is more than a mere technicality or a minor revision on the periphery of existing theory; the assumption becomes an integral part of the story.

In the pages ahead, we will try to show how statistical and empirical concerns interact in research on punishment and social control. The basic question: What kinds of social processes are assumed by the application of conventional statistical techniques to convenience samples? Our answer will be that the assumptions are quite unrealistic. If so, probability calculations that depend on the assumptions must be viewed as unrealistic too.[4]

TREATING THE DATA AS A POPULATION

Suppose that one has data from spouse abuse victims currently residing in a particular shelter. A summary statistic of interest is the proportion of women who want to obtain restraining orders. How should potential uncertainty be considered? One strategy is to treat the women currently residing in the shelter as a population; the issue of what would happen if the study were repeated does not arise. All the investigator cares about are the data now in hand. The summary statistics describe the needs of the women in the dataset. No statistical inference is needed since there is no sampling uncertainty to worry about.

Treating the data as a population and discarding statistical inference might well make sense if the summary statistics are used to plan for support services needed by current shelter residents. A conclusion that "most" want to obtain restraining orders is one thing; a conclusion that a "few" want to obtain such orders has quite different implications. But there are no inferences about service needs of women who might use the shelter in the future, or women residing in other shelters. While such limitations may have no impact for shelter staff, they are obstacles to scientific inquiry.

ASSUMING A REAL POPULATION AND IMAGINARY SAMPLING MECHANISM

Another way to handle uncertainty is to define a real population and assume that the data can be treated as a random sample from that population. Thus, current shelter residents could perhaps be treated as a random sample drawn from the population of residents in all shelters in the area during the previous twelve months. This "as-if" strategy would seem to set the stage for statistical business as usual.

An explicit goal of the "as-if" strategy is generalizing to a specific population. And one issue is this: Are the data representative? For example, did each member of the specified population have the same probability of coming into the sample? If not, and the investigator fails to weight the data, inferences from the sample to the population will likely be wrong.[5]

More subtle are the implications for estimates of standard errors.[6] The usual formulas require the investigator to believe that the women are sampled independently of one another. Even small departures from independence may have serious consequences, as we demonstrate later. Furthermore, the investigator is required to assume constant probabilities across occasions. This assumption of constant probabilities is almost certainly false. Family violence has seasonal patterns; Christmas is a particularly bad time. The probabilities of admission must vary over the course of the year. In addition, shelters vary in catchment areas, referral patterns, interpersonal networks, and admissions policies. Thus, women with children may have low probability of admission to one shelter, but a high probability of admission to other shelters. Selection probabilities depend on a host of personal characteristics; probabilities must vary across geography and over time.

The independence assumption seems even more unrealistic. Admissions policies evolve in response to daily life in the shelter. For example, some shelter residents may insist on keeping contact with their abusers. Experience may make the staff reluctant to admit similar women in the future. Likewise, shelter staff may eventually decide to exclude victims with drug or alcohol problems.

To summarize, the random sampling assumption is required for statistical inference. But this assumption has substantive implications that are unrealistic. The consequences of failures in the assumptions will be discussed below.

AN IMAGINARY POPULATION AND IMAGINARY SAMPLING MECHANISM

Another way to treat uncertainty is to create an imaginary population from which the data are assumed to be a random sample. Consider the shelter story: The population might be taken as the set of all shelter residents that could have been produced by the social processes creating victims who seek shelter. These processes might include family violence, as well as more particular factors affecting possible victims, and forces shaping the availability of shelter space.

With this approach, the investigator does not explicitly define a population that could be studied, even with unlimited resources of time and money. The investigator merely *assumes* that such a population exists in some ill-defined sense. And there is a further assumption, that the dataset being analyzed can be treated as *if* it were based on a random sample from the assumed population. These are convenient fictions. Convenience will not be denied, but why are these fictions? The reasons are not subtle: (1) The population does not have any empirical existence of its own; (2) the sample was not in fact drawn as a random sample.

In order to use the imaginary-population approach, it would seem necessary for investigators to demonstrate that the data can be treated as a random sample. It would be necessary to specify the social processes that are involved, how they work, and why they would produce the statistical equivalent of a random sample. Vague rhetoric seems inadequate, and we doubt the case could be made for the shelter example or any similar illustration.

Nevertheless, reliance on imaginary populations is widespread. Indeed, regression models are commonly used to analyze convenience samples; as we show later, such analyses are often predicated on random sampling from imaginary populations. The rhetoric of imaginary populations is seductive because it frees the investigator from the necessity of understanding how data were generated.

WHEN THE STATISTICAL ISSUES ARE SUBSTANTIVE

Statistical calculations are often a technical sideshow; the primary interest is in some substantive question. Even so, the methodological issues need careful attention, as we have argued. However, in many cases the substantive issues are very close to the statistical ones. For example, in litigation involving claims of racial discrimination, the substantive research question is usually operationalized as a statistical hypothesis: certain data are like a random sample from a specified population.

Suppose, for example, that in a certain jurisdiction there are 1084 probationers under federal supervision: 369 are black. Over a six-month period, 119 probationers are cited for technical violations: 54 are black. This is disparate impact, as one sees by computing the percentages: in the total pool of probationers, 34% are black; however, among those cited, 45% are black.

A t-test for "statistical significance" would probably follow. The standard error on the 45% is $\sqrt{.45 \times .55/119} = .046$. So, $t = (.45 - .34)/.046 = 2.41$, and the one-sided p is .01. (A more sophisticated analyst might use hypergeometric distribution, but that would not change the outlines of the problem.) The null hypothesis is rejected, and there are at least two competing explanations: either blacks are more prone to violate probation, or supervisors are racist. It is up to the probation office to demonstrate the former; the t-test shifts the burden of argument.

However, there is a crucial (and widely ignored) step in applying the t-test: translating the idea of a race-neutral citation process into a statistical null hypothesis. In a race-neutral world, the argument must go, the citation process would be like citing 119 people drawn at random from a pool consisting of 34% blacks. This random-sampling assumption is the critical one for computing the standard error.

The t-statistic may be large for two reasons: (1) too many blacks are cited, so the numerator in the t-statistic is too big, or (2) the standard error in the denominator is too small. The first explanation may be the salient one, but we think the second explanation needs to be considered as well. In a race-neutral world, it is plausible that blacks and whites should have the same overall citation probabilities, at least in some average sense. However, in any world, these probabilities seem likely to vary from person to person and time to time. Furthermore, dependence from occasion to occasion would seem to be the rule rather than the exception. As will be seen below, even fairly modest amounts of dependence can create substantial bias in estimated standard errors.

In the real world, over the past five years, the proportion of federal probationers convicted for drug offenses has increased dramatically. Such probationers may be subjected to drug testing, and are often required to participate in drug treatment programs. The mix of offenders and supervision policies has changed dramatically. The assumption of probabilities constant over time is highly suspect. Likewise, an assumption that all probationers face the same risks of citation is almost certainly false. Even in a race-neutral world, the intensity of supervision must be in part determined by the nature of the offender's crime and background; the intensity of supervision obviously affects the likelihood of detecting probation violations.

The assumption of independence is even more problematic. Probation officers are likely to change their supervision policies, depending on past performance of the probationers. For example, violations of probation seem likely to lead to closer and more demanding supervision, with higher probabilities of detecting future violations. Similarly, behavior of the probationers is likely to depend on the supervision policies.

In short, the translation of race-neutrality into a statistical hypothesis of random sampling is not innocuous. The statistical formulation seems inconsistent with the social processes on which it has been imposed. If so, the results of the statistical manipulations—the p-values—are of questionable utility.

This example is not special. We suspect that for most convenience samples, the social processes responsible for the data will be inconsistent with what needs to be assumed to justify conventional formulas for standard errors. If so, translating research questions into statistical hypotheses may be quite problematic: much can be lost in translation.

DOES THE RANDOM SAMPLING ASSUMPTION MAKE ANY DIFFERENCE?

For criminal justice research, we have tried to indicate the problems with making statistical inferences based on convenience samples. The assumption of independence is critical, and we believe this assumption will always be difficult to justify.[7] The next question is whether violations of the independence assumption matter. There is no definitive answer to this question; much depends on context. However, we will show that relatively modest violations of independence can lead to substantial bias in estimated standard errors. In turn, the confidence levels and significance probabilities will be biased too.

Violations of Independence

Suppose the citation process violates the independence assumption in the following manner. Probation officers make contact with probationers on a regular basis. If contact leads to a citation, the probability of a subsequent citation goes up, because a law enforcement perspective is reinforced. If contact does not lead to a citation, the probability of a subsequent citation goes down (a law enforcement perspective is not reinforced). This does not seem to be an unreasonable model; indeed, it may be more reasonable than independence.

More specifically, suppose the citation process is a "stationary Markov chain." If contact leads to a citation, the chance that the next case will be cited is 0.5. On the other hand, if contact does not lead to a citation, the chance of a citation on the next contact is only 0.1. To get started, we assume the chance of a citation on the first contact is 0.3; the starting probability makes little difference.

Suppose an investigator has a sample of 100 cases, and observes 17 citations. The probability of citation would be estimated as $17/100 = .17$, with a standard error of $\sqrt{.17 \times .83/100} = .038$. Implicitly, this calculation assumes independence. However, Markov chains do not obey the independence assumption. The right standard error, computed by simulation, turns out to be .058. This is about 50% larger than the standard error computed by the usual formula. As a result, the conventional t-statistic is about 50% too large. For example, a researcher who might ordinarily use a critical value of 2.0 for statistical significance at the .05 level should really be using a critical value of about 3.0.

Of course, investigators who are on their toes might notice the breakdown of the independence assumption: the first-order serial correlation for our Markov process is about .40. This is not large, but it is detectable with the right test.[8] The dependencies could easily be more complicated and harder to find, as the next example shows. Consider a "four-step Markov chain." The probation officer judges an offender in the light of recent experience with similar offenders. The officer thinks back over the past four cases and finds the case most like the current case. If this "reference" case was cited, the probability that the current case will be cited is 0.5. If the reference case was not cited, the probability that the current case will be cited is 0.1. In our example, the reference case is chosen at random from the four prior cases.[9] Again, suppose an investigator has a sample of 100 cases, and observes 17 citations. The probability of citation would still be estimated as $17/100 = .17$, with a standard error of $\sqrt{.17 \times .83/100} = .038$. Now, the right standard error, computed by simulation, turns out to be .062. This is about 60% larger than the standard error computed by the usual formula.

In short, conclusions are much the same as for the first simulation. However, the four-step Markov chain spreads out the dependence so that it is hard to detect: the first-order serial correlation is only about 0.12.[10] Without a priori knowledge that the data were generated by a four-step Markov chain, a researcher is unlikely to identify the dependence.

Similar problems come about if the Markov chain produces negative serial correlations rather than positive ones.[11] Negative dependence can be just as hard to detect, and the estimated standard errors will still be biased. Now the bias is upward, so the null hypothesis is not rejected when it should be: significant findings will be missed.

Of course, small correlations are easier to detect with large samples. Yet probation officers may use more than four previous cases to find a reference case; they may draw on their whole current case load, and on salient cases from past case loads. Furthermore, transition probabilities (here, 0.5 and 0.1) are likely to vary over time in response to changing penal codes, administrative procedures, and mix of offenders. As a result of such complications, even very large samples may not save the day.

The independence assumption is fragile. It is fragile as an empirical matter because real-world criminal justice processes are unlikely to produce data for which independence can be reasonably assumed. (Indeed, if independence were the rule, criminal justice researchers would have little to study.) The assumption is fragile as a statistical matter, because modest violations of independence may have major consequences while being nearly impossible to detect. The Markov chain examples are not worst-case scenarios, and they show what can happen when independence breaks down. The main point is that modest violations of independence can introduce substantial biases into conventional procedures.

DEPENDENCE IN OTHER SETTINGS

Spatial Dependence

In the probation example, dependence was generated by social processes that unfolded over time. Dependence can also result from spatial relationships rather than temporal order. Spatial dependence may be even more difficult to handle than temporal dependence. For example, if a researcher is studying crime rates across census tracts in a particular city, it may seem natural to assume that the correlation between tracts depends on the distance between them. However, the right measure of distance is by no means obvious. Barriers such as freeways, parks, and industrial concentrations may break up dependence irrespective of physical distance. "Closeness" might be better defined by travel time. Perhaps tracts connected by major thoroughfares are more likely to violate the assumption of independence than tracts between which travel is inconvenient. Ethnic mix and demographic profiles matter too, since crimes tend to be committed within ethnic and income groups. Social distance rather than geographical distance may be the key. Our point is that spatial dependence matters. Its measurement will be difficult, and results may depend on how distance itself is defined. Whatever measures are used, spatial dependence produces the same kinds of problems for statistical inference as temporal dependence.

Regression Models

In research on punishment and social control, investigators often use complex models. In particular, regression and its elaborations (e.g., structural equation modeling) are now standard tools of the trade. Although rarely discussed, statistical assumptions have major impacts on analytic results obtained by such methods. Consider the usual textbook exposition of least-squares regression. We have n observational units, indexed by $i = 1, \ldots, n$. There is a response variable y_i, conceptualized as $\mu_i + \epsilon_i$, where μ_i is the theoretical mean of y_i, while the disturbances or errors ϵ_i represent the impact of random variation (sometimes of omitted variables). The errors are assumed to be drawn independently from a common (Gaussian) distribution with mean 0 and finite variance. Generally, the error distribution is not empirically identifiable outside the model, so it cannot be studied directly—even in principle—without the model. The error distribution is an imaginary population, and the errors ϵ_i are treated as if they were a random sample from this imaginary population—a research strategy whose frailty was discussed earlier.

Usually, explanatory variables are introduced, and μ_i is hypothesized to be a linear combination of such variables. The assumptions about the μ_i and ϵ_i are seldom justified or even made explicit.[12] For one representative textbook exposition, see Weisberg (1985). Conventional econometric expositions are for all practical purposes identical (e.g., Johnston 1984; Fromby, Hill, and Johnson 1984). Structural equation models introduce further complications (Freedman 1987; Berk 1988; Freedman 1991; Berk 1991), but random variation is represented in a similar manner. Although the models seem sophisticated, the same old problems have been swept under the carpet. Why do μ_i and ϵ_i behave as assumed? To answer this question, investigators would have to consider, much more closely than is commonly done, the connection between social processes and statistical assumptions.

Time Series Models

Similar issues arise in time series work. Typically, the data are highly aggregated. Each observation characterizes a time period rather than a case;

rates and averages are frequently used. There may be T time periods indexed by $t = 1, 2, \ldots, T$. The response variable y_t is taken to be $\mu_t + \epsilon_t$ where the ϵ_t are assumed to have been drawn independently from a common distribution with mean 0 and finite variance. Then, μ_t will be assumed to depend linearly on values of the response variable for preceding time periods and on values of the explanatory variables. Why such assumptions should hold is a question that is seldom asked, let alone answered.

Serial correlation in residuals may be too obvious to ignore. The common fix is to assume a specific form of dependence between the ϵ_t. For example, a researcher might assert that $\epsilon_t = \gamma \epsilon_{t-1} + \delta_t$, where now δ_t satisfy the familiar assumptions: the δ_t are drawn independently from a common distribution with mean 0 and finite variance. Clearly, the game has not changed except for additional layers of technical complexity.

RECOMMENDATIONS FOR PRACTICE

Convenience samples are a fact of scientific life in criminal justice research; so is uncertainty. However, the conventional techniques designed to measure uncertainty assume that the data are generated by the equivalent of random sampling, or probability sampling more generally.[13] Indeed, probability samples have two great benefits: (1) they allow unbiased extrapolation from the sample; and (2) with data internal to the sample, it is possible to estimate how much results are likely to change if another sample is taken. These benefits, of course, have a price: drawing probability samples is hard work. An investigator who assumes that a convenience sample is like a random sample seeks to obtain the benefits without the costs—just on the basis of assumptions.

If scrutinized, few convenience samples would pass muster as the equivalent of probability samples. Indeed, probability sampling is a technique whose use is justified because it is so unlikely that social processes will generate representative samples. Decades of survey research have demonstrated that when a probability sample is desired, probability sampling must be done. Assumptions do not suffice. Hence, our first recommendation for research practice: whenever possible, use probability sampling.

If the data generation mechanism is unexamined, statistical inference with convenience samples risks substantial error. Bias is to be expected and independence is problematic. When independence is lacking, the p-values produced by conventional formulas can be grossly misleading. In general, we think that reported p-values will be too small; in the social world, proximity seems to breed similarity. Thus, many research results are held to be statistically significant when they are the mere product of chance variation.

We are skeptical about conventional statistical adjustments for dependent data. These adjustments will be successful only under restrictive assumptions whose relevance to the social world is dubious. Moreover, adjustments require new layers of technical complexity, which tend to distance the researcher from the data. Very soon, the model rather than the data will be driving the research. Hence, another recommendation: do not rely on post hoc statistical adjustments to remove dependence.

No doubt, many researchers working with convenience samples will continue to attach standard errors to sample statistics. In such cases, sensitivity analyses may be helpful. Partial knowledge of how the data were generated might be used to construct simulations. It may be possible to determine which findings are robust against violations of independence. However, sensitivity analysis will be instructive only if it captures important features of the data generation mechanism. Fictional sensitivity analysis will produce fictional results.

We recommend better focus on the questions that statistical inference is supposed to answer. If the object is to evaluate what would happen were the study repeated, real replication is an excellent strategy (Freedman 1991; Berk 1991; Ehrenberg and Bound 1993). Empirical results from one study can be used to forecast what should be found in another study. Forecasts about particular summary statistics, such as means or regression coefficients, can be instructive. For example, an average rate of offending (commonly called λ) estimated for teenagers in one neighborhood could be used as a forecast for teenagers in another, similar neighborhood. More demanding, perhaps, are forecasts of individual values rather than summary statistics. Using data from one prison, for instance, a researcher might predict which inmates in another prison will be cited for rule infractions. Correct forecasts would be strong evidence for the model.

Cross-validation is an easier alternative. Investigators can divide a large sample randomly into two or more parts. One part of the data can be used to construct forecasting models that are then evaluated against the rest of the data. This offers some degree of protection against bias due to overfitting or chance capitalization. But cross-validation does not really address the issue of replicability. It cannot, because the data come from only one study.

CONCLUSIONS

We have tried to demonstrate that statistical inference with convenience samples is a risky business. While there are better and worse ways to proceed with the data at hand, real progress depends on deeper understanding of the data generation mechanism. In practice, statistical issues and substantive issues overlap. No amount of statistical maneuvering will get very far without some understanding of how the data were produced.

More generally, we are highly suspicious of efforts to develop empirical generalizations from any single dataset. Rather than ask what would happen in principle if the study were repeated, it makes sense to actually repeat the study. Indeed, it is probably impossible to predict the changes attendant on replication without doing replications.

ACKNOWLEDGMENTS

The authors wish to thank Sheldon L. Messinger for helpful comments and suggestions.

NOTES

1. Random sampling has a precise, technical meaning: sample units are drawn independently, and each unit in the population has an equal chance to be drawn at each stage. Drawing a random sample of the U. S. population, in this technical sense, would cost several billion dollars (since it requires a census as a preliminary matter) and would probably require the suspension of major constitutional guarantees. Random sampling is not an idea to be lightly invoked.

2. As we shall explain below, researchers may find themselves assuming that their sample is a random sample from an imaginary population. Such a population has no empirical existence, but is defined in an essentially circular way—as that population from which the sample may be assumed to be randomly drawn. Regrettably, inferences to imaginary populations are also imaginary.

3. Of course, somewhat weaker assumptions may be sufficient for some purposes. However, as we discuss below, the outlines of the problem stay the same.

4. As indicated above, we use *random sampling* to mean sampling with replacement from a finite population: each unit in the population is selected independently (with replacement) and with the same probability of selection. Sampling without replacement (i.e., simple random sampling) may be more familiar; in many situations, sampling without replacement is very close to sampling with replacement. We use the term *parameter* for a characteristic of the population. A *sample statistic* or *estimate* is computed from the sample to estimate the value of a parameter.

5. Weighting requires that the investigator know the probability of selection for each member of the population. It is hard to imagine that such precise knowledge will be available for convenience samples. Without reweighting, estimates will be biased, perhaps severely.

6. The standard error measures sampling variability; it does not take bias into

account. Our basic model is random sampling. In the time-honored way, suppose we draw women into the sample one after another (with replacement). The conventional formula for the standard error assumes that the selection probabilities stay the same from draw to draw; on any given draw, the selection probabilities do not have to be identical across women.

7. "[I]ndependence seems rare in nature" (Kruskal 1988:934).

8. On the other hand, even if the serial correlation were detected, the conventional corrections (e.g., ARIMA models) would not apply here.

9. In other words, the "most similar" recent case is equally likely to be any of the four prior cases; this is no more unrealistic than standard models based on independence.

10. The standard error is affected not only by first-order correlations, but also by higher-order correlations.

11. We believe this will be relatively rare in criminal justice data.

12. Again, minor correlations in the ϵ_i can create major bias in estimated standard errors for coefficients.

13. With a probability sample, there is a well-defined population; units are drawn into the sample by some objective chance mechanism, so the probability that any particular set of units falls into the sample is computable. Generally, each sample unit will be weighted by the inverse of the selection probability.

REFERENCES

Berk, R. A. 1988. "Causal Inference for Statistical Data." Pp. 155–72 in *Handbook of Sociology*, edited by N. J. Smelser. Beverly Hills: Sage.

———. 1991. "Toward a Methodology for Mere Mortals." Pp. 315–24 in *Sociological Methodology*, Volume 21, edited by P. V. Marsden. Washington, DC: The American Sociological Association.

Berk, R. A., and A. Campbell. 1993. "Preliminary Data on Race and Crack Charging Practices in Los Angeles." *Federal Sentencing Reporter* 6(1):36–38.

Ehrenberg, A. S. C. and J. A. Bound. 1993. "Predictability and Prediction." *Journal of the Royal Statistical Society* Series A, Part 2, 156:167–206.

Fromby, T. B., R. C. Hill, and S. R. Johnson. 1984. *Advanced Econometric Methods*. New York: Springer Verlag.

Freedman, D. 1987. "As Others See Us: A Case Study in Path Analysis" (with discussion). *Journal of Educational Statistics* 12:101–223.

———. 1991. "Statistical Models and Shoe Leather." Pp. 291–358 (with discussion) in *Sociological Methodology*, Volume 21, edited by P. V. Marsden. Washington, DC: The American Sociological Association.

Gross, S. R., and R. Mauro. 1989. *Death and Discrimination*. Boston: Northeastern University Press.

Johnston, J. 1984. *Econometric Methods*. New York: McGraw Hill.

Kruskal, W. 1988. "Miracles and Statistics, The Casual Assumption of Independence." *Journal of the American Statistical Association* 83(404):929–40.

MacKenzie, D. L. 1991. "The Parole Performance of Offenders Released from Shock Incarceration (Boot Camp Prisons): A Survival Time Analysis." *Journal of Quantitative Criminology* 7(3):213–36.

Meehl, P. E. 1978. "Theoretical Risks and Tabular Asterisks: Sir Karl, Sir Ronald, and the Slow Progress of Soft Psychology." *Journal of Consulting and Clinical Psychology* 46:806–34.

Nagin, D. S. and R. Paternoster. 1993. "Enduring Individual Differences and Rational Choice Theories of Crime." *Law & Society Review* 27(3):467–96.

Weisberg, S. 1985. *Applied Linear Regression*. New York: Wiley.

15
Stability of Punishment: What Happened and What Next?

ALFRED BLUMSTEIN

INTRODUCTION

The one occasion I have had to engage in formal public debate in print with Sheldon L. Messinger was over a paper I wrote with Jacqueline Cohen in 1973 (Blumstein and Cohen 1973) proposing a theory of the stability of punishment. Eight years later, Messinger joined with Richard Berk and Berk's then-student, David Rauma, and Thomas Cooley, in a paper (Berk, Rauma, Messinger, and Cooley 1981) that analyzed California data on prison admissions, and argued that these data did not confirm the stability-of-punishment hypothesis. Their challenge was based mostly on the technical aspects of the definition of "stability" in a time series and was based on data from California.[1] My colleagues and I raised some objections to the challenges raised (Blumstein, Cohen, Moitra, and Nagin 1981), and we thought they were appropriate, but I have no desire here to reopen that discussion.

I have had many stimulating and much more fundamental debates with Messinger, and I was surprised to find him as a party to this rather technical one. But his involvement gives me an excuse to revisit this issue, which I believe to be important, not only for insights into processes of social control—an issue that is close to his heart—but also for possible policy implications.

The stability-of-punishment hypothesis was stimulated by some ideas of Durkheim and by examining the time series of incarceration rates in the United States from the 1920s through the early 1970s, which displayed an impressive stability over that period. The U.S. incarceration rate averaged

110 per 100,000, with a coefficient of variation over that fifty-year period of only 8 percent.[2] When the same pattern was repeated in some foreign countries over even longer periods, that gave rise to some attempts to figure out what processes could account for that seemingly very stable pattern.

Even though subsequent events have certainly made it clear that we are no longer in a stable-punishment regime, I continue to believe that the arguments advanced in that original paper and in a number of succeeding papers refining aspects of the theory were a reasonably valid assessment of the processes at work at the time. It is clear, however, that whatever stability prevailed in the fifty years leading to 1973, they certainly do not prevail today.[3] The U.S. incarceration rate at the end of 1993 reached a level of 351 per 100,000 in state and federal prisons (Gilliard and Beck 1994), with an additional 50 percent in local jails. This rate is more than three times the rate that had prevailed for the fifty years prior to 1973, and reflects an exponential growth rate averaging 6.5 percent per year since 1973.

In this paper, I would like to revisit that initial hypothesis, explore some of the earlier debate, and examine what happened to take us from the originally stable regime (stable in at least some reasonable definitions) to one that now seems to be out of control. I would then like to examine where our current policies might be taking us, and what possible restoring forces might yet appear to tame this exponential growth, at least to some degree.

THE STABILITY-OF-PUNISHMENT DEBATE

The Original Hypothesis

In examining a time series of incarceration rates in the United States, I was struck by how little variation they displayed. Figure 15.1 presents that information from 1925 to 1975. Looking at those data, it is striking how closely they adhered to the mean of 108.5 per 100,000 and how well the great majority of the points stayed within even *one* standard deviation of 11.0.[4] The most significant deviation (after the early years of the series, which started in 1925 with a rate of 79 per 100,000) was in the late 1930s, when the Great Depression gave rise to a maximum deviation of 137 per 100,000 in 1939. This was followed by a rapid decline during World War II, when the nation had much better uses for its young men of prison age, and the incarceration rate dipped to a local minimum of 100 (still well within one standard deviation of the mean rate) in 1945.

The only other deviation was in the late 1960s, when the move to community-based treatment and "prison reform" led to a dip to a rate of 94 in 1968. This low rate could also be partly artifactual because of the small

Stability of Punishment

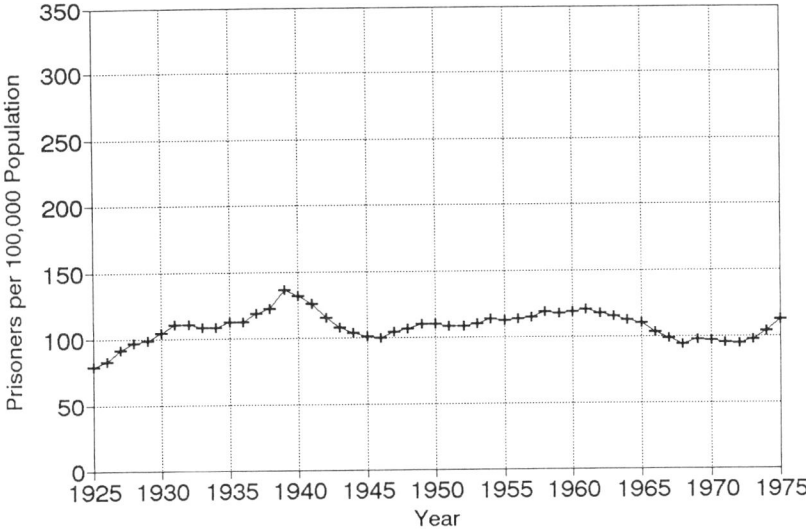

Figure 15.1. Incarceration rate by year 1925–1975.

cohort sizes in the prime imprisonment years at that time as a result of the low number of births in the later depression years and the wartime years.[5]

We were struck by the flatness of this curve, by its trendlessness, and by the presumed existence of "homeostatic" forces that kept this process in reasonable balance. The fact that a similar pattern was displayed in Norway over even a longer period (1880 to 1964) albeit at a lower rate (52.5 per 100,000 with a standard deviation of 8.2), and in other Scandinavian countries as well, strengthened the conviction that there must be some kind of stabilizing process at work, and led to a search for explanation and interpretation.

The hypothesis, in short, recognizes the possibility that crime rates would be climbing and falling depending on a wide variety of social conditions that were far less amenable to control than would be the case with prison populations. The proposed mechanism was one of shifting thresholds. As crime rates went up, the threshold of the seriousness of the offense or of the offender's prior criminal history (or other attributes that might enter into sentencing decisions) would be raised in order to avoid imposing an excessive burden on the prison system. This recognized a degree of common interest that was shared by judges and prosecutors (who were generally far more subservient to judges in those days). With indeterminate sentences (one year to life was not uncommon in states like California), parole boards had a broad range of discretion. They, too, could shift thresholds on their readiness to tolerate risk in the released offenders as necessary to accelerate departures when admissions were increasing in order to avoid overcrowding of the state's prisons.

The process could also work similarly when crime rates were decreasing. If crime rates were to decline appreciably, then behaviors that were tolerated but widely objected to would become candidates for passing new laws or more aggressively enforcing old laws (e.g., laws prohibiting drugs or prostitution).

This is a modification of the Durkheim ([1938] 1964) argument that *crime* (rather than punishment) is a natural—and even in some sense desirable—aspect of society, and that societies without crime will seek to redefine certain behaviors as crimes partly to reinforce the norms in that society. This is an argument that was developed in rich detail by Kai Erikson in *The Wayward Puritans* (1966).

With a variety of other collaborators, I pursued the issue to provide more elaborate structure of the dynamics of the process maintaining a homeostatic relationship (Blumstein, Cohen, and Nagin 1977). Some of that work explored the stability phenomenon within individual states and the similarity across neighboring states of the nature of their individual incarceration rate time series (Blumstein and Moitra 1979).

The Challenge by Berk, Messinger, et al.

The principal issues in the challenge by Berk, Messinger et al. (1981) and in a separate paper by David Rauma (1981), derive from an analysis of a long time series, more than twice as long as our fifty-year series for the United States as a whole, and hinges on an elaborate analysis of the autoregressive integrated moving average (ARIMA) time series model outlined by Box and Jenkins (1976), and a finding that the longer time series for California was not "stationary" in the terms of that model. Our response (Blumstein et al. 1981) was to argue that this technical definition of "stationary" was not the principal relevant criterion, but rather that our emphasis was on trendlessness and small variation around that trend. We argued that the time series we were studying both in many of the states as well as in the nation as a whole displayed those aspects of "stability." Of course, this is not the time to reopen that old debate. Rather, I wanted to use this as a departure point for examining what has happened since.

Figure 15.2 extends the graph of Figure 15.1 to 1993. It is difficult to pinpoint the precise year in which the dramatic growth of the right-hand portion of the graph began, but it does appear to be in the period 1973 to 1975, and so we can identify 1974 as an important turning point, but with significant acceleration beginning in 1981.

Even the simplest examination of that figure would challenge any pre-

Stability of Punishment 263

Figure 15.2 Incarceration rate by year 1925–1993.

sumption of stability after 1980. The period between 1974 and 1980 might be argued as within the reasonable range of the prior stable rate. But that would be reasonable only if the rate had turned down after 1980 instead of accelerating upward.

Knowing Sheldon L. Messinger's views on the political nature of punishment policy and his concern that it does more harm than it does good, I am certain that the trend over the last two decades must have distressed him considerably, and certainly far more than the questions of "stationarity" compared to "stability" in our original debate. He must be very concerned about the forces that have given rise to this dramatic growth in incarceration that had over one million people in state or federal prisons by the end of 1994, with another half-million in local jails.

SUBSEQUENT DEVELOPMENTS IN THE INCARCERATION RATE

It is clear that whatever forces maintained the seeming homeostatic process from the 1920s through the mid-1970s, had been fractured by 1975 and totally abandoned by 1980. Several factors have contributed to that shift.

Ironically, most of the initial attacks on the stable process appear to have come from the liberal Left, which generally is hostile to any increase in punishment. This opening was exploited by the conservative Right, which seems to have an insatiable demand for more punishment.

Some of the initial assault on the previous regime of control by parole boards was stimulated by a succession of findings through the 1960s that reported on various kinds of experimental and quasi-experimental evaluations of correctional treatment alternatives. Most of these found a null effect, or no difference between the innovation being tested and any other approach.[6] The accumulation of these null-effect results led to a clamor that "nothing works." The initial response by the Left to these findings argued that, since the correctional system could not claim to rehabilitate (then the reigning ideology of corrections), then one ought to intervene less in the lives of those convicted. Exemplars of this stance were Robison and Smith (1971), who made this reduced-intervention argument particularly vigorously.

Such an argument was clearly in conflict with the view of the Right, whose perspectives were certainly enthusiastically endorsed by the public more broadly. At that time, in the early 1970s, crime rates were soaring significantly from the low rates characteristic of the early 1960s to the values that prevailed in the mid-1970s. That growth was attributable to a mixture of the arrival of the baby boom cohorts (starting with the 1947 cohort, which reached age fifteen in 1962 and nineteen in 1966) into the peak crime ages of fifteen to nineteen. That demographic shift gave impetus to the "crime in the streets" theme of Barry Goldwater's 1964 presidential election campaign. That growth continued with the increasing cohort sizes until the largest cohorts (those born around 1960) began to recede from the high-crime ages after 1980.

Those demographic shifts were exacerbated by the disruptions and challenges to forces of authority that characterized the 1960s. The most salient challenges were associated with the civil rights struggles in the early 1960s and the protests against the Vietnam War in the late 1960s and early 1970s. The effects of the changing demographic composition (more people in the high-crime ages) were augmented also by the contextual effect of larger cohort sizes, which increased the age-specific crime rates within the high-crime ages. Both the compositional and the contextual effects contributed to higher aggregate crime rates.

With crime an increasing concern to the general public, and with the traditional crime control methods and prison populations maintained in a stable mode by the now discredited "corrections" functionaries, the policy issues were fully ripe for major reconsideration. There was little doubt that the arguments for punitiveness would prevail. An article entitled "Lock 'Em Up" by James Q. Wilson (1975) articulated very well the incapacitation argument: an offender in prison cannot be committing the crimes in the community that he might have committed if he were free.

The deterrence argument also has a natural appeal to legislatures and to the middle-class perception generally. With the growth of the public's concern, there followed an intense battle among political figures to show who is acting more "tough" on offenders, and a corresponding scramble for political opportunities to label their opponents "soft" on crime. Aside from its symbolic nature, this battle to be the toughest candidate seems to be based largely on a presumption of the deterrent effectiveness of toughness. The underlying presumption is that increasing the threat of criminal sanctions (usually articulated in terms of sentence severity) is a very powerful influence in inhibiting criminal activity.

While there is little doubt that deterrence works to some degree, there must be important differences in its effectiveness in conventional middle-class populations—who have so much to lose from the condemnation and relative deprivation associated with a prison sentence—compared to the lower-class populations that comprise the great majority of the offenders who engage in the crimes that lead to imprisonment. The political effectiveness of the toughness stance must derive from the projection of their own response to the deterrent threat of the bulk of the middle-class voters, and their difficulty in appreciating the diminished responsiveness of the principal targets of the threat. They recognize that the threat of imprisonment keeps *them* from committing crimes, and so it should work comparably with others who commit crimes. They then seem to take the position that, if current sanctions are not working, they should be increased in order to cross a response threshold. For offenders, that threshold would probably be somewhat higher, but not necessarily out of reach.

It does not seem to enter the public debate that the rational weighing of costs and benefits—a salient characteristic of middle-class behavior—is not necessarily characteristic of everyone's decision to engage in a criminal offense. Or that actions that could lead to gaining "respect"[7] would have great saliency to some people, enough to warrant risking their lives, let alone risking imprisonment. Or that the loss in personal well-being (or "utility" in terms of the cost-benefit calculation) associated with imprisonment is considerably greater for a person who is employed and lives with his family than it is for an unemployed person with no such stable attachments. Indeed, the opportunity for reasonable room and board in prison may not be much worse than life on the streets, especially if one has some protective affiliates in prison who will serve as a shield against the predators that make prison life so threatening to many.

The attempts to curry favor with the electorate also give rise to efforts to point to individual cases where an offender who committed a serious crime was let out on probation or was given a surprisingly small sentence.[8] Given the diversity of judges, their values, and the variety of variables that they take into account, it is not surprising that such cases can readily be found in any jurisdiction. Pointing to such errors of commission[9] usually leads to a further call for toughness in limiting the opportunity to release a prisoner. It also gives rise to a growing cry for "mandatory-minimum" legislation, which requires judges to sentence all offenders convicted of a particular offense specified by the statute to a specified minimum sentence, regardless of whatever mitigating circumstances might be present in the case.

Along with this came a general scapegoating of judges as being too "lenient," a cry that was often encouraged by prosecutors, many of whom harbor ambition for higher office.[10] These mandatory minimum sentences started as low as one year in the 1970s (or even thirty days for drunk driving convictions) and have escalated in the past decade to values as high as ten years or more, most notoriously for drug offenses. These are offenses for which incarceration is so largely an inappropriate and ineffective sanction because the offenders deterred by the threat of the sanction or incapacitated by its imposition are readily replaced from a willing labor market.

Another means by which the conservative perspective has come to hold greater sway in the development of punishment policy also derives from the concerns about "disparity," the fact that two offenders equally placed (the ideal case where the two crimes are identical and the offenders' prior records and other relevant attributes are identical) receive different punishment, perhaps because they came from different jurisdictions (urban areas tend to be more lenient than rural areas for the same offense) or because they face judges who use different criteria. The pressure for reducing disparity gave rise in some places (most notably California) to determinate sentencing laws, which tried to specify by statute a sentence to be associated with each of the major offense categories. Of course, given the variety of burglaries, and prior records, and other relevant offender characteristics, this introduced its own form of disparity by bringing cases that were unlike into the same box. It also provided an opportunity for the political pressure toward greater severity to ratchet up the prescribed sentence for any particular offense. This could happen, for example, when a particularly heinous version of the offense was reported in the morning newspaper or—with much greater impact—on the evening television news. There would then follow a rush by many legislators to get into the hopper their own bill calling for an increase in the prescribed sentence for that generic offense class.

This introduction of determinate sentences was also usually associated with elimination of the parole function, and the parole release decision in particular. Parole boards, charged with making the release decision within the boundaries of the indeterminate sentences prescribed by the judges, were branded fully as much as judges as evildoers. The public could always be reminded that they made a decision that in retrospect was wrong when a released prisoner recidivated by committing a serious felony.[11]

The next stage in the escalation of sanctions, and its assault on judicial leniency was the mandatory-minimum sentencing law. If it could be shown that an offender put on probation (for a first offense with mitigating circumstances, say) committed a serious crime while on probation, then that was taken as proof of judges' leniency, and so the legislature would require that all such offenders would have to go to prison for at least the prescribed minimum sentence. This would apply to all offenders convicted of the specified crime, regardless of the mitigating circumstances; only the prosecutor, with discretion over the charges filed, could make any such accommodation. With others, I have recently been examining the prior records of people sentenced under mandatory-minimum sentencing laws; they tend to have appreciably less serious prior records compared to others sent to prison (Blumstein, Cohen, Nagin, and Pogarsky 1995).

The large majority of people sentenced to prison under mandatory-minimum laws are those sentenced for drug selling offenses. These are demonstrably the offenses for which prison is least appropriate in terms of incapacitation (because someone else will replace that drug seller as long as the demand persists and as long as there is a willing queue of candidates for the position) as well as from the viewpoint of deterrence (since those driven out of the business by the threat of extremely high sanctions will also be replaced by others whose disutility for prison may be lower or whose view of other forms of gainful economic activity is less rich). If the intention is less utilitarian and more retributive, even then the hostility to the drug seller seems largely to have abated in the general public. The evil represented by the leading character in *The Man with the Golden Arm* no longer seems to represent the general public view of a drug seller, especially at the retail level on the street. Rather, the public has come to view the seller as one more individual willing to take the risks in order to pursue that line of economic activity, either for large economic gain or merely for sustenance.

The latest weapon in the armamentarium of those intent on greater use of incarceration is the "three strikes and you're out" laws that were passed by public referendum in Washington in 1993, subsequently in California, and included in the Federal Violent Crime Control and Law Enforcement Act of 1994. Variants of this principle (mandatory life imprisonment without parole for conviction of a third "strike"—a third conviction of one of a set of specified serious offenses), clearly based on the ambiguously applicable baseball metaphor, are being considered in a number of states.

It is not clear to what extent the three-strike laws are intended to achieve retribution or crime control. If the latter, it would be through deterrence and incapacitation. For either, this is a relatively inefficient means for achieving those effects. If the laws are focused on the most serious violent felonies, the twice-convicted offender should already be facing a long sentence, and it is not clear that much more deterrent threat will be added by extending this to life. In terms of incapacitation, the laws keep people in prison well after

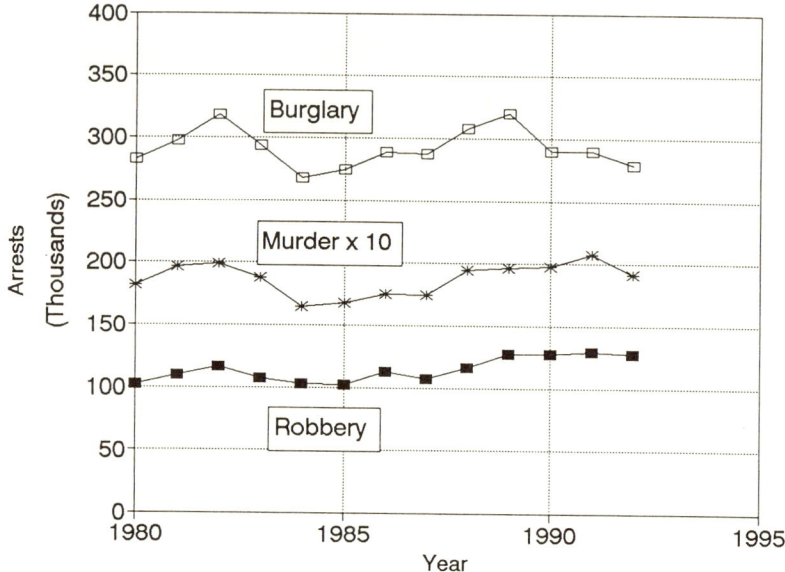

Figure 15.3 Arrests by crime type by year.

their active criminal careers have ended—very likely by age fifty, almost certainly by age sixty. If the choice arises about whom to release—a currently violent offender not under such a mandatory law or an aging one imprisoned under a three-strikes law—the system will have to release the currently serious offender. Once such laws are passed, even when restricted to the most serious offenses, they then provide a platform for expanding the scope of offenses that can be counted as strikes. Indeed, the federal law initially was confined to serious violent felonies, but ended up permitting drug convictions to be counted as one of the strikes. One can reasonably anticipate seeing other kinds of offenses added in the future as they capture the attention of the moment.

In 1994, over 60 percent of federal prisoners and about one-quarter of state prisoners were there on a drug charge. Many of them are first offenders serving time under a mandatory-minimum sentence. Approximately half of the growth in the prison population since 1985 is attributable to the growth in drug offenders, who comprised only about 6 percent of prison populations in 1979. Thus, the obsession with the drug war has been a major contributor to the growth in prison populations.

There has also been some growth in the general sanction level since the early 1970s, but the period since about 1980 has been very stable for all the crime types that are important for prison. This is reflected in Figure 15.3, which shows the number of arrests for murder, robbery, and burglary, the three most prevalent offenses in prison aside from drugs, and Figure 15.4, which presents the commitments per arrest for these three crime types. Figure 15.5 shows the same trend data for drugs, which has moved dramatically upward in both arrest rate and commitments per arrest.[12]

One other important source of growth in prison population is the level of recommitment of parolees—an issue that Messinger and I talked about pursuing together. Parole boards have received the same political message that they too ought to become tougher to keep up with the political tenor of the times and indeed have been more aggressive in performing urinalysis on parolees, in delaying release decisions, and in making recommitments for technical violations.

Another factor that was a significant contributor to the growth in prison populations through the 1980s was the same demographic shift that contributed to the growth of crimes in the 1960s and 1970s: the baby boomers. Since the peak age for crime occurs in the late teens, and the peak age for imprisonment is in the late twenties, the population bulge associated with that generation was expected to impact the prison population about a decade later than it impacted the crime rates.[13] The impact of that demographic shift on prison populations was relatively small, however, compared to the shift associated with the drug war, and in the same order of magnitude as the shifts in the punishment of the more common street crimes. In any event, those effects should have saturated by the early 1990s as the baby boomers

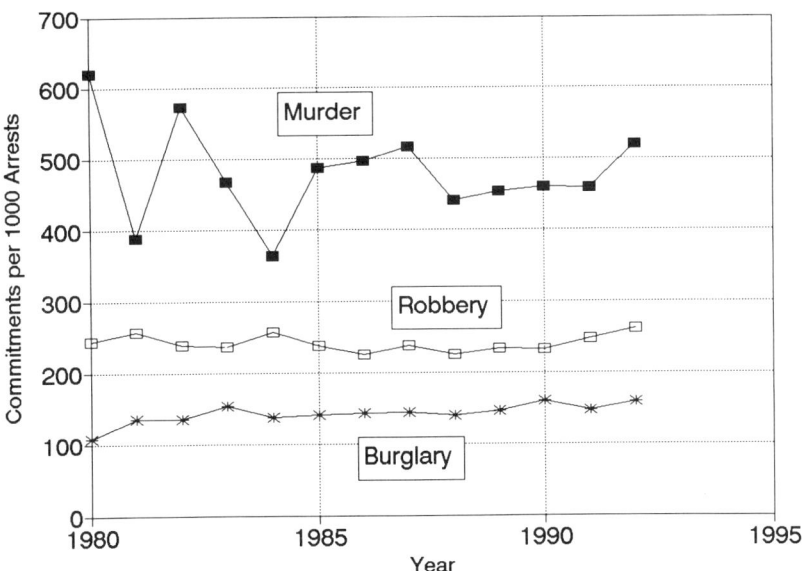

Figure 15.4 Prison commitments per 1000 arrests.

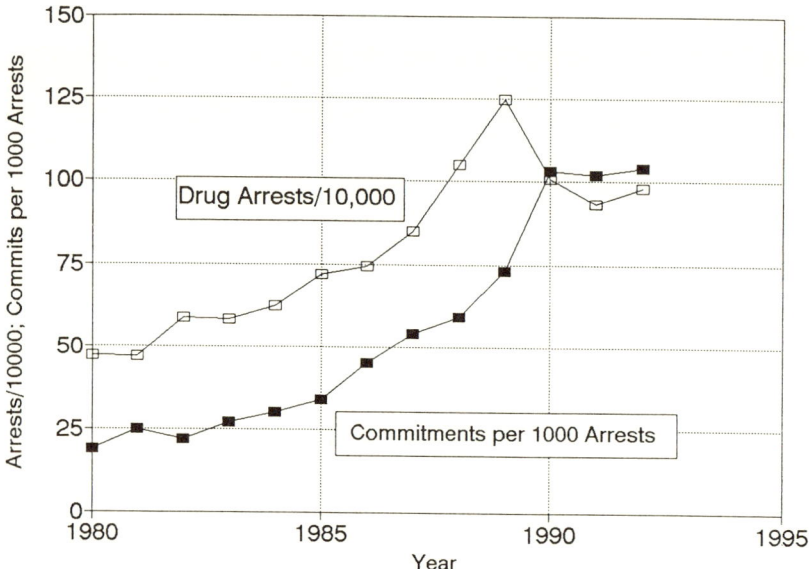

Figure 15.5 Drug arrests and commitments per arrest.

passed out of the high imprisonment ages, and should already have begun working the other way, waiting for the arrival of the echo boom following the demographic trough associated with the 1976 cohort, the smallest cohort in the U.S. population under age forty.

TOWARD THE FUTURE

This process of escalating incarceration must certainly pain an individual like Sheldon L. Messinger, with his deep concerns about social justice. He would certainly want to seek ways to reverse this trend toward open-ended growth in punitiveness. The number of options, however, are limited.

One approach that might be pursued is finding means of enhancing public education so that the naive reaction to the argument that more punishment will lead to less crime, regardless of the social dynamics of the particular crime (the substitution in drug markets, for example) or the offenders on whom the punishment is targeted (offenders with relatively low disutility for prison, for example). Somehow, the subtleties of those differences have not been able to get through the emotion and the rhetoric of sanction policy. It does appear that too much of the policy debate is from the perspectives of the ideological poles: arguing broadly for more incarceration at one extreme (with no concern for where it can be most effectively applied) or, at the other extreme, against incarceration as a broad generality rather than with a sharp focus on where it is least effective and most wasteful.

In economic policy, in contrast, there still remain sharp ideological differences between the Left and the Right, but there has emerged a level of theoretical agreement and strong empirical observations that have brought the poles much closer together than has been the case in criminal justice policy. In part, this is attributable to the much more backward state of empirically grounded theory in criminology, which could force resolution on at least some aspects of the debate. A major rise in the level of support for research in the whole area of crime and crime control through the National Institute of Justice (whose annual budget has been about twenty-two million dollars for a number of years, in marked contrast to the eleven billion dollars for the National Institutes of Health) could help move that process forward.[14]

In policy terms, one could argue for more widespread use of sentencing commissions as an instrument for generating at least some degree of coherence in sentencing structures. It represents an antidote to the passionate response to a particular crime, or the mood of the moment, and could sometimes serve as an inhibitor of the frequent legislative response of mandatory-minimum sentences. That approach is limited, however, because even sentencing commissions have to respond politically (in most cases, their guidelines must be approved by the legislature). Sentencing commissions that operate under capacity constraints make even more sense because the capacity constraint imposes a discipline that even the most conscientious sentencing commissions are sometimes forced to ignore. It is rare that a sentencing commission hears a demand for reduction of any sentences. Almost all the communications call for increased sentences, and so the capacity constraint provides a basis for asking for which offenses the sentence should be reduced in order to provide the capacity for the sentence to be increased.

One might also require the development of prison impact statements to be provided to the legislature before any change in sentencing policy is enacted. This is done as a natural matter of course for other programs that involve budgetary implications (and the Congressional Budget Office was established by the Congress for this purpose), but changes in sentencing policy and its costs and prison population impacts rarely come onto the same table for joint consideration. Changes in the legislative process here might force more responsible consideration of sentencing policy.

Probably the most likely prospect for change in consideration of sentencing will be through the emergence of a coalition between fiscal conservatives (who will one day become appalled at the costs of incarceration, and the inefficiency associated with much of that) and liberals (who want to reduce sentences and use the funds for other social programs that might promise to reduce crime in the longer run). There are some glimmerings of the emergence of those coalitions, and one might hope to see them coalesce over the next decade.

Maybe one day we might even revert to a new stable regime of incarceration rate, although I have my doubts that that will happen as long as sentencing policy remains a salient aspect of the political process. And that is likely to continue as long as crime rates are a troubling part of life in America— and they seem to be destined to continue for at least the next decade.

While this is not the way Sheldon Messinger would wish to see things, I am sure that he would be pleased to see any responsible process emerge that diminishes some of the irrationality that is driving current sanction policy. I hope that he will devote at least some of his time to these issues in the coming decades, when he does not have the obligations of classes and other traditional demands on his time.

NOTES

1. One could readily concede that California could be an exception to almost any social theory without seriously threatening the validity of the theory.

2. The coefficient of variation of the series is the ratio of the standard deviation of the observations to their mean.

3. Since our initial paper was written in 1973, this may be just one more example of perverse nature rebelling as social science tries to pin down its behavior.

4. The numbers used here are more recent ones, and are slightly different from those used in the original paper. They are based on Cahalan (1986:Table 3-7). Information for more recent years was obtained from annual BJS updates, the latest of which is Gilliard and Beck (1994).

5. The denominator of the incarceration rate is the total national population. A more appropriate denominator would be a population weighted by some measure of the age-specific incarceration rate, which tends to peak in the midtwenties. To some limited extent, this would boost the rate during the 1960s and reduce it during the 1980s when the peak of the baby boom generation moved into the peak imprisonment ages.

6. A paper by Robert Martinson (1974) attracted considerable attention to the null-effect findings. His paper was based on a more comprehensive survey in Lipton, Martinson, and Wilks (1975).

7. See Elijah Anderson's (1994) discussion of the importance of "respect" to the people he characterizes as "street people."

8. The case of Willie Horton, who gained such prominence in the Bush campaign of 1988, is probably the most famous such example.

9. The errors of omission—failure to release an offender who is a good risk and would not recidivate—are never seen.

10. Can one require an oath of further political celibacy from prosecutors?
11. Willie Horton was a notorious example of such a release that led to a heinous recidivist offense. That occurrence was eventually used to condemn the Massachusetts governor at the time, Michael Dukakis, who was running for president.
12. The data for Figures 15.3, 15.4, and 15.5 are drawn from U. S. Department of Justice, Bureau of Justice Statistics Report No. NCJ-147036, *Prisoners in 1993*: June 1993.
13. These impacts of the demographic shifts on crime and on prison populations are examined in some detail in Blumstein, Cohen, and Miller (1980).
14. Joan Petersilia and I have argued for an annual doubling of the NIJ budget to a level of $1 billion per year. See Blumstein and Petersilia (1994).

REFERENCES

Anderson, Elijah. 1994. "The Code of the Streets." *Atlantic Monthly* 273(May): 80–94.
Berk, Richard, David Rauma, Sheldon Messinger, and Thomas Cooley. 1981. "A Test of the Stability of Punishment Hypothesis: The Case of California, 1851–1970." *American Sociological Review* 46(December):805–29.
Blumstein, Alfred and Jacqueline Cohen. 1973. "A Theory of the Stability of Punishment." *Journal of Criminal Law and Criminology* 64(Summer):198–207.
Blumstein, Alfred, Jacqueline Cohen, and Harold Miller.1980. "Demographically Disaggregated Projections of Prison Populations." *Journal of Criminal Justice* 8(1):1–26.
Blumstein, Alfred, Jacqueline Cohen, Soumyo Moitra, and Daniel Nagin. 1981. "Testing the Stability of Punishment Hypothesis: A Reply." *Journal of Criminal Law and Criminology* 72(4):1799–1808.
Blumstein, Alfred, Jacqueline Cohen, and Daniel Nagin. 1977. "The Dynamics of a Homeostatic Punishment Process." *Journal of Criminal Law and Criminology* 67(3):317–34.
Blumstein, Alfred, Jacqueline Cohen, Daniel Nagin, and Greg Pogarsky. 1995. "Prior Records of Sentenced Offenders: Mandatory and Non-Mandatory Sentences, Drug and Non-Drug Offenses." Working paper, Carnegie Mellon University, Heinz School, Pittsburgh, PA.
Blumstein, Alfred, and Soumyo Moitra.1979. "An Analysis of the Time Series of the Imprisonment Rate in the States of the United States: A Further Test of the Stability of Punishment Hypothesis." *Journal of Criminal Law and Criminology* 70(3):376–90.
Blumstein, Alfred and Joan Petersilia. 1994. "Investing in Criminal Justice Research." Pp. 465–87 in *Crime*, edited by Joan Petersilia and James Q. Wilson. San Francisco: ICS Press.
Box, G. and G. Jenkins. 1976. *Time Series Analysis*. San Francisco: Holden-Day.
Cahalan, Margaret. 1986. *Historical Corrections Statistics in the United States, 1850–1984*. Report No. NCJ-102529, Bureau of Justice Statistics, Washington, DC.

Durkheim, E. Emil. [1938] 1964. *The Rules of Sociological Method*, translated by S. Solovay and J. J. Mueller. Chicago: University of Chicago Press.

Erikson, Kai. 1966. *The Wayward Puritans*. New York: Wiley.

Gilliard, Darrell K. and Allen J. Beck. 1994. "Prisoners in 1993." *BJS Bulletin* NCJ-147036(June).

Lipton, D., R. Martinson, and J. Wilks. 1975. *The Effectiveness of Correctional Treatment: A Survey of Treatment Evaluation Studies*. New York: Praeger.

Martinson, Robert. 1974. "What Works? Questions and Answers about Prison Reform." *Public Interest* 35(2):22–54.

Rauma, David. 1981. "Crime and Punishment Reconsidered: Some Comments on Blumstein's Stability of Punishment Hypothesis." *Journal of Criminal Law and Criminology* 72:1772.

Robison, James O. and Gerald Smith. 1971. "The Effectiveness of Correctional Programs." *Crime and Delinquency* 17:67–80.

Wilson, James Q. 1975. "Lock 'Em Up." *New York Times Magazine*, 9 March.

VI
EPILOGUE

Criminology occupies an uneasy place among the disciplines concerned with systems of punishment and social control. Sociology, as much as it may be drawn into public controversy and internal debates about "value-freedom," can always fall back on its academic identity in the social sciences. Law, which stands with medicine as the most established and prestigious of all professions, is secure enough to allow any theoretical scrutiny of its identity.

Criminology, however, is neither a "pure" academic discipline nor a profession that offers an applied body of knowledge to solve the crime problem. The history of criminological thought has left an insistent tension between the drive to understand and the drive to be relevant. The most radical resolution of this tension has been for applied interests to split themselves away into areas such as "criminal justice studies." This resolution, however, perpetuates rather than solves the tension. The turmoil in American society in the midsixties—the anti–Vietnam War protest, campus radicalism, social unrest, violence in the ghettoes—exacerbated this tension in yet another way. Should the connection between criminology and agencies of social control (police, courts, prisons) be used neither for "pure" knowledge nor to help these practitioners, but in support of a wider program of social justice, even at the expense of antagonizing the dominant political powers? What happens when criminologists become social critics?

We include Gilbert Geis's epilogue about the dramatic story of the Berkeley School of Criminology at the end of the sixties, not just because Messinger played a role, but because this remains a living illustration of the internal contradictions in criminology. Like the narrative of all such fractious episodes, this narrative will be disputed—as Geis is aware—by many of the participants. Twenty-five years later, the story is still able to provoke the raw emotions of loyalty and betrayal. The narrative is worth recounting, however, not to settle old scores, but to remind us how relevant these tensions remain. In a public discourse driven by fear of crime and an ethos of economic rationality, the space for independent academic work is becoming smaller. Schools and departments of criminology and other academic disciplines that are without either outside support or a strong intellectual tradition are just as vulnerable as the Berkeley School of Criminology was twenty-five years ago.

16
The Limits of Academic Tolerance: The Discontinuance of the School of Criminology at Berkeley

GILBERT GEIS

It is almost two decades now since the closing of the School of Criminology at the University of California, Berkeley. The details of the school's end, vivid and traumatic, remain deeply fixed in the minds of many who participated in the emotional events that sought, fruitlessly, to forestall the demise of the forty-two-year-old academic unit, the first of its kind in the country. Ask one of those at the center of the conflict to tell you what happened and you are likely to get some variation of a common response: "Do you have two or three weeks just to listen?"

Again and again, persons involved in the events that preceded the phasing out of the School of Criminology insisted—almost pled—that an adequate analysis must thoroughly appreciate the heady atmosphere, the fierce, intense mood of rebellion, the camaraderie, the sense of power, and the wild, often reckless extravagance of the period. No words, they say, can satisfactorily capture the tone, the feelings, the excitement, and the hopes of so many associated with the upheaval that contributed to the closing of the school. To overlook or undervalue the significance of this atmosphere, they emphasize, is to neglect the most crucial component of the story. The politicalization of the School of Criminology, all agree, created tremendous tensions within the faculty and among students. "You had to take a position," one participant remembers. "You had to sign a petition." "You had to march or not march." "You were either for or against the dissidents. It was very, very difficult to sit on the fence, to stand aside." If students chose to work with a member of one faculty group, I was told, they often felt compelled to make certain that no one from the other group was involved.

To several readers of an earlier draft of this paper—those involved in the Berkeley events at that time—the preceding few paragraphs, representing an effort to convey the spirit of the times, fell short. The *Rashomon* nature of recollections and the strength of feelings found expression in their written responses: "My initial reaction was not to comment and/or make any suggestions—to let dead dogs lie as they were," Gregg Barak, a School of Criminology student from 1967 to early 1974, wrote, "but over the next twenty-four hours things kept coming to mind." The depiction of the period at Berkeley, he noted, "did not capture the 'zeitgeist' of the School during these times. . . . [It] seems to be in black and white and needs coloring in, if you will" (personal communication, December 8, 1993). For Barak, what was memorable was that the School of Criminology was a beehive of scholarly and applied work, a place of resort for internationally known scholars, and, for students, a source of invaluable field training at prisons, at state hospitals, and with parole and probation departments. Barak remembers the school as vibrant and invigorating, and he believes that it "was destroyed in its infancy by people who were too narrow to tolerate true diversity and academic freedom" (ibid.).

Similarly, another correspondent thought that it would be helpful to try to put the Berkeley situation into a larger context:

> The Crim School was not unique. All over the country, leftists lost jobs and/or didn't get tenure. With the dissolution of the student movement after Vietnam, oppositional intellectuals no longer had an activist base of support. Whatever the details of the Crim School, there was a backlash all over the country against Ethnic and Women's Studies, against Marxists, etc. (Anthony M. Platt, personal communication, October 30, 1993).

For others, there was a failure in those paragraphs to capture satisfactorily the chaotic and unacceptable character of what went on at the time in the School of Criminology. "The piece does not adequately convey the way the endless efforts made by a core group to hold the place together were frustrated by militant faculty and students," one person noted (Thomas Blomberg, personal communication, January 12, 1994). Another thought that adequate attention had not been paid to the view that the rebels' "street tactics and arrant anti-intellectualism deprived [the school] of just claim to membership in this community. They were largely a propaganda agency. . . . The history of the bad odor of the Criminology School is something you don't make enough of" (Sanford H. Kadish, letter to the author, December 8, 1993).

Finally, one writer said:

> I do not believe you devoted enough effort to telling it like it was for those of us who were not of the persuasion to get class credit for assisting in demonstra-

tions, or who did not wish to politic for professors who had a political agenda. Classes were cancelled or curtailed for long periods (weeks) to satisfy personal desires. When many of us went to class, we expected the subject matter to be discussed in some way, not tirades against this or that, the value of drugs and pot, or the next demonstration that would be coming up. Enough instructors were involved to cast a very serious pall over the school. Your paper does not convey this. . . . [T]o me, the situation was very severe. (George Felkenes, letter to the author, December 16, 1993)

Two decades later, obviously, memories continue to cut deep, allegiances remain strong, and emotions intense. We will come back to these issues in the concluding section, after the story of the demise of the school has been told.

THE NATURE OF THE DEBATE

The issues concerned with the closing of the School of Criminology seem clear enough. Neither those pressing for its disestablishment nor those seeking to let it be, as I see it, lied in any significant manner; that is, they did not make allegations that were not accurate, though reasonable people might differ somewhat about this or that emphasis. The sins almost invariably were those of omission. The difficulty, therefore, did not overly concern whether what was being said was true (though much was not proven), but rather which set of truths was to prevail. Each side mulishly refused to grant legitimacy to the concerns of the other, but rather took refuge behind its own rhetoric, a rhetoric that sometimes was bombastic, sometimes bureaucratically bland. Each side, bullheadedly, insisted that its facts alone, without consideration of the other facts, were sufficient to support the conclusion that it advocated.

Because neither side at the time conceded the relevance or virtue of the other's position, the essential nature of the conflict never was clarified so that there could be agreement on the relevant issues and, on this basis, on a common agenda. That agenda, to my mind, should have been built around several basic propositions, including: (1) there were difficulties in faculty quantity and quality and, perhaps, curriculum integrity in the School of Criminology; (2) while the university administrators found obnoxious some of the public actions of the school's students and faculty, it was necessary in an academic environment to put up with these behaviors, however discomforting they might be. It was important, nonetheless, to reach an agreement regarding tolerable and intolerable classroom and public behavior, drawing upon academic freedom guidelines; (3) the School of Criminology had performed, at the moment did perform, and could continue to perform a valuable intellectual and public service, though it needed shoring up. The final item would deal with whatever measures needed to be taken to make certain that the school met the reasonable requirements of one of the country's leading universities.

Those who condemned the School of Criminology found it, among other things, "isolated" from the local law enforcement community, duplicating a curriculum that was readily available in the state university and community college systems, and staffed by a faculty that, in terms of the flagship campus of the University of California, was in some instances of unsatisfactory quality and was too small to warrant school standing. These are not facts that can readily be disputed today, nor could they have been at the time they were alleged as sufficient grounds for the disestablishment action that was taken.

Those hoping for the school's survival, for their part, emphasized its virtues and, most particularly, called attention to what they said were the true motives of those seeking to jettison the school. The school's defenders (who had the enrollment numbers to prove it) maintained that it was very popular with students, while its grading was pretty much in line with that of the rest of the university. They further argued that several of the faculty, admitted Marxists, provided heady intellectual classroom fare and were perfectly willing to entertain and discuss contrary viewpoints. They stressed that the issues of crime and criminal justice were of deep importance in contemporary American life and deserved the kind of specialized emphasis that the school alone could provide, particularly during this time of fervent civil protest, moral indignation, and the reassessment of the rights of blacks, students, and other historically belittled groups.

The school's advocates spelled out in some detail the case for its controversial focus in a document prepared shortly before it was officially eliminated:

> It is not an especially radical program, but it represents a substantial departure from the usual indoctrination which passes for higher education.
> The program is different in two important ways. First, the School of Criminology includes courses which raise questions about the nature of society and suggest that the elimination of crime requires an economic, political and cultural transformation of the established order. Second, crime is dealt with from a broad historical perspective which contrasts sharply with the kind of professional specialization characteristic of much of graduate and undergraduate education. From this viewpoint, crime cannot be understood (nor eliminated) without examining the political economy. "Theft," for example, cannot be analyzed without understanding how property and possessions are accumulated in a capitalistic economy. (Committee to Save the School of Criminology, undated a)

The school's most vocal adherents maintained that the demise of the unit was not a consequence of the premises stated by its opponents, but rather that these premises camouflaged what was an act of retaliation for highly publicized acts of political protest by students and by a core of faculty members. These people had made themselves highly visible and, from the viewpoint of the university administration, embarrassingly unpopular not only with it, but also with the local law enforcement establishment. They also had offended the conservative administration of the state under Ronald Reagan, who was represented by Edwin Meese III, then the governor's legal affairs secretary, on the school's advisory council.

What we had, then, was a jousting match, often tasteless, at least if dignity is the judgment criterion, that was characterized on one side by intense partisan feelings and beliefs and, on the other, by rather implacable insensitivity. There was no question where the ultimate power lay, though those who lost out seemed astonishingly unaware of this, or perhaps they were indifferent or sacrificial. Those who had the power used it effectively. They never descended to the barricades (where at least a vital part of the issue lay), but rather relentlessly set forth a persuasive critique whose only false note was that in some important measure it was besides the point.

The closing of the School of Criminology was a wrong decision, and it seems clear that behavior that the university deemed politically unsavory contributed to the end of the school. Nonetheless, the school was vulnerable on the grounds of academic unsuitability and weakness that were alleged as sufficient to support discontinuance. But these shortcomings obviously were remedial disabilities. In the name of academic freedom and tolerance, the university administration should have been especially resistant to its impatience with the legitimate expression of dissent as well as the shenanigans—both silly and, at times, meanly vicious—associated with the school.

THE SCHOOL OF CRIMINOLOGY (1916–1973)[1]

The School of Criminology traces its roots back to 1916, when August Vollmer, the city of Berkeley's chief of police, and Alexander M. Kidd, a law professor, began a summer program in criminology to train candidates for law enforcement positions. The course was offered annually through 1931, when funds became available to launch a criminology program during the regular session. A Bureau of Criminology was established in the Department of Political Science in 1939, and eleven years later a self-standing School of Criminology began to offer degrees. Strong leadership was provided by Orlando W. Wilson, who had been a patrolman in Berkeley, and subsequently chief of police in Fullerton, California, and Wichita. Wilson was appointed a professor of police administration at Berkeley in 1939, and served as dean of the School of Criminology from 1950 until he accepted the position in Chicago in February 1960 as superintendent of police.

In 1961, Joseph D. Lohman was appointed dean of the school. Lohman ran the unit like a patronage operation, with little faculty democracy. He sought, in line with a 1961 order from the administration, to alter its curriculum from an emphasis on law enforcement and technical offerings in forensics (though these continued to be taught) to a heavy focus on social science. Students were required to take their first two years of work in general education before pursuing a criminology major, though the school provided a number of extremely popular undergraduate courses. A master's degree (Masters of Criminology) and doctorate (Doctor of Criminology) were offered; Lohman was eminently successful in securing grant money to subsidize both faculty research and graduate education.

Lohman died at the age of fifty-eight in April 1968, a crisis year at Berkeley and throughout the country. His death occurred at the early edge of the period when the school's fate began to come under scrutiny, and his departure left an enormous leadership gap. A large, hugely exuberant man, Lohman from 1939 to 1959 had been on the fringes at the University of Chicago of the inner circle of sociologists—by common consent the most eminent faculty in the discipline in the nation. Unable or unwilling to complete his doctorate, he entered upon a political career that led to his election as sheriff of Cook County (1954–1958), then state treasurer (1959–1961), and, almost, candidate for governor of Illinois. Had Adlai Stevenson, his political ally, won the presidency, Lohman believed that he might well have been named secretary of Health, Education and Welfare. When Stevenson's political career reached a dead end, Lohman accepted the position at Berkeley as dean of the School of Criminology. He was recruited by Herbert Blumer, a preeminent sociologist who had moved to California from the University of Chicago. Blumer, an impressive man both physically (he had played professional football) and intellectually, held an adjunct appointment in criminology, and had considerable clout in the Berkeley campus power structure.

It is quite possible that Lohman, a highly experienced and very adroit political manipulator, his skills honed in one of the most demanding arenas in the country, backed by Blumer's prestige and connections, would have effectively resisted the demise of the School of Criminology. He might have dictated internal reforms or conciliated or browbeaten his opponents. On the other hand, once a favorite with the top administrators at Berkeley, Lohman had fallen from grace when university administrators came to regret following his advice to call in the police during the early student uprisings. Also, by common agreement of those who worked closely with him, Lohman had grown weary of the battles that raged within the school. Besides, the steps he had taken to enhance the academic respectability of the school had alienated much of his police support; Berkeley law enforcement in earlier times had regarded the school as something of a police clubhouse; this was no longer true.

The 1969–1970 School of Criminology catalog provides a sly hint of the nervous ambiance that prevailed in Berkeley: "[T]he campus retains the pleasant atmosphere of a park, with wooded glens, spacious plazas, and picturesque Strawberry Creek running westward through the length of the campus," it is noted, followed by the piquant observation, "One is impressed by the vitality of [the] campus. Political tables and noontime speeches that make news are, of course, part of the story" (University of California 1969:5).

During the 1969–1970 academic year, Bernard Diamond, a psychiatrist who also held appointments in the law and medical faculties, was acting dean of the School of Criminology, and Paul Takagi, a tenured associate professor, was assistant dean. Takagi had come to Berkeley from a position in the research division of the Department of Corrections in Sacramento. Diamond had replaced Leslie Wilkins, who was acting dean in 1968–1969. Wilkins, an exceptionally competent British scholar (who, like Lohman, did not have a doctorate), had left for a position in the School of Criminal Justice at the State University of New York, Albany. His departure, Wilkins tells colleagues, followed on the heels of a request that deans report to campus administrators the names of all faculty not meeting classes during the campus protests against the Vietnam War. Rather than do so, Wilkins accepted a long-standing offer to relocate in Albany (cf. Laub 1983:74). Diamond would be replaced for 1970–1971 as acting dean by Sheldon L. Messinger, who would have the *acting* removed from his title the following year. In 1972–1973, when the school was under the administrative microscope, there were six tenured faculty members, only four of whom had a full-time commitment: Messinger, Takagi, Jerome Skolnick, and M. Edwin O'Neill, the last an associate professor of criminalistics who would retire at the end of the school year. Diamond was with the school two-thirds time, while law professors Arthur Sherry (half-time) and Caleb Foote (quarter-time) were the other tenured faculty. Nontenured spots were held by Barry Krisberg, Anthony Platt, and Herman Schwendinger; there also were a number of temporary appointments and visiting professors, including Robert Fisher, Richard Korn, a psychoanalyst-criminologist, and Lloyd Street, a W. E. B. DuBois student who now teaches at Cornell University. Prominent overseas criminologists also came in considerable numbers to spend time at the school.

PLATT AND PEOPLE'S PARK (1971)

The activities and academic credibility of Platt and Schwendinger constituted a vital unstated issue that permeated—if only by their flagrant avoidance—reviews and other documents relating to the School of Criminology. Both were dedicated, outspoken Marxists. Platt, English-born, had read law at Oxford and received a 1966 Berkeley doctorate in criminology. He was, some believe, "the best student the School of Criminology ever had" (Jerome H. Skolnick, personal communication, October 27, 29, 1993).[2] After Berkeley, Platt held a postdoctorate at the University of Chicago, working under Norval Morris until the two had a falling out over the management of a research grant evaluating aid to blacks. Morris, Platt says, thought the project ought to be terminated and the findings written up; Platt thought otherwise (Anthony M. Platt, personal communication, October 30, 1993).

Platt (1991:226), who traces his political perspective to his family and to his identification with the student and antiwar movements, was a fiery left-wing favorite of the students in the School of Criminology. Schwendinger was politically and theoretically experienced in left-wing politics before he came to Berkeley. Takagi lined up with Platt and Schwendinger. The roots of Takagi's radicalism grew out of his experience of imprisonment as a Japanese-American during the second world war (Platt 1991:226). As a tenured associate professor, Takagi lay beyond the reach of reviewers.

Platt's campus notoriety peaked when he was arrested twice while participating in 1971 in the second anniversary celebration in Berkeley's People's Park, a site synonymous with the upheavals of the times (see, e.g., Peterson 1992:198). The park, 450 by 270 feet, a five-minute walk from the campus, had been regarded as "the scene of hippie concentration and rising crime" (Rapoport 1970:20) before the university bought the land; its aim was to build dormitories on it. At 4:45 in the morning of May 15, 1969, two hundred police officers raided the site, evicted fifty squatters, and circled the area with an eight-foot fence. By noon, students had gathered to "reclaim" the park. The Alameda sheriff's department, attempting to hold back the crowd, killed one person, blinded another, and wounded thirty persons with buckshot.

A week later, 482 demonstrators were arrested in another police sweep, though no charges were filed against them; later, a grand jury would indict a dozen deputies for violating the demonstrators' civil rights. On Memorial Day in 1969, thirty thousand people paraded at the park, demanding that it be turned over to the community (cf. Gitlin 1987:353–61). The university soon after installed facilities to make People's Park a multipurpose recreational facility, but it was boycotted by student and community groups, despite the pressing shortage of intramural athletic space. Persons using the parking facility that had been erected nearby found their license numbers printed in the underground paper, *The Berkeley Tribe* (Rapoport 1970).

Platt was arrested while he was part of the second anniversary protest crowd that included Tom Hayden, now a California legislator. He was charged with vandalism of a car (four of its tires had been slashed), but that allegation was dropped when it became clear that the car in question was Platt's own. A second charge, interfering with an officer, was dismissed by the court in the middle of a jury trial when the police refused to hand over relevant documents that apparently included the name of an officer who had beaten Platt. Afterwards, Platt's suit for false arrest and battery—filed in part to clear him in the eyes of university authorities—was settled out of court for $2,500 and, reports have it, several policeman were fired. Platt also received an official apology from the Berkeley campus police chief (Friedman 1974:3).

Before this episode, Platt had been recommended for tenure by all levels in Berkeley's personnel review process. That recommendation was in the process of being forwarded by Chancellor Roger Heyns[3] to the regents. After Platt's arrest, Heyns withdrew the tenure recommendation. Lore (which may be true) has it that Heyns did so when he was notified of Platt's arrest by a telephone call while he was on his way to the regents meeting. Critics, looking back, wonder why Platt could not have played it cool and behaved peaceably until the tenure recommendation received the routine approval for which it was destined. Platt bristles at this idea. "I didn't go to People's Park to get arrested," he says. "You must understand my frame of mind, my belief in the need for political integrity" (Anthony M. Platt, personal communication, October 30, 1993).

The following year, Albert H. Bowker, a mathematical psychologist recruited from City University of New York, succeeded Heyns. His appointment provided demonstrators with a new refrain for their chants: "Bow-wow Bowker is a running dog," they now barked. Bowker initiated a second review of the Platt case. The results again favored tenure though the vote now was divided. Bowker demurred. In a 1972 letter to the university committee that adjudicated tenure cases—appropriately written on May 1—Bowker noted of Platt's major scholarly work, *The Child Savers* (Platt 1969),[4] a revisionist history of the origins of the juvenile court, that he found "very little that differed from the orthodox Marxism of the 30's" and that he considered the study "sharply biased" (Goodman 1992:24). Two years later, in a tape-recorded interview with Platt, Bowker backed away, calling his statement "ill-considered" (Committee to Save the School of Criminology undated b).

Bowker also relied in his decision against tenure on evidence of Platt's active role in the effort to decentralize the Berkeley police force and to restrain it from using helicopters. Oddly, he indicated in a written memorandum on Platt's case that he would not criticize a professor of mathematics or physics and perhaps not even one of psychology for taking a leading role in such issues, but that he found it divisive for a professor of criminology to do so. Then there was this dialogue:

Platt: Then you think that a professor in the School of Criminology should support the local police?
Bowker: No, I think that's an irrelevant issue. It has, however, been harmful to the University.
Platt: If it's an irrelevant issue why did you include it in this memo to the [university tenure review] committee?
Bowker: I probably didn't use very good judgment in that memo. (Committee to Save the School of Criminology undated b:2)

These kinds of considerations in time became moot as the university began to employ the argument in the Platt case that it would be foolhardy to award tenure to a professor in a school on the verge of becoming defunct. Platt was supported, unsuccessfully, by the American Civil Liberties Union and by the University Council of the American Federation of Teachers, whose president called the action against him "the most shocking violation of academic freedom in many years" (Committee to Save the School of Criminology undated a:2). But the courts found no ground for interfering with an administrative decision that had followed stipulated procedural guidelines (Goodman 1992:24).[5]

The decision in the Platt tenure case, to my mind, remains indefensible. The university lost a competent scholar, who, working under more difficult conditions at California State University, Sacramento, would continue to make noteworthy contributions to the field, both in research and teaching (Platt would win awards for teaching several times) and by means of critiques of the administration of criminal justice in the United States.

Writing recently, Platt reflected on the protest movement and the shortcomings of the blueprint that fueled it:

> The theoretical weaknesses of radical criminology in this country were in part the result of an emphasis on short term activism and idealist expectations about the impact of social protest on the established political structures. They also reflected anti-intellectual tendencies within the overall New Left, the lack of a Marxist tradition in American universities, the discrediting of the theoretical legacy of the Old Left, and the institutional hostility of Cold War liberals to any kind of radical theory in the social sciences. (Platt 1991:227)

Consequently, he notes, "radical criminology in its earliest days tended toward ultraleftism, romanticism, and a messianic utopianism" (ibid.).

In a late 1993 discussion, Platt said that, if he had it to do over, he would seek to form better strategic alliances to try to guarantee the school's survival. But he also stresses the mood of the times:

> We thought we would be successful; we were optimistic in the way that utopians often are. Obviously, from the way things turned out, we were misguided; otherwise we wouldn't have done it. But it seemed like a time to

stand and I felt like part of a very large body. We would have played it more shrewdly. (Anthony M. Platt, personal communication, October 30, 1993)

In personal terms, Platt observes that he would prefer a lower course load than he has today as a faculty member in the California state college and university system and that he misses working with doctoral students. But he is emphatic in his overall assessment of the events in which he played so prominent a part: "I have no regrets," he says.

Tenure also was denied to Schwendinger. The magnetic pull of Schwendinger's intellect becomes evident when you talk to those who have taken his classes or worked with him. He was, one former student maintains, "one of the most brilliant men I've ever known" (June Kress, personal communication, October 30, 1993), while another insists that Schwendinger, without question, was the intellectual leader of the school, that "the other faculty members deferred to him; he was the intellectual heavyweight" (Gregg L. Barak, personal communication, November 4, 1993). Platt (Anthony M. Platt, personal communication, October 30, 1993) insists that Schwendinger was "the smartest person" in the school and notes that he could be "scathing intellectually."

Schwendinger had taken a high-risk strategy, basing his case for tenure almost exclusively on *The Sociologists of the Chair* (1974), coauthored with his wife, Julia. Most assistant professors churn out a series of articles, often based on their dissertation, rather than take the chance that a monograph will not get completed in time or will not be accepted for publication. *The Sociologists of the Chair* is a vast compendium of the history of sociological endeavor in the United States as seen from a Marxist perspective. Some of the reviews were scathing. "This book is an interesting propaganda piece for sectarian socialists but difficult to take seriously as a work of historical scholarship," the reviewer for the *American Journal of Sociology* (Baker 1975:1487) maintained, adding that "it compensates for its limited evidence with ample doses of rhetoric" (p. 1489). The reviewer also pinpointed a good deal of sloppiness, such as the identification of one American president as "Robert" McKinley (for a later critique of factual mistakes in the book see Deegan 1988:31). Favorable statements about the book, where offered in mainstream journals, were usually grudging and hedged: terms such as "overwritten," "turgid," and, most often, "dogmatic" were applied to the volume (*Book Review Digest* 1975:1125). One always has to wonder, though, whether a record relatively similar to Schwendinger's but with a doctrinaire liberal leaning would have passed muster.

Schwendinger spent most of the remainder of his career at the State University of New York campus at New Paltz, where he published two books, *Rape and Inequality* (1983) and *Adolescent Subcultures and Delinquency* (1985), both in collaboration with his wife. As with his other work, these found great favor with those who shared his ideological viewpoint;[6] others typically believed that the books selectively mined information that supported preconceptions.[7]

THE MORRIS IMBROGLIO (1971)

In 1971, Messinger and Norval Morris, a professor of law at the University of Chicago, were candidates for appointment as dean of the School of Criminology. Morris (personal communication, October 12, 1993) remembers that before his two-day visit to the Berkeley campus he was "seriously interested in finding out what they wanted. . . . I knew that there was a desperate condition at the School."

Morris, born in New Zealand, is a distinguished criminal law scholar, and a cheerfully friendly and highly articulate man. He has law degrees from the University of Melbourne and a doctorate in criminology from the London School of Economics. Later, he would serve as dean of the law school at Chicago for four years. Before coming to the United States, Morris had been director of the United Nations Institute for the Prevention of Crime and the Treatment of Offenders in Tokyo and, on the basis of this experience, he was sympathetic to the protest movement, with Berkeley as one of its major epicenters, that deplored continuing American involvement in Vietnam.

Morris's visit to Berkeley was a disaster, though memories about the precise details of what went on vary. Sanford Kadish, then dean of the law school, who sponsored Morris, recalls that the students' behavior toward Morris was "disreputable" and "embarrassing." It was a "descent into anti-intellectualism," marked by an "absence of civility." For Kadish the memory is like a "pain in my heart" (Sanford H. Kadish, personal communication, October 13, 1993). Another observer recalls that Morris was "Mau-mau-ed" (Jerome H. Skolnick, personal communication, October 27, 29, 1993). A statement to students by Morris that he had no serious interest in the position is remembered by another observer as a major impetus for their hostility (Julius Debro, personal communication, November 11, 1993). Platt (Anthony M. Platt, personal communication, October 30, 1993) says that, though there was "bad blood" between Morris and him, he kept his distance from the fray: no one to whom I talked disputed that claim. Platt believes that the basic issue was that students defined Morris as a centrist liberal, one of the enemy.

Morris (personal communication, October 12, 1993) says that he thought that the general mood of the students in the School of Criminology was "exaggerated and unreasoning," and he believes that for at least some of them the aim was "to bring down the school."[8] Nonetheless, he remembers a reasonably polite reception, except for a few notoriously rude students.

Morris found himself unsympathetic to their hyperbole: laconically, he observes today: "I did not believe that the cutting edge of social revolution was in the criminal justice field." Morris was attacked verbally during his colloquium when he discussed what he called "the crime-prone years," the period between fifteen and twenty-four years, when young men record their highest rate of street offenses. Students accused him of advocating a biological view of crime causation. Quotations from his book (with Gordon Hawkins) *The Honest Politician's Guide to Crime Control* (1970) were used against him.[9] In addition, students interpreted Morris's statement that he believed he could obtain research funding to help support them as a form of bribery, and they would have none of it.

Shortly after he returned to Chicago, Morris received a telegram signed by a group of students saying that they would not tolerate his appointment. Gregg Barak (personal communication, November 4, 1993), then a graduate student, believes that the telegram contained threats of violence against Morris were he to accept the position. Morris's memory is of a more benign communication. What he mentions is that the telegram was replete with errors, mis-citing the titles of his books and misquoting his opinions. By then, "it was quite clear that I did not want the job and that I wouldn't get it" (personal communication, October 12, 1993).

Then there is a pause as Morris reflects on the whole matter. "I think I could have saved the School," he says finally. "I'm not sure I could have, nor whether it was worth saving, but I have a vague sense that I had the skills to bridge the conflicting parties" (ibid.).

THE SINDLER REPORT (1973)

The Sindler committee, appointed by the Graduate Council, was an eight-person ad hoc group, chaired by Allan Sindler of the Public Policy program, and including such Berkeley stars as political scientist Nelson Polsby and sociologist Reinhard Bendix. Sindler, a political scientist with a Harvard education, had taken his position at Berkeley only the year before, after teaching at Cornell. His major book, *Huey Long's Louisiana State Politics, 1920–1952* (1956), undoubtedly provided him with the background to appreciate the seamier side of academic in-fighting.

The committee's charge included an item that asked it to consider "[t]he appropriateness of the subject and of the School of Criminology for a University campus, i.e., for Berkeley" (Sanford S. Elberg and Nicholas V. Riasanovsky, letter from the president, dean, and the chair, Graduate Council, to Allan P. Sindler et al., December 20, 1972). This charge indicates that the demise of the unit was already under serious consideration. Indeed, four months after the Sindler committee was organized, the chair of the Committee on Educational Policy requested that a member of his group be added to its ranks since "amongst the issues considered by the review committee was that of the appropriateness of Criminology as a subject (discipline) for the Berkeley campus" (Charles A. Dekker, letter to Allan P. Sindler, March 9, 1973).

At the end of the 1973 academic year, the Sindler committee submitted a seventy-seven-page report (plus another ten pages of single-spaced appendices) (Sindler et al. 1973). Unanimously approved by the committee members, the report virtually sealed the fate of the School of Criminology. It is prolix and often obtuse, and focuses myopically on the fact that the School of Criminology had become heavily overloaded on the academic side. In one of its few italicized statements, which appears in the early pages, it asks: "[I]s Criminology's exclusive academic commitment compatible with its mission and structure as a separate professional school?" (p. 7). Committee members searched diligently for information to adjudicate this issue, never questioning whether it truly was the matter of utmost importance. It found only evidence that led it to a negative answer, and it heralded such evidence, again and again, in a tone much like that of someone declaring triumphantly: Gotcha!

The committee relied upon internal memoranda from Dean Messinger to the school faculty telling it to get its curriculum act together. For instance, one such memorandum in March 1973 accused the school of failing to meet the challenge to formulate a clear-cut educational mission and, instead, acting "with determined vacillation" (p. 12). The committee used evidence that there had been an ever-increasing proliferation of social science courses in the school to toll its death knell. At one point, the report thundered about "the School's rejection of its professional mission" (p. 47), as if this were, as it would turn out to be, a capital offense.

The committee took passing note of the considerable irony that the school's tilt toward academic emphasis came in the wake of a recommendation in 1961 by the Academic Senate that it be discontinued because it was too vocational, too much like a police academy to deserve a niche at a prestige university. Survival, therefore, had come through a commitment to deeper intellectual fare in the curriculum.

The Sindler Committee handled more gingerly, almost delicately, the question of course content: it must be remembered that the student uproar was making powerful noises at Berkeley. It granted that on the basis of statistical measures of faculty-student ratios criminology's enrollment was the highest, or among the highest, of all campus units. But with barely concealed disdain, it noted that there was a heavy concentration on teaching about "sex, drugs, and race" (p. 25), and it faulted the school for not containing its enrolment growth as it earlier had been told to do. The report found safest refuge in the conclusion that the courses were all over the place, none built upon another, and that together they offered a disorganized "cafeteria" or "smorgasbord" selection. To epitomize its concerns, the committee picked on the introductory course:

> The ostensible logic or design of the major is more nominal than real, if one assumes that there are really supposed to be beginning, middle, and end courses. The introductory course, taught by a temporary faculty member, was a fairly conventional survey of the major concepts, types and issues in crime. In 1972, taught by a trio of regular faculty [Platt, Takagi, and Krisberg], it was a tremendously popular success with its emphasis on the "crimes of imperialism, racism and sexism." What it will be in 1973 probably depends on who wants to or who can be persuaded to teach the introductory course. The faculty's difficulty in implementing its commitment to a consistent foundation course is symptomatic of other similar problems in curriculum development. (p. 26)[10]

Putting aside the tone of this observation—its condescension and thinly concealed ridicule—what is lacking—as in the total report—is direct, honest attention to basic issues, rather than the kind of oblique distaste that reminds a reader of the reaction of a fastidious gentleman confronted with a sidewalk saturated with dog poop. The Sindler report often is marked by *hauteur*, the French word that "Americans use to describe an arrogant, studied politeness" (Green 1992:375). And, of course, the alleged deficiencies in the introductory course in criminology are duplicated in innumerable departments in any large university.

Again and again, the Sindler committee identified the failure to mount a curriculum servicing the professional community as the core problem of the School of Criminology, the essence of its "troubled history" (p. 59) during the past dozen years, The professional commitment was declared to have been "rejected." And since the "consequences of this . . . decision are so obviously critical for the question of the school's continuance, the committee cannot emphasize strongly enough that its interpretation [of this neglect of professionalism] is not idiosyncratic" (p. 9). Since the question posed virtually dictated the answer accorded, the committee conclusion is not surprising: "Since a professional school cannot be maintained in the absence of a professional commitment, the review committee must recommend, reluctantly but inescapably, that the School of Criminology be discontinued" (p. 14).

The critical reaction to the Sindler report by Caleb Foote is understated: "It sometimes reads more like a lawyer's brief for disestablishment than an objective evaluation of the School's difficulties, achievements (apparently there are none) and failures" (Committee to Save the School of Criminology undated a:2).

Foote's words were echoed in stronger language by Dean Messinger: "I cannot refrain from saying that the ad hoc review committee seems to me to have avoided almost all hard and significant educational and administrative issues in its desire to justify the demise of the School of Criminology" (Committee to Save the School of Criminology undated a:2).

POSTMORTEM LIVIDITY (1973–1976)

The School of Criminology did not fade away quietly, though the Sindler report virtually dictated its demise. Torrents of words were written into the record between the end of 1973 and July 15, 1976, when the guillotine finally dropped by formal approval of the regents.

For their part, the students launched a series of demonstrations in 1973, demanding tenure for both Platt and Schwendinger, the appointment of a new dean by a committee with 50 percent student membership, and support of ethnic studies and "student power" within the university (Friedman 1974:4).

The intensity of identification of a cadre of students with these demands can be gathered from the recollections of a graduate student who was at Berkeley from the fall of 1971 through the summer of 1976. She had been an undergraduate at New York University, where she studied with Richard Quinney, an early leader of the critical school of criminology, but it was not until coming to Berkeley that she joined the ranks of the radicals: "I am incredibly biased," she says as she begins her reminiscences. "I chose sides and I never wavered":

> I was profoundly influenced by my work at the School. Not just in academic pursuits but in my world view. The closing of the School was a terrible loss. The School politicized a generation of criminologists. I felt that I was committed to something greater than myself. I thought we could change anything, and I learned that you have to do political acts, you just can't sit on the sidelines and write about it. (June Kress, personal communication, October 30, 1993)

As did all the rebels to whom I talked, this former school student said that she harbors no regrets. Those were exhilarating times that brought her alive and taught her essential things that she has never forgotten. She grants though that today she would do things differently. "I've become a consensus builder. It comes with aging. If you plunked me back there now, I'd say, let's sit down and let's talk it over" (ibid.).

The Sindler report was followed in 1974 by a report from the Committee on Educational Policy (Dekker 1974), the group responsible for making the final faculty recommendation on the school's fate. The committee report contained three sections: a majority view, a minority position, and a separate statement by the three student members. The nine-person majority asked for additional study and fretted that criminology might no longer be taught at Berkeley, a matter that it regarded as a potential significant loss since "the study of criminal behavior and of systems of criminal justice manifestly incorporates and addresses issues of paramount social importance" (p. 1). It also argued that "Berkeley's distinctive contributions are to be made in the area of scholarship rather than professional training" (p. 1).

The two-person minority insisted that the university get on with the demolition and in passing fired a few pot shots at the school's quality, noting that "the sociological investigation of crime and society in existing courses falls far below expected and necessary scholarly norms of the University" (ibid., Minority Report p. 2). The minority report also offered the only truly head-on reference to the political basis of the conflict, though the context leaves it uncertain whether it objected to the Marxist emphasis in the school (which was not omnipresent) or to the dominance of sociological viewpoints in criminology, though perhaps the minority believed that they were one and the same thing: "We think that the standards of University scholarship are badly served if an instructional/research unit of the University is permitted to install an exclusive ideological orthodoxy and to exclude major, important, or contradictory approaches" (p. 3). Even this strong and impatient dissent closed with the statement that "we cannot minimize our view that the field merits serious and careful endowment" (p. 4).

The dissenting report by the student members of the Committee on Educational Policy argued forcefully that the reviews had established only that the school as it presently existed should not be continued. This conclusion, it was insisted, "still permits the option of a *strengthened* School," a strategy that the students thought eminently desirable (ibid., Student Report, p. 1). The students maintained that "no one has questioned our contention that the programs in the school are comparable (in strength and in weakness) to programs in the social sciences offered elsewhere on campus" (p. 2). They then added: "[B]ecause of the field's changing and multidisciplinary character it faces problems that older disciplines avoid, but that is no cause for the . . . harsh, unsupported, and we believe, untrue assessment. It may, in fact, indicate a need for special *support* for the unit" (p. 3).

Additional agitation on the school's behalf came from John Vasconcellos, a powerful member of the State Assembly, who visited the criminology program in mid-April 1974. Writing to Bowker, Vasconcellos said that he had been told by a faculty opponent of the school that it was "isolated." Vasconcellos conveyed his reply:

> Well, there is a high student demand for programs of the school and no evidence of student dissatisfaction with its programs, so I'd conclude it's not

isolated from the students. Its graduates are quickly and well placed in jobs in society, so I'd conclude it's not isolated from the work world. So what is it isolated from?

The response he had been given, Vasconcellos wrote, was "from the rest of us faculty" (John Vasconcellos, letter to Albert H. Bowker, May 9, 1974). To Vasconcellos this interchange epitomized the conflict. "I found no evidence of partisanship or external politics. I found no evidence of ill will." Rather it was a matter of philosophy and ideology: "the seeming unorthodoxy of the School of Criminology according to academic models of learning." Why, he asked, could not the University of California be "big enough" to tolerate some variation to its traditional situation? (ibid.).

Bowker replied almost immediately. Soothingly, he went through the restructuring plans that would allow the study of criminology to continue on the campus, but under different arrangements, arrangements that he believed "have the support of most of the faculty in Criminology and a good number of students," though he regretted "the resulting student activities" and, with an obvious sigh, concluded: "hopefully we'll get through it" (Albert H. Bowker, letter to John Vasconcellos, June 6, 1974).

Restructuring plans for criminology ran through much of the debate. Attempts to becalm critics of the closing of the school often offered assurances that the undergraduate teaching of criminology would find a prominent— indeed, an enhanced place—in other university settings. It is difficult in retrospect to judge whether these promises were scraps thrown to try to quiet opposition or whether they were sincerely meant. If the aim was to dismantle a politically unpopular unit and jettison some troublesome faculty, there would be no reason not to reconstruct criminology in another guise. Numerous arrangements were proposed, though, in the end, undergraduate instruction in criminology was abandoned.[11]

A jurisprudence program was expanded in the School of Law, which attended to only a very limited extent to issues of crime and even less to the relationship between social injustice and illegal behavior. Phillip Selznick, who headed the new program, was quoted as saying that he had been told by the chancellor that "he wanted to play down the criminal justice angle symbolically" (Committee Secret Tapes, undated:3). Critics of the administration believed that they understood what was meant by this:

> The reason for "playing down the criminal justice angle" is that these professors don't want to make it look as though the reason for eliminating the School was to remove the radicals within the School. Obviously, keeping a curriculum similar to that of the School would prove that this was the case. So, the committee is caught up in a double bind of having to design a program that would look like it was replacing Criminology while not making it so identical that people could see that the only difference was the *people* and not

the program content. ("Committee Secret Tapes Talk of Dumping Crim" undated:4)

By mid-1974, the issue of the school's fate seemed settled, but matters moved slowly. It was not until two years later, in May 1976, that the Committee on Educational Policy, with new members, unanimously recommended abolition of the School of Criminology. The committee's authority lay in its right to rule on any significant—above 10 percent—budget changes for a school or college. Chancellor Bowker announced that he would make his final decision on the school's fate shortly. A hastily formed Committee to Save the Crim School sought to mobilize support. On May 29, it occupied Haviland Hall, where the school was housed. At two o'clock the following morning the police entered and arrested 139 people.

Five days later, on June 4, Bowker announced the end of the School of Criminology, citing budgetary constraints and the "isolation" of its faculty from the remainder of the university as his reasons (Silverstein 1975).

DEAN MESSINGER'S AUTOPSY REPORT (1975)

On the occasion of Sheldon Messinger's retirement in 1992, it was written that he showed "calm and fortitude in an especially difficult time" and that during the awful times in the School of Criminology "he lost no friends and even picked up a few" (Skolnick 1992:308). Others may use lesser or stronger terms of praise, but I have encountered no dissent that throughout his tenure in the school, to fuse a number of panegyrics, Messinger was "a very likeable, engaging, empathetic human being, very tolerant." To be so regarded in such times is no mean achievement.

When he became dean in 1971, Messinger could claim considerable understanding of the power intricacies of the Berkeley campus. He had worked as vice chair in the Center for the Study of Law and Society at Berkeley from 1961 until then, doing both scholarly and administrative work. He did not, however, have the personal standing or the clout that would make the authorities wary of crossing him, as they might have been with Lohman or Morris.

In 1975, while he was a visiting fellow at the Institute of Criminology in Cambridge, Messinger discussed with its students and staff his understanding of what had gone on back home. His observations are contained in a six-page single-spaced memorandum (Messinger 1975) that begins with a discussion of the role of the Board of Regents and an outline of the administrative and faculty committee structure at Berkeley, particularly as these relate to the "saga of the School [of Criminology]." Then there is a roster of the school faculty, and the observation that it is "probably the smallest of the

15 or so professional schools and colleges," followed by a thorough discussion of the curriculum and student requirements. This is marked by the observation that there was no orderly progress of students from "beginning courses" to "end courses," in part because "we couldn't see that it made much difference" which courses students took and because "[i]nstructors in some cases refused to check to see that students had met the prerequisites for registration in the 'end course.'" Another problem was that many courses were "swamped" by students who were not criminology majors because "some instructors refused to limit the size of their classes."

These introductory observations in place, Messinger got to more controversial concerns, beginning with what he labeled "the Platt Case." Platt, Messinger observed, "was influential, and controversial, as a student, and has remained so as a faculty member." Messinger wrote that he would expand on this judgment if it was desired; otherwise, he satisfied himself with a "bare bones" sketch. That sketch noted that the entire faculty, himself included, had recommended Platt for tenure at the time that Platt was a visible and vocal supporter of an amendment to the Berkeley City Charter, which would have split the police department into several units, each to be governed by a community council. The measure, placed on the ballot, had been voted down by a large majority.

The chancellor, Messinger said, had changed his mind about recommending Platt for tenure when Platt was arrested for participating in a riot. Though the charges were dismissed, Heyns now supported his denial on the ground, he had told Messinger, that Platt was "immature." Messinger summarized his view of the "Platt case" in these terms:

> Platt is, without doubt, the most widely known member of the School's faculty—particularly by law enforcement personnel, for whom he is total anathema. He is very popular with some students, particularly some undergraduates. One theory has it that the Chancellor has decided to close the school to get rid of Platt. Besides the fact that closing the School may *not* get rid of Platt, I think this theory a bit exaggerated.

Messinger then indicated that, though Platt and Takagi viewed Schwendinger as "the fount of Berkeley's version of 'the new criminology'," Schwendinger had been turned down by the tenured faculty for advancement on two occasions. Some saw this as a "political decision," Messinger noted, adding, "My view differs." Messinger declared that in 1972 an internal school dispute over a proposal by the dissidents to admit only Third World students to the unit and to appoint a black female (who many faculty thought unqualified) had led "certain key faculty members [to] withdraw from serious participation in School affairs."

Messinger closed with a four-paragraph analysis of his view of the school's situation. The initial paragraph noted that in general the establish-

The Limits of Academic Tolerance

ment and survival of enterprises in a university setting involved looking into "going conceptions among the ruling classes of what it means to be a 'civilized' person." When such conceptions change, traditional academic units can find themselves in trouble, as had the language departments at Berkeley. "Often or usually," Messinger noted, "what these groups seek is some claim on privilege, and one of the ways to make such a claim is to develop a relatively esoteric body of 'knowledge' and hold that only those with such knowledge can practice (and be paid or claim fees for) whatever it is the group's members do or claim to do."

Berkeley's criminology school, Messinger then pointed out, had been at first closely connected to the aspirations of the police and later to those of corrections, especially probation. Under Lohman, and even more under his own leadership, this practical orientation had shifted to an academic emphasis; and "through the activities of some faculty, the school came to be defined as antagonistic to these [criminal justice] trades." Ultimately, "the program as a whole was, perhaps correctly, assessed as one a first-rate university could, after all, exist without." Financial problems and the proliferation of criminal justice programs in lesser state institutions contributed to that judgment. Finally, Messinger said:

> Let me put it all somewhat differently, and then stop. There is continuous pressure on the Chancellor to allocate positions, that is, to re-allocate them. Given the financial situation, he could only do so by taking them from one place and putting them in another. If I were he, I should have looked for units with no great amount of outside support that was politically influential, with no great number of tenure-rank faculty to shift to other units, with internal conflict, whose program in the eyes of traditionalists was not any great shakes anyway. Clearly Criminology (as well as some other units) fit that bill to a tee.

There is no arguing with the accuracy of Messinger's analysis of the vulnerability of the School of Criminology. Nor is there any escaping the conclusion that he had been sorely worn down by an unwillingness of those in the school to pull together to save it.

L'ENVOI

The moves that led to the demise of the School of Criminology cannot legitimately be described as a *putsch*. They did not involve cold-blooded duplicity and hardball tactics. Rather they lacked goodwill and grace. They were the result of a sad failure to truly value academic freedom. The Berkeley administrators were unable to overlook their distress with the School of Criminology, based on real and imagined considerations, and to help to move it toward the level of excellence that would have made the university proud. There was, in this regard, a notable lack of either imagination or prescience. Nobody foresaw the enormous surge that the study of criminology would enjoy in the academic world and the pressing need for well-trained teachers and researchers. The Sindler report claimed, probably accurately at the time, that "the field of criminology enjoys no high repute for its quality" and that "there appears to be no first-rate academic unit of criminology in the country" (Sindler et al. 1973:59). What it failed to foresee was the forthcoming decline in the appeal of academic sociology and the elevation of studies of crime and criminal justice. Had criminology been given the kind of support at Berkeley it needed, the university would have assumed a major role in a flourishing intellectual enterprise.

The record indicates that Berkeley administrators were willing to suffer through the agitation that came in the wake of their decision to jettison the school because they believed that they could weather that short-term uproar and then could enjoy the long-term relief from the embarrassment that the school was causing at the moment and presumably would continue to cause if left unmolested.

They failed to see, of course, the swing in political mood that would mark the next decade and to take heed of the common axiom that should underlie university forbearance that, after all, obstreperous students soon graduate or depart. The faculty sources of embarrassment—most notably Platt and Schwendinger—were silenced at Berkeley; but their opinions might better have been allowed to play out as they might in the marketplace of ideas.

IN MEMORIAM

How best can we wrap in theoretical garb the story of the disestablishment of the School of Criminology at Berkeley? One reader of an earlier version of this paper demanded that his name be removed from the list of those to whom I had talked. The paper, he wrote scornfully, transmitted the message that the powerful always win. This is the kind of cautionary nonsense, he added, that tenured professors convey to newcomers to keep them in their place.

Such a critique is tautological since the standard definition of power is that it is the attribute characterized by the ability of its possessors to get what they want. At Berkeley, the established powerful assuredly got their way, but to say that the established forces won is to focus upon only a single criteria of triumph. Much that happened at the school had an endless eddying effect, though far beyond any hope of empirical demonstration. There were casualties, but those years also left some participants with new

The Limits of Academic Tolerance

strengths, new resolutions, perhaps greater wisdom. There is compelling truth in Hemingway's much-quoted observation that you become strongest in those places where once you have been broken.

These were years of ferment, in which the School of Criminology reflected a broader cultural and intellectual context marked by emergence of the counterculture, the wider student movement, and antipositivism in the social sciences. In criminology, alternative ways of looking at offenders and the criminal justice system gained widespread support (Cohen 1988). Todd Gitlin's (1987) sophisticated retrospective analysis of the sixties offers further insights about the nature of many of the events associated with the disestablishment of the School of Criminology. Gitlin (1987:242) too, as I have done, frets over his inability to convey satisfactorily the temper of the times: "How can I convey the texture of this gone time so that you and I, reader, will be able to grasp, remember, believe that astonishing things actually happened, and made sense to many who made them happen and were overtaken by them?" He then adds: "It was as though they were living in color while the rest of America was living in black and white" (Gitlin 1987:28). "What evolved from the blur of strategy and identity was, in a sense, its own program," Gitlin notes (p. 286). "It did not merely want you to support a position; it wanted you to dive in, and the more total the immersion, the better. The link between feeling and action was a short fuse." Yet Gitlin also is remorselessly honest in his inventory of the failures and the aberrancies of the time, particularly the insularity, the unreality, the wildly inaccurate estimates of likely allies, the backlashes, and, perhaps most notably, the absence of a sensible blueprint of what it was that was desired and how it would come about. It was much easier to document the faults of the system, much more demanding to provide alternatives that were something more than slogans and cliches. In time too, Gitlin observes, the early idealism of the movement came apart because of "its commitment to an impossible revolution" and in the wake of this its "passionate hairsplitting, irresponsible leaders, desperado strategy, insupportable tactics" (Gitlin 1987:375–76).

Similarly, Stanley Cohen, looking back on his own writings during this unsettled period, notes that they seem "so brash, simplistic, and tendentious." But this, he adds, "is how we spoke and wrote." Cohen offers an exegetic lesson on how the emergent women's movement, with its focus on rape, trashed the radical movement's romantic portrait of criminals as politically oppressed, deserving of sympathy. He provides a bittersweet summary of those times as seen in these times:

> Critical scholarship has well exposed the problems of this original agenda, but the very effectiveness of the demystification job is a little embarrassing. One has to distance oneself from those original ideas and reforms: dismiss one's

enthusiastic support for them as matters of false consciousness or perhaps a product of overenthusiastic youthful exuberance. Life seems more complicated as you get older; about that early love you say, "Well, yes, I wasn't really in love at the time, I only thought I was." (Cohen 1988:220–21)

Nonetheless, Cohen warns against radical impossibilism, which asserts that all reforms are doomed. There is evidence enough that the upheavals of the sixties produced meaningful change. But how does it all add up? Gitlin's wry observation will do: "Those who want simple conclusions should forget politics and stick to arithmetic" (1987:249).

For me, one of the best summary statements regarding the final solution for the School of Criminology is found in the response by a university-wide administrator to a 1978 report written by an assistant vice president at a Big Ten university. The University of California commissioned the report because it wanted to review the adequacy of the disestablishment procedure and to locate guidelines for such decisions.

The consultant's analysis essentially recites and supports the findings of the Sindler Committee. Normally, it would be expected that the report would receive a polite acknowledgment and then be consigned to the oblivion of the archives. However, Sandra Smith, one of the three administrators to whom the report was sent, chose to respond in unbureaucratic fashion. Smith was a senior administrative analyst in the systemwide Office of the Academic Vice President. Earlier, she had been one of the three student members of the Committee on Educational Policy who had objected to the drive toward disestablishment of the School of Criminology. "The only major concern I have about your paper [she wrote] is that the intangibles (the spirit of the moment, the ideological disputes, the personalities involved) that aren't reported in documents or in interviews with politically careful administrators, are downplayed in favor of the analysis that appears in written, rational reports." She went on: "Instead of concentrating on the differences between 1961 [when it had been unsuccessfully recommended that the school be closed] and 1973, you may find it more revealing to ask why, given the whole array of possible solutions to the 1973 problem, the committee, the Graduate Council, the Graduate Dean, and the Chancellor chose to 'tough it out' through sit-ins and demonstrations, insisting on discontinuance" (Sandra Smith, letter to Edward Dougherty, September 18, 1978).

Smith offered her own interpretation: "My feeling is that the outcome was due less to 'leadership' (such a positive term!) than to 'stubborn conviction' backed up by the ability to rationalize it and the power to enforce it."

"There were no angels in this situation," she concluded. "As a case study of the limits of academic tolerance, it will continue to fascinate me for a long time."

ACKNOWLEDGMENTS

I want to express my appreciation to Harold Becker, Thomas Gitchoff, Ann Goolsby, Dale Sechrest, David Shichor, and to the university archivist, for supplying material on the School of Criminology at Berkeley. I also want to thank those persons cited in the references who kindly discussed with me various aspects of the school's story. I am grateful to all of these persons for reviews of an earlier draft of the manuscript, which was also critiqued by Frank Cullen, Joseph DiMento, Colin Goff, Ted Huston, Paul Jesilow, Robert Meier, and Richard Moran. The judgments and interpretations made in the text are, of course, wholly my own responsibility.

NOTES

1. A comprehensive history of the School of Criminology was set out by Frank Morn in a paper at the 1985 meeting of the American Society of Criminology. Most of this material is incorporated in different parts of his book, *Academic Politics and the History of Criminal Justice Education* (1994).
2. The other candidate often mentioned for this distinction is Michael Hindelang.
3. Heyns, a clinical psychologist, had intimate knowledge of the world of criminology and corrections, since his father, Garrett Heyns, had served as prison warden at Ionia in Michigan, as head of the Michigan Department of Corrections for seven years, and as director of the Washington State Department of Corrections for a decade after that.
4. The book subsequently would be translated into Italian, Spanish, and Japanese.
5. The landmark statement on academic freedom, issued in 1915 by the Committee on Academic Freedom and Tenure of the American Association of University Professors, endorses professors "lending their active support to organized movements which they believe to be in the public interest," though it adds that a professor has "a peculiar obligation to avoid hasty or unverified or exaggerated statements, and to refrain from intemperate or sensational modes of expression" (Metzger, 1956:411; see also MacIver, 1955).
6. Commenting on this point, Barak observes: "[C]an't you say that about most works that are not conventional or mainstream? People have strong reactions—pro and con—to the kind of work done by people working in the margins or interdisciplines as it were, as opposed to those working in the safer or traditional domains of a field" (Gregg Barak, personal communication, December 8, 1994).
7. The Schwendingers, responding to an earlier manuscript version of this article, inform me that they plan to publish what they believe will be a more objective review of the issues considered in the present piece. They request that they be contacted at the Sociology Department, State University of New York, New Paltz, NY 12561, for information on where their article can be found.

8. This claim is echoed by Skolnick: "The students couldn't take it over, so they wouldn't let it function," he observes (personal communication, October 27, 29, 1993).

9. Paradoxically, snippets from the same book brought Morris to grief at the hands of conservatives when he appeared before the Senate Judiciary Committee in 1978 as a candidate, ultimately unsuccessful, to head the Law Enforcement Assistance Administration. A dispatch from the *New York Times News Service* and the *Associated Press* (September 29, 1978) noted: "Morris was questioned repeatedly about books in which he has written that he favors decriminalization of some drugs and sexual offenses and believes police should spend more of their time fighting violent crime."

10. Another take on the School's ethos has been offered by Sanford Kadish (1975), who then was dean of the law school at Berkeley: "[I doubt] that an academic criminology with so much passion and so little discernment is likely to make much of its new enlightenment by way of scholarly contributions, however much its practitioners may contribute to political action and rhetoric" (p. 842).

Kadish, writing in 1975, lamented the "stridency and vacuity of the current debate" at Berkeley in the School of Criminology (p. 844), but referred to Sykes (1974) for a sophisticated statement contrary to his own. At about the same time, Platt (1974) was writing that radical criminology had to resist attempts such as Sykes's to co-opt their realm. "Our liberal critics," Platt wrote, "have not only become instant experts on a correct class analysis but they are also trying to divide us against each other" (p. 8). For the position of the radical criminology students at Berkeley see Schauffler (1974) and Schauffler and Hanningan (1974).

11. Today, Legal Studies 170, Crime and Criminal Justice, is one of the 39 upper division offerings in the Legal Studies program. Virtually all courses in Legal Studies, however, deal with subjects such as legal theory, lawmaking, legal and moral responsibility, and law and economics.

REFERENCES

Baker, Paul J. 1975. Book review. *American Journal of Sociology* 80:1487–89.
Book Review Digest. 1975. Bronx, NY: H. W. Wilson.
Cohen, Stanley. 1988. *Against Criminology*. New Brunswick, NJ: Transaction.
Committee to Save the School of Criminology. No date a. "Defend the Crim School." Flyer, Author, Berkeley.
Committee to Save the School of Criminology. No date b. "Quotations from Chairman Bowker." *Defend the Crim School 2*.
"Committee Secret Tapes Talk of Dumping Crim." No date. *People,s [sic] Crim*. 1:1,3,4.
Deegan, Mary Jo. 1988. *Jane Addams and the Men of the Chicago School, 1892–1918*. New Brunswick, NJ: Transaction.
Dekker, Charles A. 1974. "Recommendations Regarding the Future of Instruction and Research in Criminology on the Berkeley Campus." Committee on Educational Policy, March 1.

Friedman, Joel. 1974. "Criminology's Ball and Chain: Which Way to Go?" *Daily Californian* (Oct. 23):3–4.
Gitlin, Todd. 1987. *The Sixties: Years of Hope, Days of Rage.* New York: Bantam.
Goodman, Paul. 1992. "Academic Prejudice: The Unfair Silence in Tenure Decisions." *Sacramento Bee* (Feb. 1):24.
Green, Julian. 1992. *The Distant Lands*, translated by Barbara Beaumont. New York: Marion Boyars.
Kadish, Sanford H. 1975. Book review. *Harvard Law Review* 88:840–44.
Laub, John H. 1983. *Criminology in the Making: An Oral History.* Boston: Northeastern University Press.
MacIver, Robert M. 1955. *Academic Freedom in Our Time.* New York: Columbia University Press.
Messinger, Sheldon. 1975. Memorandum to Students and Staff of the Institute of Criminology. Cambridge University, January 10.
Metzger, Walter P. 1956. "The Age of the University." Pp. 275–506 in *The Development of Academic Freedom in the United States*, edited by Richard Hofstadter and Walter P. Metzger. New York: Columbia University Press.
Morn, Frank. 1985. "The Rise and Fall of the School of Criminology at the University of California—Berkeley." Paper presented at the American Society of Criminology annual meeting, San Diego.
———. 1994. *Academic Politics and the History of Criminal Justice Education.* Westport, CT: Greenwood.
Morris, Norval and Gordon, Hawkins. 1970. *The Honest Politician's Guide to Crime Control.* Chicago: University of Chicago Press.
Peterson, Brenda. 1992. *Duck and Cover.* New York: HarperCollins.
Platt, Anthony M. 1969. *The Child Savers: The Invention of Delinquency.* Chicago: University of Chicago Press.
———. 1974. "Prospects for a Radical Criminology in the United States." *Crime and Social Justice* 1(Spring–Summer):2–10.
———. 1991. "If We Know, Then We Must Fight: The Origins of Radical Criminology in the United States." in *Radical Sociologists and the Movement: Experiences, Lessons, and Legacies*, edited by Martin Oppenheimer, Martin J. Murray, and Rhonda F. Levine. Philadelphia: Temple University Press.
Rapoport, Roger. 1970. "No One Plays in No Man's Land." *Sports Illustrated* 32(June 15):20–21.
Schauffler, Richard. 1974. "Criminology at Berkeley: Resisting Academic Repression." *Crime and Social Justice* 1(Spring– Summer):58–61.
Schauffler, Richard and Michael, Hannigan. 1974. "Criminology at Berkeley: Resisting Academic Repression. Part II." *Crime and Social Justice* 2(Fall–Winter): 42–47.
Schwendinger, Herman, and Julia Schwendinger. 1974. *The Sociologists of the Chair: A Radical Analysis of the Formative Years of American Sociology (1883–1922).* New York; Basic Books.
———. 1983. *Rape and Inequality.* Beverly Hills: Sage.
———. 1985. *Adolescent Subculture and Delinquency.* New York: Praeger.
Silverstein, Stuart. 1975. "Anatomy of a Failure: The Attempt to Save Berkeley's Crime School." *UCLA Daily Sun* (March 31):31,34.

Sindler, Allan P. 1956. *Huey Long's State Politics, 1920–1952*. Baltimore: Johns Hopkins University Press.
Sindler, Allan P., et al. 1973. Report on the School of Criminology, University of California, Berkeley. Submitted by the Ad Hoc Review Committee of the Graduate Council and of the Senate Committee on Educational Policy (June 15).
Skolnick, Jerome H. 1992. "The Retirement of Sheldon L. Messinger." *California Law Review* 80:307–9.
Sykes, Gresham M. 1974. "The Rise of Critical Criminology." *Journal of Criminal Law and Criminology* 65:206–213.
University of California, Berkeley, 1969–1970. 1969. School of Criminology 63 (August 20):1–32.

Biographical Sketches of the Contributors

Richard Berk is Professor in the Department of Sociology and the Interdivisional Program in Statistics at the University of California at Los Angeles. He also serves as the Director of the Center for the Study of the Environment and Society, and previously served on the Board of Directors of the Social Science Research Council. He has been a visiting scholar at the GAO, has served as chair of the Research Advisory Committee for the U.S. Sentencing Commission, and in 1993 was given the Paul F. Lazarsfeld Award by the American Sociological Association for contributions to research methods. He has published on a wide variety of criminal justice topics, including domestic violence, hate crimes, sentencing practices, prison crowding, and the death penalty. Among his recent methodological interests are causal inference with non-experimental data and statistical inference when random sampling does not apply.

Egon Bittner received his Ph.D. in Sociology from UCLA in 1961. After brief periods of teaching and research at the University of California campuses in Riverside and at the Medical School in San Francisco, he moved to Brandeis University, where he was the Harry Coplan Professor in the Social Sciences until his retirement in 1991. Most of his writings about police are contained in a volume entitled *Aspects of Police Work* (1990).

Thomas G. Blomberg received his Bachelors, Masters and Doctorate from the University of California at Berkeley, and is currently Professor of Criminology at Florida State University. His major research interest has been concerned with the meaning and consequences of penal reform. He has published numerous articles, chapters and books including *Courts and Diversion* (1979), *Juvenile Court and Community Corrections* (1984), and *American Corrections: Past, Present and Future* (forthcoming).

Alfred Blumstein is J. Erik Jonsson University Professor at the H. John Heinz III School of Public Policy and Management of Carnegie Mellon University. His Cornell University degrees are Bachelor of Engineering Physics and Ph.D. in Operations Research. He has had extensive experience in both research and policy with the criminal justice system. He is a Fellow of the American Society of Criminology, was the 1987 recipient of the Society's Sutherland Award for contributions to research, and was the president of the Society in 1991–92. His research and publications over

305

the past twenty years have covered many aspects of criminal justice phenomena and policy, including crime measurement, criminal careers, sentencing, deterrence and incapacitation, prison populations, demographic trends, juvenile violence, and drug-enforcement policy.

Pat Carlen is Professor, and Head of Department, of Criminology at Keele University, England. She has published eleven books on crime and criminal justice, including *Magistrates' Justice* (1976), *Women's Imprisonment* (1983), and *Women, Crime and Poverty* (1988). She was Visiting Fellow in the Department of Legal Studies at La Trobe University, Melbourne, in 1981, and Exxon Fellow at the Institute for the Study of Women and Gender at Stanford University in 1987. In 1993, she delivered the Fourth Bonger Lecture in Amsterdam. She is currently writing a book about homelessness.

Stanley Cohen is Professor of Criminology at the Hebrew University, Jerusalem, Israel and has also taught in Britain and the United States. He is published widely in the fields of criminological theory, deliquency, prisons, social control, violence and human rights. His books include *Folk Devils and Moral Panics* (1972); *Psychological Survival: the Experience of Long Term Imprisonment* (1973); *Escape Attempts* (1976); *Social Control and the State* (1983); *Visions of Social Control* (1985) and *Against Criminology* (1988). He is currently working on the subject of human rights violations.

Malcolm Feeley is a Professor of Law in the Jurisprudence and Social Policy Program at the University of California at Berkeley. Two of his books, *The Process is The Punishment* (1974) and *Court Reform on Trail* (1983) received awards from the American Bar Association.

David Freedman received his B.Sc. from McGill and his Ph.D. from Princeton. He is Professor of Statistics at the University of California at Berkeley, and has been chairman of the department. He has published several books and many papers in probability theory and statistics. His current research interests are in the foundations of statistics and policy analysis. He has worked as a consultant to the World Health Organization, the Bank of Canada, and the U.S. Department of Justice.

David Garland is Professor of Penology in the Faculty of Law, University of Edinburgh. He has taught at New York University and at the University of California at Berkeley, and has held a Davis Fellowship at Princeton University. He is author of *Punishment and Welfare* (1985), *Punishment and Modern Society* (1990), and, with Antony Duff, *A Reader on Punishment* (1994). He writes on social theory, the history of criminological thought, and on the sociology of punishment.

Gilbert Geis is Professor Emeritus, Department of Criminology, Law and Society, University of California, Irvine. He is former president of the American Society of Criminology and recipient of its Edwin H. Sutherland Award for research. Other research awards include: Donald R. Cressey Award (Association of Certified Fraud Examiners); Stephen Schafer Award (National Organization for Victim Assistance);

Paul Tappan Award (Western Society of Criminology); and the Richard A. McGee Award (American Justice Institute).

Andrew von Hirsch is Professor at the School of Criminal Justice, Rutgers University. He is also Senior Research Fellow at the Institute of Criminology and Fellow of Fitzwilliam College, Cambridge University. He has published a number of books including *Doing Justice* (1976) and *Censure and Sanctions* (1993).

James B. Jacobs is Professor of Law and Director, Center for Research in Crime and Justice, New York University School of Law. He earned the B.A. at Johns Hopkins University and the J.D. and Ph.D. (sociology) at the University of Chicago. He has written extensively about prisons and is the author of *Stateville: The Penitentiary in Mass Society* (1977), *Guard Unions and the Future of the Prisons* (1978), and *New Perspectives on Prisons and Imprisonment* (1983). His most recent book is *Breaking the Mob: U.S. v. Cosa Nostra* (1994).

Gary T. Marx is Professor Emeritus at the Massachusetts Institute of Technology, Professor and Chair of the Sociology Department at the University of Colorado at Boulder, and Director of the Center for the Social Study of Information Technology. He received his Ph.D. from the University of California at Berkeley. He is the author of numerous books, including *Undercover: Police Surveillance in America* (1988). *Undercover* received the Outstanding Book Award from the Academy of Criminal Justice Sciences and he was named the American Sociological Association's Jensen Lecturer for 1989–1990. He received the American Sociological Association's Distinguished Scholar Award From its section on Crime, Law and Deviance, and the Silver Gavel Award from the American Bar Association. Major work in progress concerns new forms of surveillance and social control across borders.

David Matza is Professor Emeritus of Sociology in the Department of Sociology at the University of California at Berkeley. He received his Ph.D. from Princeton. He has been a Research Associate at the Center for the Study of Law and Society and the Institute for the Study of Social Change at the University of California at Berkeley. He received a Guggenheim Fellowship and was the first winner of the C. Wright Mills Award from the Society for the Study of Social Problems. His books include *Delinquency and Drift* (1964) and *Becoming Deviant* (1969).

Patricia Morgan is Associate Professor of Public Health at the University of California at Berkeley. She received her Ph.D. at the University of California, Santa Barbara in 1978. She has published extensively in the areas of drug and alcohol, legal policy, deviance and social problems, and directed major cross-cultural and community-based research on illicit drug use. She has received several fellowship awards, including a Fulbright, to conduct international comparative research on policy issues related to both alcohol and illicit drugs.

David J. Rothman is Bernard Schoenberg Professor of Social Medicine and Director of the Center for the Study of Society and Medicine at the Columbia College of Physicians and Surgeons, and Professor of History at Columbia University. Trained in social history at Harvard University, he has explored American practices toward the deviant and dependent. His books include *The Discovery of the Asylum* (1971), co-winner of the Albert J. Beveridge Prize, *Conscience and Convenience* (1978), and with Sheila M. Rothman, *The Willowbrook Wars* (1984). His more recent research and publications have addressed issues in the history of human experimentation, the history of drug regulation and clinical trials with particular focus on AIDS, and the barriers to national health insurance. In 1991, he published *Strangers at the Bedside: A History of How Law and Bioethics Transformed Medical Decision-Making*.

Philip Selznick is Professor Emeritus of Law and Sociology in the School of Law (Boalt Hall) and the Department of Sociology, University of California at Berkeley. He was founding chair of the University of California's Center for the Study of Law and Society, and of the Jurisprudence and Social Policy Program in the School of Law. His books include *TVA and the Grass Roots* (1949), *The Organizational Weapon* (1952), *Leadership in Administration* (1957), *Law, Society, and Industrial Justice* (1969), *Law and Society in Transition* (with P. Nonet) (1978), and, most recently, *The Moral Commonwealth: Social Theory and the Promise of Community* (1992).

Jonathan Simon is Associate Professor of Law at the University of Miami. His book, *Poor Discipline: Parole and the Social Control of the Underclass, 1890–1990* (1993), was the co-winner of the 1994 Distinguished Book Award given by the Sociology of Law Section of the American Sociological Association. He is currently studying the emergence of risk as a pervasive framework of evaluation in contemporary society.

Jerome H. Skolnick is Claire Clements Dean's Professor of Law, Jurisprudence and Social Policy, Emeritus, at the University of California at Berkeley. For ten years he was Director of the University of California's Center for the Study of Law and Society. He has been reappointed as a Professor of the Graduate School at the University of California at Berkeley and served as President of the American Society of Criminology in 1993–94. He is the author of numerous books, articles and edited books, including *Above the Law: Police and the Excessive Use of Force* (with James Fyfe) (1993) and a third edition of *Justice Without Trial: Law Enforcement in Democratic Society* (1993).

Gresham Sykes received his AB in Sociology from Princeton University and his Ph.D. in Sociology from Northwestern University. He taught at Princeton University, Northwestern University, Dartmouth College, University of Denver, University of Houston, University of Iowa, and the University of Virginia. He was Executive Officer of the American Sociological Association, 1963–1965. He served as editor or associate editor of American Sociological Review, Journal of Criminal Law, Criminology and Police Science and American Sociologist. His books include *The Society of Captives* (1958), *Crime and Society* (1967), *Social Problems in America* (1971), *The Future of Crime and Criminology* (1980), and *Criminology* (1978), Second Edition with Francis T. Cullen (1992).

Index

AA (See Alcoholics Anonymous)
ACLU National Prison Project, 68
Addiction, 231, 235, 236–238
AIDS, AZT treatment for, 31
Alcoholics Anonymous (AA), 233–234
Alcoholism, 233–235
Alcohol use
   addiction and, 231, 235
   as pathology, 233–235
   danger rated to, 230–231
   "demon rum", 231
   driving and, 235
   "good creature of God", 231
   post-Prohibition, 233
   post-World War II, 234–235
   transition from tolerance to intolerance of, 231–233
   treatment for, 233–234
   "undeserving" poor and, 232
Antisocial control, 211–214 (See also Women, Social Control)
   exclusion of women from corridors of power and, 225
   reality of male violence and, 225
   reduction of, 224–225
ARIMA (autoregressive integrated moving average), 262
Attica, report on, 33
Autoregressive integrated moving average (ARIMA), 262

Barry case, 98
Bell v. Wolfish, 70
Berkeley School of Criminology
   aftershocks from, 292–295
   analysis of story of, 277–279, 297–298
   Committee on Educational Policy and, 292–293
   debate of issues surrounding, 279–281
   development of, 281–283
   financial problems and, 297
   Gitlin, the 1960s and, 299
   history of, 281–298
      Vollmer and, 281
      Lohman and, 282
      Blumer and, 282
      Skolnick and, 283
      Diamond and, 283
      Takagi and, 283
      Wilkins and, 283
      Foote and, 283
      O'Neill and, 283
      Sherry and, 283
      Krisberg and, 283
      Heyns and, 285
      Morris and, 288–289
      Messinger and, 295–297
      Platt and, 283–288
      Schwendinger and, 283
      Bowker and, 285–286, 293–295
   interpreting story of, 298–300
   "new criminology" and, 296
   People's Park demonstration and, 284–288
   Sindler report and, 289–292, 298
Block v. Rutherford, 70
Boot camps, 166
Born criminal crime representations, 157–158

Bounds v. Smith, 70
Brown v. Board of Education, 64, 70
Burger court, 70

Campaign for an Effective Crime Policy, 40–41
Capitalism, 22
Carceral society, 22–23
Career criminal representations, 164–165
Carter administration, 38
Chicago school, 5, 158, 166
Chinese-box model, 7
Civil disorder, 20–22, 107
Civil society, 22–23
Committee on Educational Policy report, 292–293
Community corrections, 189–190
Community policing, 166
Conformity, 5
"Continuum of care" philosophy, 55
Convenience sampling, 246, 254–255
Correction establishment, prison reform and, 69
Correspondence model and alternatives to, 12–13
Courts (*See* Judicial impact on prison reform; Women)
Covert operations (*See* Undercover policing)
Crime (*See also* specific types)
  control, 195–196
  deviance and, 12–13
  drug, 21, 22
  Durkheim's argument of, 262
  effective representations of, 173
  employment and, 21–22
  expert discourse of, 151, 152
  fear of, 153–155, 166, 196
  in free society, 163
  gangs and, 22
  ghetto and, 21, 156
  measuring, 243
  minorities and, 21–22
  nationalism and, 159–161
  national problem of, 168–169
  new penology's representations of crime and, 163–169
  in 1960s, 20–22
  politics, 168
  Progressive Era's representations of, 155–158
  protest and, 20–22, 107
  public discourse of, 151–152
  public perception of, 160–161
  Rothman's work on, 155–158
  social control and, 12–13
  social problem of, 22–24, 168
  structural analysis of, 170
  toughness on, 48–49, 53, 131–132, 133–134
  truth of, 150, 195
  undercover policing and, 100–103
  violence in, 152–153
Crime Act of 1994, 41–43, 167
Criminal career representations, 164–165
Criminal Justice Act of 1991, 126
Criminal justice policies
  administration of, 32
  Campaign for an Effective Crime Policy and, 40–41
  Crime Act of 1994 and, 41–43, 167
  Criminal Justice Act of 1991, 126
  demoralization of, 199
  drug control and, 36–37
  fear of crime and, 153–155
  Federal Crime Act of 1994, 166, 167
  federal sentencing codes and, 37–39
  history of, 29–30
  ideas and, interfacing, 11–12
  ineffectiveness of, 29, 30–31
  Messinger's work on contemporary, 17–20
  minorities and, 29, 31–32
  nationalism and, 159–161
  prescriptions for, 39–41
  proportionate sentence and, 125–127
  reform of, 32–36
  social welfare and, 168
  three strikes legislation, 17–19, 23, 132, 152–153, 165, 267–268
Criminal justice system
  growth of, 167–168

new penology and, 167–168
Progressive Era of penology and, 161–163
public face of, 85
women and, 215–216, 224–225
Criminal (*See* Offender)
Criminogenic neighborhood crime representation, 156

Death penalty, 173
Deception, undercover policing and, 104–106
Delinquent area crime representations, 156
Dependence statistical assumption, 252–254
Desert model, 127–129
Deterrence, 125, 265
Deviance
 crime and, 12–13
 Durkheim's view of, 12
 punishment and, 12–13
 social control and, 5–6, 12–13
 undercover policing and, 100–103
Deviance-control paradigm, 6, 10
Discretion, 162–163
Drug dealing, 21, 22
Drug testing, 166–167
Drug use (*See also* Alcohol use) addiction and, 231, 236–238
 broader concept of, 237
 Bush strategy against, 103, 131–132
 controlling, 36–37, 146, 239–240
 "criminal addict", 232
 marijuana, 231, 233
 minimalist concept of, 237
 new penology and, 166–167
 opiates, 232
 overuse, 237
 pathology of, 236–238
 penal sanction and, 240
 post-Prohibition, 231–233
 post-World War II, 234–235
 Progressive Era of penology and, 167
 Prohibition and, 229–230
 psychoactives, 230
 public health approach to, 235

public policy toward, 230–231
social control and, 231–233
tobacco, 230–231
treatment of, 167, 233–234

Enlightenment liberalism, 186–187, 188, 202
Enlightenment tradition, 186, 187, 189, 193
Estelle v. Gamble, 70

Fear of crime, 153–155, 166, 196
Federal Crime Act of 1994, 166, 167
Feminism, 9, 145 (*See also* Women)
Flogging case, 173
"Friendly fire" shootings, 104

Gangs, 22
Gates v. Collier, 67
General Education Diploma (GED), 58
Ghetto, 21, 156
Governmental power, crisis of, 168
"Gray Bar Hotels", 108
Guthrie v. Evans, 70

Hewitt v. Helms, 70
Home confinement program, 58–59
Hudson v. Palmer, 70

Ideas and policy, 11–12
Ideological contractions, piling-up-of-sanctions process and, 57
Illinois v. Perkins, 99
Imaginary population, 248–249
Incapacitation, 125–126, 264
Incarceration costs, 31
Incarceration rates (*See also* Prisons)
 future approaches to, 270–273
 prisons and, 31
 stability of punishment and, 263–270
Independence statistical assumption, 252–253
Individual delinquent crime representations, 156
Intermediate punishment program, 54–56

Jacksonian era of penology, 155, 158–159
Jack the Ripper case, 160
Jails, 60
Judicial impact on prison reform
 assessing problems in, 65–68
 Burger court, 70
 courts, decriminalization and desegregation, 69–70
 criticism of, 63–65
 litigation's impact and, 67–69, 70
 lower courts and, 69–71
 Rosenberg's work on, 63–69, 70, 71–72, 72–74
 "significant" social reform and, 65, 68
 successes vs. failures and, 71–72
 Supreme Court and, 69–70
Just-deserts theory, 127–129, 130–131
Juvenile delinquents, 161
Juvenile diversion program, 50–51

Kennedy sentencing bill, 37–38
Kerner Report, 21
Klaas case, 18, 152–153

Labeling theory, 5
Laws on crime (*See* specific names)
Legislation on crime (*See* specific names)
Limiting retributivism, 128
Litigation-generated prison reform, 67–69, 70

MADD (Mothers Against Drunk Driving), 236
Managerialism, 190–191, 201
Mandatory-minimum legislation, 132, 133, 266, 267
Marijuana use, 231, 233
Messinger's work on social control
 background of, 15–17
 criminal justice policies and, contemporary, 17–20
 developments of social control and, 5, 7
 recognition of, 23–24

Metaphors (*See* penal reform)
Minorities
 crime and, 21–22
 criminal justice policies and, 29, 31–32
 drug control and, 37
 in prisons, 31–32
 violence experienced by, 154
Miranda ruling, 99
Misdemeanors, 54–55
"Mixed" models, 128–129
Modern penality
 Benthamite utilitarianism and, 199
 concept of, 184–186
 "crisis of penal modernism", 202
 criticism of, 198
 culture of, 186–189
 Enlightenment tradition and, 187
 "floating norms" and, 202–203
 persistence of, 196–205
 politics of, 188–189
 punishment in, 196
 rehabilitative ideal, decline of, 202
 self-reflexive institution and, 204
 transformation of, theories of, 186, 189–192, 203
 waning of, 196
"Modified" desert model, 128
Morales Feliciano v. Romero Barcelo, 70
Mothers Against Drunk Driving (MADD), 236

NARCO, 137
National Academy of Sciences report on incapacitation, 125, 126
Nationalism, 159–161
Negativism, proportionate sentence and, 134–135
New penology
 career criminal crime representations and, 164–165
 civilizing process of society and, 171, 173
 crime as national problem and, 168–169
 crime politics and, 168

Index

criminal career crime representations
  and, 164–165
  criminal justice system and, 167–168
  cultural failings of, 171–173
  debate of, 148–149
  defined, 147
  discontents and, 169–174
  discourses of, 147–148, 149–150,
    167–169, 172, 191–192
  drug testing and, 166–167
  drug use and, 166–167
  features of, 52, 147–148, 191
  Feeley and Simon's view of, 190–
    191, 201
  governmental power and, crisis of,
    168
  Great Society and crime, 161–163
  implications of failures of, 169–174
  objectives of, 148
  Progressive Era of penology and, 163
  public opinion and, 151–155
  representations of crime and, 163–
    169
  social control and, 145
  stakes of, 173–174
  techniques of, 148
  theory of, 148–150
  underclass crime representations
    and, 165–168
  volitional theories and, 170–171

Offender
  circumstances, 56–57
  conceptions of, 194–195, 199
  noncompliance, 58
Opiate use, 232
Organizational convenience, piling-up-
  of-sanctions process and, 57
Ortega case, 102–103

Parole, 33, 131, 166, 191
Parsimony in proportionate sentence,
  129
Penality, 192 (See also Modern penality; Postmodern penality)
Penal modernism (See Modern
  penality)

Penal postmodernism (See Postmodern
  penality)
Penal reform (See also Judicial impact
  on prison reform)
  "accelerated social control" meta-
    phor, 47, 50
  actors in penal system and, 55–56
  alternative approach to studying,
    53–59, 60
  "bankloading", 52
  collapse, 193–194
  "dispersal of discipline" metaphor,
    45, 46, 190
  foreign analysis of, 30
  history of, 29–30
  home confinement program and,
    58–59
  ideological contradiction model, 46,
    47, 51
  in 1970s and 1980s, 194
  interpreting outcomes of, 50–53
  "maximum-security society" meta-
    phor, 45
  measuring outcomes of, 57–59
  metaphors, 45–60
  "minimum security society" meta-
    phor, 45
  misdemeanors and, 54–55
  "net-widening" metaphor and, 46–
    49, 60
  "new penology" metaphor (See also
    New penology), 45, 52
  offender circumstances and, 56–57
  organizational convenience model,
    46, 47, 51
  "piling up of sanctions" metaphor
    and, 49, 55–58
  policy and, interfacing ideas with,
    11–12
  political economy model, 46, 47, 51
  politics and, 155
  "post-modern penology" metaphor
    (See also Postmodern penality),
    52
  professional interest model, 46, 47,
    51
  progress model, 46

Penal reform (cont.)
  questions regarding consequences of, 59
  research on, 45–47, 59
  social control and, 45–46
  studying outcomes of, 47–50
  theoretical models of, 45–46, 57, 59
  "transcarceration" metaphor and, 51, 53
  victims' bill of rights, 53
  "wider and stronger nets" metaphor, 45, 47, 48
  "words and deeds", 47–53
  work release program and, 58
Penological modernism, 186–187
Penology, eras of, 155 (See also specific eras)
Policing (See also Undercover policing)
  community, 166
  private, 85, 106–108
  problem-oriented, 91–94
  professional education and, 94
  professionalization of, 88–91, 94
  recruitment of personnel for, 88–91
  reform in, 87–88, 91–92
  research on, 85
  responsibilities of, enlarging, 93–94
  "slam bang" style, 93
  undercover, 95–119
  view of, common, 91
Politically-generated prison reform, 67–69
"Politics of Protest," 22
Ponte v. Real, 70
Postmodern penality
  "autopoietic", 195, 206
  concept of, 181–184, 193
  "nothing works" and, 194
  phenomena of, 193–196
  transformation to, theories of, 186, 189–192, 203
President's Commission on Law Enforcement reports, 163
Prisoners' rights, 66–67, 70
Prisonization, 79
Prisons (See also Judicial impact on prison reform; Penal reform; Structural-functional perspective on imprisonment)
  academic studies on policy of, 83–84
  alternatives to, 40
  costs of, 31, 73
  Crime Bill of 1994 and, 42
  destabilization of, 68
  in drug use control, 239–240
  durability of, 27
  foreign analysis of, 30
  Foucault's view of, 19–20
  incarceration rates and, 31
  interest in, 78–79
  middle-range theory and, 80
  minorities in, 31–32
  nature of changes in, 83
  overcrowding in, 54, 66
  perspective on, changes in, 79–81
  population of, 49, 54–55, 60, 268–270
  problems in reform of, 65–68
  reliance on, American, 30–31
  social reform in, "significant," 65
  violence in, 67–68
  women in, 219–224
Private policing, 85, 106–108
Probation, 130, 166, 191
Professional interests, piling-up-of-sanctions process and, 57
Progressive Era of penology
  born criminal crime representations and, 157–158
  crime as national problem and, 168–169
  criminal justice system and, 161–163
  delinquent area crime representations and, 156
  discretion and, 162–163
  drug use and, 167
  failure of, 171
  features of, 158
  individual delinquent crime representations and, 156
  juvenile delinquents and, 161
  nationalism and, 159–161

Index   315

new penology and, 163
post-World War II, 161–163
public discourse of, 171
reform in, 168
representations of crime and, 150, 155–158
retooling, 161–163
successes of, 158–161
time frame of, 155
working classes and, 158–159
Prohibition, 229–230
history of, 230
Proportionate sentence
criminal justice policies and, 125–127
desert model and, 127–129
deterrence and, 125
in England, 137–139
in Sweden, 137–139
in United States, 135–137
fairness and, 123–125
influence of, 123
"limiting retributivism" and, 128
Minnesota and Oregon Sentencing Commissions, 126
"mixed" models and, 128–129
"modified" desert model and, 128
negativism and, 134–135
parsimony in, 129
priorities and, 127
punishment and, 129–131
punitiveness, justifying, 129–131
punitiveness, politics of resentment, 131–134
rehabilitation and, 125
Protest, 20–22, 107
Public opinion, 151–155
"Punish and treat" concept, 49, 54, 57
Punishment (See also Stability of punishment)
death penalty, 173
deviance and, 12–13
discourses of modern, 147–148, 149–150
for drug crimes, 37, 239–240
in modern penality, 196
intermediate, 49, 53–57, 58

just-deserts theory and, 130
master shifts, 10–11
objectives of modern, 148
pain delivery and, 130
proportionalism in, 124–125, 129–131
proportionate sentence and, 129–131
resentment and, politics of, 131–134
social control and, 9
social trends and, 8–9
stability of, 259–272
techniques of modern, 148
Putative reform (See Penal reform)

Ramos v. Lamm, 67
Random sampling
imaginary population and, 248–249
real population and, 247–248
statistical assumptions and, 245–246, 250–252
RAND study, 21, 22
Real population, 247–248
Regression models, 253
Rehabilitation, 30, 125, 134–135, 202, 204
Research methodologies (See Statistical methods and Statistical assumptions)
Responsibility, 192
Restorative-justice conceptions, 134–135
Retribution, 192
Reynolds case, 152
Rhem v. Malcolm, 70
Rhodes v. Chapman, 70
Rodney King, beating of, 29
Roe v. Wade, 64, 70
Ruiz v. Estelle, 67–68, 70

Sanctions, 266–267, 268–269
Sentencing (See also Proportionate sentence)
aims, 126–127
Campaign for an Effective Crime Policy and, 40–41
determinate, 34, 266

Sentencing (cont.)
  deterrence and, 125
  fairness and, 123–124
  federal codes of, 37–39
  fixed, 32–33
  foreign analysis of, 30
  formulas, 40
  get tough policies, 53–54
  guidelines, 32, 38–39, 124–127, 133, 136
  incapacitation and, 125–126
  indeterminate, 30, 32–33, 34
  judges and, 32, 38–39, 40, 134
  Kennedy bill on, 37–38
  parole and premature, 33
  political coalitions, 271–272
  reform, 32–36
  rehabilitation and, 125
  Reno's views on, 41
  research on, 85
  Rothman's work on, 133–134
  sentencing policy, 270–272
    use of prison impact statements and, 271
    use of sentencing commissions and, 271
  utilitarian vs. nonutilitarian rationales of, 85
  Washington state practices of, 34–36
  women and, 222
Sindler report, 289–292, 298
Singapore flogging case, 173
Slum, 21, 156
Social control (See also Messinger's work on social control)
  academic work on, directions of, 8
  antisocial control and, 211–214
  changes in, 10–11
  concept of, 4–5
  crime and, 12–13
  defined, 213
  deviance and, 5–6, 12–13
  discourse on, 5–9
  drug use and, 231–233
  feminism and, 9, 145
  Foucault's work on, 7–8
  individualizing, 233–235
  levels of, 6
  measuring, 243
  metaphors and (See also Penal reform), 45–60
  new penology and, 145
  penal reform and, 45–46
  policy and, interfacing ideas with, 11–12
  punishment and, 9
  research on, 145
  Rothman's work on, 7
  social trends and, 8–9
  sociological meaning of, 9
  women and, 215
  Woolf's book about, 211–213
Social trends, 8–9
Social welfare, 168
Spatial dependence, 252–253
Stability of punishment
  challenges to, 262–263
  conservative attacks on, 264
  determinate sentencing and, 266
  deterrence and, 265
  economic policy and, 271
  incapacitation and, 264
  incarceration rates and, 263–270
  judges and, diversity of, 265–266
  liberal attacks on, 263–264
  mandatory-minimum legislation and, 266, 267
  original hypothesis, 260–262
  sanctions and, 266–267, 268–269
  theory, 259–260
  three-strikes legislation and, 267–268
  Violent Crime and Law Enforcement Act of 1994 and, 267
Statistical assumptions
  as empirical commitments, 246
  confidence interval, 245
  convenience sampling, 246, 254–255
  police use of force and, 246
  prison good time and, 246
  prosecutors' charging decisions and, 246
  conventional statistical inference, 246

Index 317

data as population, 246–247
dependence, 252–254
imaginary population, 248–249
independence, 251–252
real population, 247–248
regression models, 253
spatial dependence, 252–253
standard errors, 245
substantive research and, 249–250, 255–256
time series models, 253–254
Statistical methods
cross validation, 255
data in hand, 246
micro studies, 47
microempirical measurements, 113
p-values, 245, 250, 254
probability samples, 254
random sampling, 245–246, 250–252
"tabular asterisks", 245
tool-kit approach, 54
t-tests, 245
Statistical significance, 245, 249
Structural analysis of crime, 170
Structural-functional perspective on imprisonment
development of, 78–81
emergence of, 77
insights of, 81–83
interest in prisons and, 78–79
Supreme Court, 69–70, 99 (*See also* specific cases)
Surveillance, 95–96

Three strikes legislation, 17–19, 23, 132, 152–153, 165, 267–268
Time series models, 253–254
Tobacco use, 230–231
Total institutions concept, 33, 190
Truth of crime, 150, 195
t-tests, 245, 249–250

Underclass crime representations, 165–166
Undercover policing
agents and, effects on, 104

as necessary evil, 115–116
Barry case and, 98
concerns regarding, 112–118
crime and, 100–103
deception and, 104–106
deviance amplification and, 100–103
FBI and, 97
  CISPES, 99–100
  COINTEL, 99–100
  forfeitures and, 99–100
Florida Mi-porn case and, 106
"fluffing the evidence" and, 104
"friendly fire" shootings and, 104
humor in, 108–109
myth of surveillance and, 101
Ortega case and, 102–103
"people watchers" and, 108
private, 106–108
quotations regarding, 109–112
restrictions on, 99
support for, new, 99–100
surveillance and, new, 95–96
Twentieth Century Fund and, 117–118
Undercover study and, 96–97, 102, 104
use of, 96
Wackenhut Corporation and, 106

Violence
in crime, 152–153
male, female and, 218–219
minorities experiencing, 154
in prisons, 67–68
Volitional theories, 170–171

Wackenhut Corporation, 106
Washington state sentencing practices, 34–36
Whitley v. Albers, 70
Wickersham Commission, 30
Willie Horton case, 131
Wolf v. McDonald, 70
Women
antisocial family and, 216
antisocial masculism and, 218–219

Women (cont.)
  antisocial state and, 217–218
  child-centeredness and the control of, 214
  courts and, 215–216, 219–224
  criminal justice system and, 215–216, 224–225
  formal and informal control of, 215–224
  good parenting and the control of, 214
  in prisons, 219–224
  in regulatory agencies, other, 219–224
  sentencing and, 222
  social control and, 211–215
Working classes, 158–159
Work release program, 58